P9-CFB-385

DISCARD

# ★ BETABALL ★

# BETABALL

★ ★ ★ ★ ★ ★ ★ ★

## HOW SILICON VALLEY AND SCIENCE
## BUILT ONE OF THE GREATEST
## BASKETBALL TEAMS IN HISTORY

# ERIK MALINOWSKI

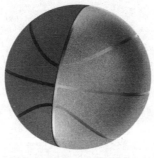

**ATRIA** BOOKS
New York • London • Toronto • Sydney • New Delhi

**ATRIA**
BOOKS

An Imprint of Simon & Schuster, Inc.
1230 Avenue of the Americas
New York, NY 10020

Copyright © 2017 by Erik Malinowski

All rights reserved, including the right to reproduce this book or portions thereof in any form whatsoever. For information, address Atria Books Subsidiary Rights Department, 1230 Avenue of the Americas, New York, NY 10020.

First Atria Books hardcover edition October 2017

**ATRIA** BOOKS and colophon are trademarks of Simon & Schuster, Inc.

For information about special discounts for bulk purchases, please contact Simon & Schuster Special Sales at 1-866-506-1949 or business@simonandschuster.com.

The Simon & Schuster Speakers Bureau can bring authors to your live event. For more information, or to book an event, contact the Simon & Schuster Speakers Bureau at 1-866-248-3049 or visit our website at www.simonspeakers.com.

Interior design by Dana Sloan

Manufactured in the United States of America

10 9 8 7 6 5 4 3 2 1

Library of Congress Cataloging-in-Publication Data is available.

ISBN 978-1-5011-5819-3
ISBN 978-1-5011-5821-6 (ebook)

R0450296100

*To Becca and Tomás,*
*my everyday MVPs*

# CONTENTS

# ★ BETABALL ★

# PROLOGUE

As the ball left Stephen Curry's hands, I was certain the shot was good.

The Golden State Warriors' season had come down to this one history-shifting play, a long, somewhat frantic three-pointer with 33 seconds remaining in Game 7 of the NBA Finals. It was June 19, 2016, and over the past 236 days, the Warriors had played some of the most dominant basketball the world had ever witnessed. They started 24-0, then 36-2, 48-4, and 62-6. By season's end, thanks to a four-game win streak heading into the playoffs, the Warriors had won 73 games against only nine losses, a mark no NBA team had pulled off in the league's 67-year history.

To cap off that milestone with a championship—which they'd done just a year earlier—seemed all but academic.

And through a regular season in which the Warriors didn't lose back-to-back games, Curry was the catalyst that kept the team humming. After winning the NBA's Most Valuable Player Award for the 2014–15 season, Curry was even more spectacular in his encore performance.

He served up a 40-point, seven-assist, six-rebound breakout on opening night against New Orleans. After a 53-point conflagration in the Warriors' third game, Curry was the league's top scorer every day through to the schedule's final game. Curry was an offensive dynamo who could not be slowed for months; he not only broke his own NBA record of 286 three-pointers in a season but obliterated the mark, swishing 402 such shots during the season. Curry also led the league in both steals and free-throw percentage for the second straight season, while also finishing eighth in assists. For much of the year, his Player Efficiency Rating—an analytical measure of a player's overall effectiveness—hovered above the all-time mark set by Wilt Chamberlain more than 50 years earlier. Alas, Curry's PER merely ended up the eighth-best in NBA history.

As his stats further pushed the boundaries of reason, Curry witnessed his star status grow into that of a full-fledged supernova. When the Warriors came out for warm-ups two hours before a home game at Oracle Arena, more than a thousand fans would congregate around the periphery of the court, often jostling for position and craning their necks for just the right angle to witness Curry's 20-minute warm-up, often an entire show unto itself. His two-handed dribbling drills under the basket. His effortless threes from the center-court logo, often nailed in rapid succession. All capped off by the customary three-point attempt from the side tunnel that leads down to the Warriors' locker room. It's a 45-foot heave that he doesn't always convert—Curry is only human, after all—but when the ball goes in, a crowd 90 minutes before any basketball game has never sounded more alive.

As much as the fans in Oakland would eat up Curry's pregame ritual, fans on the road could be just as insatiable. With every ensuing win and Curry highlight, the Warriors became a traveling road show, like an All-Star baseball team barnstorming the country back in the 1930s. During the playoffs, ESPN dedicated a camera feed strictly to showing Curry's midcourt warm-up heaves so it could then push the video link to subscribers of its mobile app. With all this attention, all the accolades and superlatives, there was a sense this was all building to . . . something. The Warriors, both individually and as a group, had made so much history in such a compact time that the season seemed destined to culminate in a memorable finish of *some* kind—either resounding triumph or unfathomable horror.

And it all came down to this shot from Curry, which looked on target as it angled toward the rim along its natural arc. Aside from a smattering of visiting fans here and there, most of the nearly 20,000 people inside Oracle Arena figured the shot would go through. You could excuse the assumption. They had been conditioned to believe this. Since Curry arrived in the Bay Area in the summer of 2009, he'd shown glimpses of becoming this kind of player, someone who could decide championships with an unforgettable game, a marvelous quarter—even a single, dead-aim shot from 25 feet out.

. . .

The story of how the Golden State Warriors found themselves one shot away from NBA immortality is one of meager beginnings, like so many compelling stories, but the thing about the Warriors is just how fast all this success came about. Five years ago, they were deep in the midst of one of the most prolonged stretches of suckitude any NBA team had ever endured, permanent residents beneath the NBA's subfloor. Entering the 2012–13 season, Golden State had made the playoffs once in the past 18 seasons. To put that in perspective, only one NBA team has *ever* suffered through a more sustained slump. From 1976–77 to 1990–91, the Los Angeles Clippers didn't make the playoffs at all—15 straight years missing out on any chance for a title. Considering eight of 15 teams from the Western Conference make the postseason every April, the odds should be on a team's side a bit more often than that, no matter how ineptly they play.

Not so for the Warriors, who were owned by one of the most re-viled men in all of the sport. From 1995 to 2010, fans in the Bay Area wished day and night for his removal from ownership. Once in a while, there'd be a rumor or a whisper about some potential deal that might be in the works, but it never seemed to materialize, and many Warriors fans couldn't imagine when better days might be imminent. It seemed preposterous that this poorly run team with bottom-rung talent could possibly compete for anything worthwhile any time soon.

That all started to change in the summer of 2010, when a new owner-ship group paid a record amount of money to buy the team and immedi-ately began changing the culture. They assessed every employee's place in the company but waited six months before implementing any sweep-ing changes. Any workers dissatisfied with their role were summarily shipped off to other competitors. Office space was renovated and rebuilt to improve workflow, communication, and trust. A greater emphasis was placed on finding technological solutions to lingering problems and using proprietary analytics to unearth latent advantages their employ-ees already possessed.

Sounds a lot like a tech company, right? That's because Joe Lacob, Golden State's new majority owner, happened to be one of Silicon Val-ley's most experienced and successful venture capitalists. His co-owner, Peter Guber, was one of Hollywood's most famous and prolific produc-ers. Along with a team of tech-minded investors sprinkled across the Bay Area, they spent nearly a half-billion dollars just for the right to try to turn one of the most moribund, unimpressive franchises in all of professional sports into something successful.

The first couple of years didn't go so well. Two seasons in, two seasons still out of the playoffs. Fans remained agitated and impatient, but the new owners were committed to seeing their vision through. There were missteps, turns gone wrong that led to harsh lessons. But there were also glimpses of a brighter future, brought about by savvy evaluations, and the kinds of twists of fate that seem to come only when you're in the absolute best position to accept them. Both men had found success outside sports through constant innovation; both were convinced they could apply that same principle to construct a championship-caliber team. They would urge employees to speak out; encourage cross-collaboration; invest in bold, new technologies that could flame out; and never resist the urge to adapt. In the tech industry, the term for this stage of development is "beta"—never fully baked, always in flux, focused yet open to change.

That strategy? It worked beyond their wildest imagination. The Warriors captured their first championship in 40 years and followed that up with the greatest regular season in NBA history. Curry was a global megastar. The Warriors were raking in millions in pure profit, faster than any other franchise. And the winning seemed to come so easily, as if it was all preordained.

. . .

Now, in the waning moments of Game 7, the Warriors teetered on the precipice of all-time greatness, one final three-pointer from a couple dozen feet out that would decide whether Golden State completed a scintillating storybook run or summoned forth a monstrous wave of second-guessing that few teams had ever experienced. As the tenths of a second ticked off, the oxygen sucked itself out of Oracle Arena, the ball fell toward the rim, and we all waited to see what the fates would decide. It was the culmination of a six-year odyssey to build the best basketball team ever assembled.

But to really fathom what came next, we need to go back to how the Golden State Warriors, against all odds, arrived at this most improbable and momentous point in time.

# 1 ★ ★ ★ ★ ★ ★ ★

# NEW BLOOD

## From Chris Cohan to Joe Lacob

**W**hen Joe Lacob's ownership group paid unprecedented money for the Warriors in 2010, it had purchased not only one of the worst teams in all of professional sports but one of the oldest and most historically significant teams in the NBA. The Warriors actually predate the league itself.

In 1946, as America was recovering from the chaos of World War II and once again returning its collective gaze to pro baseball and football, the upstart Basketball Association of America was presenting big-time hoops as a real and viable sporting alternative. With franchises in all the major northeastern seaboard cities, the BAA had to contend only with the more established National Basketball League, a loose collection of midwestern teams that were forged from the revenues of late thirties corporate giants such as General Electric and Goodyear. For three years, the two entities operated independent of each other, rivals jockeying for the same talent pool. And due to its urban locales, the BAA often attracted the best talent flowing in from the college ranks.

As one of the BAA's charter organizations, the Philadelphia

Warriors—so named for a long-gone team part of yet *another* early professional league—were a powerhouse, finishing second in their division
during the inaugural season of 1946–47. The team ahead of them in the
standings, the Washington Capitols, was coached by future Boston Celtics legend Red Auerbach and went 49-11, a full 14 games better than Philadelphia. Nonetheless, it was the Warriors who won the first-ever BAA
championship, knocking off the Chicago Stags, four games to one, in the
Finals. Leading the way for Philadelphia was a 25-year-old rookie out of
Murray State in Kentucky named Joe Fulks, who would play eight seasons
(all with the Warriors) and eventually earn his induction into the Hall of
Fame.

Fulks was a bona fide star that first season, averaging more than 23
points a game. Such a feat was remarkable on a number of levels. First,
most teams back then typically scored only in the 70s on any given night;
one player supplying a solid third of your total scoring has scarcely happened in any era. Second, Fulks's production was more than six points
higher per game than the next-closest player—38 percent more, to be
precise, than Washington's Bob Feerick. And though Fulks made more
field goals and free throws than any other player, it was not the result of
some freak physical prowess, as fans would witness in such future stars
as Bill Russell and Wilt Chamberlain. Fulks stood 6-foot-5 but weighed
less than 200 pounds, scrawny even for his day (and unthinkably so in
modern times).

No, Fulks was the BAA's first superstar—once dubbed "the Babe
Ruth of basketball" by the *Saturday Evening Post*—because he had mas-
tered a skill few others even attempted. More than any other professional
player of his day, Fulks, undersized and unsuspecting, had popularized
the use of a jump shot.

In the earliest decades of professional basketball, scoring was largely
the result of either layups close to the basket or flat-footed set shots from
the outside. Some college players could pull off one-handed set shots, but

it wasn't until Kenny Sailors, a 5-foot-10 point guard at the University of Wyoming, unleashed the infinite possibilities of a one-handed jump shot, in which the ball is flicked from one's wrists at the apex of one's leap, that basketball started to undergo a paradigm shift. Sailors, himself a rookie in that BAA season of 1946–47, finished second in the league in assists and averaged nearly 10 points per game for the Cleveland Rebels, but Fulks, with his height advantage, was able to better exploit the shot's potential in a way that Sailors could not. Edward Gottlieb, the Warriors' coach, would later say Fulks had "the greatest assortment of shots I've ever seen in basketball." Fulks's single-game NBA record of 63 points, set in February 1949, stood until Elgin Baylor bested him by a point a decade later. The Warriors' proclivity for embracing era-defining jump shooters, it seems, was present in the franchise's DNA from the get-go.

Several modern-day teams can still trace their roots back to those upstart days, but few were as dominant in that proto-NBA as the Philadelphia Warriors. After the BAA's third season, the league agreed to merge with the NBL and, in a meeting held high in the Empire State Building in August 1949, the NBA was born.

As the league evolved, the Warriors held their place as one of its premier teams, making the playoffs in nine of the league's first 13 seasons and winning a second title in 1955–56. Hall of Famers such as the aforementioned Chamberlain, Nate Thurmond, and Rick Barry all helped keep the team relevant and competitive in the years following the team's move to San Francisco (starting with the 1962–63 season) and subsequently to Oakland (for 1971–72). The San Francisco Warriors were rebranded as the Golden State Warriors, a name that was expected to give off a more communal and inclusive vibe, and played in the relatively new Oakland–Alameda County Coliseum Arena, built in 1966 and a stone's throw from the home of the Oakland Athletics, who were about to run off a streak of three straight World Series titles and establish a brief baseball dynasty.

The Athletics' new neighbors held up their end by winning the 1974–75 Finals, led by Barry's sublime play and the head coaching of 39-year-old Al Attles, who had lost twice in the Finals as a backup point guard for the San Francisco Warriors in 1963–64 and 1966–67.

With a championship, stable ownership, star power to spare, and a fervent fan base, the future looked rosy for the Warriors as the eighties approached.

But Barry's departure for the Houston Rockets in the summer of 1978 signaled an inexorable shift downward in the franchise's fortunes, and as the NBA moved forward on the backs of budding stars like Magic Johnson, Larry Bird, and Michael Jordan, the Warriors were left behind. They missed the playoffs in nine consecutive seasons, an astonishing feat of badness, considering that by the 1985–86 season (the last in that lamentable streak), eight of the 12 Western Conference teams qualified for the playoffs every April. Fortunately for Golden State, that was the year a hotshot rookie out of St. John's University named Chris Mullin gave the team a vital infusion of youth and attitude. With players like Mullin, point guard Tim Hardaway, and shooting guards Mitch Richmond and Latrell Sprewell, the Warriors made the playoffs five times in an eight-year span. They went 55-27 for the 1991–92 season, cracking 50 wins in a season for the first time in 16 years. Once again, it seemed as if a run of sustained competence—if not outright excellence—might be in the offing.

After posting a 50-32 record for the 1993–94 season, the Warriors dropped off a cliff, finishing 24 games worse the following year. In a league now carried by dominant centers across the country—from Orlando's Shaquille O'Neal to San Antonio's David Robinson to Houston's Hakeem Olajuwon and more—the Warriors were once again relegated to the league's dingy basement. Only the historically abysmal Los Angeles Clippers and Minnesota Timberwolves had worse records in the Western Conference.

Appropriately enough, that precipitous downfall into oblivion co-incided with the arrival of a new majority owner—a man who would quickly become the bane of every Golden State fan's existence.

· · ·

In the summer of 1994, the Warriors were enjoying something of a renaissance—not quite a full return to the halcyon days of the mid-seventies, but there wasn't much to complain about if you were a Golden State fan. Coming off a 50-win season and their fifth playoff appearance in eight years, the Warriors' roster contained a compelling blend of veteran scorers and young stars that looked like a foundation for years of success to come. With Mullin, Sprewell, and No. 1 overall pick Chris Webber leading the way, watching Golden State play could be pure ecstasy. They were a top-five scoring team for five years running, leading the league twice over that time. Thanks to head coach Don Nelson and his high-octane up-and-down approach—dubbed "Nellie Ball"—few teams were as consistently exciting to watch as the Warriors.

At the top, the team was controlled by chairman Jim Fitzgerald and team president Dan Finnane, who were generally well respected around the league and avoided unnecessary headlines, but they didn't quite have the lovability factor of previous owner Franklin Mieuli, who facilitated the franchise's move from Philadelphia to San Francisco in 1962 and then became majority owner until 1986, when he sold to Fitzgerald and Finnane. Mieuli, with his trademark deerstalker cap, was a Bay Area icon who had made his fortune in TV and radio. He was a visible and beloved part of the Warriors mystique, often seen sitting in the front row at home games even after he sold his stake. And though the Warriors were frequently competitive in those intervening years, Fitzgerald and Finnane, in time, felt a financial crunch, enough so that they grew eager to sell a minority share of the team and bring in an infusion of fresh cash.

Enter Chris Cohan, a cable TV magnate who had founded Sonic Communications in 1977 and turned a small, regional collection of broadcast systems into one of the largest cable operators in the United States. After his parents divorced, Cohan spent his childhood in Salinas, deep in the heart of Monterey County, and then later north in the Bay Area. He graduated from Los Gatos High School in 1968 and earned a degree in recreation from Arizona State in 1973. His father, John, died a few months later and left him with an inheritance of money and communications infrastructure that was worth, according to a *San Francisco Chronicle* investigation some years later, as much as $10 million. Cohan turned that considerable head start into a widespread cable conglomerate, allowing him the kind of capital that can secure a 25 percent stake in an NBA team during a relaxed round of golf, which was exactly what Cohan did with Fitzgerald in the spring of 1991. Cohan paid $21 million for the privilege. He was now a minority owner in the NBA.

More important, Cohan said the handshake deal (which was never put into writing) came with an assurance that he would be allowed to buy the remaining 75 percent of the team in about two years' time. When that didn't happen, Cohan sued Fitzgerald and Finnane to dissolve the team's corporate partnership, an effort to forcibly wrest the team from their control.

When news of the suit broke in July 1994, it was a bombshell. Cohan had alleged not only bad faith and broken promises but also that Fitzgerald and Finnane were giving themselves fat bonuses and actively trying to circumvent the NBA's salary cap. The Warriors called the suit "frivolous," and a trial date was scheduled in San Francisco Superior Court for October 11, the day after the Columbus Day holiday.

But on October 8, that Saturday before, the Warriors' owners announced they were selling the remaining 75 percent stake in the team to Cohan. The amount of the sale was later reported to be $110 million, putting Cohan's total investment at around $130 million. Everyone in Golden

State's orbit was stunned, from the fans to other team owners to Warriors employees, who immediately began asking anyone in sight for some shred of intel on the new owner. In three years as minority owner, Cohan had been like a ghost to many in Oakland. Despite owning a quarter of the franchise, his name didn't even appear in the team's media guide.

And while whispers turned to rumors, Cohan tried his best to assuage concerns about what new ownership might herald. "I want to assure our many fans," he said in a statement, "that I am committed to keeping this team in the Bay Area and look forward to working with Don Nelson and the players and staff to ensure that the Warriors' franchise continues to be, in every way, a first-class organization." Two days later, Cohan spoke publicly for the first time as the Warriors' sole owner and again sought to allay lingering fears. "I guess I've been in business long enough," he said from the floor of the arena, "and I don't try to fix anything that isn't broken."

Five weeks later, the Cohan era had its first of many catastrophes. Chris Webber, who averaged 17 points, nine rebounds, and two blocks per game in his rookie season as the Warriors' starting center, openly clashed with Nelson, claiming the head coach was needlessly verbally abusive to him during practices. Webber had signed a 15-year contract before his rookie season but exercised an out clause and became a restricted free agent after just one year. He held out at the start of the season when the Warriors wouldn't offer a shorter, more player-friendly deal. Cohan eventually met with Webber, became convinced that the situation could not be resolved, and traded him to Washington for shooting guard Tom Gugliotta and three future first-round picks. Cohan undermined Nelson publicly by confirming Webber's beef was solely with the head coach, and the Warriors ultimately lost a future five-time All-Star who would average more than 20 points and nearly 10 rebounds a game over 15 seasons. Nelson privately told his coaching staff that the hullabaloo over the trade meant his own dismissal might be sooner than later.

A month after losing Webber, Cohan further alienated fans when, in a newspaper interview, he floated the possibility of moving the Warriors 40 miles south to San Jose. (Golden State's home arena in Oakland could seat only some 15,000 fans, thousands fewer than most other teams' buildings.) Meanwhile, the Warriors struggled mightily on the court, losing 14 of 15 games after starting off with a promising 7-1 record. And by the time the NBA's board of governors approved Cohan's purchase of the team on January 4, 1995, the Warriors were knee-deep in chaos.

Golden State had just 14 wins against 31 losses heading into the mid-February break. At the All-Star Game in Phoenix, Cohan deftly evaded a couple of Bay Area reporters attempting to confirm whispers that Nelson was already ousted as head coach. Cohan, holding his wife by the hand, maneuvered his way through a crowded concourse—the kind of pursuit you might see through a bustling European train station in a Jason Bourne movie—and escaped to a secured area. The next day, the Warriors announced that Nelson was "stepping down" as head coach. The team, as Cohan explained then, "didn't appear to be responding to Don Nelson, for whatever peculiar reason."

The hits kept coming. Nelson was replaced by Rick Adelman, who was canned after one season in favor of P. J. Carlesimo, who was brought on as the kind of stern taskmaster who could impose discipline. (Some Portland Trail Blazers, whom he had led to three straight playoff appearances, called him "Policimo.") And just 14 games into the 1997–98 season, with the Warriors sitting at 1-13, Latrell Sprewell assaulted Carlesimo during a practice, choking him and leaving visible bruising on his neck. Cohan terminated Sprewell's contract and the NBA shelved him for a full year, the longest suspension in NBA history. In offering a defense, Sprewell told reporters, "I just got to the point where I couldn't take it anymore."

The Warriors were embroiled in one controversy after another. Cohan sued Nelson, trying to recoup more than $1.5 million in wages from his ex-coach (and lost). The team battled with both the city council and the Oakland–Alameda County Coliseum Authority (the entity that owns the arena and the land beneath) over bonds that were issued to pay for $140 million in arena renovations that moved the Warriors to San Jose for the 1996–97 season. Then Cohan threatened to dismiss season-ticket holders who didn't renew their seat licenses for that season of displacement. (The policy cost the team thousands of season-ticket holders. Cohan later characterized the move as "a horrible reaction that I wish I could take back.")

The Warriors were also found in breach of contract with the OACC to the tune of some $20 million, regarding unpaid rent and other revenues from premium seating. Cohan even sued the Warriors' former lead counsel, Robin Baggett, who was a childhood pal and the best man at his wedding, over a sketchy land deal gone south. An investigation by the *San Francisco Chronicle* in 2002 found that Cohan had often wielded litigation as a weapon when he was chief executive of Sonic Communications. As OACC president Scott Haggerty told the *Chronicle*, "Why can't somebody good buy our team?"

But what truly sank the Warriors in those early years of the Cohan era was that they were terrible at basketball. A significant reason was that most of their top draftees didn't become the foundational players everyone hoped for:

- With the No. 1 overall pick in 1995, they picked Joe Smith. He was traded three seasons later.
- In 1996, with one of the picks from the Webber trade, general manager Dave Twardzik could've selected future Hall of Famers Kobe Bryant or Steve Nash, but instead took Todd Fuller. He was traded after two seasons.
- In 1997, they took Adonal Foyle with the eighth pick. Future Hall of Famer Tracy McGrady went No. 9 to Toronto.

- In 1998, they traded away No. 5 pick (and future Hall of Famer) Vince Carter plus cash to Toronto on draft night for No. 4 pick Antawn Jamison. Future Hall of Famers Dirk Nowitzki and Paul Pierce went back-to-back four picks later.

By virtue of all those high draft picks in succession, the Warriors seemed destined to acquire at least *one* legitimate franchise face—maybe even a future Hall of Famer!—but few truly panned out.

All the losing, all the missteps finally came to a head on February 13, 2000. What should've easily been the high point of the Cohan era—hosting the NBA All-Star Game in Oakland—instead turned out to be its nadir. Midway through the fourth quarter, a ceremony took place to signify the passing of the torch from the current All-Star host city to the following year's. Cohan stood at center court with Michael Jordan, the president of basketball operations for the Washington Wizards, who were hosting the 2001 All-Star Game. "As soon as the roar for Jordan subsided and Cohan's name was mentioned," Ray Ratto wrote in the *San Francisco Examiner*, "the boos rolled down the aisles like spilled beer, and though Cohan held his stage smile, he was plainly stung, again." As Cohan felt the humiliation build inside, he could see his wife sitting courtside straight in front of him, her head dropped in horror. Cohan himself could take the punishment, but what really gutted him was that his five-year-old son, Dax, was standing right next to him on the court. That deluge of hate raining down, with his son standing *right there*, that's what stung Cohan to his core. After that day, the relationship between Cohan and Warriors fans was irrevocably broken.

Cohan retreated from public view, often watching games not from courtside but from his owner's suite on the second level. He gave an extended interview to the *Contra Costa Times* in late 2001—"Do I like litigation? Absolutely not. I try to avoid it at all possibility" was just one of several choice sound bites—but as he took a step back, one of his protégés moved to the fore. It's easy to blame the revolving door of general managers for the Warriors' continued failure with personnel decisions—sportswriter Ralph Wiley famously wrote that Twardzik told him he didn't draft Kobe Bryant because the high school phenom "didn't catch my eye"—but now there would be one constant in the years to come, someone who, against all odds, ultimately outlasted Cohan himself.

. . .

Robert Rowell was just 27 when Cohan hired him as the team's assistant controller in 1995. He'd been the associate athletic director at Cal Poly–San Luis Obispo, in the area where Sonic, Cohan's cable giant, began its formidable rise so many years before. (To this day, Cohan's name still adorns the performing arts center in SLO.) Rowell was regarded as a man with a keen business acumen, who, despite a lack of interpersonal skills, could become a rising star in sports business. After overseeing the financials involving the arena renovation, Rowell was named Golden State's vice president of business operations in 1998. Three years later, Rowell (still just 33) was named chief operating officer. And in 2003, after the Warriors improved by 17 games, Rowell was promoted to team president, a position he would hold for the remainder of his time in Oakland. Most critically, the bump in title gave him control over all aspects of business and basketball operations. Cohan was, more or less, done with running the Warriors. Nothing happened now without Rowell's say-so.

Revamping the Warriors would've been a monumental task for anyone. From 1997 to 2002, the Warriors won between 17 and 21 games in each season, which, to this day, remains five of the seven worst seasons in Warriors history. The 2000–01 season was a particularly horrific affair: Golden State dropped eight in a row after the All-Star break, won a game, then dropped 11 straight, won another game, then lost 13 in a row to end the year. That's a second-half record of two wins and 32 losses, some of the most putrid basketball ever played in the modern era.

So Rowell had nowhere to go but up, and he did—for a time. Golden State won at least 34 games in each of the next three seasons. Then came the remarkable 2006–07 campaign—the "We Believe" season, as it's known. Nelson was back for his second go-round as head coach and, led by an inspired core of Baron Davis, Matt Barnes, Jason Richardson, and Monta Ellis, the Warriors won nine of their final 10 games to sneak into the playoffs for the first time in 13 seasons. And as the No. 8 seed in the West, they executed one of the league's most improbable upsets, knocking off the 67-win Dallas Mavericks (coached by former Warriors guard Avery Johnson) in six games.

Utah stopped Golden State's miracle run in the next round and the Warriors soon fell back into their old habits. The major rumblings that summer revolved around Kevin Garnett being Oakland-bound in a blockbuster trade with the Minnesota Timberwolves, but Cohan put the kibosh on that. And despite an uptick to 48 wins in 2007–08, Golden State fell victim to a hypercompetitive Western Conference and missed the playoffs by two games.

The Warriors were bullish on the future and on Ellis's role with them, so much so that they signed him to a six-year, $66 million contract that July. But any ability to build on the momentum of the prior season was quashed a few weeks later when Ellis reported to the Warriors that he had hurt his left ankle while training offseason at his home in Mississippi. The diagnosis was a torn ligament that would keep him sidelined for three months.

Shortly thereafter, Ellis said he was actually injured while playing pickup ball. Then ESPN reported that not only had Ellis suffered a kind of injury (torn deltoid ligament plus a high ankle sprain) that is not often caused by basketball, but the 23-year-old also had cuts and scrapes on his legs that were inconsistent with any kind of basketball-related injury.

In October, Ellis finally came clean to the team and admitted that he hurt the leg riding his moped—an activity prohibited by the parameters of his newly signed deal. Golden State could've tried to void the entire contract but settled on suspending Ellis for 30 games without pay.

The incident also exposed a widening fissure between Rowell on one side and Chris Mullin and Don Nelson on the other. Rowell actually used the announcement of the suspension to publicly chastise Mullin, who had lobbied for leaner discipline. "Chris Mullin made it perfectly clear to both Mr. Cohan and myself that he didn't think this was a big deal at the beginning, and we happen to think it's a very big deal," Rowell said. "We happen to think that it's a big deal for our fans, it's a big deal for our season ticket holders, it's a big deal for our business partners, it's a big deal for the Warriors organization." Ellis returned to the lineup in late January and played 25 games, but the season was already lost. In 2008–09, Golden State lost 19 more games than the season before.

With the Warriors, the good times never lasted long, mostly because Rowell was not a very good evaluator of basketball talent and his misjudgment often resulted in disastrous business decisions. In 2001, Cohan signed Antawn Jamison to a six-year contract extension worth $83.7 million, the most lucrative in Bay Area sports history—more than Chris Mullin, Barry Bonds, Joe Montana, or Jerry Rice had ever earned—with one stroke of a pen. Two years later, in one of his first acts as team president, Rowell traded Jamison and three others to Dallas for 31-year-old Nick Van Exel and three more players. He then signed Corey Maggette in the summer of 2008 to a five-year deal worth around $50 million.

But the truly baffling move came 10 games into the 2008–09 season when Rowell signed Stephen Jackson to a three-year contract extension worth nearly $28 million . . . when Jackson still had two years left on his current deal. In the NBA, this was considered tantamount to management malpractice. "We view this as a win-win for everyone," Rowell said in a statement. Exactly one year later, Jackson was traded to Charlotte after begging for his release. "I wanted to be out pretty bad," Jackson proclaimed. "Things were going bad. I was getting blamed for everything. I wasn't seeing eye to eye with the team. I got fined in preseason, which was ridiculous. It was just a lot of things that I didn't agree with that was going on."

And as Rowell stacked the roster with overpaid malcontents, the Warriors' best players often struggled before being dumped elsewhere, with little or nothing in return for Golden State:

- Derek Fisher, who had won three titles as the point guard for the Shaq/Kobe-led Lakers, was signed in July 2004 to a six-year deal worth $37 million. By opening night, Don Nelson had relegated him to the bench in lieu of Speedy Claxton. Fisher started only 32 games that season and 36 the next before being traded to Utah.
- Baron Davis, the life force of the "We Believe" season, was acquired from New Orleans in February 2005 for Claxton and Dale Davis. But when he was offered a three-year extension in 2008, it was for only $39 million. The Los Angeles Clippers signed him the following summer for $65 million.
- Jason Richardson was a stellar first-round selection in 2001, but six years later he was traded on draft night to Charlotte for No. 8 overall pick Brandan Wright, who didn't last three seasons.
- Gilbert Arenas, a second-round pick in 2001, blossomed over two seasons into a multidimensional point guard who could score, pass, and defend, but he went east in 2003 for $65 million from Washington, just five months after Rowell promised season-ticket holders the team was "not going to let that guy walk away without an offer."

The second-rate players were rewarded; the potential cornerstones eventually fled. Such was life with the Warriors in those days.

By the time the 2009–10 season concluded, the Warriors consisted of only a couple of faint bright spots engulfed by a mishmash of unproven draftees and high-priced, underachieving misfits. They were the second-highest-scoring team in the NBA but the second-worst at defense. *Maybe* a pearl of greatness existed within this roster somewhere, but that can be hard to pluck out when you're posting the fourth-worst record in the NBA, just 26 wins across 82 games.

More than 15 years since Chris Cohan bought the Warriors outright, since he promised to keep the Warriors a "first-class organization," they had made the playoffs just once. For the better part of two decades, the Warriors earned a reputation as one of the worst (and worst-run) franchises in all of American professional sports.

. . .

The first rumblings that Cohan might be getting serious about selling the team hit the local papers in time for the Fourth of July weekend of 2009. Even if fans were already delirious at the prospect of someone—anyone!—replacing Cohan for good, it wasn't a surprising development. Not only did Cohan give day-to-day control to Rowell in 2003, but he also sold 20 percent of the team to a group of four investors in 2004. They were well-known executives in the tech industry, but none wielded decision-making power. It was another infusion of cash for Cohan, who had sold Sonic Communications in 1998 for some $200 million. But then the Internal Revenue Service came after him in 2005, alleging the use of three illegal tax shelters to handle the transaction. The government sought more in total damages than Cohan had pocketed, so the windfall from a Warriors sale could be quite helpful. Throw in the decade and a half of unrelenting criticism from fans and media members and it's easy to see why Cohan wanted out when he did. By the spring of 2010, it was time for prospective bidders to name their price.

The most logical suitor was Larry Ellison, the founder and chief executive of financial software giant Oracle, which already owned the naming rights on the Warriors' home arena. With a net worth of $28 billion, Ellison was the third-richest man in America. It was hard to envision any price too high. Ellison was passionate about sports, having just bankrolled an America's Cup–winning sailing team that February, and had even tried to own an NBA team in the past. In 2006, Ellison reportedly tried to buy the Seattle SuperSonics for $425 million and move them to San Jose. (Instead, they sold for $350 million and moved to Oklahoma City two years later.)

Business was Ellison's livelihood, but sports was a true passion. And once you factor in all those billions, anyone else jumping ahead in the auction process would be an upset akin to those No. 8 seed Warriors in 2006–07 not only knocking off Dallas but winning the whole damn thing.

On July 15, 2010, the team announced that Cohan had officially sold the Golden State Warriors for $450 million. That was more than three times his initial investment and more than anyone had ever paid for the right to own an NBA franchise.

And it wasn't Ellison with the winning bid.

The Warriors were sold to an ownership group composed of Joe Lacob, a longtime Silicon Valley venture capitalist; Peter Guber, the famed Hollywood producer; and a gaggle of minority investors, including YouTube cofounder Chad Hurley, Zappos founder Nick Swinmurn, TIBCO founder Vivek Ranadivé, philanthropist Erika Glazer, and prominent Bay Area VCs such as Juvo Capital's Harry Tsao, Oak Investment Partners' Fred Harman, Oaktree Capital Management's Bruce Karsh, Fort Mason Capital's Dan German, Redpoint Ventures' John Walecka, and Kingsford Capital Management's Dave Scially.

Ellison released a statement saying Cohan had left money on the table in accepting Lacob and Guber's bid: "Although I was the highest bidder, Chris Cohan decided to sell to someone else. In my experience this is a bit unusual." Sal Galatioto, who handled the sale for Cohan, explained to a local paper that Ellison's bid had come in too late and that considering his bid, which he conceded was higher by a few million, would have been poor form: "Chris and I both felt that the moral and ethical thing to do was to honor the deal we had. It just wouldn't have been morally right."

And because Ellison's bid didn't represent a substantial increase over the other suitors—not even eclipsing $500 million—it was easier to enforce the lapsed deadline. But a source close to Cohan told me the owner would've given Ellison more consideration had the money been there: "I think if the bid was *significantly* higher, yeah, Chris would have definitely thought about it."

Among the other bidders were Mark Mastrov, the Bay Area businessman who founded 24 Hour Fitness, and David Bonderman, the founder of the San Francisco–based private equity firm TPG Capital— both of whom exceeded $400 million in their offers. But after increasing their initial bid, Lacob and Guber were informed by Galatioto they had won.

As the paperwork was finalized, Lacob was vacationing in Greece with Nicole Curran, his fiancée, and about to board a helicopter for Delphi, once the home of the all-powerful, all-knowing Oracle.

Now, Lacob's next destination would be Oracle Arena.

. . .

Born in January 1956, Joseph Steven Lacob lived his earliest years in New Bedford, Massachusetts, nestled south of Boston in a working-class coastal enclave that's actually closer to (and much more identifiable with) Providence, Rhode Island. For more than a century, New Bedford was one of the East Coast's primary whaling hubs, and it was a tough place to grow up in those post–World War II years. Lacob's mother, Marlene, worked long hours at a grocery store; his father, Sid, worked the factory floor at a local paper plant. For years, the city was defined by the dozens of textile mills that dotted its geography, but jobs would become scarce. The Lacobs lived around the corner from a hospital in what, Joe once recalled, "wasn't the easiest neighborhood."

Like so many New England youths of the 1960s, Lacob was enchanted by the success of his beloved Celtics. When he was nine years old and first walked onto the hardwood flooring of a local gym, it was as if he was teleported 58 miles north onto the Boston Garden's iconic parquet, the same one graced by Bill Russell, John Havlicek, and Sam Jones, among so many other greats. The story Lacob likes to tell is that it was in that moment he knew he would one day own an NBA team.

Not *play* in the NBA, but *own* a franchise.

It was a more absurd wish than what most kids his age would normally conjure, but that improbable eventuality was first set into motion when Lacob was 14 years old and his father's position was transferred 3,000 miles west to a plant in Anaheim, California. "One of the great breaks in my life," Lacob has said. "California is where the new stuff happens, right? God forbid I would've had to end up staying in New Bedford."

For Lacob, the move to Anaheim meant a world of new possibilities and he soaked it all in. Since the family home was just a mile from Anaheim Stadium, Lacob got a job working concessions at California Angels games. He started out with Cokes and then ice-cream sandwiches before working his way to peanuts—a far more lucrative treat, not just because you could throw them but because the bags could be double- and triple-stacked upon one another, allowing Lacob to carry a bigger load and sell more on every trip into the Anaheim Stadium stands. And since he was getting a 14 percent commission on every sale, those peanuts really added up over the course of a game.

As a standout student at Katella High in Anaheim, Lacob played junior varsity hoops and, later, varsity tennis, but he was drawn to science in the classroom. Upon graduating in 1974, he chose biological sciences as his major at the University of California–Irvine. Lacob kept his night job in Anaheim throughout most of his undergraduate studies—seven years of selling peanuts actually paid his way through school—and he became not only an Angels fan, witnessing Nolan Ryan in his freakish prime, but also a massive Lakers fan, back when Gail Goodrich, Wilt Chamberlain, and Jerry West ruled the Forum.

While at Irvine, Lacob lived at home for his freshman and sophomore years to further save money. He would be the first from his family to graduate from college and wanted to make the most of the opportunity. He also took a mathematics class taught by Edward O. Thorp, who, in 1962, had authored *Beat the Dealer*, perhaps the best-selling book on gambling ever published. Thorp wrote about the methods behind card-counting and how algorithmic models could help players beat the major casinos at their own game. By the time Lacob arrived in his classroom, Thorp, who would chaperone his students on field trips to Las Vegas to put his lesson plan to practical use, had already delved into the even more controversial study of ace prediction in blackjack. His ideas had a deep influence on how Lacob approached risk, reward, and the innate tension between them. "The big thrill," Thorp once recalled, "came from learning things nobody else in the world had ever known."

As Lacob approached his graduation from UC-Irvine in 1978, he focused on going to medical school and pursuing the chance to become a doctor. (He even coauthored studies that were published in the journals *Psychopharmacology* and *Physiology & Behavior*.) But there were two problems with his plan. The first was that no one would accept his med school applications. For two years, he applied to dozens of the top universities—47, by his own count. He got waitlisted at one (Washington University in St. Louis) that eventually passed. The second hiccup was he didn't really want to become a doctor anymore. His girlfriend (and future wife), Laurie Kraus, told him flat out that he'd make a terrible doctor. "Hell of a good piece of advice," Lacob conceded years later, but he knew it, too. He'd worked several jobs as an undergrad, including a stint in the morgue, which cemented his hunch that he needed a new direction. "I liked the science," Lacob said in 2012, "but I didn't really like the idea of treating people and being involved in all that." For the first time in years, Lacob faced an uncertain future, but he earned a master's in public health from UCLA in 1979 and went to work for FHP International, one of the country's first big HMOs.

Then Lacob came to what he's deemed his turning point in life. Encouraged by the idea that he needed *some* kind of management experience if he was going to be the kind of success he envisioned, Lacob started applying to business schools and, this time, actually was accepted to a few. He relocated to the Bay Area, and by the time he graduated from Stanford in 1983 with his MBA, Lacob was already director of marketing for an up-and-coming biotech firm called Cetus.

Based in Emeryville, a then-growing Oakland suburb and future home of animation powerhouse Pixar, Cetus became known in tech circles in March 1981 when it pulled off what was hailed in the *New York Times* as the largest-ever IPO in the history of corporate America, raising nearly $120 million in its first day of public trading. That smashed the old record of $101.2 million set just a few months earlier by another scrappy Bay Area startup: Apple Computer.

Though scientists James Watson, Francis Crick, and Rosalind Franklin had discovered the foundational elements of DNA back in 1953, the biotech industry was finally booming by the mid-eighties, with investors pouring millions of investment dollars into the field. It was those kinds of cash infusions that allowed Cetus to make some of the most groundbreaking advancements in biotech history. In 1983, a Cetus scientist named Kary Mullis conceived of a method to copy DNA and synthesize unlimited amounts of genetic material from just a single strand. The technique, dubbed polymerase chain reaction, eventually earned Mullis the Nobel Prize in Chemistry. "I was in the right place at that point with the right time with the right educational experience," Lacob later said.

It was these serendipitous circumstances that led to Lacob (who had formed his own startup by now) getting hired as a director and partner by the prestigious Silicon Valley venture capital firm of Kleiner Perkins Caufield & Byers in May 1987. As one of the most accomplished VC giants on Sand Hill Road, Kleiner Perkins let Lacob apply his backgrounds in biotech and life sciences to the business world—and sports often made a cameo appearance in his investments. Lacob quickly built a reputation on making sound investments that were buoyed by a healthy dose of inherent risk. He was one of the earliest backers of the news site SportsLine.com (now owned and operated by CBS) and the e-commerce hub Autotrader.com. Across more than 20 years, Lacob would invest Kleiner's money in dozens of companies centered on life sciences, alternative energies, and medical devices.

In Silicon Valley, no one has a batting average close to perfect. The best you can hope for is not to have any one failure blow up into a major scandal. But in 2009, Lacob got burned by an oil-and-gas-drilling startup called Terralliance, which claimed to use satellite imaging to more efficiently find pockets of untapped fossil fuels under the surface. They accepted millions in funding from numerous firms and investors. Former secretary of state Colin Powell was listed as an adviser. By 2006, the company was valued at roughly $1 billion. The next year, Lacob, then a Terralliance board member, was breathlessly quoted in the *Times* about how the somewhat surprising investment in a company dependent on fossil fuel production didn't undermine Kleiner's commitment to eco-friendly investments: "We're extremely committed to that investment thesis."

There were two main problems with Terralliance. One was that it was spending its investment dollars far too rapidly—akin to "a drunken sailor," said one report. But more damning perhaps was that its satellite imaging tech didn't quite provide the results they had claimed to Kleiner and other investors. As a result, the company was in free fall by 2009. The CEO was fired for misconduct and later sued for stealing intellectual property to create a competing company. Terralliance changed its name in early 2010 and again the following year. It remains one of the biggest busts to happen since the financial meltdown of 2008. So when Lacob's purchase of the team was made public, it's understandable that the *Wall Street Journal*'s headline was less than subtle: LET'S HOPE JOE LACOB'S GOLDEN STATE WARRIORS IS NO TERRALLIANCE.

Lacob had also struck out on a high-profile sports venture. In November 1997, he led a group of investors who put $3 million into the upstart American Basketball League, a professional women's league that would compete with the WNBA. After the ABL's inaugural season, Lacob became the controlling owner of the San Jose Lasers and his group held a 20 percent stake in the league itself. He said the inspiration to invest came from attending USA men's basketball blowouts at the 1996 Summer Olympics in Atlanta and being more entertained by the women's games. "We compete with Bill Gates every day at Kleiner Perkins," Lacob told the *Los Angeles Times*. "Here we're competing against David Stern."

The ABL, with its league offices in Palo Alto, filed for Chapter 11 bankruptcy protection a few days before Christmas 1998 and ceased operations immediately. It had run out of money. The ABL All-Star Game—slated for San Jose in January 1999—never happened.

Lacob eventually wised up on his sports investments. In 2006, he purchased a minority stake in his original hometown team, the Boston Celtics. "I am glad to welcome my longtime friend Joe Lacob to our ownership group," said Celtics co-owner Irv Grousbeck in a statement.

"He has a passion for sports and a distinguished record of success in business, and I know he will be an excellent partner." Lacob was content to stay on the West Coast and watch mostly from afar as the Celtics built their own super-team—led by Paul Pierce and new acquisitions Kevin Garnett and Ray Allen—and advanced to the 2008 Finals against the Los Angeles Lakers. It was a conflicting moment for Lacob, who sat in the front row at the Staples Center cheering on the team that taught him to love basketball versus the team he cheered as a Southern California teenager. Boston won the title in six games.

All the while, as he was learning the ins and outs of NBA owner-ship, Lacob remained a longtime season-ticket holder of another fran-chise, one that would hit the market not two years later. By that time, Lacob seemed ready for a new phase in his life. He'd done venture capi-tal for some 23 years. He and his wife, Laurie Kraus Lacob, had divorced and their four kids—Kirk, Kent, Kelly, and Kayci—were grown and college-aged. He'd won an NBA title as a minority owner, albeit with little influence. And as a Bay Area resident for nearly 30 years, Lacob knew what it would mean to take ownership of the Warriors and, dare to dream, win a championship.

Buying the Warriors was a calculated risk, the biggest of Lacob's ca-reer. At a cost of nearly a half-billion dollars to himself and his investors, Lacob couldn't afford to fail.

.   .   .

On the day the sale was announced, Cohan released his final statement as Warriors owner: "As I conclude my tenure as owner of the Warriors, I wanted to take this opportunity to express my sincerest gratitude, and to personally say thank you to the best fans in all of sports. It's a phrase that is too often utilized by players, coaches, executives, and owners in all sports leagues, but I can say without reservation and unbridled con-viction that Warriors fans have earned the sole right of that honor and distinction. Thank you for making Golden State Warriors basketball the incredible fan experience that it has become." Cohan has not spoken publicly since that day.

Lacob also released a statement to mark the occasion, one enveloped in optimism and hope: "I am incredibly excited to have the opportunity to be the next steward of this storied NBA franchise. This is my dream come true. Peter and I intend to do what we do best—innovating and building. It is our passion to return the Warriors to greatness and build nothing short of a championship organization that will make all of us in the Bay Area proud."

Beat writers were shocked when Lacob returned their calls that same day, stressing that the purchase wasn't some vanity project for him and Guber. "We did our due diligence. I think we wanted it more than the other guys and I think we are more knowledgeable about basketball than all these other guys," he told one writer. "We think it's a very good opportunity as a business enterprise and the potential is there. But this is all about winning. We're going to change the course of this franchise."

But to turn around one of the most hapless teams in basketball would require, among many other things, a leader on the court, a star who could pull others into his orbit, an icon they could sell to the public. Pulling off nothing less than one of the great turnarounds in NBA history would hinge entirely on finding such a player and getting him to come play in Oakland.

Little did Lacob and Guber know such a man was already in their employ.

# 2 ★ ★ ★ ★ ★ ★ ★ ★

# IN THE NAME OF
# HIS FATHER

### The 2009–10 season

**W**hen Wardell Stephen Curry II made his NBA debut for the Warriors on October 28, 2009, he was still years away from changing the way we watch and think about professional basketball. In due time, Curry would mix a breathtaking blend of technique, fearlessness, and bravado into a brew that served to intoxicate hoops-watchers the world over. He would break league records, then rebreak them himself before the NBA had time to rise to his level. His jump shot became unfathomably reliable as Curry routinely produced highlights destined to be discussed and dissected for years to come. If you've watched any appreciable amount of basketball over the past few years, you have at least one memorable moment in mind.

But when the Warriors drafted him, Steph Curry was seen as a scrawny college star who performed feats that couldn't be replicated in the pro game. Curry could score, pass, and capably defend, but the likelihood of his ever eclipsing the career of his father seemed remote and, in almost all ways, impossible.

Dell Curry was a standout at Virginia Tech, a First-Team All-American who would go on to play 16 years in the NBA for five different teams. Curry was a reliable outside shooter in college and, upon entering the league in 1986, quickly cemented his place in a new wave of players who came up with the three-point line as a way of life rather than a novelty. When Dan Majerle of the Phoenix Suns set the NBA single-season record for threes in 1993–94 with 192, Curry was third in the league with 152. He was also clutch; it was Curry's two late free throws that snapped Chicago's record 44-game home win streak in 1996. When he retired after the 2001–02 season, Curry was the Charlotte Hornets' all-time leader in points scored. He had also swished the 10th-most threes (1,245) in NBA history.

So from the start, with such an accomplished father, Steph Curry's path to the NBA seemed preordained. He was born on March 14, 1988, at the same Akron, Ohio, hospital where LeBron James had been delivered just three-plus years earlier. But whereas James was born to a single mother and endured a childhood that was both nomadic and hellish—"I saw drugs, guns, killings; it was crazy," James told *Sports* Illustrated— Curry's upbringing was of deep privilege. Dell was a 23-year-old shooting guard playing for the Cleveland Cavaliers when his first son came along. But when Steph was three months old, the Hornets selected his father with their first pick in the expansion draft, so the Currys headed 500 miles south to North Carolina, laying down familial roots that anchor the family there to this day.

Dell played 10 years in Charlotte, so little Steph often got to see his father at work as one of the league's deadliest long-range shooters. Less a star than a role player, Curry started only 99 games out of 1,083 over his career, but as a sixth man he thrived. His three-point percentage topped 40 percent for eight years in a row, leading the league once with a 47.8 percent clip. His free-throw rate was outstanding—Curry stands comfortably among the top 100 in NBA history from the charity stripe—and his steal rate was above average. The 6-foot-5 Curry, for the most part, was a proficient and reliable player. And lasting in the NBA for 16 seasons is no small accomplishment, with the league's average career flickering out in fewer than five. On contracts alone, Dell Curry made nearly $20 million over his career.

Steph was there to see much of it unfold, either during home games in Charlotte or even on the road once Dell signed free agent contracts elsewhere, first with Milwaukee (for one season), then Toronto (for three, which meant frequent one-on-one showdowns with Vince Carter before Raptors games). Steph, who idolized guards like Allen Iverson, Steve Nash, and Reggie Miller, developed a jump shot that could turn grown-ups agape, a pull-up that, on first glance, feels awfully reminiscent of what Warriors fans could describe in the here and now. "I found myself subconsciously picking up things that [my father] used to do," Curry later remembered.

But the problem back then was both physical and mechanical. Curry was puny by any real measure. He was 5-foot-5 in sneakers by eighth grade and still only 5-foot-8 (and maybe 150 pounds) by his sophomore year at Charlotte Christian School. He was the star, leading CCS to a conference title, even if his jumper started down low at the waist and steadily heaved upward like a conveyor belt, a choreographed move that would be easy for average defenders to shut down. Maybe physical stature would come in time, maybe not, but his father knew that elite Division I schools—let alone the NBA—would not come calling on a shot such as his.

In the summer of 2004, Dell, a full two years retired from the league, was fully available to teach his eldest son the ways of the jump shot. Ground zero was the half-court adjacent to their Charlotte home, and the two spent hours each day forging a new kind of jumper—a more traditional style that depended on the top-of-the-jump wrist flick most NBA stars prefer—that would give Steph a truly lethal weapon in his arsenal. His ball-handling, his court vision, his passing were all clearly at the level you'd expect from the son of an NBA two-guard, but they would mean little without a proper jumper. It was an excruciating experience for all involved. "The summer of tears," they dubbed it.

But the basketball boot camp worked. Curry emerged with a fluid, arching shot now also fueled by an irrational confidence. Coaches witnessed in him a focus and maturity that belied his youthful countenance, and CCS thrived under his ascension, going 31-3 during his senior season. Curry ended his high school career with school-record 170 three-pointers and 232 steals over three varsity seasons. "The gifts that he has," Shonn Brown, his high school coach, once said, "I truly believe he's like, 'Lord you have blessed me with these gifts and talents, I'm going to utilize them to the best of my ability.'" His senior-year page in the yearbook included a quote attributed to Michael Jordan: "I've always believed that if you put in the work, the results will come. I don't do things half-heartedly. Because I know if I do, then I can expect half-hearted results." It was indicative of an ethic that extended to the classroom as well, where Curry exhibited a joie de vivre that counteracted the seriousness with which he often consumed basketball. "If I had to summarize Stephen Curry in one word," said Chad Fair, his drama teacher, "it would be *joyful*. He loves being wherever he is."

Curry would have given anything to catch on at a top Division I university, the kind of program that could develop his skill set and mold him into the NBA-caliber player he knew he was. With his father's pedigree and revered status in the Charlotte community and beyond, this seemed like the surest of outcomes. But Curry, barely 6 feet tall and only starting to fill out his upper body, was summarily ignored by all the big-time schools. Virginia Tech, his father's alma mater, barely gave Steph a sniff. They would not offer a scholarship unless he sat out his freshman year. (The family stopped regularly attending Hokies games after that.) Curry was left scrambling for how to continue his higher basketball education. "Sometimes," Brown recalled later, "kids don't pass the eye test." His mother, Sonya, has been more blunt: "A lot of Division I schools were supposed to have a great ability to assess talent, but they missed his."

One school noticed. Davidson College, a small liberal arts college with an enrollment below 2,000 students, didn't command a modern reputation for top-flight basketball—the legendary Lefty Driesell did coach the school to back-to-back Elite Eight appearances in 1968 and 1969—but it was Division I and only a 20-minute drive from the Currys' home in Charlotte.

Bob McKillop, who'd coached the Wildcats since 1989, had been aware of Curry's athletic potential for nearly a decade. His son Brendan played with Steph on a state-title-winning summer league baseball team when both were 10 years old; the coach remembered seeing Curry run down fly balls in center field. So by the time Curry finished his freshman year of high school and was concentrating fully on basketball, McKillop began his long recruitment. Whereas most other schools saw an undersized guard who'd have trouble beating larger upperclassmen to the rim, McKillop was not deterred. As the coach once told ESPN, "I saw brilliance."

Curry's decision came down to Davidson, Virginia Tech, Virginia Commonwealth, and Winthrop. On September 16, 2005, with McKillop and his assistant making their last, best pitch while seated in Dell and Sonya Curry's living room, Steph gave him his verbal commitment to Davidson. The coaches practically danced around the room, delirious from relief. A player such as Curry could lift a scrappy program like Davidson's to new heights. In NCAA hoops, all you need is one star-level talent to make a splash.

A year later, Curry matriculated at Davidson and began preparing for his freshman season. The Wildcats had gone 20-11 and made the NCAA tournament the season before, losing to Ohio State in the first round, but the departure of seven seniors meant a lack of depth on McKillop's roster. Thus, Curry was installed as the starting two-guard from the get-go and thrown into the fire on the road against Eastern Michigan in the season opener.

The first half of Curry's debut was a disaster, thanks to nine turnovers. The Wildcats were down by 16 at the half and McKillop was already wondering if the advanced maturity he'd assessed in Curry had been blindness on his part, but he stuck with his freshman and let him start in the second half. Curry responded by spurring an 18–4 run that helped tie the game. Eastern Michigan recovered and would lead again by as much as 10, but Curry would not be denied. He swished a three with 2:35 left to play that gave Davidson a lead it would not relinquish.

Curry finished with 15 points and 13 turnovers, but the Wildcats were winners, 81–77. The next night, facing a tough Michigan squad, Curry scored 32 points and nearly coordinated another epic second-half comeback before Davidson succumbed by 10.

Curry's play—and Davidson's season—only got better as the year progressed. After dropping early games to top schools like Missouri and Duke, the Wildcats rolled through their Southern Conference schedule. In the conference championship game against the College of Charleston, Curry played all 40 minutes and scored a game-high 29 points to go with eight rebounds and three assists. (He had only two turnovers.) The Wildcats were 29-4 and finished conference play at 17-1. For all their success, they were selected only as a No. 13 seed in the NCAA tournament and lost to No. 4 seed Maryland, 82–70, though Curry was sensational with a game-high 30 points that kept Davidson within striking distance the whole game.

For the season, Curry averaged 21.5 points, good enough to finish ninth in the country and second among all freshmen, trailing only a lanky University of Texas phenom named Kevin Durant. His 122 three-pointers were the most of any freshman in NCAA history. His averages of 4.6 rebounds and 2.8 assists showed that his game had depth, that he wasn't simply a volume scorer who racked up empty points. And the loss to Maryland, though disappointing for its competitiveness, made Steph Curry into a national name. "He's for real," Maryland coach Gary Williams said afterward. "I told him after the game, 'You could play anywhere.' "

Though expectations were raised for his sophomore season, Curry was even better. The Wildcats went undefeated in conference play (20-0) and won the Southern Conference title again, heading to the NCAA tournament with a 29-6 record and riding a 22-game win streak. But even with Curry, who stayed at shooting guard and was a top-10 scorer for much of the season, the No. 10 seed Wildcats weren't expected to go far, being such a small school from a conference few could name. Their first opponent was No. 7 seed Gonzaga, which had become famous over the years for two things: producing Hall of Famer point guard John Stockton and upsetting other schools in the NCAA tournament.

Nonetheless, the Wildcats, led by Curry's 30-point second-half explosion, prevailed in an opening-round shocker, 82–76. It was Davidson's first NCAA tournament win in decades, and Curry was the breakout star of March Madness. His game-high 30 points against No. 2 seed Georgetown two nights later secured a 74–70 win and Davidson's place in the Sweet 16. Five days later, Curry pumped in another 30 to lead all scorers and propel Davidson to a 73–56 laugher over No. 3 seed Wisconsin. (The game was tied at halftime before the Wildcats blew up.) As proclaimed by ESPN anchor Scott Van Pelt on *SportsCenter*, Curry was "the star of the tournament whose legend continues to grow." It was an eight-day span that forever changed the trajectory of Curry's life, altering his status from an intriguing, under-the-radar prospect to a future NBA lottery pick who might experience a career arc on par with his father's.

The Wildcats then had to contend with No. 1 seed Kansas, regarded as the best team in the country. With four future NBA players in their starting lineup, the Jayhawks were looking to become the fourth No. 1 seed of the tournament to make the Final Four—a grouping that, somehow, had never occurred before—while Curry's crew was looking for the single-greatest win in Davidson program history.

With Kansas up by only two at halftime, the second half was a frantic back-and-forth that wasn't decided until the very end. With Kansas up by five, Curry came off a screen, pulled up from 24, and buried a long three to cut Davidson's deficit to 59–57.

With five seconds left and a chance late to win the game on a buzzer-beating three, Curry was double-teamed up high and forced to pass the ball to teammate Jason Richards, whose 25-footer went wide left of the rim. It was a deflating finish, with Curry, who led all scorers (yet again) with 25 points, unable to attempt a final shot when it mattered most. "We expected to win," McKillop said after the loss. "It came down to one final play. That's the beauty of this game that we play." Eight days later, Kansas won the national championship.

In the aggregate, Curry's stats were superlative. He finished fourth in the nation in scoring with 25.9 points per game—which helped Richards, the starting point guard, lead the nation in assists—and was selected as a Second Team All-American. Curry's 162 three-pointers were an NCAA single-season record. More important, he had shown a national audience that his skills could translate to the NBA.

And yet, the entire history-making season almost never happened.

Though Curry started all 36 games his sophomore season, he was almost knocked out for the year back in the schedule's earliest moments. After a 64-point thrashing of Emory in the season opener, the coaching staff discovered Curry had torn cartilage in his left wrist. It was on his nonshooting hand and could potentially heal on its own, but the pain would be constant through the season. Plus, because it was so early in the year, Curry could get surgery and, per NCAA rules, sit out the season as a redshirt, thus retaining a year of eligibility. After a discussion between McKillop, the medical staff, Steph and Dell Curry, and the Wildcat seniors, the decision was made: Curry would not get surgery. They would tape his wrist, up and around his thumb, and wait for the cartilage to heal itself with time.

Davidson's next game was on the road against No. 1 North Carolina, a nationally televised ESPN game. Playing against fellow future lottery pick Tyler Hansbrough and the Tar Heels—one of the schools Curry yearned to play for as a high school prospect—Curry missed his first four shots, keeping his dribble contained to his right hand whenever possible. As usual, Curry led all scorers, with 24 points, but he missed 10 of 12 three-point shots and the Wildcats came up short, 72–68. However, his nonshooting hand had proof of life. Curry could play with the injury, and by midseason the wrist was healed sufficiently that he stopped taping it.

There wasn't much question that Curry would return to Davidson for his junior season; the only mystery was what he'd decide in a year after that. Following one more healthy season, chances were that Curry would depart for the NBA, so McKillop switched him to point guard. Curry could better show off his passing and defense and become familiar with the position he'd likely play in the pros. At 6-foot-3 and 180 pounds, Curry was too small to compete as a shooting guard on the NBA level.

But even as he switched to a position better suited to his ball distribution, Curry's offense soared. He led the nation with 28.6 points and nearly doubled his nightly assists to 5.6. His efficiency came down a few ticks, but his overall game was more suited to what the NBA expected of him: a slightly undersized point guard with explosive scoring potential and above-average passing and defense. When Davidson, with a 26-6 record, was upset in the semifinals of the Southern Conference tournament—meaning there'd be no return trip to the NCAA tournament—Curry's future was sealed and college basketball lost one of its most exhilarating acts. "Curry is less athlete than folk hero," wrote Tommy Craggs in *Slate*, "a star who shares a strand of DNA with the knife throwers, crack shots, and pool-hall massé artists of the world."

During Curry's three seasons at Davidson, the team compiled an 85-20 record, including an astounding 55-3 in conference play. Curry was selected as a First Team All-American and left school as the 25th-best scorer in NCAA men's basketball history. His 414 threes were fourth-most all-time, just 43 behind Duke's J. J. Redick for the top spot. Curry played 104 games for the Wildcats and scored in double digits in 102 of them. Just one month after Davidson's season ended, Curry and his family agreed there was little else he could accomplish in school. He declared for the NBA Draft.

"I'm mentally and physically ready to make that jump," he told reporters. "This is a dream of mine since I was a little kid." Several Charlotte TV stations carried the press conference live. Their hometown hero was officially off to the NBA.

. . .

"His first step is average at best, and considering his skinny frame and poor explosiveness around the basket in traffic, it's unlikely that he'll be able to get to the free throw line anywhere near as much in the NBA as he does in college." That comes from the scouting report posted on DraftExpress.com—widely recognized as the leading authority in NBA Draft analysis—on February 28, 2009, with just a few games to go in Curry's collegiate career. The follow-up assessment posted in early May was kinder, though it still concluded that Curry's NBA prospects were, at best, "an interesting case." The report on NBADraft.net was more scathing: "Far below NBA standard in regard to explosiveness and athleticism. . . . He's not a natural point guard that an NBA team can rely on to run a team." And ESPN's Doug Gottlieb, while conceding that Curry made his teammates better, still ran down a litany of his perceived shortcomings: "Was Curry capable of blowing by defenders in college? No. Is he big enough to shoot over NBA players? No. Does he have a defined position at the NBA level? No. Can he contain the basketball? No."

But these conclusions didn't reflect how Larry Riley thought of Curry. He saw Curry's flexibility between point and shooting guard fitting in perfectly with Don Nelson's up-and-down, high-tempo offense. Riley believed Curry could be the franchise cornerstone Golden State so desperately coveted.

The Warriors couldn't afford to screw up this pick. They had the seventh choice in the 2009 draft, thanks to a 29-53 record, and Riley, who had decades of experience as a scout and coach in both college and the NBA, was promoted to general manager after the season. This draft choice would be his first major decision as the person in charge of player personnel, and the Warriors needed lots of help.

A few weeks before the draft, Riley still hadn't settled on anyone. He would happily take a point guard, but he also wanted to beef up the frontcourt, maybe with a physical center who could operate under the rim. Riley also thought about seniors, who were becoming increasingly rare in the draft as more players declared earlier in their collegiate careers. The Warriors had the fifth-youngest roster in the NBA, so a more polished prospect might be preferable to a "project" player who required development.

Riley felt no small amount of pressure. "A draft pick is an asset," he said. "You're focusing on next year *and* five years down the road at the same time." At the multiteam predraft workout held in Oakland, Riley joked with reporters about the tenuous position of picking so late. "Seven—it's a great *number*," he told one. "I don't know if it's a great pick."

This was not only the most important decision in Riley's professional life but the culmination of a career that almost never happened.

Riley and his twin brother, Mike, grew up the sons of farmers in Whitewater, Indiana, harvesting corn, wheat, and soybeans while raising beef and dairy cattle. Instead of taking over the family business after high school, both boys enrolled at Chadron State College in Nebraska, an 1,100-mile drive west by car. Like their father at the University of Wyoming after the war, Larry and Mike were skilled at basketball and baseball, which they both played at CSC. Larry, who also ran cross-country, then headed for graduate school at Southeast Missouri State and coached a few seasons of high school basketball in Indiana. He hopped from one collegiate assistant coaching job to another before getting a call from his old coach at Chadron, offering him the head coaching job. Riley took a 25 percent pay cut and headed from Mercer University in Georgia back to Nebraska. That gig led to the head coaching job at Eastern New Mexico, where Riley patrolled the sidelines for 10 seasons. While there, Riley coached two sons of Del Harris, the Milwaukee Bucks head coach who had employed his twin brother years earlier at a small Indiana college. In 1988, Harris hired Riley as a Bucks video scout. He soon became Harris's top assistant, but in 1994 general manager Stu Jackson hired Riley to be an executive with the expansion Vancouver Grizzlies. Riley was regarded as one of the NBA's top discerners of talent and his job took him across the country.

On January 9, 1997, Riley's life changed in an immeasurable way. While on a scouting trip for the Grizzlies, his flight from Cincinnati to Detroit was delayed by 30-mph winds and freezing snow showers in the area. At the gate, Riley was chatting lightheartedly with other passengers, the way you do when you're all antsy to just get home already, when he heard a voice inside his head: *Go home.* He brushed it off the first time, but then the voice spoke again. As a religious man, Riley would not shrug off what had just happened. He asked the gate agent to refile his ticket for back home.

When Riley deplaned for his layover at Seattle-Tacoma International Airport, he turned on his cell phone and it started ringing. Stu Jackson, his boss, was on the line, sounding panicked.

"Where are you?!?" said Jackson, before informing Riley that his original flight, Comair 3272, had crashed in whiteout conditions while flying to Detroit. All 29 souls on board were lost.

Riley still had to catch a smaller regional flight to Vancouver, but he did and made it home when, by all rights, he never should've been alive to do so. He hugged his daughter and wife that night, vowing to make the most of his life, to never let those closest to him down. "It reinforced my faith," he said years later, "and reinforced that you should treat everyone as well as you can."

In 2000, Don Nelson brought Riley aboard to the Dallas Mavericks and he spent six seasons there, mostly as an assistant coach and scout. And in August 2006, when Nelson was rehired by the Warriors as head coach, Riley followed two days later. After three years on the bench—including the "We Believe" season of 2006–07—Riley was bumped up to the front office as Chris Mullin was let go.

As general manager, the 64-year-old Riley would run point on the Warriors' draft strategy.

He had six weeks to prepare.

Even without the luxury of spare time, Riley was determined to take his time and do this pick right. "The worst decisions, to me, are knee-jerk reactions," he said before the draft. "We're not going to get into something that we haven't had a chance to evaluate." And yet, even as two dozen prospects went through drills at the team's practice facility, Curry worked out neither there nor one-on-one for the Warriors. All they had to go on was a sit-down with him at the NBA Combine in Chicago less than a month before the draft, what they (and other teams) could publicly observe over those three days of drills—"Curry looked smooth, smart, and extremely talented in pretty much everything he did," concluded one report—and, well, three years of Davidson highlight reels.

Riley had also scouted Curry in person, during his junior season when the Wildcats went to Indianapolis to play Purdue five days before Christmas. The Boilermakers were a tough foe—ranked No. 13 in the country—and Curry played awful, missing 21 of 26 shots from the floor, including 10 of 12 threes. Davidson lost by 18, but Riley left impressed with Curry's confidence and demeanor in one of the most dreadful performances a First Team All-American could produce.

By draft day, Riley had grown slightly more optimistic that Curry could fall in Golden State's lap at No. 7. That's because Minnesota was sitting in front with both the No. 5 and No. 6 picks, thanks to a late trade with the Washington Wizards. ("I didn't feel like there was anybody at the five spot who could fit into our rotation," said Wizards general manager Ernie Grunfeld in justifying the predraft trade. "I don't think there are any guarantees in the draft.") That the Timberwolves would pick Spanish star Ricky Rubio with one of them felt all but certain, but the calculus was whether that selection of one young point guard then might dissuade them from looking at Curry. Perhaps, at that point, the Timberwolves might opt for someone like Jordan Hill, a bruising power forward from Arizona. The likelihood was that the Warriors' selection would come down to either Curry or Hill. Riley put on a brave face, but his gut told him it'd be Hill. The Warriors' own website even had compiled mock drafts from around the internet, thereby exciting fans by hyping potential picks such as Hill, UCLA's Jrue Holiday, Italian import Brandon Jennings, Memphis's Tyreke Evans, Syracuse's Jonny Flynn, and Arizona State's James Harden. There just seemed no conceivable way Curry would fall to No. 7.

As the Warriors' brain trust assembled in their war room in Oakland, Curry made his way from his hotel room to the draft inside Madison Square Garden. He could feel the butterflies puttering around his stomach and knew not just that his life would be inexorably changed in a few hours but that he had no control over any of it. Riley, too, had endured a few sleepless nights himself. In short order, all would be decided, one way or another.

. . .

When NBA commissioner David Stern stepped to the podium to announce that Minnesota had selected not Stephen Curry but Syracuse point guard Jonny Flynn with the No. 6 pick, the boos rained down from Knicks fans who knew that Curry would be scooped up by Golden State, one pick ahead of their own team. The Knicks would have to settle for Jordan Hill, the Arizona power forward who played all of 24 immaterial games before being traded halfway through his rookie season. Their fans knew, in that moment, what had slipped their grasp. Still, Knicks brass thought the Warriors wouldn't necessarily go for Curry. They already had Ellis. What did they need with another small point guard?

Out in Oakland, when Flynn was picked, there was immediate befuddlement. Then, maybe a second later, exaltation. Travis Schlenk, the assistant general manager who was on the coaching staff during the "We Believe" season, grinned from ear to ear. To his right, Larry Riley and Robert Rowell shared a fist bump. Don Nelson clapped heartily, and someone from the back of the room let out a "Wooooo, baby!" Riley was relieved. The weeks of worry and due diligence would not be in vain. "There we go," he said, to no one in particular.

Five minutes later, Curry was announced as the No. 7 selection, going to the Golden State Warriors, and boos again flooded the theater at MSG. Knicks fans had steeled themselves on the hope that Curry, who had shimmied his way into their hearts by driving Davidson's comeback win over the University of West Virginia at Madison Square Garden in December, might be theirs by day's end. As the jeers subsided in New York, Riley bounded out of Golden State's draft bunker in Oakland like a gambler who had finally beaten the house. Curry would soon jet off to Oakland to begin his professional career in earnest.

Or would he? Behind the scenes, Jeff Austin, Curry's agent, had done everything in his power to prevent his client from ever becoming a member of the Warriors. He wouldn't let Curry work out privately for the Warriors, in the hope of dissuading Riley and the front office from picking him. Austin had other plans for Curry. "I respect you a lot," he told Riley some time before the draft. "Don't take Steph. This is not the right place for him." Riley also recalled Dell Curry as "cold" toward him. Both father and agent wanted Steph playing home games at MSG as Broadway's newest star. Most critically, Curry *himself* preferred to play for the Knicks, liking what he saw in Mike D'Antoni's high-scoring offense. Austin pleaded with the Knicks to trade up ahead of the War-riors.

While Riley rejected Austin's repeated overtures, he was also hold-ing secret discussions with Phoenix regarding a potential blockbuster trade that would send Curry (provided he fell to No. 7) to the Suns in a package centered on Amar'e Stoudemire, already a four-time All-Star at 26 and primed for the best years of his career—provided his knees held up. The Suns, in turn, saw Curry as a potential successor to two-time MVP Steve Nash.

In the end, the transaction never materialized for numerous rea-sons, but there was a point when Steve Kerr, the Suns general manager trying to finagle the trade into existence, thought they essentially had a done deal. "We had a lot of discussions, Larry and I," Kerr said years later. "Until something is approved by the league office, you can't count on it. We felt pretty good about it, though."

So good that when Flynn was announced at No. 6, the Suns' press corps could swear they heard cheering from the team's war room two floors away. Splashed across the *Arizona Republic* sports section the next morning was a hopeful headline: A NEW LOOK IN THE WORKS.

Upon landing in San Francisco the next day with the Currys, Austin got a call from someone in the Suns front office urging them not to go to the introductory press conference, that a trade was all but a formality. But there had been no such indication from the Warriors, and Steph Curry had already grown accustomed to the notion that he would, in fact, play for Golden State for the foreseeable future. Seated at the presser later that day, he spoke highly of Don Nelson, announced that (same as at Davidson) he'd be wearing No. 30 to honor his father, and said that he was excited to be in the Bay Area.

Despite the best efforts of everyone not named Larry Riley, Curry was neither a Sun nor a Knick but a Warrior, at least to start his four-year rookie contract. And even if he was, at last, warming to the idea of leading Golden State into a new phase, the same could not be said for one of the men with whom he'd share a locker room.

. . .

Entering the 2009–10 season, Monta Ellis was the man in Oakland. The first high schooler the Warriors ever drafted, back in 2005, Ellis was, much like Curry, a scrawny combo guard who could play the point, score, and, above all else, chuck it up from long range whenever humanly possible, even if his shooting percentages were never efficient enough to warrant such volume. He was a 21-year-old starter during the "We Believe" season of 2006–07 and would develop a knack for reeling off 30- and 40-point games with ease while chipping in the requisite assists for which any good point guard could be counted upon. By the time Curry was drafted, Ellis was the most-tenured Warrior and his words, in that thick Mississippi drawl of his, carried weight with the team.

But there were theoretical difficulties in having Ellis and Curry on the same roster. The problem, observers saw, was that they played the same part. Both were shoot-first, pass-second, and literally occupied the same physical footprint on the court—6-foot-3 and 180 pounds. They could be counted upon for steals but not a whole lot of defense otherwise. And it's not as if the Warriors needed to groom Curry as some kind of successor; Ellis would be only 24 when the season tipped.

The Warriors, fans, and local press corps didn't have to wait long to gauge Ellis's reaction. In late September, with everyone gathered for media day and wanting to talk about Curry's arrival, Ellis told reporters he didn't envision the two being able to play much together right away, that the Warriors were "not going to win that way." A season barely begun had already, by all appearances, started to sour. "You can't put two small guys out there and try to play the one and the two when you've got big two-guards in the league," he added. "You just can't do it."

In truth, Ellis's point was plenty valid—that in a league where taller shooting guards had come into vogue, a smart team would prioritize getting more height into the lineup—but all anyone heard was that he and Curry shouldn't play together, that such a pairing wasn't a winning formula. Never mind that Don Nelson's long coaching career included plenty of three-guard lineups and other creative solutions to roster problems. Storm clouds had gathered on the season before a single game was played.

To smooth over the hullabaloo, Ellis gave a sit-down interview to the Warriors' team website after practice the next day and chalked it up, as athletes often do, to his comments' being taken out of context. He emphasized that everyone just wants the team to get better and that if two guys are vying for the same position, that's just the reality of their chosen profession. "Everybody knows it's a business," he said. Ellis put on a good face and said what he needed to say, but it was clear he felt threatened by Curry, who took it as a veteran player making it known whose team this still was.

On top of Ellis's cold welcome to Curry, Golden State was also dealing with a disgruntled Stephen Jackson, who had signed a contract extension not a year earlier (even though he still had two years remaining on his original deal) yet taken his demand for a trade public. "I'm 31 years old. I have four or five years left, I want to be in a situation where I can continually be in the playoffs and get another ring," he said in an interview a month before training camp opened. The NBA fined him $25,000 for those comments. Jackson was then suspended by Nelson for two preseason games after a particularly nasty performance against the Lakers in which he committed five fouls, plus a technical foul, in less than 10 minutes of action. He then bolted for the locker room and never returned to the sidelines.

It was the first time Nelson, in his 31 years as a head coach, had ever suspended a player. Jackson relinquished his role as team captain, which was maybe the smartest move he made during this sequence of events. "I can't be a role model to guys who make the same amount of money as me," he told reporters. "I don't want to be a role model." He also could barely hide his bitterness at Curry's privileged upbringing. "I'm kind of jealous because I was raised in a household with just my mom, and he had both his parents," Jackson told the *New York Times* early in the season. "I had to work, didn't go to college, came up the hard way."

There were some moments of levity as the season approached—Curry even led a spirited rendition of "Happy Birthday" to Ellis during an open practice, complete with the sight of a slightly befuddled Ellis holding balloons and an oversized sheet cake at center court—and opening night could not come fast enough. Two days after Ellis's semi-public fêting, the Warriors rang in the season at home against the Rockets. Curry was the starting point guard, Ellis the shooting guard. With the hotshot rookie at the one and the undisputed team leader at the two, the Warriors set out to find what kind of team they would be in the season's early going.

Seconds after the tip, Curry corralled the ball and ran pick-and-roll with Jackson, who glided to the hoop for the season's first two points and Curry's first NBA assist.

So far, so good.

Curry, antsy about his debut, took a three-hour nap that afternoon that helped calm his nerves. His mother, Sonya, who was staying with him, cooked his ritual pregame spaghetti before he made the drive to Oracle Arena. The traffic was more than he expected, and when he made his way to the players' entrance in back, a film crew from NBA.com was waiting for him. By the time he finished pregame warm-ups 90 minutes before tip, Curry felt fully wired; it was anticipation drawn from excitement. All the summers with his dad, all the doubters through high school and college, all of the sweat and agony led to this moment. He'd wanted to be in the NBA, like his dad, for as long as he could remember.

Finally, that moment had come.

Two and a half minutes into the game, Curry moved from the top of the three-point line, crossed over to his right to take Trevor Ariza off the dribble, angled around a high screen from Andris Biedriņš, and popped a jumper from just above the free-throw line that swished through with a snap. Curry's first two points in the NBA looked as effortless and confident as anything he'd tried at Davidson. The NBA often moves too quickly for rookies, even those drafted with lofty expectations. For Curry, this felt like any other night.

The Warriors led by 10 at the half, but Houston stormed back with a 35–19 third quarter that put Golden State in a hole for the remainder of the evening. Still, the Warriors had a chance in the final seconds to walk off their home court as winners. With 6.6 seconds left to play and down by three, Stephen Jackson inbounded the ball to Anthony Morrow, who heaved up a desperation three from straightaway that bounced down to Curry under the rim. With just a couple of seconds on the clock, Curry's only logical move was to kick the ball back out to Ellis, who was open in the corner. But Curry absentmindedly just laid the ball up and in, giving Golden State two points . . . except it needed three.

The buzzer sounded. Ellis and Jackson skulked off. The Warriors had lost, 108–107. Curry finished with 14 points, seven assists, and four steals. He missed his only three-point attempt.

Curry went home to his Oakland apartment that night day frustrated but undeterred. His girlfriend, Ayesha Alexander—an old church group acquaintance and aspiring actress who was in town from Los Angeles—cooked him a postgame meal, and Curry fell asleep watching highlights on TV. There were 81 more games to play, and these Warriors, talented but dysfunctional, would test the limits of everyone's patience soon enough.

. . .

With four losses over the first five games, Stephen Jackson had had enough. As the Warriors wrapped up a dispiriting 120–107 road loss in Sacramento, Jackson's agent, Mark Stevens, gave an interview to ESPN to rip Don Nelson and again try to force the team to trade his client. Two days later, when reached on the phone at an Indianapolis bar while sipping scotch, Nelson told KNBR the team was doing all it could to hasten Jackson's departure but that "it's harder than hell to trade that guy."

Meanwhile, the Warriors careened toward rock bottom. Jackson played only 18 minutes in a lifeless 108–94 loss to Indiana on the road. Nelson said it was because Jackson had a gimpy back. Jackson reiterated after the game that he was fine and wanted out of town more than anything. "Everybody knows the situation here. I'm just going to continue to play. I know a lot of people expected me to blow up when coach took me out of the game, but for what? It is what it is." As the *San Francisco Chronicle* wrote, "What it is could be defined as garbage, and it's spilling over to the other players."

After starting the first six games, Curry was held out of the initial lineup against the Pacers and scored only six points in just over 21 minutes off the bench. He didn't make a three, and had only five thus far in seven games. The papers all saw him going through the motions on the bench in Indianapolis. That night, Curry tweeted, "Promise to all the Warrior fans . . . we will figure this thing out . . . if it's the last thing we do we will figure it out." In Golden State's next game, at Madison Square Garden against the Knicks, the team he had so hoped to play for, Curry was buried on the depth chart, with 25 family and friends who'd requested tickets sitting in the MSG stands. He played less than three minutes of garbage time to conclude the game, after the Warriors' victory was all but certain, and didn't attempt a shot. He did, however, block Knicks power forward David Lee for his first career rejection. Whatever Curry yelled at Lee in that moment caused the All-Star power forward to jaw in his face for a few seconds once play was paused.

The next night in Milwaukee, rookie guard Brandon Jennings had his instantly famous 55-point performance in a 129–125 win over Golden State. Curry again didn't start, but he did score 14 points on nine shots. At practice the next morning, Nelson announced to the team that Jackson's time as a Warrior had come to its merciful end, that he'd been traded to the Charlotte Bobcats. What was coming back to the Warriors wasn't an impressive package of talent (Raja Bell and Vladimir Radmanović), but the move was addition by subtraction. Ellis wasn't thrilled that his friend Jackson was jettisoned, but it suited Curry just fine.

The rookie had been, at the suggestion of his agent, watching old footage of his Davidson days for a confidence boost. And after the bus ride down to Cleveland, Curry later met up with an acquaintance who also bolstered his morale: LeBron James.

In the summer after his sophomore year at Davidson, after the team's magical run to the Elite Eight, Curry attended the Nike-run LeBron

James Skills Academy, a high-profile prospect camp held at the University of Akron. James and Curry, the two Akron natives, had already hit it off when James came to see Curry play in the Sweet 16 in Detroit—the Cavaliers were in town to play the Pistons the night after—and Curry returned the favor the following week when Cleveland came to Charlotte. It was the start of a budding friendship between the league's present and future. And James knew well of Curry's penchant for heroics. In the first game of the summer camp, with James teamed up with the New Orleans Hornets' Chris Paul on one side, it was Curry, playing for the opposing team, who sank a contested three-pointer for the win.

So with Golden State scuffling and Curry about to play his first professional game at Quicken Loans Arena in Cleveland, the rookie stopped over at James's house the day before for a little decompression. They talked about who was playing on TV that night and about their favorite shows. They dueled for a few frames in James's personal bowling alley. They chatted about everything *except* the next day's contest. For Curry, who'd done an admirable job of keeping his early-season frustrations in check, this was a glimpse at how top-tier superstars lived their life away from basketball. It was also a healthy reminder to *have* a life away from basketball.

Nelson put Curry back in the starting lineup against Cleveland, and he responded with 14 points and seven assists. The Warriors lost by six, but Curry was recharged. He made at least one three in each of the next eight games. In the last game before the All-Star break, with Ellis out nursing a sprained knee, Curry notched his first NBA triple-double (36 points, 10 rebounds, 13 assists). With his 43 percent shooting beyond the arc, Curry was selected for the Three-Point Shootout—as his father had been twice before—and led all scorers after the first round before falling to Boston's Paul Pierce in the finals.

After the All-Star break, Curry averaged more than 22 points, nearly eight assists, and two steals, starting in every game he played. After

Curry went for 31 points and 11 assists during a March loss in Atlanta, Corey Maggette sensed the rookie was special. "There is something bright at the end of the tunnel," Maggette said after the game. "Even in the darkness, you notice the way Steph is playing. You see flashes of greatness. We're watching an All-Star forming."

In the end, Don Nelson barely got the 24 wins he needed to become the NBA's all-time winningest coach, but the Warriors barely resembled what you'd consider a competitive team. A pileup of injuries even forced them, at one point, to use what's known as a hardship waiver to sign a player just so they could satisfy roster requirements. Rowell, in his infrequent public statements, never seemed overly concerned with the growing meltdown. "We've got a little hiccup here," he told one ESPN writer after a mid-November loss in Milwaukee. "I'd say our problems have a lot more to do with not having a healthy center than anything else."

The Warriors finished with 26 wins and 56 losses, three games worse than the previous year. It was a desultory time from start to finish—except for Curry's play. He was named Western Conference Rookie of the Month three times; led all rookies in assists and steals, while finishing second in scoring; was runner-up for Rookie of the Year to Sacramento's Tyreke Evans; and was a top-10 player in steals per game as well as three-point and free-throw percentage. And aside from missing two games in mid-March with a sprained left ankle—a flare-up of the same injury he had suffered 13 months earlier during his junior year at Davidson—Curry played in every game of the season.

In the season finale, Curry played all 48 minutes—as did three other Warriors, which still wasn't as weird as Devean George being forced (by a shortage of able bodies) to play the last few minutes *after* he had fouled out—and finished with 42 points, nine boards, and eight assists, the first rookie to do so in a game since Hall of Famer Oscar Robertson in 1961. "That kind of summed up our season," he said afterward. "For us to finish like this in the last game of the year in my rookie season—

and considering everything that has happened this year—it's definitely something to remember."

In completing the most impactful season of any Warriors rookie since Chris Webber 16 years earlier, Curry surpassed expectations and validated general manager Larry Riley's stubborn belief that, with the seventh pick, he had nabbed the draft's best player not named Blake Griffin, who went No. 1 to the Los Angeles Clippers.

And yet, Curry's emergence wasn't even the most welcome development for the franchise that season. That moment came on March 22, a few hours before a 133–131 home loss to Phoenix, punctuated by 34 points from beloved ex-Warrior Jason Richardson and 37 from Amar'e Stoudemire, the man nearly traded for Curry himself.

The press release on this morning, in fewer than 200 words, brought news that no loss, no matter how karmically painful, could overshadow. The headline read WARRIORS RETAIN GALATIOTO SPORTS PARTNERS TO CONDUCT SALE OF TEAM.

# 3 ★ ★ ★ ★ ★ ★ ★

---

## BETABALL

### The 2010–11 season

**E**ven though the $450 million sale of the Warriors wasn't finalized until November 12, some four months after Chris Cohan had agreed to the offer, Joe Lacob and Peter Guber were already well under way with the business of remaking the Warriors in their own image. In fact, their first personnel move occurred a few days *before* they technically owned the team.

On July 8, 2010, the sports world was transfixed on the Boys and Girls Club of Greenwich, Connecticut, where LeBron James announced to Jim Gray, live to 13 million watching on ESPN, that he was absconding with his skills and heading south to play for the Miami Heat. It was a seismic moment in NBA history, one with reverberations that resonate to the present day. But later that night, with the state of Ohio and other sporadic pockets of the sports world nursing a LeBron-size hangover, news broke of another deal that was slightly less dramatic.

The Warriors and Knicks, whose respective destinies diverged over the course of a few minutes during the 2009 draft, completed a sign-and-trade that would send Anthony Randolph, Ronny Turiaf, Kelenna

Azubuike, and a future draft pick to New York for David Lee, an All-Star power forward who could score and rebound in bunches. His proclivity for double-doubles represented the kind of consistent front-court presence the Warriors so painfully lacked. And even though Riley's efforts made the deal happen, Lacob himself personally signed off on the deal a full week before it was public knowledge he was the new owner. Almost more than anything else, Lacob wished to rebuild the Warriors roster with an emphasis on defense and rebounding, and, in his mind, Lee was the perfect first move. The real irony, though, is that the Knicks were inclined to deal away Lee only because they'd just given $100 million to Amar'e Stoudemire, whose creaky knees had scared the Warriors a year earlier off a potential trade for Curry. By eschewing Stoudemire and waiting a year to acquire Lee, the Warriors still got a dependable frontcourt player but one who was accompanied by a fair, long-term contract—Lee agreed to the deal on the condition of six years and $80 million from Golden State—and a reliable pair of knees.

Better yet, the Warriors didn't have to deal Curry to get him.

Lee's arrival was the splashy on-court roster move that served to define the start of the Lacob era, an unambiguous line of demarcation from the Cohan-riddled past, but the other key move, this of the off-court variety, came just a few days before training camp was slated to begin. Wanting to start fresh with a new head coach on the bench, Lacob bought out the final year of Don Nelson's contract, effectively forcing the NBA's all-time winningest coach into early retirement, for $6 mil-lion. In doing so, he promoted Keith Smart, who'd been an assistant in Oakland for the past seven seasons, to the top job. Best known for hit-ting the game-winning shot for Indiana in the 1987 NCAA champion-ship game, Smart was familiar to the team, young, likable, and, at worst, could act as a placeholder for the upcoming season. (Plus, he surely cost a lot less than $6 million.) Nelson retired for good to Hawaii, where he could sit on his back porch and smoke cigars as the whales swam by, maybe take in a poker game with his good friend and neighbor Willie Nelson. Smart, meanwhile, was thrown into a coaching situation as chaotic as any in the league.

But as much as fans and employees expected Lacob to clean house as soon as possible, that wasn't his style. What Lacob valued above all was data and information. Risk, especially for a venture capitalist, can never fully be eliminated, but you can certainly minimize its effect by accumulating information about what your employees are responsible for, how efficient the business side is, where the potential lies for growth. All these questions and more would be addressed swiftly . . . in six months' time. Everyone would get the season to show their value, what they could do in this new administration going forward. Robert Rowell would stick around as team president but was stripped of his decision-making power. Larry Riley stayed on as general manager, but Lacob's eldest son, Kirk, a 2010 Stanford graduate who grew up cheering general manager Billy Beane's Oakland A's of the "Moneyball" era, was named director of basketball operations.

The other reason Lacob didn't want to rush into anything was that the Warriors were known for *exactly* those kinds of mistakes in the past. The organization clearly needed new leadership, but Lacob cited Mullin's hiring as executive vice president in 2004 as a cautionary tale. The former Warriors star made a splash that summer with trades and free agent contracts that seemed ill-advised in the moment and only soured over time.

Besides, as important as certain changes would be, Lacob also had to recognize what did *not* need changing. He knew that as vital as Curry was to the Warriors' long-term success, a happy Ellis was paramount to team chemistry in the short term. He wanted to avoid a repeat of what happened to start the 2009–10 season. As a season-ticket holder since 1998, he had seen how the season was sabotaged long before opening night. After the sale was announced, Lacob made a point of talking up not just Ellis's talent but his leadership and maturity. "He is just so impressive," Lacob told reporters. "He's so team-oriented right now, you've got to be impressed with it." Lacob even took Ellis, his wife, Juanika, and their son, Monta Jr., to a 49ers football game that fall, in an effort to get to know him and his family.

Curry, after an impressive rookie season that showed glimpses of the electricity he displayed at Davidson, was eager to start the season. More than any other Warrior, he'd been able to wipe the stink of the past year away by playing for Team USA in the 2010 FIBA World Championship in Turkey. For a two-week span stretching from late August into mid-September, Curry played alongside veterans like Chauncey Billups and Andre Iguodala and fellow future stars such as Kevin Durant, Kevin Love, and Russell Westbrook. The United States easily won gold, even as Curry barely averaged 10 minutes of action and five points. He distributed a game-high five assists in a 37-point opening-round blowout of Iran but tallied only seven threes across eight games. Still, the international experience proved invaluable for both Curry's immediate confidence and the Warriors' future personnel moves. He had bonded with Iguodala and Durant, often attending chapel services with them as time allowed.

With training camp starting up just a couple of weeks after the tournament's conclusion in Istanbul, Curry had to acclimate to a lower quality of hoops. But even with no expectation of making the playoffs, the Warriors were undoubtedly a better team than a year ago. They found trade partners for both Stephen Jackson and Corey Maggette, whose bloated contracts were a drag on roster flexibility. Lee, a former All-Star, gave the team size down low. Ellis was entering year two of his great chemistry-building experiment with Curry. Smart was a fresh-faced, energetic coach. Free agent guard Dorell Wright was signed to a reasonable three-year contract worth $11 million. It was a concoction of talent that, Riley hoped, would rebound and defend better while scoring more efficiently.

Before the sale was approved—merely a formality in any sense—the Warriors started the year by winning four of their first five games before dropping three of five on their first road trip. Ellis was sensational, averaging 26.5 points, five assists, and nearly three steals, and Wright already looked a true Warrior, with nearly 60 percent of his 15-point scoring average derived from threes.

Lee's tenure also started strong, with more than 14 points and 11 boards per game. But during a five-point win in New York against his old team, Lee suffered a gruesome injury when he accidentally nailed Knicks forward Wilson Chandler in the mouth with his left elbow. One of Chandler's teeth became lodged in Lee's skin and the wound became infected over the next day. Lee needed an intense regimen of antibiotics (plus two surgeries) to fix the issue; doctors even warned him that his career could be over if the infection reached a certain area of his triceps muscle, which would then have to be removed. For a while, it felt like the same unbelievably bad luck that the Warriors had faced for 20 years. Lee missed almost three weeks but recovered and quickly regained his form as a double-double machine, finishing seventh in the league with 33.

Curry also had early season travails to overcome. In a late preseason game against the Lakers down in San Diego, Curry rolled his right ankle while on defense and was diagnosed with a sprain. Curry missed several practices but was back for the season opener at home against Houston, when he came down from shooting a three and landed on Aaron Brooks's foot. He then injured the same foot a third time when, in the very next game, against the Clippers, he maneuvered around a Blake Griffin screen and rolled the ankle merely by shifting his weight. His lower leg was so thick with tape after the game that it looked as if Curry had been fitted for an ankle cast. He missed the next two games but soon returned to his reliable, 20-points-a-night form.

Finally, on November 12, 2010, the NBA approved the sale of the

Warriors to Lacob and Guber's group by a unanimous vote. Lacob called it "a great day for me and my family, and a great day for Warriors fans" and said he was "incredibly anxious and excited to take the helm," even though he'd already been making crucial decisions for months.

The two friends who'd spent the better part of a decade hoping to buy an NBA team had finally done so. They could now get down to the business of introducing themselves to the Warriors' fan base, a first impression four long months in the making.

. . .

"I don't think I could write a script that would be any better than this."

As Joe Lacob said those words, sitting on a stool across from fellow co-owner Peter Guber, the acclaimed Hollywood producer, it represented the fulfillment of a 50-year dream. Lacob told the story of how he had longed to own his own team, as local media and dignitaries chowed down on a lavish three-course meal prepared by award-winning chef Jan Birnbaum. Beyond the windows of Epic Roasthouse, diners were treated to a stunning view of the Bay Bridge.

But this posh soirée wasn't in Oakland.

That Lacob and Guber opted to have their introductory luncheon in one of the toniest eateries along San Francisco's Embarcadero, in a building that had signified, according to reports a few years earlier, "the first privately owned, ground-up construction on San Francisco's waterfront in 100 years," was no accident.

Moving back to the Warriors' original Bay Area home city was always part of the plan; Lacob even admitted a move was "possible" when asked about it that day. He never hid his intentions, obvious as they were. "We are in the greatest city in the world," Lacob said, pointing toward the windows off to his side. "Take a look. It's incredible. Who wouldn't want to be here?"

After a beat, once more for emphasis: "Who would *not* want to be here?"

Still, the theme of the event was not relocation but something more like resurrection. "This is not the cure for cancer," Guber told the gathering. "Might be the cure for Cohan, but it's not the cure for cancer."

Lacob said they'd be "very involved," that this wouldn't be the kind of ownership that "would be coming in once a month." Guber, for his part, talked about improving the "fan experience" and the desire to examine and improve every aspect of how someone attends a Warriors game, from buying the tickets to paying for snacks to going home after the fourth quarter ends and feeling that you weren't swindled. That was where Guber's expertise lay, while Lacob's task was to construct an elite team on the court and in the front office. "There's no reason we can't turn this into a championship franchise," he said. "This is where it starts. It starts today."

That night, the two men met the Oracle Arena crowd and stood on the court as owners for the first time. "You are the best fans in the NBA," Lacob said. "If you look up there, that is a very lonely flag. We want another one!" Guber took the mic and declared his new favorite colors to be blue and yellow and his new favorite letter to be *W*—"Lots and lots of Ws! Go get 'em Warriors!"

Lacob thanked the crowd and both men took their courtside seats again. Guber turned to Lacob. "Be careful," he said, as the cheers died down. "All glory is fleeting." It was, of course, a memorable movie line, the final words spoken in the Oscar-winning film *Patton*.

The Warriors were up by 13 after one quarter and would lead by as many as 32 points just before halftime. The Detroit Pistons, however, would cut that deficit to two with just a few seconds remaining in the game. Golden State barely held on for a nervous 101–97 win. Curry and Ellis combined for 48 points, as the Warriors finished with more rebounds, steals, and blocks than the Pistons.

And yet, while Golden State's lead was slowly bleeding out, Lacob turned to Guber at one point and mumbled what so many Warriors fans had screamed aloud for two decades: "They are *terrible*."

. . .

"Well, you're going to have to look down if you want to see the camera."

Travis Schlenk didn't give off the impression of someone you'd care to defy. Beefy and bald, with a penchant for wearing cowboy boots instead of designer shoes, Schlenk was wrapping up his seventh season with the Warriors when we met on April 13, 2011. It was his second year as the team's director of player personnel. Two months later, he would be promoted to assistant general manager. It was an impressive rise for the Selden, Kansas, native who caught on with Golden State after working four years with the Miami Heat as their video coordinator. He then paid his dues as a video scout and assistant coach with the Warriors. Schlenk is, perhaps due to his midwestern upbringing, reserved in conversation—"one of those guys who flies under the radar," according to Jerry West—and that reticence served him well in becoming the Warriors' resident stats nerd in those first few months under the Lacob regime. Someone who's ostensibly in charge of your team's nascent analytics buildup is not someone who should be gabbing to the press when it's not his place.

But Schlenk was doing me a service this day, as we walked along the catwalks suspended some 80 feet above the Oracle Arena flooring. A few hours before the Warriors' final regular-season home game of the 2010–11 season, a dance team down below was squeezing in last-minute practice before the 7:30 p.m. tipoff against Portland. The Trail Blazers, sitting on 48 wins, were looking ahead to the playoffs, where they'd face the Dallas Mavericks, while the 35-win Warriors were looking ahead to a summer of golf and general uncertainty about what changes might befall the franchise.

For now, Schlenk was willing to show me what I'd asked to see. As Lacob prepared to head off to Boston for the MIT Sloan Sports Analytics Conference several weeks earlier, I'd read a news story that the Warriors had installed motion-capture cameras inside Oracle Arena as part of a data-gathering effort called SportVU. The hope was that this budding technology might usher in a movement that would revolutionize how basketball is analyzed, how the game is taught to the next generation.

For some, this represented nothing less than the future of the NBA.

Despite its name, SportVU didn't originally develop from anything sports-related. The firm was founded in 2005 by Miky Tamir, an Israeli entrepreneur who earned a PhD in physics and worked for the Soreq Nuclear Research Center in Israel for 10 years. His specialty was advanced optical recognition and image processing, and Tamir founded the company based on missile-tracking technology he had developed. And in the way you can track a missile based on motion capture, you can also track a player or a ball during a sporting event, and that seemed like a more profitable and practical application.

SportVU started analyzing soccer games by recording ball and player motion more than a dozen times per second. The footage would be piped through SportVU's proprietary algorithms to plot the data on a three-dimensional grid. What resulted were not only custom animations and tailored scouting reports, but also virtual reams of spreadsheet data that could be further parsed by the teams themselves, provided you had a stable of quants who knew what the hell to do with all the information.

Most American audiences probably learned about SportVU for the first time during the 2008 U.S. presidential election, when it partnered with a graphics firm named Vizrt to provide CNN with its Jedi-like holograms of anchor Jessica Yellin during the network's coverage. A month after Barack Obama was elected president and the need for political holograms had dissipated, SportVU was acquired by a company with three decades of expertise in sports and statistics. Stats LLC, which was jointly owned by the Associated Press and Rupert Murdoch's News Corporation, bought out Tamir and other minority investors. For a year, the Chicago-based Stats had been looking to move into motion-capture technology if it could acquire the right company.

That company was SportVU.

The first task was deciding which sport to target. Baseball was cornered by a Silicon Valley company named Sportvision, better known for its "glowing" hockey puck, the virtual first-down line on NFL telecasts, and (more pertinent to Stats' interests) the location and speed for every pitch thrown in every Major League Baseball game. Football was an option, but the sport boasted too many variables. A single play could evolve in an endless number of directions, affected by myriad circumstances that would have to be considered ahead of time. As nice as it would be to gain a foothold in a market built upon an $8.5 billion business, the NFL was out.

But the NBA, then a $4 billion industry on the rise, presented a host of opportunities. The sport was fluid but defined. (A round ball? Five players on each team? Compared to other sports, that was analytical heaven.) The court size was also manageable from a data standpoint— only 4,700 square feet, compared to an NFL field that encompasses 57,600 square feet, end zones included. And there were some teams already in line to come aboard as early adopters. As the 2010–11 season approached, the task fell to Brian Kopp, Stats' vice president of strategy and development, to get at least a handful of teams to commit. To do that, he'd have to first convince them of the data's utility. "You don't want to come in and say, 'Look at all this cool technology. Look at all this data it can spit out,'" Kopp told me. "People think that's cool, but teams had one of two reactions. One is, 'That's great, but I don't understand what it means.' The other was, 'What am I going to do with that?'"

Four teams initially signed on for the 2010–11 season as SportVU guinea pigs: the Dallas Mavericks, Houston Rockets, Oklahoma City Thunder, and San Antonio Spurs. For a new tech-centric movement to hit the NBA, this was as perfect a starting foursome as you could orchestrate. San Antonio had quietly maintained a modern-day dynasty by eschewing the usual dictums of modern NBA strategy and roster development; this seemed the next logical step. Dallas was owned by Mark Cuban, a dot-com billionaire who was an active investor in analytics companies. Houston was led by general manager Daryl Morey, the MIT grad and Sloan conference cofounder. And Oklahoma City was being molded into a perennial contender by general manager Sam Presti, who started out as a $250-a-month intern with San Antonio before getting hired by Seattle in 2007—at the ripe age of 30—as the second-youngest GM in league history. These were the first four teams to embrace a style of tech they hoped could take their organizations to new heights.

The Warriors, with nothing to lose, were the fifth.

SportVU first came on their radar in mid October, with opening night for the 2010–11 season still 11 days away. Pat Sund, Golden State's basketball operations coordinator and son of then–Atlanta Hawks general manager Rick Sund, was at the (deep breath now) Northern California Symposium on Statistics and Operations Research in Sports, held at Menlo College in the affluent Silicon Valley suburb of Atherton.

While soaking up all the sports geekery one could consume, Sund bumped into Dean Oliver, a former director of quantitative analysis for the Denver Nuggets. Oliver, who, in 2002, literally wrote the book on basketball analytics (*Basketball on Paper*) and who would later become ESPN's first-ever director of production analytics, talked up the SportVU system to Sund, who then took that info back to Schlenk and Kirk Lacob. Within weeks, the Warriors' staff agreed to move forward on the tech and contacted Stats. A technician was flown in from Chicago to assess Oracle Arena for a potential fitting. It would be SportVU's first placement on the West Coast.

By the time the SportVU cameras were fully operational in mid-January and ready to feed game data back to the Warriors' front office, the team was already 15-23 and scuffling mightily under the direction of new coach Keith Smart. After starting the season with six wins over their first eight games, the Warriors cratered, losing 16 of their following 19 games.

But on January 14, 2011, when the Warriors smacked the Clippers, 122–112, thanks to a barrage of 14 threes on 26 attempts, it was with six SportVU cameras fully operational and preparing to feed in-game data to the front office in Oakland as soon as possible. For the rest of the season, with every home game captured by SportVU's eyes in the sky, the Warriors won 20 games and lost 23. Even Curry's shooting percentage went up a not-insignificant three percentage points. Schlenk told me then that Smart and his coaching staff weren't doing a whole lot with the data coming in. That was to be expected when you combine a first-year head coach and a technology still in its infancy. But the Warriors were finally building a foundation of data that could be used to their advantage down the line.

And SportVU was capturing the Warriors at the right time, just as they started playing their best basketball in years.

. . .

In the infancy of his ownership, Lacob tried to maintain a visible public presence, especially when it came to the fans, while Guber, from his years as a Hollywood producer and studio head, recognized the value in promoting a good story. The two men, more than anything, wanted to help fans forget the years when Chris Cohan would watch games from his Oracle Arena owner's suite in self-imposed exile. They set up an email address where fans could send questions directly, and Lacob did an hour-long Q&A on KNBR, the Warriors' flagship radio station, answering dozens of questions on everything from how he handled the constant losing ("I get home and I'm kind of depressed") to the strategy for attracting big-name free agents ("We're going to sell the city. . . . We're going to sell the environment. . . . We're going to sell Peter Guber and his ability to help you get whatever in Hollywood") to his assessment of Keith Smart ("I think he's really doing what he thinks it takes to win a game").

Most important, Lacob offered his take on the continued coexistence of Stephen Curry and Monta Ellis and whether one of them ultimately had to go: "Unless we got offered a tremendous deal—where we got clear value in excess in return—Steph Curry is going nowhere. Monta Ellis is going nowhere. These guys are my kind of guys. I love them. They're fantastic players. They're the best offensive backcourt in basketball."

It was hard to argue with Lacob on that last point. Though the Warriors' record stood at 19-26, Ellis was one of the league's top scorers with nearly 26 a game and Curry was second on the team with nearly 19 points a night. They had roughly the same shooting percentage, though Curry did better from three-point land. While Ellis was forcing contact, drawing fouls, and getting to the free-throw line more often, Curry was already the league's best free-throw shooter. In fact, his 93.4 percent clip would end up as the best free-throw percentage by a second-year player in NBA history, breaking the old mark of 91.3 percent set by Chauncey Billups, his teammate at the FIBA World Championship the summer before. Ellis looked like a high-volume scorer, Curry the young protégé.

The old truism in basketball—especially at the NBA level—is that no matter how many talented players you have, there's still only one ball. And that ball, for now, belonged to Ellis.

At least the team was now essentially drama-free. The extracurricular sideshows that turned the previous season into a traveling circus were snuffed out with Smart's arrival. Lacob, as the owner, could do only so much from his perch. It's up to the head coach to keep the locker room peace, to keep tension and egos from sabotaging the on-court play, and Smart had a deft hand for giving everyone a role to play and then keeping them in their place.

Unfortunately, that diplomacy didn't always translate to the most successful brand of basketball. The renewed emphasis on defense and rebounding wasn't quite yielding the results Lacob expected. Yes, Ellis and Curry were prolific scorers, but the Warriors were being outscored when those two were in the game. The duo ended the season with a net rating of –1.8, meaning their lineups were outscored by nearly two points per 100 possessions played. (This might seem like a trivial deficit, but stretch it out over a season and it adds up.) Their most frequent five-man starting lineup—Ellis, Curry, David Lee, Dorell Wright, and Andris Biedriņš—had a net rating of –4.6. Their team defensive rating—how much opponents scored every 100 possessions—was only a point better than the year before and still ranked 26th out of 30 teams. For the fifth year in a row, they gave up the most rebounds. On offense, they fell from second to seventh, even as they both attempted and made more shots than any other team in the league. It was a lack of efficiency—evinced by Smart's dearth of a cohesive game plan—that doomed their season, even as they ultimately finished at 36-46, 10 games better than the year before but still 10 games out of the playoffs.

But with the Warriors stumbling through another year rife with underachievement, Lacob kept hopes buoyed. This was a transition year, after all. There were still major personnel moves to be made, both with the roster and in the front office. And those new SportVU cameras, which became fully operational in January, would soon be pumping gigabytes of raw data to the team's data analysts.

And what better place to pump up the Warriors' burgeoning tech bona fides but the MIT Sloan Sports Analytics Conference, held every March in Boston since 2007. It's the epicenter of where technology and

sports intersect. If you were running a sports franchise and not sending at least a few of your top front office people there, you were getting
left behind. Daryl Morey, the Houston Rockets general manager and
MIT grad, was a cofounder and frequent panelist. Lacob, with his deep
Boston roots, was a popular figure at Sloan and was invited to speak at
the 2011 conference on a panel dubbed "New Sports Owners: The Chal-
lenges and Opportunities." After staying close to local media for his first
few months of ownership, this was Lacob's first industry-wide splash as
the Warriors' chief executive.

The appearance didn't go well. During the panel, a few writers in
attendance started tweeting out comments Lacob had made about fan
loyalty. "There's a lot of pressure from the media to make quick trades,
from the internet bloggers, which I'm not sure are the real fans," he said.
"I check out whether they have season tickets; they don't usually. So
there's a lot of pressure on that. But we think we've got a good core and
we're going to take our time a little bit and see what we can do with that
and add to it and we have a plan for how we're going to do it.

"And on the business side, I could have come in and fired everybody
day one. There were a lot of media that wanted me to do that, too, because there were certain people that for whatever reason people think
need to be changed. Again, got to take a year, go through the season—
like you would with any other business—evaluate what you have, and
then at the appropriate time here make some changes if we need to. So I
don't feel any great rush to do it.

"One fortunate thing we have is, we have a team that even though
has not been winning . . . I do think you should make the postseason
every other year on average in basketball, since 16 teams out of 30 make
it. And in our case, once in the last 16 years, that's pretty pathetic, it's not
good. So I think that we do feel a great pressure to fix that, but we also
came in, we have a great fan base. And we don't have any tremendous
rush on the business side to go and just drastically alter things. So I'm

going to take my time, like I would with any other business, evaluate, put a solid plan in place that gets us there."

There was a lot to unpack in Lacob's comments, but the one that went viral was his insinuation about people (in this case, bloggers) not being "real fans" if they didn't buy season tickets. Lacob emailed beat writers the next day to clarify what he said and did damage control interviews, but the honeymoon phase with Warriors fans was over.

It wasn't just the crack about season tickets being a determinant of fan loyalty. Lacob also gave the impression that the team was taking the fans' passion for granted, perhaps not feeling a pressure to make bold roster changes (as he'd promised from day one) since fans will put butts in the seats no matter what, as they did through the dreadful Cohan years. The Warriors stood pat at the trading deadline, seemingly content to ride out the season with what they had, which, beyond Curry, Ellis, and Lee, wasn't much.

Before he left the Boston Convention & Exhibition Center that day around lunchtime, Lacob mingled in the halls to take questions from passersby. Such a scene, for myriad reasons, would've been unfathomable with Chris Cohan, but here Lacob was. No doubt his inquisitors felt they were learning something from Lacob's answers, but, in all likelihood, he was learning just as much.

Regardless, Lacob's task as steward of the franchise, certainly from a public relations perspective, had just become a lot tougher.

. . .

Five weeks after Sloan, the season was over and the team started overhauling its downtown headquarters, the fifth and sixth floors above the Oakland Convention Center parking garage. What was billed as a $1.6 million renovation of some 17,000 square feet of office space was a sign that the initial assessment period had essentially come to an end. That meant, beyond just a change in personnel, a change in office culture. It was one of the surefire ways Lacob had seen startups work in Silicon Valley. You had to facilitate a positive working environment for people to be afforded a chance to contribute their best. Cubicles were rearranged. Dividing walls were removed. Efficient, high-density lighting was installed. A cavernous, central conference room was constructed. (There were also little design quirks sprinkled throughout, like wall-to-ceiling photos of the scene inside Oracle Arena on game night and a mini free-throw line painted on the floor of the break room to equate the act of dumping your garbage or recycling with Curry shooting from the charity stripe.) And Warriors memorabilia was hung throughout the corridors. Lacob wanted team employees to take pride in their work, to feel that they were part of something that was getting better all the time. Insofar as the Warriors needed to sell the merits of the team to the public, Lacob first had to sell the Warriors to his own people.

Curry sure was buying in. He raised his scoring average from 17.5 to 18.6 points, and his shooting efficiency improved across the board. But the bugaboo again was that right ankle, which he sprained multiple times during the season, causing him to miss eight games in all. Curry finally had his first ankle surgery, in Charlotte on May 25, six weeks after the season ended. The hope around team headquarters was that he'd be ready and healthy for the fall.

His nagging lower-extremity issues aside, Curry, when he was mobile, seemed reinvigorated with the joys of basketball that eluded him during his rookie year. With a calmer locker room and more roster stability, Curry was more relaxed, more his natural self. Goofing around during one February practice, he let one fly from the other end of the court, slinging the ball from 90 feet out like a jai alai player letting loose his pelota, and the ball swished through with ease. He turned and jumped onto one of the Warriors' media relations staffers and started yelping, "I *told* you that would happen! I told you!"

"That was no camera dubbing, no visual effects, no Adobe Photoshop," Curry said after regaining his composure. "None of that. That was just pure . . ."

He paused for a moment, then shrugged, as if he'd searched for an explanation that might suffice but came up empty.

"I guess it's luck, but hey."

# 4 ★ ★ ★ ★ ★ ★ ★

## GROWING PAINS

### The 2011–12 season

Even with a 10-game improvement over the previous season, the Warriors were, as of April 2011, an organization still without clear direction. Stephen Curry and Monta Ellis formed what had the potential to become a fearsome backcourt, the kind that could go out and score 40, 50, even 60 points on any given night—a lethal combination that can engineer wins in the NBA. Throw in David Lee with nearly 17 points and 10 rebounds per game and suddenly you've got a somewhat dependable core.

Off the court, Lacob finally started establishing a new front office team. It wasn't any great surprise when, on the night of the Warriors' season finale on April 13, news leaked that the Warriors had hired a new assistant general manager, someone who might stick around for a year or two, learn how things were done in Oakland, and then take over for Larry Riley, who would presumably move laterally to another position or retire.

Nor was it surprising that the new hire didn't have much management experience. Lacob made it clear early on that he would value a fresh perspective from any relevant field. In startup culture, you can't predict which person in the room is going to give a voice to your next big idea. Could be your chief technology officer or a junior engineer still years away from a windowed office.

But this hire was jarring in that the new guy had often sat across from the Warriors at the negotiating table, trying to scrape together every dollar for his clients.

Bob Myers, the new assistant general manager, was a player agent.

For 14 years, Myers had built a rep as one of the brightest young sports agents in the industry, but his upbringing was rooted in both basketball and the Bay Area. He was a rabid Warriors fan who grew up in nearby Danville and played ball at Monte Vista High School. Myers enrolled at UCLA and walked on to the basketball team under head coach Jim Harrick. When Myers was a sophomore, UCLA won the 1995 national championship. In his senior year, they advanced to the Elite Eight, but Myers was never much more than a role player, scoring 104 points *total* over 76 career games as a Bruin.

On the cusp of graduating with a degree in economics, Myers was at a loss. In the spring of 1997, Harrick facilitated a meeting with the legendary super-agent Arn Tellem and the two hit it off. Soon, Myers was faced with a decision. He could intern at financial giant Bear Stearns, an opportunity that would prove lucrative sooner rather than later, but Tellem was offering a gig as a junior agent—pay was a $2,000-a-month stipend, no benefits. One choice offered a fast route to stability and a seven-figure salary, the other was loaded with uncertainty.

Myers chose Tellem's firm and began to learn the industry from one of its best. It was educational from the start, with Kobe Bryant stopping by during Myers's first day in the office. Wearing a Joe Montana jersey, Bryant was just a rookie but affable and confident to the hilt. "How's it going?" he said to Myers, who reciprocated the question. "Good," Bryant replied. "I'm gonna win 10 championships and then I'm gonna retire."

Myers knew big-time basketball culture from his years at UCLA, but this was a whole new world.

Myers proved to be a calm, diplomatic foil for Tellem, who could be emotional as only the most celebrated super-agents are. Myers earned a law degree at night from Loyola Marymount—he was often seen wearing his Warriors sweatshirt around campus—and eventually became a vice president at Tellem & Associates, later named SFX Sports. When Wasserman Media Group acquired the firm in 2006 for a reported $12 million, Myers was named a managing executive. By the spring of 2011, he'd successfully negotiated some $575 million in contracts. His clients included NBA players such as Brandon Roy, Robin and Brook Lopez, Kendrick Perkins, DeAndre Jordan, Dorell Wright, and Jarron Collins. He also represented Tyreke Evans, the Sacramento guard who had edged out Stephen Curry for Rookie of the Year a season earlier.

The recommendation of such an unconventional pick was months in the making. As soon as the Warriors sale was finalized, Lacob got a call out of the blue from Danny Ainge, the Celtics general manager with whom Lacob was still close from his days as minority owner. Ainge said he should look closely at Myers if he was preparing to fill any executive-level positions over the coming months. In fact, Myers himself asked Ainge to put in a good word with Lacob, as the prospect of working for his boyhood team—and under ownership that seemed poised to turn the franchise around—was tantalizing. Lacob had never heard of Myers, but Guber, through his deep UCLA connections, knew of him.

Myers and Lacob finally met in December 2010. Though the sit-down went well, Lacob held firm to his self-imposed six-month personnel freeze. During that time, he thought about the risk of such an unorthodox hire. Sure, Lacob had promised a bold, fresh approach to running the Warriors, but bringing a sports agent into the upper management fold seemed a little nutty. Myers had sensed that reluctance, calling his father after the meeting to tell him that, despite a pleasant face-to-face, he didn't think there was any way the Warriors would hire him.

But as Lacob interviewed more prospective candidates over the coming months, he couldn't stop thinking about Myers, who had amassed an extensive network of contacts through the years. His age was an asset; with his youthful countenance and svelte frame, Myers looked more like a Half Moon Bay surf shop owner than a front office executive in Oakland. He had the swagger that comes from playing college ball yet grasped the diplomacy needed to push a deal to fruition. The lack of practical NBA front office experience didn't sit totally right with Lacob, but maybe there was a way around this hang-up. He proposed to Myers something like an apprenticeship: Work under Riley for a year or two as assistant general manager and, if everything seems to be working out, the GM position would be his.

Myers invited Tellem to dinner in Los Angeles, to personally break the news to his longtime mentor that he was leaving the agency. Tellem, as if acting on that instinct that makes agents good at their jobs, knew something was up. "You're taking a job with an NBA team," he said.

Myers was stunned. When Tellem asked who the lucky suitor was, Myers told him to guess. The super-agent knew right away it could only be the Warriors. This was more than a career move for his protégé. This was a homecoming long overdue.

Word leaked on the night of April 13, as the Warriors were wrapping up the season at home against Portland, that the longtime agent would be coming aboard as Lacob's first major hire.

Although the basketball world was floored by the news, anyone who knew Myers's state of mind in those days before the announcement wouldn't have found the news so shocking. Perhaps it was the knowledge that his departure from the sports agent profession was imminent, but Myers had exhibited a very public frustration with the field in which he'd spent more than a decade of his professional life. Just five days before his hiring was announced, Myers appeared at the Southwestern Law School Sports Law Symposium in Los Angeles as part of a panel discussion dubbed "Pre-Professional Athletes in an Amateur World: NCAA Rules, State Laws, Agents and Extra Benefits." Those in attendance described someone who clearly looked as if he had had enough with being an agent, especially when Myers spoke of the endless, media-driven fervor surrounding BYU sensation Jimmer Fredette and the frenzy to secure his representation.

But more than just what Myers's presence meant for the franchise's future prospects, his arrival in Oakland meant that ownership had moved to a new phase. The season had wrapped. Evaluations were being made. People would be fired. It was time for Lacob and Guber to start molding the Warriors in their own image.

The rebuild was officially on.

. . .

Two weeks after the season ended, Keith Smart was let go as head coach. He'd performed ably as a post–Don Nelson stopgap, but Lacob wasn't convinced he was the long-term answer as coach, so the team didn't pick up the option on his contract. Lacob had long seen companies flounder when execs were slow to replace top leadership. Same for the NBA, so Smart was cut loose and the Warriors were, once again, on the hunt for a new coach.

On the front office side, Lacob followed up hiring Myers—a relatively inexperienced executive—by bringing aboard a man with some of the most impressive credentials in NBA history. A week shy of his 73rd birthday, Jerry West, a man so enmeshed in the fabric of basketball history that his likeness graces the NBA's own logo, was appointed to the Warriors' executive board. As a player, West played 14 seasons, all with the Lakers, and made the All-Star Team every year, won 33 consecutive games and a title in 1972, and retired as the third-highest scorer in league history.

After a two-year break to decompress—and in need of fresh income following a costly divorce settlement—West returned to the Lakers in 1976 as their head coach and spent the next 24 years with the club in various management roles; the organization won six more championships over that time, including four while West was either general manager or executive vice president of operations. He was the man who convinced Shaquille O'Neal to head west from Orlando. He also later molded the Memphis Grizzlies into a viable NBA franchise.

By the spring of 2011, there was nothing West yearned to accomplish in any basketball-centric capacity. He'd been retired for four years. That was when longtime Warriors public relations chief (and former Lakers PR staffer) Raymond Ridder put his old boss in touch with his newest one.

The offer from Warriors management proved too tempting, but the gig came with conditions from West. He'd report directly to Lacob and Guber but would not have decision-making powers of any finality; West knew and respected Myers from past contract negotiations and didn't want to undermine his apprenticeship. He had also known Riley for many years and considered his judgment beyond reproach. Plus, West had had his fill of being the kind of organizational top dog who could swing fortunes with a single word. "I never want to get back to where I go to bed at night, never go to sleep," he said after the hiring, "worrying about one play that a player makes that might cost a game."

But West did know that he could contribute real guidance to a franchise that was still in a state of infancy, learning how to win. He knew the Warriors were close; maybe his player evaluation skills could tip the scales. (The Bay Area media also had written of his interest in potentially joining the Warriors for nearly a decade.) After an evening-long conversation with Joe and Kirk Lacob, Peter Guber, and Travis Schlenk, West was convinced the arrangement could work.

Convincing someone of West's caliber to join a fledgling organization was a classic Silicon Valley power move on Lacob's part. He had helped dozens of companies come to fruition, and each one needed a collection of board members who were both disparate and cooperative. They needed to buy into the culture. They needed to be united in the company's mission. Of course, it also doesn't hurt if you can put a splashy name on the roll. Among basketball fans, Jerry West was about as splashy as it gets, between his Hall of Fame playing career and two-plus decades of success in the front office. And as one of the all-time great talent evaluators in league history—the man who, on draft night in 1996, traded for a Philly-area high school phenom named Kobe Bryant, who would go on to break his Lakers franchise scoring record—West believed this Warriors roster was ripe for a full-on transformation.

In Curry, West found a kindred spirit. Fifty years before Curry won back-to-back Southern Conference Player of the Year Awards, West did so while starring at West Virginia. Both came into the league as heralded first-round picks who overcame slight height disadvantages to make their names as elite sharpshooters. But West also made the All-Defensive team five times in 14 seasons, and he knew the Warriors would go only as far as an improved and retooled defense would allow them.

The question was, who could play such a style? In that vein, West began dropping hints about future strategy from his first moments as a team employee. "I've seen teams trade players that score tons of points and people say, 'How in the world can you trade that player?'" West said at his introductory press conference. The public perception was that Monta Ellis, a scoring-first/defense-last kind of two-guard, would soon be on his way out, and that the Warriors might view the upcoming draft, just a month away, as a means to pair Curry with a taller shooting guard who could play both ends of the floor. "When I look at this team," West said, "obviously they need more size."

But regardless of when (not even if, by that point) Ellis was traded, the Warriors still needed stability at the head coaching position, and Lacob settled on his man in early June: Mark Jackson, who played 17 seasons in the NBA, made the playoffs 14 times, and retired in 2004 with the second-most assists in league history, behind only John Stockton, was named head coach of the Warriors, ending his seven-year stint as an on-air analyst for ESPN.

Though he had never coached professionally, Jackson was one of the league's most recognizable and likable broadcasters. At only 46, Jackson wasn't far removed from his playing days and maintained a deep rapport with many current players. Lacob considered him a fresh face, one who could help the Warriors mold an identity of fast-paced, gritty, competitive hoops. And he was a proven winner, having played in 131 playoff games over his career—more than twice the collective postseason experience of his roster.

On the surface, it was a risky play for Lacob, who could've gone for someone with an actual iota of coaching experience on his résumé, but Jackson ticked all the boxes he needed. He knew about the modern game. He was a point guard for more than 20 years between college and the pros, so he knew the intricacies of both offense and defense. He had credibility to spare. And Jackson was almost hired by his hometown New York Knicks in 2008 when they had their own vacancy, but they opted instead for Mike D'Antoni, who had quit as Phoenix Suns head coach after an immensely successful five-year reign. Jackson, to his credit, waited for another prime opportunity to come along. Three years later, he landed in Oakland, with the bright lights (and blinding expectations) of Broadway firmly behind in a reality that never came to pass.

It had now been almost a year since Lacob and Guber had been announced as the new owners, and almost every key management position had been addressed—except one. On June 21, just two days before the 2011 draft, the most prominent face of the Chris Cohan era was finally scrubbed away. "One week ago, for my first time as a Warriors fan, the air smelled fresh," wrote one local blogger. "The hope in my chest, the hope that is so often restrained by realism, bloomed fully. Joe Lacob made the most significant move he will ever make as owner of the Golden State Warriors: he fired team president Robert Rowell."

To the surprise of not a single soul, Rowell was finally relieved of his Warriors employment after 16 years, the final eight as team president. There was no press availability, no conference call. Just a statement from the team and Rowell. The company line was that Rowell had stepped down, but the subtext was unambiguous.

"We spent a lot of time evaluating this decision and believe that now is the appropriate time for the new ownership team to put our complete stamp on the entire organization," Lacob's statement read. Rowell thanked the team for the "opportunity to have worked with the best, brightest, and most dedicated staff in professional sports," but he would not be remembered for his marketing wizardry, for finding ways to keep fans in the seats during even the most putrid times. Instead, Rowell's legacy would be one of public feuds, involving both players and executives, of miserable personnel decisions, of looking like the propaganda minister of what, in time, took on the form of a shadow ownership group. Lacob still needed to retool the business side, and whoever he chose to replace Rowell would have immense responsibilities from the start, chiefly to serve as the point person overseeing the campaign for a new arena.

That man, Lacob announced in the fall, would be Rick Welts, the former president and CEO of the Phoenix Suns. It was a momentous decision for several reasons. Welts, then 58, was an NBA lifer, coming to love the NBA thanks to his father's Seattle SuperSonics season tick-

ets. He started out as a ball boy for the team as a teenager, then became
the team's head of public relations, and eventually the No. 3 man in the
league office in Manhattan, behind only commissioner David Stern and
deputy commissioner Adam Silver. He was the brains behind the creation of the annual Dunk Contest that precedes the All-Star Game. He
helped brand the 1992 Olympic men's basketball team as the "Dream
Team." Welts left the NBA in 1999 but returned in 2002 to join the Suns'
front office. Over the next nine years, Phoenix made the conference Finals three times and won 50 or more games five times.

But Welts's professional life collided with his personal when, in May
2011, he came out as gay. In a *New York Times* article, Welts talked about
the pain of living in the closet for decades, feeling unable to speak up in
a culture not altogether friendly to homosexuals. (The day after Welts
came out to Stern in April, Kobe Bryant was overheard directing an
antigay slur at a referee. Bryant was fined $100,000 by the league.) Welts
told the *Times* his hope was "to be a mentor to gay people who harbor
doubts about a sports career, whether on the court or in the front office."
Less than four months later, Welts resigned from the Suns to move to
the Bay Area and live with his partner, Todd Gage. He had hoped to take
some time off to decompress, plan his next career move, and get to know
Gage's two children from an earlier marriage.

That was when Lacob came calling with an opportunity. He had
started cleaning house by the time Welts came aboard, but allowed his
new team president not only the freedom to pick from who was left
standing—to uncover, in Welts's words, "some real gems"—but also to
recruit from the sports and business worlds. It was, Welts recalled later,
"the easiest recruiting job in the history of sports." Two weeks later, he
was the highest-ranking out-gay team executive in American professional sports—a distinction he holds to this day.

With Rowell's departure, there were now just a couple of executives
left over from the Cohan regime. That was assistant general manager

Travis Schlenk, who had established himself as a shrewd evaluator, and his boss, Larry Riley, the general manager who had drafted Curry (then resisted trading him) two years earlier and given the Warriors the shot of new energy they so craved. And over the course of the next year, Riley would orchestrate moves that would both enrage fans to the point of near-mutiny and put the team in a position to experience, before too long, unprecedented levels of success.

. . .

As Lacob made moves to shore up the Warriors off the court, there was much still to be decided on the court. With Myers on board as the GM-in-waiting and Jackson behind the bench, a new kind of brain trust was formed that could help Joe and Kirk Lacob, Larry Riley, and Travis Schlenk decide the next major player acquisition, which would come via the draft on June 23.

Five weeks earlier, the Warriors found out where their pick would land when Lacob attended his first draft lottery. Golden State finished 12th out of 15 Western Conference teams, but four wins in their last six games meant that they ended up with only the 11th-worst record in the NBA. That gave them less than a 1 percent chance of earning the No. 1 pick in the draft lottery, but you never know with these things. Each team chooses its own representative to attend the lottery; Lacob chose to go himself. After arriving at the northern New Jersey headquarters of NBA Entertainment, Lacob made his way toward a tented cocktail reception. Once inside, he'd heard that Kyrie Irving, the Duke point guard widely believed to be going No. 1 to whoever was lucky enough to hold that spot, was somewhere nearby and asked to meet him. A few minutes later, Irving and Lacob were making benign small talk about being a couple of first-time lottery attendees, impossibly unaware of how their fates would dramatically intertwine just a few years later.

Lacob gamely held his smile onstage that night as deputy commissioner Adam Silver announced the Warriors would draft at No. 11, their draft slot staying put in accordance with their final record. Afterward, someone informed Lacob that the Warriors had nailed three of the four numerical combinations necessary to land the No. 1 draft position. They were just one uncooperative ping-pong ball shy. Instead, the top pick went to the Cleveland Cavaliers, who slogged through a dismal 19-63 season after losing LeBron James to Miami. "You've got to be happy a little bit—a *little* bit—for Cleveland," Lacob conceded, "given what they went through this last year."

Even at No. 11, the Warriors could make an impactful pick. A year earlier, they dropped from No. 4 to No. 6 in the draft lottery and general manager Larry Riley, amidst a period of extreme presale uncertainty, took 6-foot-10 Baylor center Ekpe Udoh with the pick. After an underwhelming rookie year of averaging fewer than five points and four rebounds over 58 games, it was clear Udoh would not be solving the Warriors' size problem. They needed to be more dynamic. They needed someone who could play both ways in Mark Jackson's dual-focused system. And while the days of Don Nelson's free-flowing "Nellie Ball" were long gone, Golden State still needed scorers. Curry needed help, preferably someone bigger, someone who didn't need much space to produce his own shot. The team wanted someone of high character, someone who wouldn't be overwhelmed by the rigors of the NBA.

When the No. 11 pick came around, there was no question who should be taken. Klay Thompson, a slick-shooting two-guard from Washington State, was perfect for the Warriors. He was 6-foot-7 and possessed a lethal three-point shot, swishing 242 of them across three collegiate seasons. He wasn't an elite one-on-one defender, but he could get up and down the floor and defend more than capably in a structured system. And the NBA was firmly in Thompson's DNA. His father, Mychal, had been drafted No. 1 overall by the Portland Trail Blazers in 1978 and played 12 seasons in the league as a 6-foot-10 power forward/center, eventually winning two titles with Magic Johnson's Showtime Lakers in the mid-eighties. Mychal retired before Klay was even two years old, so his son didn't have quite the memories Stephen Curry did of Dell's NBA exploits, but Klay Thompson was still plenty familiar with league culture and the expectations therein. And despite his preference for long threes and the confidence required to hold that mindset, Thompson wasn't cocky, at least not outwardly. He was laid-back and reserved, in that typical Southern California kind of way. Thompson just wanted to play ball; most everything else was secondary.

Inside the Warriors, Thompson had no greater champion than Jerry West himself, who was the Lakers' general manager when Mychal Thompson was on the team and later grew to know Klay when he was still just a boy. West was convinced Thompson would be available when Golden State picked at No. 11 and that he could solve a multitude of their issues. A week before the draft, Thompson worked out in Oakland in front of the Warriors' staff, everyone from Lacob on down to Jackson. West took aside Bill Duffy, Thompson's agent, before the workout had concluded and told him in confidence, "That's our guy."

The Warriors had other players high on their board who were available at that position—Kawhi Leonard of San Diego State and Chris Singleton of Florida State were two in particular that Riley eyed—but the front office felt neither was good enough for that draft slot and that they could take either one only after first trading down a few spots. But when Jimmer Fredette went at No. 10 to the Milwaukee Bucks, picking Thompson was a no-brainer. The idea of pairing up Curry with a taller guard who was projected as a fearless shooter was too enticing. His pedigree and attitude were perfect for Lacob's new-look Warriors. Just minutes after being drafted, Thompson met the media and talked about his offensive prowess and passing abilities but also about the idea of team-first basketball and how he wasn't "out to get mine." Golden State had hosted far too many of those players in recent years.

Thompson's selection seemed, on the surface at least, to fly in the face of the stated mission of improving team defense and rebounding. Yes, Thompson was a towering guard (6-foot-7) and a capable defender, but whether he could lock down the league's best scorers in one-on-one situations was an open question.

His arrival also seemed to make Monta Ellis an obvious redundancy. Thompson was younger, was taller, and possessed a more lethal three-point shot. Perhaps it would take a few months, but Ellis's tenure with the Warriors, the only team he'd ever known, suddenly felt more tenuous than ever. Riley's public contention was that the team did not feel more inclined to trade Ellis and that Thompson could easily slide up and play small forward in Jackson's system.

But any appreciable development from Thompson would instantly make Ellis the team's most attractive asset come next February's trading deadline. And if Riley could use him to obtain the legitimate center that Lacob craved, all the better.

· · ·

One immense complication figured to stall all the Warriors' machinations toward a more hopeful future, and that was a lengthy, bitter work stoppage. Unable to come to an agreement on a new collective bargaining agreement, the NBA owners locked out the players on July 1, claiming that they had lost nearly $1 billion over the last three seasons alone. They sought to cut the players' share of basketball-related income (BRI) from 57 percent down to 47 percent. The players refused, countering with 53 percent. What followed was months of rancor, accusations, and late-night negotiations that kept basketball writers bleary-eyed as they staked out hotel conference rooms desperate for any morsel of new info. The low point came in mid-November, when the first round of scheduled player paychecks didn't go out. The average NBA player lost $220,000 of income as a result, and the length of the season was being shortened by the day. Back and forth they went, haggling over the BRI split, the provisions of the salary cap, players' contractual rights, and more arcane yet important minutiae. Commissioner David Stern told an ESPN audience that the NBA was approaching a "nuclear winter."

By that point, dozens of players had opted to play overseas, stay in shape playing for an Asian or European club team, and await word about when they should return home for the NBA season. Some All-Stars even made the jump abroad: Tony Parker went to France, Andrei Kirilenko played in Russia, Deron Williams and Mehmet Okur went to Turkey, and Kenyon Martin went to China. Some Warriors did the same. Ekpe Udoh, Golden State's 2010 lottery pick, went to Israel, while 2011 second-round pick Charles Jenkins opted for Italy.

But most NBA players, including all of the league's biggest stars, stayed stateside and found other ways to maintain their endurance and stamina amid uncertainty about when a new NBA season would actually begin. Klay Thompson, bored out of his mind, kept busy working out in Southern California. For Stephen Curry, the Warriors' most important player, the lockout essentially amounted to an extended rehab from his ankle surgery back in May. The procedure, which required two ligaments in his right ankle to be rebuilt, limited Curry's mobility for a large part of the summer, so he spent much of that downtime near his home in Charlotte. Sandwiched around his July wedding to Ayesha Alexander, Curry worked to get back into top form, even if the season's status remained in perpetual limbo.

During that rehab, a chance encounter changed Curry's career trajectory. While working out at a clinic in Charlotte with Harrison Barnes (a standout University of North Carolina small forward who was projected as a future lottery pick) and several members of the Charlotte Bobcats, Curry met a local sports trainer named Brandon Payne. The founder of Accelerate Basketball Training in Fort Mill, South Carolina, about 30 minutes south of Charlotte, Payne didn't look like your average trainer. He was stocky, with a military-style buzz cut, not the image of the sweaty, hyper-inspirational yelling type. After that day's workout, Payne introduced himself to Curry, gave him his number, and said to call him if he wanted to work on skills more specific to his game. All Curry could do, thanks to his mending ankle, was work on ball-handling while sitting down, but he was intrigued. That night, Payne received a call from Curry and the two met again early the next morning. It was the genesis of a years-long relationship that continues to this day.

Payne, a Charlotte native and son of a coach, played Division II basketball an hour away at Wingate University and graduated in 2001 with a bachelor's in sports management. He stayed on staff as an assistant coach for two seasons and, while in that role, became interested in the training side of the game, in how you could blend strength and conditioning with skill development. Payne researched the latest technology that was being used in basketball-centric drills. The regimens he developed were designed to push players to their limits while maintaining a youthful love for the game. Payne sought to improve their cognitive decision-making as well as confidence through repetition. In time, he would dub this as an effort to improve players' "neuromuscular efficiency." That concept might sound like empty jargon, but it was gaining traction with NBA players who needed to stay in shape. For Accelerate, the lockout was a serendipitous boon to its business.

Curry bought in right away. Three months after surgery, the newlywed could finally participate in full basketball drills, and since the lockout prohibited him from practicing in Oakland, Curry made full use of Payne's attention and expertise. Between Accelerate's headquarters in a nondescript industrial-park space in unincorporated South Carolina and a full-service gym encased within a nearby marketing company, Curry spent hours a day getting into the best basketball shape of his life. "His desire to learn more," Payne says, "his desire to understand how the body operates has led him to be incredibly detailed."

His shooting stroke was soon back. His ankles felt strong as Payne's associates smacked him with foam pads as he drove to the rim. One of Payne's signature drills, where you dribble a basketball in one hand and toss a tennis ball back and forth to a trainer with the other, helped fortify Curry's hand-eye coordination. Payne also impressed upon him the importance of off-ball anticipation and putting his body in a position to excel before the pass even reached him. In mid-October, Curry posted a YouTube update from a recent training session that effectively doubled as Accelerate's first major client endorsement.

Aside from the basketball component, Curry also liked that he could bounce ideas off Payne and address specific skills that needed fine-tuning, such as moving to his right with the ball and exploding toward the rim. And since Curry had no time yet to work with Mark Jackson or the new coaching staff, Payne was the closest thing he had to a head coach at that time. That would change once the season started, but the lockout held everything up. As October became November, all Curry and the rest of the players could do was wait.

Finally, an agreement was reached. As announced at 3:40 a.m. on November 26, the 149th day of the lockout, the league would play a 66-game season, instead of the usual 82. Players would start off with a 51.5 percent slice of the BRI pie, and that number would scale down slightly over the next few years. The parameters regarding player contracts were constructed so as to incentivize them to stay with their original teams, which could offer more years and money than other suitors. It was a clear response to how Chris Bosh and LeBron James had essentially timed their free agency so they could unite in Miami with Dwyane Wade, and the NBA had no desire for the league's best talent to concentrate so heavily in any one space. Changes in revenue-sharing also benefited small-market teams. Stern was trying to level the NBA playing field in the best way he could. In turn, everyone would ideally be earning more money than ever before, although the consensus opinion was that the players, at least in the near term, had caved, unable to exert any great leverage on the 30 team owners. In the end, the lockout forced a two-month delay from when the schedule normally started.

Ready or not, the truncated season would tip off on Christmas Day.

. . .

Stephen Curry's right ankle didn't even make it through the preseason.

In the final tune-up before a marquee Christmas Day matchup against the Los Angeles Clippers, Curry was defending Jimmer Fredette late in the second quarter when he shuffled his feet back on defense and his right ankle rolled over. Curry didn't return for the second half, and suddenly his status for opening night was in doubt. "I'm disappointed. We need him back quick," Mark Jackson said after the game. "We hope Steph comes back quick because everybody knows we are a better basketball team with him."

Far from 100 percent, Curry was hurried back for the opener and played miserably in a 19-point home loss to the Clips, shooting 2-of-12 from the floor and finishing with only four points and four assists. The following night against the Chicago Bulls, Curry was matched up against Derrick Rose, the reigning Most Valuable Player. He was sublime for much of the evening, scoring 21 points, dishing out 10 assists, stealing six passes, and holding Rose to only 4-of-17 shooting and 13 points. Two minutes in, Curry launched an alley-oop pass from half court to a gliding David Lee, who slammed it home. Early in the fourth, with the Warriors up 15, Curry threw a pass from 70 feet out that Dorell Wright dunked on the fly.

But a few minutes later, Curry drove to the rim and his right foot came down on Kyle Korver's and rolled yet again. He hobbled off to the locker room and didn't return as the Warriors closed out a 99–91 win for Jackson's first career coaching win at any level. "He ran his basketball team," Jackson said. "He did a great job of being an extension of me on the floor." In the locker room, Curry immersed his fragile limb in a large Gatorade container filled with ice water, all too aware that this season was cascading yet again into another series of inexplicable injuries that threatened to forever define his pro career.

Curry sat out one game but returned on New Year's Eve to face Andre Iguodala and the Philadelphia 76ers at Oracle Arena. The Warriors were without Monta Ellis, whose grandmother had died, and Klay Thompson, making his first career start, was not up to the task, scoring just three points in 26 minutes. Curry moved well enough, dropping 10 points in the first quarter alone, but the Warriors were listless from the get-go, so much so that Joe Lacob was, as one news report said, "slumped in his courtside chair, arms folded in frustration." After the Warriors led by 10 after one quarter, Philadelphia outscored them by 36 over the final three.

The Warriors then dropped a game in Phoenix before flying to San Antonio, where they hadn't won a game since 1997. Golden State was competitive well into the third quarter and Curry was once again playing smart and efficient basketball, with 20 points on 11 shots, along with eight assists.

That's when Curry's ankle gave out again. As he faked a pass downcourt and reestablished his dribble, it looked as if Curry's tiptoes caught just enough of the court to roll his foot out unnaturally. Curry once again limped off, unable to put much weight on the leg. "Oh, my goodness!" team broadcaster Jim Barnett yelped when Curry came up lame. "Oh, this is just *heartbreaking*." After the game, Curry was at a loss to explain how this could keep happening: "It's been one of those things that's been chronic with me. I've been trying to nip it in the bud, but it seems to be coming back."

Curry missed eight games and needed eight more after that to really find his shot again. Then a 36-point effort in Denver, enough to seal just Golden State's ninth win in 23 games, seemed to signal he was back for good. But two weeks later, Curry strained a right-foot tendon in Phoenix and missed the entire second half of a game won on an Ellis 20-footer with one second to play. That was the final game before the All-Star break, so Curry rested for six days before missing a 24-point loss in Indiana and then weirdly subbing in for only the final three seconds of an 85–82 win in Atlanta. Curry played sparingly off the bench the next two games before starting again at home against Dallas on March 10. Midway through the third, in an otherwise normal sequence where he dribbled into a defender's body and then away, Curry shifted his weight on the wrong spot and his right ankle again rolled out. He limped to the bench and slammed a chair in frustration. This recurring nightmare would not stop.

Curry started the next night on the road against the Clippers, but he was clearly affected by the injury, going scoreless in nearly 10 minutes. The Warriors were up by 17 when Jackson pulled him, and Golden State held on for a 97–93 victory. "I just felt it wasn't right to throw him out there," Jackson said. "He looked like he was gutting it out."

That Warriors win on March 11 would mark Curry's last game of the season. It was clear that he was severely compromised. Curry's right ankle was a chronic issue that needed to be definitively addressed before it completely derailed his promising career. The team would have to soldier on in his absence, and a decision about surgery would be made after the season.

Despite Curry's dropping in and out of the lineup so often, the Warriors had persevered. They were 17-21 and not entirely out of the playoff picture. David Lee was averaging nearly 20 points and 10 rebounds, while Ellis was scoring some 22 points a night.

But there would be no playoffs this season, no triumphant underdog story played out. Unbeknownst to many, a bombshell would soon drop. It landed on March 13—just two days after Curry took his leave for the season—and would shake the entire Warriors organization to its core.

. . .

Joe Lacob was anxious heading into the 2011–12 season, what with all the turnover, but at least the prime executive positions were filled. Bob Myers was in line to replace Larry Riley as general manager one day, if all went well, and Rick Welts was in place as team president. Meanwhile, the team pressed on in its rebuilding of fan trust. The team website unveiled the Owners' Box, a dedicated section where fans were encouraged to email Lacob and Guber, who promised to read every submission and respond to as many as they could. The page went up in January 2011 with the first Q&A following in July, a few weeks after the draft.

Most of the fan questions included the kind of affirmations you'd expect, with people largely gushing over the new ownership. The last query did inquire about the most difficult part of running a professional sports franchise. Here, Lacob was somewhat revealing.

"The most challenging aspect of owning the Warriors has been the patience that I've had to exercise," he said. "From the beginning, I understood that everything can't be changed overnight. It's a process. Like most fans, I'd love for us to immediately be a 50-win team and a championship contender. The reality is that it's not that simple. We will do our best to make this a very good team in as short amount of time as possible, but we will be smart in our decision-making, which will enable us to sustain our growth and be competitive each and every season."

The patience may have been challenging, but it was also the very public nature of the whole endeavor that Lacob was still grappling with. Every move the team made was reported and dissected at light speed. That May, before Mark Jackson was hired, Lacob was driving to the airport to fly to San Antonio and interview Spurs assistant coach Mike Budenholzer for the vacancy. He turned on KNBR, the local sports radio station, and the host was referencing an online report that disclosed Lacob's plans. He was shocked to his core. The media were reporting something as he was literally in the act of doing it. Upon returning from San Antonio, Lacob fired two staffers over the leak.

But as the lockout came to an end and Lacob could survey the roster heading into the abbreviated season, everyone from the fans to the media to the highest-tier executives could see the glaring needs. It didn't require a front-page newspaper scoop to see that the Warriors still needed a more traditional center to fortify the frontcourt, someone who could not only rebound and protect the rim but competently pass. And if Klay Thompson developed into the kind of perimeter shooter the Warriors hoped he would be when they drafted him, that meant one notable player above others was expendable: Monta Ellis.

The problem was that Lacob, from the start, was publicly adamant that the Warriors were not looking to trade Ellis. It's a sensible strategy, since to suggest otherwise might've fomented a full-on fan mutiny, and by looking as if you're resisting any calls to trade a scorer like Ellis, you're actually gaining leverage, forcing prospective trade partners to sweeten their offers.

And Lacob played the role perfectly. Speaking to KNBR in June, two days before the team drafted Thompson, Lacob tried to stamp down speculation that any selection they made signaled which way the wind blew on dealing Ellis. "I think you can very, very much clearly presume that we value him very highly," he said, "and that he is arguably our best player. He's certainly one of our best players, and we are not trying to trade him."

Lacob then blamed the media for all the speculation: "This is not coming from us. This is not coming from us. The media is out of control, I mean, to be quite frank, compared to what it used to be. People write stories based on one little fact or something that's hearsay. It's not based on fact at all, and then other people repeat it, and then it becomes fact."

But at the same time, Lacob was sowing the seeds for moves to come later, emphasizing that, somehow and some way, the team needed to get bigger up front—and if that meant entertaining deals for a popular player like Ellis, so be it. "If we got offered a fantastic deal for any player, we would have to consider it," Lacob said. "We have been offered, by the way, for Monta Ellis in particular. So it's something we have to listen to . . . but the truth of the matter is—and I believe this personally—that we have a terrific backcourt, one of the best in the NBA, and I don't believe this stuff about it being a small backcourt at all. It's not small. Dallas just won a championship with a much smaller backcourt, with guys that couldn't shoot as well as ours." Lacob concluded the reason the Mavericks were so successful "was the fact they had two 7-footers in the middle. We don't."

A few months later, in January 2012, with Ellis shooting better than 51 percent from the floor and averaging 19 points a game, Lacob again boosted Ellis's bona fides in a video interview given to the team website. "Monta Ellis is a great player. Some people believe that he's the third best shooting guard in the league. I think it's very likely true," Lacob said. "Monta is definitely rounding his game, he's getting better as the years go on. He certainly has a lot of heart." In that same sit-down, perhaps Spidey-sensing the potential turbulence to come, Lacob made another public plea for patience.

"I would just encourage everybody, as hard as it may seem sometimes, and I know it's been hard for all of us Warriors fans for a long time, stick with it. Stick with us," he told Warriors radio broadcaster Tim Roye. "We're doing everything possible to build a winning team and a winning organization and we're going to get there."

Behind the scenes, the Warriors, and Larry Riley specifically, had spent the season trying to finagle a deal for a center, and Ellis was always at the center of such proposals. As time went by, one player became the singular focus: the Milwaukee Bucks' Andrew Bogut, who had been a forceful if ephemeral star over his seven seasons in the league. With the ball, Bogut could command a double-team down low, thus opening up a shooter (be that Curry or Thompson) somewhere along the perimeter, and his passing ability would space the floor more than ever. As the first No. 1 overall pick out of Australia, Bogut represented a legit, All-Star-caliber low-post presence—the Warriors' first such player in decades.

Riley felt this opportunity was one the Warriors could not pass up. He had started conversations with Bucks general manager John Hammond the year before. The Bucks had said no, and as the months went by and the trade deadline drew near, Riley was convinced that Hammond would trade Bogut during the next offseason. And because the coming free agent market for centers looked thinner than usual, Riley knew he had to act decisively to make this happen.

For years, there was a long-held belief among Warriors fans that the team had to work through a bit of soul-searching, some kind of heated internal debate regarding whether they should trade Monta Ellis or Stephen Curry. The team contends to this day that it was always about Ellis, who was the only option that made any sense. Curry was younger and had a cleaner injury history (to that point), and Ellis, for all his clear talents on the court, had used up his fair share of goodwill with team management over the previous years. The moped accident. The frustration with Curry's presence as training camp opened. The years of locker room discontent that Ellis had, at best, tacitly allowed to exist as team captain.

The other complicating factor was that a former Warriors employee had filed a sexual harassment lawsuit against Ellis and the team just three months earlier. Erika Ross Smith, who worked in community relations, alleged in the suit that Ellis sent her sexually explicit text messages, including a photo of his genitals. She then claimed the Warriors fired her in August 2011 without just cause and months after she complained to the team about Ellis's clandestine missives. The suit also alleged, among other things, that Larry Riley told Ellis the matter would be "swept under the rug" and handled quietly and that Ellis's wife, believing Smith had initiated the relationship and continuing texts, assaulted her during a Warriors home game in February 2011. After a lawsuit was filed that December, the Warriors denied all wrongdoing. "When we were made aware of a consensual relationship between Mr. Ellis and the plaintiff, we did what an organization should do," Rick Welts said in a statement. "We told both to stop—promptly, directly, and fairly." Regardless of what happened, it was yet another example of the kind of controversy that had become commonplace under the old ownership group. History, it seemed, was repeating itself.

Off the court, there were benefits to subtracting Ellis. But in basketball terms, adding Bogut stood to be a boon for the Warriors' young guards. With a healthy Bogut manning the middle, the team felt as if a tremendous puzzle piece had finally been attained. It also showed that they had both the assets to make the kind of seismic trades needed to facilitate a turnaround and the gumption to actually follow through on those opportunities. So long as Bogut could produce on the court, the trade made sense.

But therein lay the biggest problem: Bogut was far from 100 percent health-wise. Two months earlier, he broke his left ankle after going up to block a shot and landing on the foot of Houston's Kyle Lowry. Bogut was ruled out indefinitely, this setback just the latest in a freaky string of maladies that had plagued his career. He missed 16 games in his second season with a sprained left foot. The next year, Bogut missed 43 more games with pain in his lower back. He then missed the Bucks' playoff series loss in 2009–10 with a dislocated elbow and broken wrist. In 2010–11, it was migraines and more back pain that added up to 17 absences. And now this broken ankle. Though none of these injuries were chronic or even connected in any tangible way, they showed that Bogut had a real propensity for missing games. When Bogut was playing, there were few true centers who could contribute in the ways he did, but he couldn't stay off the injured list.

Despite the reality that they would be without their prized center for months, the Warriors felt compelled to make the deal. If anything, the injury even worked to Golden State's advantage, since the chances of Hammond's finding a willing trade partner for an injured Bogut (as opposed to a healthy one) dropped off considerably. The Warriors' inner circle—Larry Riley, Jerry West, Mark Jackson, Travis Schlenk, Bob Myers, and Kirk Lacob—was all in on pulling the trigger, but Joe Lacob had the final say-so.

"They walked me in. They were all scared to tell me that they had come to consensus," Lacob told a rapt audience years later at Kleiner Perkins, his old venture capital firm. "I listened, and I said, *Are you serious? You want me to trade our best player for a guy that's injured, has a history of being injured?*" He knew right away that he would get the brunt of the backlash from fans, who adored Ellis, the most-tenured Warrior by that time. Lacob, channeling a mindset born of dozens of Silicon Valley board meetings, allowed his brain trust—the people he'd hired to make *precisely* these types of decisions—to present its best case, and he saw no reason to veto such a potentially franchise-altering move: "It was the right thing to do. I became convinced to do it. I had to do something to turn it around. You have to be bold. You have to take risks."

The trade was announced on March 13, 2012, just hours before the Warriors were to play in Sacramento. Ellis, who had come to the Warriors as a 20-year-old high-schooler from Mississippi and gone on to score more than 8,000 points across seven seasons, was traded along with Kwame Brown and Ekpe Udoh to Milwaukee for Bogut and who else but former Warriors captain and all-around malcontent Stephen Jackson, the same player who, according to Don Nelson once upon a time, was "harder than hell" to trade away. The Warriors, having already learned their lesson, traded Jackson to San Antonio two days later for

Richard Jefferson, T. J. Ford, and a late first-round pick in the upcoming 2012 draft.

"This kind of trade just doesn't happen every day," Lacob said when Bogut was introduced to the media. "It could have taken us three, four, five years to add this piece. We're leaps and bounds ahead of where we were a week ago."

But the Ellis trade rocked the Warriors' fan base to its core. Even Ellis seemed surprised it actually happened. "I had some great years here. I had some bad ones," Ellis said outside his locker stall for the final time as a Warrior. "I'm just thankful that I had the opportunity to do what I do for the seven years I was here." Ellis said the team hadn't notified him of the trade before it was announced. He learned of it while watching TV in the visitors' locker room in Sacramento. "I kind of figured that something bad was going to happen today," he said with a knowing smile. "I was prepared for it. I'm good."

Three days after Ellis was traded, the NBA's schedule makers showed they had a sense of humor when who else but the Milwaukee Bucks dropped in to play the Warriors at Oracle Arena. Ellis, when announced with the Bucks starters, received an emotional standing ovation from the fans. He scored the game's first points on a 15-foot jumper, finished the night with 18 points on 15 shots, and the Bucks destroyed the Warriors, 120–98. During a timeout halfway through the first quarter, the video screen played a tribute to Ellis, scored to Green Day's "Good Riddance (Time of Your Life)," which brought the crowd to a frenzy.

The blowout loss, coupled with the jarring sight of Ellis in colors other than Warrior gold and blue, underscored how fast the season was slipping away. The fan base had become a combustible stew of anger and frustration, one that boiled over just a few nights later in what would be remembered as the undisputed nadir of Joe Lacob's time as team owner.

Oh, and that sexual harassment lawsuit against Ellis? Talks between the Warriors and Smith's legal counsel began just a few days after Ellis was traded. A settlement was announced in June 2012. Terms were not disclosed, and the team again denied it did anything wrong.

. . .

### "WE WANT MONTA!"

Joe Lacob shrugged as he heard those three words cascade down from the highest reaches of Oracle Arena on March 19, 2012. What else could he possibly do? This night was supposed to be one of the bright spots in an otherwise rotten season, the night that the franchise finally did right by Chris Mullin and retired his No. 17 jersey. Lacob himself had announced to season-ticket holders back in September—a month after Mullin was inducted into the Hall of Fame—that the Warriors would raise his jersey to the rafters the following spring. The team even put a two-page promotional spread at the start of the 2011–12 media guide. This night was to be the high point of the season.

But the festivities turned into a very public and very ugly referendum on Lacob's 20 months as team owner. The team was on the verge of missing the playoffs for the 18th time in 19 seasons, yet their record was almost assuredly too good to keep their protected first-round pick come June—the result, weirdly enough, of a terrible trade Mullin had approved back in 2008 when he was the Warriors' executive vice president of basketball ops.

That time, before Curry arrived and before Lacob bought the team, felt like a lifetime ago, but the Warriors were, same as ever, still an awful basketball team. They'd lost three in a row and entered the night of March 19 with a record of 18 wins and 24 losses. Even the woeful Timberwolves, thanks to All-Star power forward Kevin Love, were having a more successful season. The Warriors were now getting leapfrogged by the perennial dregs of the Western Conference. And by this time, every Golden State fan who subscribed to *Sports Illustrated* had received in the mail not one but *two* separate issues featuring cover photos of Jeremy Lin, the Palo Alto kid and Harvard grad who'd been waived by the Warriors in the preseason and eventually picked up by the New York Knicks. "Linsanity" was at its peak in the Big Apple; Lacob had let him go for nothing.

This was rock bottom.

Lacob still had high hopes for the evening. He wanted to keep the focus on Mullin and his accomplishments as much as possible, on a 17-year Hall of Fame career built on 13 seasons in Oakland. He'd won two Olympic gold medals, his second as a member of the historic Dream Team that stormed through the 1992 Summer Games in Barcelona. Along with Tim Hardaway and Mitch Richmond, Mullin was the backbone of the Warriors' "Run TMC" trio, which played infectious, uptempo ball. With a lethal long-range jumper and iconic, close-cropped flat-top, Mullin had solidified his place in the sport by the time of his retirement in 2001.

Mullin was hired by Golden State as a special assistant for the 2002–03 season. After several years in the front office, he was canned in 2009, a year after then–team president Robert Rowell publicly ripped him following the Monta Ellis moped incident and effectively stripped him of decision-making authority. It was a sad and unbecoming end to Mullin's tenure with Golden State, a stretch that dated back nearly a quarter century by that point. In Lacob's mind, this night was an attempt to welcome Mullin back into the Warriors fold, for the team to embrace the better parts of its history.

But this management group, in the eyes of Bay Area locals, looked just as bumbling and misguided as Chris Cohan and his charges. The roster moves weren't panning out. The losing showed no end in sight. The fans were itching for some sort of release, a chance to voice their growing, collective angst.

Team management had planned an elaborate halftime ceremony

that, until Lacob took the floor, was proceeding according to plan. Various Warriors legends of the past were seated at center court as visiting dignitaries: Richmond, Hardaway, Hall of Famer Nate Thurmond, championships-winning coach Al Attles, and more. Mullin's jersey would be raised to the rafters after nearly 20 minutes of speeches and anecdotes and remembrances. Before coming out, Lacob heard the crowd boo NBA commissioner David Stern, whose prerecorded well-wishes for Mullin played on the video screen above. He thought to himself, somewhat jokingly, *Maybe I'll do better than him.*

Lacob was pelted with boos before taking the mic. He stood awkwardly for a few seconds, embraced Mullin, then stood at center court, trying to settle himself amidst a growing din of anger. As a venture capitalist, one of Lacob's core tenets was that you always need to have a backup course of action to mitigate risk: *If this goes wrong, what do I do?* But with no contingency, the jeering kept coming. Bogut was stunned. As was Mark Jackson, who played two seasons with Mullin at St. John's University. Kevin Love stood off to the corner with his Timberwolves teammates and could only giggle. The local media could think of only one prior instance that compared, when Chris Cohan was booed off the court during the NBA All-Star Game in 2000. Lacob had also forgotten the sports franchise owner's cardinal rule, as coined by Dan Rooney of the Pittsburgh Steelers: "The less you say, the better off you are."

Mullin stepped forward, mic in hand. "I got it," he first told Lacob before addressing the crowd.

"As the greatest fans in the NBA," Mullin boomed in his New York accent, "as everyone has stated, sometimes change is inevitable and it's gonna work out just fine. With your support and patience—and use that passion in the right direction—this thing is going in the right way. I've got great confidence in Joe, Mark Jackson, and everything will work out just fine. Just a little bit of patience. Use that passion!"

But when Mullin, the good cop, couldn't calm the unruly masses, that responsibility fell on bad cop Rick Barry, the tempestuous Hall of Famer who led Golden State to the title in 1975 and a man never shy to speak his mind. "One second here. C'mon, people! You fans are the greatest fans in the world!" Barry shouted. "Show a little bit of *class*. This is a man that I've spent some time talking to. He is going to change this franchise." The boos did not stop. "This is crazy. Seriously. C'mon! You're doing yourself a disservice. All of the wonderful accolades being said to you, for you to treat this man, who is spending his money to do the best that he can, to turn this franchise around, and I *know* he's going to do it. So give him the respect he deserves." Lacob had been belittled to his barest elements, and even the most defiant of Warriors fans must've felt some modicum of empathy by now.

Lacob labored through a few more prepared remarks—his hands visibly shaking at times as he read off his note cards—and Mullin's jersey was finally revealed for all to see. The theme from *The Natural* echoed throughout. Lacob stood arm in arm with Mullin and his family, an awkward, enduring image of a night that had devolved into yet another infamous moment for a franchise riddled with them.

After returning to his courtside seat early in the second half, Lacob stayed there for the rest of a dispiriting 97–93 loss. He spoke with the press after the game and admitted the obvious, that such a moment was regrettable but that it wouldn't come to ultimately define his time as Warriors owner. "I'm not going to let a few boos get me down," he said. "Winning will solve all things." Lacob knew he'd made a major miscalculation, but the part of him that was a longtime season-ticket holder understood where the fans were coming from. He knew how fans could viscerally hate an owner when the team was playing lousy. (Lacob even hated the word itself: *owner*. For him, it conjured up visions of old plantations in the Deep South.) He spent that night replying to some 400 emails that had flooded his inbox. The next day, Lacob said on KNBR that he would've booed himself, too.

"The day is going to come," Jackson said after the loss, "where he's truly appreciated around here."

. . .

After Ellis was traded away Klay Thompson thrived, finally able to show off the breadth of his skill set. In his first 38 games, all but one coming off the bench, Thompson averaged just eight points on just seven shots in 17 minutes per game. Now slotted into the starting lineup, Thompson started 28 games after Ellis's departure and averaged nearly 19 points on 16 shot attempts per game. His threes per game went from 1.3 to 2.1. David Lee's scoring average leaped to 22.1, an increase of three points. But with such a depleted roster, the remaining Warriors didn't have enough offense to compete. They won only six of 28 games after the Ellis trade and missed the playoffs for a fifth straight year.

As this torturous season came to a close, the team steeled its gaze toward a future that felt like a dream unrealized. Lacob couldn't wait to get going. Two days before the season finale, he moved Larry Riley, who had drafted both Curry and Thompson and orchestrated the Bogut trade, to director of scouting and elevated Bob Myers to the position of general manager. Still just 37, Myers became the second-youngest GM in the NBA. He had accumulated just one season of executive experience, but that didn't matter to Lacob, who preached the gospel of hiring people who might be scant on service time but long on potential. In Myers, he saw someone with the temperament—an innate penchant for diplomacy—that would prove critical to getting deals done, to building a culture within the Warriors based on teamwork and selflessness. The learning curve would be steep, and Myers didn't have the luxury of time. The 2012 draft—shaping up as one of the most important nights in Warriors franchise history—was just two months away.

Before that happened, Warriors officials topped off this hellish season with one more gut-punch to the fan base. Lacob, Peter Guber, mayor

Ed Lee, lieutenant governor Gavin Newsom, NBA commissioner David Stern, Jerry West, Mark Jackson, David Lee, and local leaders gathered on a makeshift dais along San Francisco's Embarcadero to announce formal plans to build a luxurious 19,000-square-foot arena along Piers 30 and 32 and move the team across the Bay in time for the 2017–18 season. Despite a $500 million price tag, the team would pay every penny.

After four decades in Oakland, the Warriors were now lame ducks.

Lacob spoke for six minutes and offered few specifics but confessed that a tight timeline had necessitated this move—the team's lease in Oakland would be up in 2017—and that the Warriors had labored with the San Francisco mayor's staff for five months to work out the particulars. He thanked the people of Oakland for hosting the Warriors for some 40 years, then explained how the team's fan base is split between those in Oakland and the greater East Bay and to those living in San Francisco, the North Bay, and the lower peninsula (home to Silicon Valley and most of the tech industry).

"What people don't understand is that, in fact, our fan base is really 50-50," Lacob said, "and we don't release this information all the time but it's 50-50. . . . So we are the Bay Area's basketball team, is the way we look at it. And we had to find the best site that served the majority of our fans for the very long term."

Lacob predicted this building would become one of the NBA's jewels, something that could help define the Warriors' legacy for decades to come. "We intend to build the most spectacular arena in the country . . . that all Bay Area residents can be proud of," he said.

"An architecturally significant building on truly an iconic site"—Lacob waved his hand along the stretch of land, with Oakland a distant, hazy backdrop—"it doesn't get any better than this."

# 5 ★ ★ ★ ★ ★ ★ ★

# MARK'S MEN

## The 2012–13 season

On the morning of May 30, 2012, Bob Myers sat on one of the thousands of green benches dotting New York's Central Park with a pocket full of good-luck charms and stressed about events he could not control.

The NBA Draft Lottery, now held in Times Square and broadcast on ESPN in prime time, was normally a low-key affair. The only drama came with discovering which teams the ping-pong balls (selected behind closed doors just minutes before) had been deemed worthy of the top picks. The process, of course, favors the worst teams, which receive the highest number of routes to the top pick. The Charlotte Bobcats, as the worst team during the 2011–12 season, had a full 25 percent chance of coming home with the No. 1 slot. The Washington Wizards had roughly a 20 percent chance. The Cleveland Cavaliers, who selected Kyrie Irving at No. 1 a year before, had a 13.8 percent chance, with the New Orleans Hornets close behind at 13.7 percent.

Way down the list were the Warriors, which had just a 3.6 percent chance at the top slot, a draft position they hadn't experienced since taking the forgettable Joe Smith at No. 1 in 1995.

The far more likely scenario for Golden State—60 percent, in fact— was that it would stay in the No. 7 draft position, but that possibility came with a backstory, and that's where Myers's charms took on their intangible importance.

The chain of events started four years earlier, on July 22, 2008, when the Warriors were scrambling to fill the point guard void created by Baron Davis's free agent defection to the LA Clippers. With a team that had won just 48 games, Chris Mullin gambled that this was still a team that was one or two players away from competing with the Western Conference elites, so he traded a conditional first-round pick to the New Jersey Nets for Marcus Williams, a 22-year-old who could potentially break out in Don Nelson's system. But the pairing was a disaster from the get-go and Williams was waived before the season was over.

Williams's flameout notwithstanding, the Warriors' first-round pick in 2011 now belonged to the Nets—provided the pick fell outside the top 14 picks (i.e., the draft lottery). If Golden State was bad enough to miss the playoffs and get into the lottery, the pick would move to 2012 but only be top-11 protected. If that pick was in the top 11, it would slide to 2013 and become top-10 protected. If *that* failed to happen, the Warriors would give up second-round picks in 2013 and 2015.

In September 2009, Larry Riley, afraid of losing a potentially high draft pick, made a deal himself with the Nets that nearly proved disastrous. He convinced New Jersey to bump the pick back a year, to 2012. In return, the Warriors gave up a 2011 second-round pick. And that 2012 conditional first-rounder would now only be top-7 protected, which would then be top-6 protected in 2013 and, if necessary, 2014. If the Warriors were then still inept enough to stay in that top-6 range, they would cede second-rounders in 2014 and 2016.

The Warriors drafted in 2011 at No. 11—meaning they would *not* have lost the pick, though Riley couldn't have predicted the future—and took Klay Thompson. Now Golden State had to draft at No. 7 or better in 2012 or Utah (which acquired the pick in a February 2011 deal for point guard Deron Williams) would snatch the pick, thereby benefiting from an arcane mishmash of deals four years in the making. The surefire way to do that would be to finish with at least the fourth-worst record in the league, since it's impossible to fall more than three slots in the draft lottery.

But to have a reasonable chance at getting the No. 7 pick or better, Golden State *had* to at least finish with the seventh-worst record.

Here was the problem: The Warriors were better than anyone expected. On March 13, with about six weeks left, Golden State had 18 wins and 21 losses, not nearly bad enough to get down to No. 7, and the lockout-shortened, 66-game season was wreaking havoc with the Warriors in two ways. First, fewer games being played meant more volatility and fluctuation in teams' records, wherein any streak of wins (or losses) would be more decisive in determining final win/loss records than in a typical 82-game season. Second, the 2011 lockout essentially forced several top college players to stay in college for another year to avoid the NBA's uncertain labor situation, so the 2012 draft was expected to be far deeper than usual. The No. 7 pick would carry a lot more value this time around.

The pick *had* to be kept.

And the Warriors started losing—a lot.

A four-game losing streak, capped off by the night of Mullin's jersey retirement and everything that transpired at center court, was followed by a streak of six losses, then *another* of eight. Heading into the final game of the season, at home against San Antonio, the Warriors needed to lose and hope that the Toronto Raptors won their home game against the Nets. That would leave both teams at 23-43. A coin flip, of all things, would then determine who received the No. 7 draft lottery slot. Guess right and you had a 72 percent chance of picking at No. 7 or higher. Guess wrong and you had a 72 percent chance of falling below seventh—and that would mean losing the pick altogether.

With a depleted B-side lineup that included Thompson at shooting guard alongside Chris Wright, Jeremy Tyler, Mickell Gladness, and Charles Jenkins, as well as just two bench players, Golden State lost to San Antonio, 107–101, to hold up their end of the deal. The 22 losses over their final 27 games was a tanking for the ages. The Raptors, meanwhile, sealed their fate three hours earlier by crushing a hapless Nets team by 31.

The following afternoon, inside the NBA's headquarters in Manhattan, a coin was flipped. The Warriors won the No. 7 draft lottery slot.

But that lingering 28 percent loomed over Myers like a cloud, and the only way it would dissipate was to watch deputy commissioner Adam Silver open up the comically large envelope and hope for the best. Silver started at No. 14 and worked his way up. With the eighth pick, Silver pulled out a Raptors logo and the Warriors relaxed. Seconds later, Golden State was announced as the team drafting No. 7.

Myers smiled, exhaled, and winked at a team official standing offstage. His predecessor had drafted Curry at No. 7 not long ago, so it seemed another franchise-altering talent at that spot was not out of the question.

. . .

The Warriors went into the 2012 draft with four picks. One of Lacob's earliest decrees was that the Warriors would cease trading away such assets. They would rebuild through strategic trades (such as Monta Ellis for Andrew Bogut) and the draft. Against all odds, they had kept their pick at No. 7, but they also had another first-round pick—a late one at No. 30—by virtue of the March 15 trade that shipped Stephen Jackson off to San Antonio. They had a second-round pick at No. 35, which they had acquired (along with Troy Murphy) back in February 2011, when they traded former lottery pick Brandan Wright (whom they'd acquired for Jason Richardson in 2008) to the Nets. There was one more, a late second-rounder at No. 52, but there was little hope of extracting long-term value there.

So the Warriors had three of the top 35 picks in an unusually deep draft. They already had two young snipers in Stephen Curry and Klay Thompson, a legit power forward in David Lee, a still-recovering Andrew Bogut . . . and not a whole lot else. Myers's goal was to extract as much from those three picks as could possibly be expected. He wanted high-character players who would put the team above all else. He wanted to identify talent that was overlooked by other teams. And he wanted players who projected as capable defenders in Jackson's fast-paced system. Lacob had preached defense and rebounding for almost two years. It was time to deliver on that mandate.

The Warriors brain trust identified certain targets but it would all depend on how the picks ahead of them played out. There were no guarantees at No. 7, but the first three picks, as expected, were Anthony Davis (New Orleans), Michael Kidd-Gilchrist (Charlotte), and Bradley Beal (Washington).

The next-best player on the board was Harrison Barnes, a 6-foot-8 small forward from the University of North Carolina who had long been hyped as not just a physically gifted phenom but intelligent beyond his years. "Widely touted as college basketball's most cerebral star since Bill Bradley," crowed an article in the *Atlantic* just two months before the draft. "But where Bradley devoted his analytical abilities to hoops and academics, Barnes has added a third area of interest: the business of basketball." Barnes was the platonic ideal for an emerging kind of pro athlete where the constant, real-time maintenance of one's image held an unprecedented importance. "The longer you stay in college," he told the magazine, "the better a brand you build." That part appealed to Lacob, but his athleticism and ability to defend multiple positions made him a no-brainer for any team.

But the Cavaliers surprised everyone by opting for Dion Waiters, a Syracuse two-guard with a reputation for high energy and a knack for creating his own shot. With Curry and Thompson, the Warriors didn't have a glaring need for a player like that, even as most draft boards agreed he would fall to Golden State at No. 7 after Barnes went at No. 4 to the Cavs. After Waiters went higher than expected, Sacramento took Kansas power forward Thomas Robinson at No. 5 and Portland went with Weber State point guard (and Oakland native) Damian Lillard at No. 6. That meant Barnes fell to the Warriors at No. 7. Golden State had its new starting small forward.

At No. 30—still a spot where you could hope to find a good rotation player, if not an outright starter, Myers opted for Vanderbilt center Festus Ezeli, a 6-foot-11 senior who boasted a wingspan approaching 7-foot-4. He wasn't a great scorer and was a terrible free-throw shooter, but Ezeli projected as a good rebounder, especially on the offensive end, and rim-protector. And at 22 years old, he possessed a physical maturity not seen in all first-round picks. When Bogut was healthy again, Ezeli, the team hoped, would make a capable backup center behind him.

Five picks later, the Warriors pulled off one of the most critical draft selections in franchise history, even if no one knew at the time. Myers was all too aware that this draft could offer great value at No. 35, but the choice he made for an undersized power forward from Michigan State named Draymond Green was a masterstroke, one of the all-time great second-round picks ever recorded.

As a product of one of college basketball's perennial powerhouses, Green was a solid if somewhat unspectacular player. He started less than half of the 145 games he played and averaged 10.5 points, 7.6 rebounds, and 2.9 assists over that time, as well as 36.1 percent shooting on threes. But he averaged more than 16 points and 10 rebounds in his senior season, when the Spartans won the Big Ten tournament and reached the Sweet 16 as a No. 1 regional seed. He recorded not one but two triple-doubles in NCAA tournament games over his career; only Oscar Robertson (four) and fellow Michigan State alum Magic Johnson (three) ever posted more. The National Association of Basketball Coaches named Green the NCAA Division I Player of the Year.

Measured at the NBA Combine at 6-foot-7 and 235 pounds, Green was smaller than your typical power forward but beefier than your average small forward. He had an excellent midrange jumper that could potentially extend to the NBA's longer three-point arc. On and off the court, Green was emotional, energized, moody, and just plain loud. He oozed confidence and talked trash like a veteran. In one pre-draft interview, Green said he modeled his game after "old-school Charles Barkley." He even shared a little DNA with Golden State, wearing 23 in college as an homage to former Warrior (and fellow Saginaw, Michigan, native) Jason Richardson.

But no one had any clear idea how far Green might fall. He wasn't projected to be a lottery pick by a single mock draft prognostication, despite being named a First Team All-American. There were questions about his NBA readiness, his athleticism, his positional value. Lottery picks have to be the surest things in a draft, and Green hadn't convinced the league with his breakout senior season. NBA.com predicted he'd go at No. 27 to the champion Miami Heat. *Sports Illustrated* had him going No. 26 to Indiana. But Green knew he'd had a good workout with Golden State. He figured, worst-case scenario, the Warriors would pick him at No. 30 and give him the distinction of being a first-round pick. Still, he was stressed about the uncertainty. He barely slept the night before. He forgot to eat both breakfast and lunch on the day of the draft, too preoccupied with the life-changing events just hours away. At a draft party in Saginaw with 100 friends and family, Green grew anxious as the night went on and on, with no mention of his name.

The Warriors felt they needed to take a true center at No. 30, and Ezeli was, for them, a no-brainer, no matter how highly they thought of Green. The other part of their thinking was that since Green had completely fallen out of the first round, they could take the calculated risk of hoping he'd still be there at No. 35. His versatility, to be able to play both small and power forward and switch between the two seamlessly, was something the new-look Warriors valued mightily. The NBA itself was trending toward an era in which the defined lines between positions were becoming increasingly blurred, and Green possessed the type of traits well suited to exploit that emerging philosophy.

For his part, Green thought Golden State was a perfect fit. He was keen on playing for Mark Jackson, on helping the Warriors grow. And he was already motivated to show 29 other teams how much they should regret passing on him. Green just needed that phone call, to know where he was headed next.

Finally, Deputy Commissioner Adam Silver read his name at No. 35. The party in Saginaw erupted in cheers. Green was headed across the country to Oakland.

"I got my opportunity," Green said that night, looking more relieved than elated. "It's not about where you go or what pick, it's about the fit. And I think Golden State will be a great fit for me."

. . .

In the spring of 2012, Richard Ferkel held the future of the Golden State Warriors in his hands.

Twice.

The first time occurred on April 23, a Wednesday, when he performed an exploratory arthroscopic surgery on Stephen Curry's right ankle. Curry had sought the opinions of three separate doctors before coming to the determination, along with his family, team officials, and agent, that the best option was to get in there and check things out.

There was a chance that his ankle tendons would have to be completely reconstructed. The surgery a year ago in Charlotte had failed to keep him injury-free, so Ferkel would make an incision, peek inside with a minicam, and see what he could see. When he did, the good news was that the area only required some cleanup and that Curry could be back on the court in maybe three months, four tops.

Two days later, Ferkel operated on Andrew Bogut's left ankle, a procedure that was supposed to be far less stressful for Warriors execs. The plan was for Ferkel to clean out some bone spurs, maybe scar tissue as well, and that Bogut could be back in three months or so. That meant missing the Summer Olympics in London—Bogut had played for his native Australia in two previous Olympics—but all outward indications were that the Warriors' prized springtime acquisition would be more than ready for the start of training camp in the fall.

And as ready as the Warriors were to take the next step during the 2012–13 season, what with the trio of primo draft picks and both Curry and Bogut recovering from injuries, the business side was also starting to take shape. Team president Rick Welts was now running point on the proposed San Francisco arena. Bob Myers was learning the ropes as the new general manager.

Behind the scenes, Lacob's son Kirk was overseeing the buildup of the technology and analytics team. By the time his father had bought the Warriors, every NBA team had access to StatsCube, a proprietary statistical database that was developed and maintained by the league office. But that system, which held all play-by-play data going back to the 1996–97 season, became public in April 2011. At least by then, Golden State had already installed the SportVU system in Oracle Arena and was collecting gobs of information. Now, more than a year later, the Warriors had just collected their first full season of proprietary data, which they were still trying to figure out how to integrate into the basketball side.

There were more new tech initiatives coming through the pipeline.

They developed their own internal efficiency metrics. They partnered with a company called Sports Aptitude that produced player profiles (dubbed "BBIQ") measuring 10 different personality criteria on a scale of 1 to 10. These categories ranged from "Mental Toughness" and "Internal Motivation" to "Leadership Potential" and "Influence & Presence." Kirk Lacob felt the tests, which were based on answers given to 185 questions, provided a valuable window into a player's psyche, and the team was soon consulting the BBIQ database before acquiring any player.

The Warriors were also a client of Synergy Sports, which melded play metadata with video and allowed teams to search and analyze game footage in new ways. They signed on with a group called MOCAP Analytics, run by a group of Caltech and Stanford engineers who were friends of a friend of Kirk Lacob (a Stanford alum). What MOCAP could do was take the raw SportVU data—perhaps a couple million lines of gangly spreadsheet cells—and repurpose them into heat maps, play visualizations, and other materials that could soften the learning curve for coaches and players unaccustomed to this presentation. It was all built on the mandate given Kirk Lacob by his father and upper management when he committed to building out the analytics side. "We had an ownership group who was really willing to buy into this and give us time to develop it," Lacob told a sports analytics conference in September 2012. "They said, 'We don't care if you can't figure it out in two years. Keep working, find a solution, find a way to make this, help us get better.' "

The Warriors could now pull up specific plays to gauge their underlying effectiveness, see if a player's jumper got flatter from the start of the game to the end, and much more. As Lacob told the crowd, "We need to be able to make this information useful to us and then useful to both the rest of the front office and the coaching staff, if it's going to make any sort of impact on what we're doing in the long term."

In time, the SportVU system would form the backbone of a system of digitized tracking that would reshape how basketball strategy was devised throughout the entire league. Entering the 2012–13 season, the Warriors were still trying to figure out what to do with the data they were receiving, but they knew the onus was solely on themselves to figure it out as soon as possible. Unlike other teams that had been early signatories to SportVU, Golden State execs weren't paranoid about who else had access to the system. In their eyes, the sooner every team had SportVU, the sooner there was a more complete data set for everyone to access. That meant hiring people who knew how to parse the data and how to present it to the coaches, who would then filter it down to the players.

For Kirk Lacob, there was one person who fit that description better than anyone. At the time when Joe Lacob bought the Warriors, the franchise was affiliated with a team in the Development League, which is their version of Major League Baseball's minor leagues. Some NBA franchises owned D-League teams; some merely partnered with a team, usually for geographical convenience. Such was the arrangement between Golden State and the Reno Bighorns, a four-hour drive to the northeast on I-80 East out of downtown Oakland. It was in Reno that Kirk Lacob met a newly hired team analyst named Sammy Gelfand, who bore a striking resemblance to Jonah Hill's character from *Moneyball*. Gelfand needed just five years to graduate with two bachelor's degrees (history and political science) from George Washington University and a master's in sports industry management from Georgetown. He'd interned with the Washington Nationals' media relations department and then with Octagon, the same agency that represents Stephen Curry. From there he was hired by the Bighorns in October 2010, the same month Kirk Lacob took over as the Warriors' director of basketball operations. Lacob met Gelfand in Reno on a trip there and came away impressed with both his knowledge and his demeanor.

A year later, Golden State put down almost $2 million to buy its own

D-League franchise, the Dakota Wizards in Bismarck, North Dakota. They were only the fourth NBA team to actually own and operate its own D-League affiliate, but the Warriors saw the investment as a low-cost method of developing young players who would otherwise slip their pipeline (while also growing the Golden State brand beyond the Bay Area). Kirk Lacob was installed as Dakota's general manager; Gelfand was the first person he hired. He needed someone who could act as liaison between the coaching staff and the front office, and Gelfand proved more than capable in Lacob's eyes. So when Myers was promoted to general manager the following year and the team started preparing for the 2012 draft, Gelfand was brought aboard for some extra assistance. Shortly thereafter, the Warriors moved the Wizards to Northern California, just a 90-minute drive south of Oakland into surf country, and renamed them the Santa Cruz Warriors. Gelfand was promoted to director of player personnel for Santa Cruz, but it was only a matter of time (especially with Kirk Lacob being promoted to assistant general manager for the Warriors) before he'd make the leap back to Oakland for good.

But Golden State didn't need Gelfand with the team then and there because they weren't entirely sure how best to execute their analytical advantage, though they started to figure out a few things. First was that Bogut, when healthy, would give them the defense and rebounding they craved. Second was that Curry and Thompson could form the backbone of a lethal scoring threat. Finally, that offensive attack would rely upon the three-pointer, shot with both volume and efficiency. Recognizing that the shooting percentage between a long two-pointer (say, 22 feet) and a three-pointer (24 feet, at the top of the arc) was essentially the same, you were earning a greater commission on your shot investment if you purposely tried to take threes instead of twos.

And that meant Curry was as vital to the future of the Warriors as perhaps no other player since Rick Barry back in the seventies. But there were complications. Curry was coming off the ankle surgery. More pressing, though, was that his rookie scale contract was about to expire and the Warriors wanted to lock him up to an extension, but what kind of a player would they be signing? Curry had shown flashes of the college superstar they'd taken with the No. 7 pick, the sharpshooter who was openly coveted by both Phoenix and New York. Still, could those ankles hold up through a whole season? He had already sprained his right ankle in the preseason, on October 19, and sat out the Warriors' final two exhibition games. On the day of the season opener on Halloween night—and the midnight deadline to sign such an extension—the fate of Curry and his role in the Warriors' future were still in doubt.

In the end, just hours before the deadline, Bob Myers and Jeff Austin completed an agreement that felt fair to both sides, a four-year deal for $44 million. At the time, an average of $11 million a season for a player who'd yet to prove he could produce at an elite level over 82 games seemed like a gamble, but if Curry stayed healthy and became even a fraction of the player the team envisioned back in 2009, the contract would look like a coup for the Warriors.

For Curry, regardless of whether his ankles held up, $44 million was nothing to scoff at. That was more than twice what his father had earned in his entire 16-year career, and only seven point guards in the NBA would be paid more than he would. "If you look at other people in my draft class or other people with comparable stats," Curry told reporters, "I might be below their pay grade, but I'm not really concerned with that. I could potentially be underpaid. I just don't want to be that guy who is overpaid. That's my mission." Throughout the negotiations, Curry kept coming back to a phrase his father had instilled in him: *Never count another man's money.*

On the court that night, Curry was out of sorts, missing his first 10 shots before nailing a couple of important jumpers in the final few minutes. He even missed two free throws in the last five seconds that could've iced the game, but the Warriors still eked out a victory, 87–85.

Curry missed 12 of 14 shots and finished with only five points. He missed all six of his three-point attempts.

"It was one of those games," Curry said after the win, "but it was a crazy day."

. . .

What was far more encouraging for Golden State as the season opened was that Andrew Bogut was finally in uniform and ready to roll. He played almost 19 minutes in the opener, scoring eight points and grabbing six rebounds. Bogut started four of the Warriors' first five games, but then his ankle gave way. He was shut down for the next nine games, of which Golden State won just five. There were hopes Bogut might return after Thanksgiving, but he went on local radio on November 27 and admitted the pain and swelling had not dissipated. "There's really no timetable for a return right now," he said. "It's frustrating the hell out of me. It's just taking a very slow course right now and people are speculating . . . so I haven't commented on any of that stuff that's been put out there by your counterparts, I guess, and I'm just trying to get it right to play."

At practice later that day, Bogut said the pressure to play on opening night, though he wasn't pain-free, came from him. "I wanted to play the first game of the season," he told the press. "I've never missed an opening night in my career and I didn't want to miss one. I probably was a little stupid with it, but for my mental state, I had to know where I was at. If I hadn't played a game yet, I'd still be kicking myself."

Later that night, Warriors beat writer Marcus Thompson II dropped a bombshell that Bogut's procedure had been more than a routine cleanup, that he'd actually had a version of microfracture surgery, which is much more serious, can require a year or more of recovery, and has ended careers in a blink. The next morning, Bogut walked with Bob Myers to meet the media to explain what happened all those months ago.

Before long, Bogut broke from the company line. "We don't want to fool anybody, anymore," he said. "We don't want to keep creating a little bit of excitement of, 'Hey, Andrew might be playing Saturday. It might be Monday. He's back.'" Bogut was frustrated with constant setbacks, with always moving the goalposts on when he might play again. He denied the organization pressured him to return early, but Bogut was tired of skirting the reality of his predicament. "It's enough. It takes a toll on me personally and on the organization," he added. "It got to the point that we spoke this morning and I said, 'Let's make it an indefinite leave until I'm ready.' There's no point in throwing numbers out there."

Myers tried to smooth over the situation. "On any injury, I don't think there's any attempt at deception or omission," he told the media gaggle. "We convey it how we think it's appropriate. As long as we're on the same page with the athlete per the rules, our focus is on the recovery time. . . . I'd like to think we are transparent and always will be."

It was an approach the Warriors tried to take in the immediate aftermath of the Bogut-Ellis trade, when they held a conference call for season-ticket holders two weeks after Bogut was acquired. Trying to quell concerns from longtime fans who were plunking down thousands of dollars a year, Riley, with Bogut himself on the line, impressed upon one caller after another that the big Australian was vital to their chances for success. "I was with Monta Ellis for six years," Riley explained to a fan in San Jose. "I knew him inside and out. In order to transform this team, to give us a chance to be successful as we go into next season, it was a situation where we had to make a move and set the table for a team that could be built to last.

"I went through the situation where we won one time and got into the playoffs," Riley added, "and that team was not built to last. This team is built to last."

Bogut's surgery came one month after that pronouncement, and Myers had taken over for Riley in the interim, but that promise—*This team is built to last*—was looking, in hindsight, like the kind of wishful thinking that had doomed the franchise for years.

With the controversy far from subsiding, Myers finally capitulated. Speaking on a Warriors pregame show two days later, Myers denied any cover-up but admitted the appearance of impropriety was entirely avoidable. "I know it's being perceived that it was mishandled and not handled appropriately," he said. "Ultimately, that rests on my shoulders. . . . The last thing I want to do, or anybody in the organization wants to do, is deceive the fans. So the fact that some people feel that way, I feel really bad about that. . . . It's a group of people. It's not one person in a room writing a script. . . . In this specific situation, I feel like I could've done a better job, personally, as to how it was conveyed."

That Myers had technically been general manager for all of three days when Bogut went under the knife was irrelevant. The misdirection of the last few months was an unforced error, the kind of self-inflicted screwup that became maddeningly commonplace during the Cohan/Rowell era.

From that day on, the Warriors were a changed team. Hours after Myers's mea culpa, Golden State won a squeaker at home against the Denver Nuggets, 106–105, as Andre Iguodala's last-second three was reviewed and then disallowed, the officials concluding that the shot was still cradled in his hands as the game clock hit zero. "What a bizarre finish!" howled TNT broadcaster Steve Kerr. The Warriors' on-court celebration was so effusive, one newspaper wrote, "you would've thought they'd won a playoff game."

As Bogut remained out of commission, Curry carried the team. The sprained ankle he had sustained in the preseason turned out to be an unfounded scare. Curry played in each of the Warriors' first 36 games and averaged 20.5 points, a full three points above his career mark to that point. That was due to his unyielding barrage of three-point attempts, which climbed from 4.7 per game over his first three seasons to nearly seven. Even with that rise in volume, Curry's accuracy shot up from 44.1 to 46.1 percent. In historical terms, Curry was fast becoming a more lethal three-point shooter than many NBA greats who'd made their bones on the shot, people like Ray Allen, Steve Kerr, Reggie Miller, Larry Bird—yes, even his father, Dell. And the Warriors were a better team for it, posting a 23-13 record through that early-season stretch. Curry's 113 threes were the third-most in NBA history through a season's first 36 games. Between points, rebounds, and assists, only LeBron James and Russell Westbrook bested Curry's total production on a nightly basis.

The chemistry between Curry and Thompson (who was averaging nearly 16 points) was so palpable that it birthed a meme. At halftime of a late December win over the Charlotte Bobcats, Brian Witt, who wrote for the team site and handled Golden State's social media presence, tweeted an off-the-cuff thought after Curry and Thompson combined for 25 points and seven three-pointers in the first half. He concluded his note with the Twitter hashtag #SplashBrothers. One of the great NBA nicknames was born. It was a nostalgic play on the "Bash Brothers"— Mark McGwire and Jose Canseco, who ruled nearby Oakland Coliseum in the late eighties—and the Warriors pushed Witt to keep it visible. Such a repeatable phrase played perfectly into Peter Guber's push to tell stories, to sell players in a unique and affecting way. It was the kind of organic branding that corporations lust after.

But the ankle sprains that had derailed Curry's earlier seasons would not stay in exile. During a light game-day shootaround in January, Curry landed on Festus Ezeli's ankle after chasing a loose rebound. Against LeBron James and the defending champion Miami Heat that night, a Curry-less Golden State was held to its season low in points and lost, 92–75. A few nights later in San Antonio, with Curry sitting out again, the Warriors couldn't crack 90 and lost again.

Curry was back the next night in New Orleans, pouring in 20

points and seven assists in a 116–112 win. The Warriors were an entirely different team with him on the floor, and their chances for success hinged solely on whether his health held up. A month later, on February 27, Curry played all 48 minutes, knocked down 11 of 13 three-point chances in front of 19,033 people at Madison Square Garden, and scored a career-high 54 points—the most anyone had scored at MSG since Kobe Bryant dropped 61 on the hapless Knicks in early 2009.

Golden State was benefiting from other meaningful contributions. Klay Thompson started every game as the two-guard and validated, in every way, the decision to trade Monta Ellis. Playing more than 35 minutes a night, Thompson was averaging nearly 16 points and a trio of threes per game. And David Lee, pouring in 19 points and nearly 11 boards while playing in 51 of Golden State's first 52 games, was named as a reserve for the Western Conference All-Star squad, the first time a Warrior had been named to the All-Star Team in 16 years, since Latrell Sprewell in 1997. Harrison Barnes, firmly entrenched as the starting small forward, was good for nine points and four boards a night—not the production they'd hoped for from the No. 7 pick in the draft, but they didn't need him to be spectacular. Same for fellow rookie Draymond Green, who was little more than a back-of-the-rotation role player and averaging less than four points and four rebounds as Lee's backup.

They were also playing with a toughness that Jackson had instilled in them. For years they'd been little more than pushovers and laughingstocks, a date on the schedule that opposing players could look at to pad their offensive stats. Jackson was fighting back against that reputation, game by game. The best evidence of that paradigm shift came in early February in Houston when the Warriors' defense had broken down to the point where they had allowed 23 three-pointers to the Rockets, including five from former Warrior Jeremy Lin. That had tied the NBA record for most threes by a team in one game, and Houston wanted that record for their own. But with less than a minute left—and the Rockets sure to jack up threes at every chance down the floor—Jackson instructed his team to foul before any Rockets player could shoot, which continually forced Houston to the free-throw line. The crowd laid into the Warriors, but the tactic worked. "We're not going to lay down," Jackson said after the 140–109 loss. "If you're going to try to get the record, we're going to stop it."

And in a tough late February matchup at Oracle against San Antonio, the Warriors were clinging to a three-point lead in overtime. During a timeout, Jackson implored them not to give up, drawing on a memory from his own time as a player. "I used to sit where you sit!" Jackson said in the huddle. "And after all that work, a coach would take me out and bring in somebody else." He tapped his chest. "It was disrespect to *me*! You earned the right to win the game! You earned the right! Now let's go get it!" Three seconds after the Spurs inbounded the ball, Klay Thompson stole an errant Tim Duncan pass to seal the win.

By early March, Bogut, who'd been mostly inactive since November but saw a smattering of action through January and February, was back in as the starting center on a nightly basis. With Golden State sitting on a 33-27 record, Bogut started 20 of the Warriors' final 22 games, averaging five points and eight rebounds in 25 minutes per night. As much as Australians love their beer, Bogut quit drinking during the season because the intake caused his feet to swell and throb with pain. Curry may have been the Warriors' internal gearbox, dictating the game's pace, but Bogut was the engine, providing the raw power and physicality that gave Golden State an added dimension it needed to compete with the West's titans.

The Warriors finished the season 14-8 with Bogut back and ended up at 47-35—their best record in five years and good enough for their first playoff appearance in six. They clinched a spot with four games remaining, thanks to a 16-point win over the Minnesota Timberwolves, the same team that laughed at them a year earlier as Joe Lacob was booed at center court. The Warriors skipped down the hallway to the locker room in postgame jubilation, high-fiving security guards and team officials along the way, but it was understated and almost awkward-looking, as if the team truly didn't know how to react under such positive circumstances.

Curry, who had 24 points and 10 assists, looked relieved as he sat in the locker room and took in the moment. "From where people predicted us at the beginning of the year," he said, "this is definitely hard work paying off over the course of a season."

By season's end, Curry had played in 78 of 82 regular-season games and was the league's breakout star. He averaged 22.9 points, good for seventh in the league and 4.3 points better than his previous best. His rate of 6.9 assists per game (another career-high) was 14th-best in the NBA. Curry was also the NBA's second-best free-throw shooter, behind Oklahoma City's Kevin Durant, as well as top-15 in steals.

But after that playoff clincher against Minnesota, Curry was still tantalizingly short of a record that would define his career more than any accumulation of ankle sprains. Theretofore, Curry had made 249 three-pointers, just a handful shy of Ray Allen's all-time season mark of 269, set during the 2005–06 season when he was with the Seattle Super-Sonics. Curry had four games left to make 21 threes.

Two nights later against Oklahoma City, Curry sank three in a 19-point loss. The next night in Los Angeles, he swished nine threes on 15 tries against the Lakers en route to 47 points. Golden State lost by two and was hanging on to that No. 6 playoff seeding by a hair. Curry was just nine threes shy of Allen.

At home against San Antonio three nights later, Curry made seven threes in a 10-point win over the Spurs. That left Curry just two away from breaking the mark. With Golden State needing a win in its final game, on the road in Portland, to secure that No. 6 seed, they would need all of Curry's long-range game on the season's final night.

The Warriors did win, 99–88, and though Curry wasn't dominant in the finale, scoring just 15 points on 16 shots, the single-season three-point record was his. Off a pass from Jarrett Jack midway through the second quarter, Curry drained a no-dribble three from the right wing for his 270th triple. He let out a fist-pump as he turned back on defense, his teammates on the bench holding up their last three fingers on each hand. Curry finished with four on the night, establishing the new single-season record at 272. Rerouting the offense through Curry and his long-range prowess had paid dividends far beyond anyone's expectations. They led the NBA in three-point percentage for the first time in club history.

Golden State could now turn its focus to the playoffs and a matchup with the formidable 57-win Denver Nuggets, under the direction of former Warriors head coach George Karl and the scoring and defense of Andre Iguodala, as good a two-way player as there was in the NBA. The Warriors were underdogs headed into the series, to be sure, but they were healthy, and the shooting of Curry and Thompson (who finished with 211 threes, a feat that would've led the NBA in each of the past three seasons) gave them a puncher's chance of at least stealing a couple of games.

"This was an important first step for this franchise and for this ownership group and for all these guys and the coaches," Joe Lacob said just a few feet away from Curry's locker the night they beat Minnesota to clinch a playoff spot. "Let's just build on this now."

. . .

The Nuggets were one of the most well-rounded and versatile teams in the NBA. They were the league's highest-scoring team, with 106.1 points per game. They had the fifth-best field-goal percentage and were tops in offensive rebounds, third in assists, second in steals, and third in blocks. Despite losing 6-foot-10 swingman Danilo Gallinari to a torn knee ligament late in the season, the Nuggets could put up points in a blink, thanks to Iguodala, 25-year-old point guard Ty Lawson (drafted 11 picks after Curry), and veteran Andre Miller. They also boasted an imposing collection of young bigs: Kenneth Faried, JaVale McGee, Kosta Koufos, and Timofey Mozgov. It was no wonder the Nuggets had made the playoffs in 10 straight seasons, the last nine under head coach George Karl.

But the Nuggets' shortcomings were glaring. They committed the third-most turnovers. Their three-point shooting was ranked 25th out of 30 teams, and their free-throw shooting was third-worst in the league, barely above 70 percent as a team. The Warriors' strategy would be to keep their perimeter shooters out and away from the basket but be physical if they came toward the rim. Force contact, crash the boards to nullify their offensive rebounding, and clog up those passing lanes with pressure. Most relevant to Golden State's interests, Denver gave up the second-most threes in all of basketball, an average of 8.3 per night. That was more than the Warriors averaged per game, meaning if Curry and Thompson (hell, even others) could hit shots from the outside, Denver would be hard-pressed to quell the assault.

Still, it seemed the Warriors' playoff inexperience would work against them, and the Nuggets' 57 wins were the franchise's best since joining the NBA (from the upstart American Basketball Association) in 1976. They had won 23 in a row at home, going back to mid-January. Of 18 ESPN basketball writers predicting the series, not one picked the Warriors to win.

Game 1 came down to the final play. Denver worked at the league's second-fastest pace, but this game was more measured. Curry missed his first nine shots of the night and Golden State led only 48–44 at the break, but every time the Nuggets pushed out to a second-half lead, the Warriors responded. Curry's corner three from the left side tied the game at 95–95 with less than 15 seconds to go.

Both coaches tried to game the matchups. Karl subbed in Andre

Miller, the 14-year veteran of more than 1,100 career games. Jackson put in rookie Draymond Green, the second-round pick who'd played only four minutes all night but had all the signs of a naturally gifted one-on-one defender. As if by design, the other eight players cleared out. The seconds ticked down, Miller vs. Green for the win.

Moving toward his left, Miller drove from the top of the key. As he propelled toward the rim, he switched the ball to his right hand and scooped the shot up and in with less than two seconds remaining. Green was caught going to his left and lost position as Miller drove the lane—"one slithery move," the rookie later said. Against youth, experience had won out.

Despite the 97–95 loss, the Warriors showed they could hang with the Nuggets. They just needed to firm up their focus. Curry and Thompson combined for 41 points, but totaled only six threes. The Warriors outrebounded the Nuggets by 10, but committed six more turnovers.

But far more concerning was when Golden State lost David Lee in the fourth quarter. As the All-Star collided with JaVale McGee, he fell to the ground and tore his right hip flexor. *Pop!* Lee lost all sensation in his leg.

The next day, an MRI confirmed the injury's severity. Lee, who'd led the NBA with 56 double-doubles during the regular season and had already posted one (10 points, 14 rebounds) in his first career playoff game before the fall, was ruled out for the remainder of the postseason.

Jackson had a critical decision to make. Not only was Lee gone, but Denver would be getting back Faried, its best rebounder at more than nine per game, from a sprained ankle that kept him out of Game 1. Andrew Bogut, though playing, was still feeling significant pain from a bone bruise in his troublesome left ankle. The obvious move was to slide Carl Landry into the starting lineup and hope that the frontcourt could grab enough rebounds in Lee's stead, but Landry had started only two games all year. Green would also get more minutes in Game 2, but forcing him into his first career start also seemed risky. With few other options, Lee's injury had come at a most inopportune time.

On the morning of the game, Jackson went to his coaches with a crazy proposition he was prepared to be talked out of. What about starting Harrison Barnes at power forward? He had played all season at small forward, but he was strong and a decent one-on-one defender. On top of that, they would slot backup point guard Jarrett Jack in with the starters for a three-guard alignment. Jackson had a feeling Curry and Thompson were due for a breakout. His staff thought it could work, and though Landry was announced during pregame intros as the starter, it was Jack who took his place as the ball tipped off.

Jackson's makeshift starting lineup shot 62 percent from the floor, grabbed 90 percent of available defensive rebounds, and generally stayed a step ahead of the Nuggets no matter what Karl tried. Golden State, in this unorthodox iteration, beat Denver, 131–117, to end the Nuggets' home win streak and even the series. The quartet of Curry (30 points), Jack (26), Barnes (a career-high 24), and Thompson (21) shredded the Denver defense for 101 points between them. Golden State won the rebounding edge, 36–26. Green, Landry, and rookie center Festus Ezeli all played more than 16 minutes off the bench to make up for Lee's absence. The Warriors shot 56 percent (14 of 25) on threes and a whopping 69 percent (37 of 54) on two-point shots. They had morphed into a buzzsaw that Denver couldn't contain.

After the game, Jackson was wryly asked if, in addition to his quirky lineup change, he had suggested to his team that they shoot 65 percent from the field as a means for winning. In that moment, Jackson gave rise to one of the great playoff narratives.

"In my opinion," Jackson said with regard to Curry and Thompson, "they're the greatest shooting backcourt in the history of the game and I'm a guy that's just not throwing that out there. I've followed basketball my entire life—not only played, covered, but I was a fan as a kid.

I watched the great players and these two guys are absolutely off the charts. I would've put Reggie Miller and myself in there but I held him down." Aside from a few instinctual laughs, the media contingent was left otherwise speechless. Jackson was whisked away. How could you possibly follow up on a proclamation like that? *Greatest shooting backcourt in the history of the game?* Jackson was dead serious in the moment, but if the Warriors were going to see this series through and pull off the upset, they needed to believe at least a shred of that declaration.

Curry's efficacy looked as if it might once again be limited due to (what else?) an ankle injury. He turned his left foot late in the third quarter but stayed in the game and played nearly 42 minutes. When the Warriors returned to Oakland to prepare for Game 3, Curry told reporters he wouldn't be able to play without the extra day of rest afforded by the travel schedule. His availability for Game 3 was made to look like a game-time decision, but the Warriors were hosting their first playoff game in six years. The face of the franchise would absolutely be in uniform, no doubt about it.

Once again, Jackson started Jack in lieu of Landry. It had worked so well in Game 2, so why change anything? Landry chipped in 19 points, and Jack's 23 points on 14 shots proved vital. Bogut started at center and played 29 fruitful minutes, with Green and Ezeli spelling him as needed. In the end, the outcome hinged on an Andre Iguodala halfcourt heave at the buzzer that clanged off the side of the rim. Golden State won, 110–108, to take a 2–1 series lead.

Curry was relieved he hadn't made the ankle worse, but the Warriors would've been lost without his contributions, capped off by a 16–2 run in the third that gave Golden State a one-point lead. Curry's final line (29 points, 11 assists) represented the kind of playoff performance that could steer a career toward greatness.

And the world needn't wait long for his next memorable moment. After opting against a painkilling injection before Game 3, Curry succumbed and received the shot before Game 4. He'd never had one before a game and was loath to start now, especially at such a critical time, but Curry's body urged otherwise.

He started off slowly, missing his only shot attempt in the first quarter and scoring only five points in the second, but Jack's trio of threes helped pace Golden State to a 12-point halftime lead.

Then Curry had his first true playoff awakening, a springtime act that would become commonplace before long. After Ty Lawson scored 15 points in the first six minutes of the quarter to slash the Warriors' lead to just four, Curry hit a left corner three to push the lead back to seven.

Two minutes later, Curry swished a straightaway catch-and-shoot three from 25 feet to put Golden State up by nine.

With 1:54 to go, another three for Curry, from 29 feet out on the left wing. The lead was now 11.

Curry then picked Lawson's pocket as he drove the lane, raced the other way, and launched a pull-up three from the top of the arc that sailed on through for a 17-point lead.

To cap it all off, he swept in another left corner three with 23 seconds to go.

Curry finished with 22 points in the third quarter alone and the Warriors led by 19 heading to the fourth. By night's end, Denver had come unraveled, tying its season-high in turnovers with 23. Golden State made 11 of 26 three-pointers, and Curry, who was practically comatose until well into the second half, finished with 31 points, seven assists, and four steals. Even Draymond Green posted career-highs of 13 points and four steals in 25 minutes off the bench. The Warriors won, 115–101, and took a commanding 3–1 lead as the series went back to Denver.

After the emotional highs of Games 3 and 4, Denver came ready to play for Game 5. Their fate would not be sealed on their home floor. Mark Jackson leaned on his starters, as Curry, Jack, Thompson, and

Barnes all played more than 41 minutes. Curry finished with only 15 points on 19 shots. Barnes was a much-needed catalyst, with a team-high 23 points, but the Warriors fell behind by 20 at halftime and couldn't dig out fast enough. Golden State fell, 107–100, despite a 31–21 fourth-quarter flurry. Jackson accused the Nuggets of dirty off-ball play that wasn't being called—"they tried to send hit-men on Steph"—even as both Bogut and Green were called for flagrant fouls on Faried. (For his comments, Jackson was fined $25,000 by the league.)

"Draymond Green," George Karl quipped after the game, "did he play football or basketball at Michigan State?"

Regardless, the Warriors had the upper hand going back to Oakland, with a couple more surprises in store for the Nuggets. One was that Jackson opted to go with a larger, more traditional starting lineup with Carl Landry finally stepping in at power forward, Barnes sliding down to small forward, and Jack going back to the bench. But the more dramatic reveal came just minutes before tipoff when the Warriors streamed out of the tunnel onto the court. First was Curry, but following close behind was a uniformed and ready-to-play Lee, who had torn his hip flexor just 12 days earlier. It wasn't *quite* the modern-day equivalent of Willis Reed coming out to the roars of Madison Square Garden before Game 7 of the 1970 NBA Finals, but it was enough for the Warriors.

The Nuggets led by four after one quarter, thanks to eight points from Lawson, but when Lee subbed in for Andrew Bogut with 2:23 left in the first, Oracle Arena ascended to a new level. Jackson had Curry run pick-and-roll with Lee, who missed on a midrange jumper from 18 feet, his only field-goal attempt of the evening. He exited for good after less than 90 seconds of playing time, but the Warriors were charged up. Lee resumed his sideline cheerleader role and Golden State ground down Denver in the second to trail by just two at halftime.

Curry had only six points and five assists at the break, but he had another third-quarter breakout, hitting three three-pointers in a

90-second span that turned a tie game into a six-point Warrior cushion. His three with 3:46 to go in the third lifted Golden State to its largest lead of the night at 11. With Bogut chipping in six points and seven rebounds in the quarter, the Warriors held that 11-point margin heading to the fourth.

Denver stormed back as Jackson's team started to finally show its playoff inexperience. Andre Iguodala's step-back three with 4:14 to play cut Golden State's lead to four, but the rebounding of Green and Bogut, as well as the Warriors' ability to hit free throws, saved them from an untimely collapse.

Golden State won, 92–88, and Denver was sent home for the summer. Curry finished with 22 points and eight assists but also seven turnovers. Green, in 24 minutes off the bench, set a new career-high with 16 points.

Of all the Warriors' contributions on this night, it was Bogut who, thanks to the first pain-blocking injection of his career, made the most meaningful impact. The man whose controversial arrival cost Joe Lacob every scrap of goodwill he'd accrued as owner played the game of his Golden State life, finishing with 14 points, 21 rebounds, and four blocks in 40 minutes, his lower extremities holding up under their most floor time in nearly a year and a half. The 7-footer who couldn't log 20 minutes to save his life at season's start was magnificent when the Warriors needed him most.

. . .

For all the feeling of accomplishment that comes with upsetting a major foe in the first round of the playoffs, that feeling can quickly wash away once you realize that the reward for such an achievement is the privilege of playing a much tougher opponent. So it was that the Warriors now faced the often-indomitable, never-to-be-underestimated San Antonio Spurs.

Led by 14-time All-Star Tim Duncan, the backcourt of Tony Parker and Danny Green, super sixth man Manu Ginobili, and a budding two-way stud in Kawhi Leonard, head coach Gregg Popovich's squad was the class of the league, known for its track record of excellence, its ingrained organizational culture, and systematic play that sacrificed style for efficiency. San Antonio's shooting percentage ranked third in the league. On threes, they were fourth. Free throws? Third. And no team compiled more assists.

And yet, the Spurs were known for defense, which was above average in nearly every important category. They allowed nearly five fewer points per game than the Warriors were accustomed to scoring. They allowed the fourth-lowest shooting percentage on two-point shots.

San Antonio's lone defensive weakness represented a tight needle to thread. Though they were proficient in limiting three-point attempts, opponents shot decently (35.3 percent) when they did get those shots off. That three-point defense ranked only 12th in the NBA. For the Warriors, who shot a league-best 40.3 percent from deep, that was a strategy they could exploit. With volume three-point shooting and a little luck that enough shots fell, Golden State could hang on to steal a game, maybe two . . . and then you never know what can happen.

What happened in Game 1 was a night of basketball not soon forgotten. The Warriors hadn't won in San Antonio since 1997 but were dominant from the start. They led after one quarter (28–25) and at halftime (53–49). Then Curry, in accordance with his burgeoning reputation for such outbursts, rained down all kinds of hellfire in the third, scoring 22 points on 12 shots. Entering the fourth, Curry had 32 points and eight assists as the Warriors led, 92–80. The lead swelled to 16 with just 4:30 to go. Jackson opted for a super-small lineup featuring Curry, Jarrett Jack, Harrison Barnes, Draymond Green, and Klay Thompson, who, at 6-foot-7, was the tallest Warrior on the court. Golden State, it seemed, would cruise to a series-opening win.

Then the bottom dropped out.

Thompson was called for a blocking foul on Tony Parker and fouled out with four minutes left. Suddenly, Richard Jefferson came into the game and Golden State's offense dried up. In turn, the Spurs suddenly couldn't miss. Parker scored six unanswered points over the next minute. Kawhi Leonard then put up a bank shot in the post followed by a catch-and-shoot three from 24 feet after Jefferson missed two free throws with 1:57 left that could've stalled the San Antonio spurt. Before Jack knocked down a midrange jumper with 30 seconds to go, the Spurs had executed a 15–0 run, eaten up more than four minutes of clock, and were down by one.

After Jack's shot put the Warriors ahead by three, Danny Green tied up the game on a three from the right wing with 20.8 seconds left. As the clock ran toward zero, Curry's desperation turnaround jumper from 16 feet out clanked off the back iron and overtime awaited.

San Antonio pulled off a 7–0 run after Golden State scored the first five points of overtime, but it was Jack again who gave the Warriors late life as his left-handed layup with 20.3 seconds left tied the game at 115. Manu Ginobili, from 22 feet out, had the Spurs' last shot of overtime. Draymond Green, who'd allowed Andre Miller to best him in the waning moments of Game 1 in Denver, would not allow history to repeat. He closed out hard and forced the shot askew, ensuring Golden State's first double-overtime playoff game since Game 4 of the 1976 Western Conference Finals. The stakes this time were not as pressure-packed but no less dramatic. Every move was followed by an immediate counter. Back and forth they went.

Eventually, time would run out on someone.

With both teams tightening up, perhaps from sheer exhaustion, Barnes finally got Golden State going with a three from the right corner. But a minute later, a missed Barnes three led to Draymond Green wrangling for an offensive board and getting whistled for a foul. It was

Green's sixth of the game, and Golden State's most tenacious young defender was banished to the bench.

A couple of Tony Parker jumpers, a Boris Diaw midrange, and a Danny Green three gave San Antonio a 126–121 lead with 1:06 left, but the Warriors had one frantic comeback left in them. Curry was immediately fouled on a drive in the lane and made two free throws to cut it to three. Ginobili then launched an ill-advised straightaway three from 29 feet that clanked down into Carl Landry's waiting arms. Curry dribbled up court, drove around Diaw with his left, and scooped up a finger roll with his right to cut the Spurs' lead to one with 32.8 seconds left.

On the next possession, Parker tried to run off as much time as possible with his dribble. He crossed over Kent Bazemore and, with four seconds on the shot clock and 13 left in the game, missed a sprawling layup. As Barnes grabbed the rebound and passed off to Curry, Bazemore sped down the side of the court and slipped behind the defense. By the time Curry passed to him in the paint, Diaw was so twisted around that he couldn't reach to defend the shot. Bazemore's weakside layup put Golden State ahead by one.

With 3.4 seconds left, San Antonio had one last chance.

Standing on the sideline with ball in hand, Kawhi Leonard scanned for a pair of open arms. Then he found one: Standing there on the far-side wing was Ginobili, all alone. Diaw had coerced a switch from Curry, which meant Jarrett Jack, Diaw's original defender, should've switched onto Ginobili . . . but Jack was meandering in space near the inbounds, essentially double-teaming Tony Parker, who was already being guarded by Barnes. That mixup forced Curry to lunge at Ginobili, who flicked the ball up with a hair-trigger release. The high arc of a shot—normally the kind you see only from players goofing around in postpractice cool-down—snapped through the netting with 1.2 seconds to go.

Jack's desperation three was off and the Spurs prevailed, 129–127.

Except for the final four seconds of the third quarter—and despite the lingering ankle issues left over from the Denver series—Curry played all 58 minutes, scoring 44 points and dishing out 11 assists. Barnes had 19 points in nearly 53 minutes. And Draymond Green played a career-high 38 minutes before fouling out.

The Warriors shot better (51 percent to 43.8) and won the rebounding battle (55–45), but the Spurs remained the Spurs. This was what they did in the postseason. They outlasted, outworked, perhaps even outlucked their opponents come April and May because of their personnel. Jackson tightened up to an eight-man rotation as Popovich could afford to go 10 deep. For a team as green as Golden State, the night was a crushing defeat that doubled as PhD-level coursework in closing out a playoff win. They'd just learned how from the best.

The Warriors tied up the series two nights later with a 100–91 win, paced by 66 points from the Splash Brothers. Again, Jackson stuck to his eight-man rotation while Popovich got 12 of his players into the game. Both Curry and Thompson played more than 43 minutes, and their accruing fatigue started to show in Game 3, when they made just 12 of 37 shots in a 102–92 loss back in Oakland. David Lee returned for this one but was ineffective in three minutes, his presence unable to provide the same emotional resonance as in Game 6 against Denver.

The Warriors bounced back in Game 4 with an overtime win, 97–87, to even the series at 2–2. Barnes logged more than 51 minutes and scored a game-high 26 points while Curry played a manageable 38 minutes and scored 22 points on 15 shots. The Warriors pulled down a season-best 65 rebounds, of which 18 went to Bogut. Though San Antonio led by eight with five minutes to go, Golden State went on a 12–4 run to close out regulation, all the scoring provided by Jack and Thompson.

The pain in Curry's ankle was matched only by his frustration with having to endure another nagging injury when his team needed him more than ever. "It seems like every time you get on a roll and feel somewhat healthy, there's a setback," he said after the win. "And it just tests you. It changes your routine. It changes your outlook on the game, your preparation." He credited a 2:00 a.m. text his mother sent the night before for lifting his spirits, but a little divine intervention may have also contributed.

Before the game, Jackson was heading into the Warriors' chapel, just down the hall from the team's locker room, and he saw Curry inside. When they both emerged, Curry told him he'd give him what he had, which was an immediate red flag to Jackson. "That's not the language he speaks," said Jackson, who conferred with Bob Myers before proceeding to let Curry play as much as he could handle. His Game 4 heroics (which included holding Danny Green to just 10 points and a game-low –25 point differential) were nothing short of a Mother's Day miracle. As Jackson preached after the win, "God has His hands on this team."

But the Warriors—unbroken yet banged up—were spent. While Barnes scored 25 points on 18 shots in Game 5, Curry and Thompson combined for only 13 points. The Spurs won easily at home, 109–91, and it was more of the same at Oracle Arena for the deciding Game 6. The Warriors didn't eclipse 23 points in any one quarter while all five Spurs starters scored in double digits. Curry and Thompson could only scrounge up 32 points from 37 shots, even as both played more than 40 minutes. Draymond Green played only eight minutes and was held scoreless. Even oft-ignored center Andris Biedriņš was forced into 11 minutes of action.

Golden State didn't have the depth to last much longer against a juggernaut like San Antonio, which closed out the series with a 94–82 win. Bogut admitted after the loss he was "running on fumes the whole series." He missed the fourth quarter, as did Barnes, who fell on his head in the second quarter, left to receive six stitches, and then sat out the final frame with a headache. Curry missed six of eight three-pointers, sapped of the leg strength needed to hoist those deep daggers with consistency. Watching from the owners' suite, Kirk Lacob could see that the Warriors were gassed. *Maybe it's better if we don't win one more game,* he thought to himself.

Once the game ended and the players cycled their congratulatory hugs and well-wishes, Curry grabbed the mic and thanked the fans for their support and promised to be back in the playoffs next season. He knew that could be the only goal. As bad as his ankle felt in the moment, Curry would endure no surgery that offseason, a first since after his rookie year. He'd take a couple of weeks off to recuperate, spend some time with Ayesha and their one-year-old daughter, Riley. One of basketball's fresh faces, though still not an All-Star, had made his name known to a nation. "With the way I played this season," Curry said a few minutes later, "it's setting a foundation for me."

After the loss, Joe Lacob huddled in the back of the Warriors' locker room with reporters. He spoke quietly, a hint of emotion welling up in his voice, and tried to sum up his first playoff experience in the immediate aftermath of its demise. "It was a great season for us as an organization. I think we turned it around, bottom line," he said. "This organization, this team, needed to be turned around and a lot of things had to happen for that turnaround to happen. Hiring a lot of great people on the business side, and on the basketball side, made some good trades, signed some free agents. You all know what those moves were. The Andrew Bogut–Monta Ellis, very large trade, which we got a lot of criticism for early on—I guess *I* did—proved to be, I think, the right thing to do."

Lacob spoke of a hopeful future, anchored by the youth of Golden State's budding stars—Curry was 25, Thompson and Green still 23, while Barnes was only 20. He credited David Lee with returning from injury to finish out the series against San Antonio. He lauded Mark Jackson and his staff. "We'll build on this and we'll get better next year," he added. "We'll be better than we were this year. We'll get together beyond that, and we will get what we very badly want, which is a title."

A reporter asked Lacob if he was still keen to keep improving the team as needed, willing to make tough, necessary moves to chase a championship.

"I'm ready to go," Lacob replied.

Tomorrow?

"Right now."

# 6 ★ ★ ★ ★ ★ ★ ★

# LEARNING TO FLY

## The 2013–14 season

**W**hen Bob Myers first became an agent back in the late nineties, he learned quickly that the Warriors didn't have the most pristine reputation around the league. If Golden State was being whispered as a potential free-agent destination, it was often to leverage another club into sweetening its contract offer. Some of that perception was because of inept negotiations by past front office people; some of it was because, for so long, the Warriors were one of the worst teams in the NBA, so why would anyone want to play for them?

A curious thing happens, though, when you change owners, hire a stable of competent executives, and start winning enough games that you start to look like a potential playoff team every year. All of a sudden, those free agent pitch meetings start to become more of a two-way affair.

So when the summer of 2013 rolled around, the 47-win Warriors got a seat at the big boy table for once. The No. 1 free agent was center Dwight Howard, just 27, one of the best defenders in the NBA, but saddled with a reputation for aloofness and immaturity. With Bogut on the mend, the Warriors saw a chance to not only try to attract a marquee free agent—a big guy who could dominate the paint like few others—but also show the NBA (and, by extension, other free agents) that Oakland was a destination all players should seriously consider. Howard was a long shot, but they had to try.

Eventually, Howard whittled his list of potential suitors down to three clubs . . . and the Warriors made the cut, along with the Los Angeles Lakers (his previous team, who could offer him more years and money than anyone else) and Houston Rockets, constructed by the analytically minded general manager Daryl Morey, and a team on the rise, thanks to high-scoring point guard James Harden, acquired a year earlier from Oklahoma City.

When Howard appeared bound for Houston, Myers went to his backup plan, though it was decidedly less sexy than bringing aboard one of the league's most physically imposing centers. Plan B was none other than Andre Iguodala, the leader of the 57-win Denver Nuggets that fell to the Warriors in the playoffs. Like Howard, Iguodala was a free agent who could stand to make more money by re-signing with his former team, but his situation was more complicated. Iguodala had a player option for the 2013–14 season that was worth $16.1 million. All he had to do was trigger that option and he was set for another year.

But in March, just a couple of weeks before the playoffs, Iguodala announced he would opt out. The hope, of course, was to land a long-term deal with more money per season. It was a risk, but Iguodala felt the calculus worked in his favor. He didn't have to decide on the opt-out until the playoffs had concluded, but by that time, the Nuggets had lost both head coach George Karl, who was named Coach of the Year but nonetheless fired for perpetual playoff underperformance, and general manager Masai Ujiri, who was poached by Toronto three weeks after winning the NBA's Executive of the Year.

From the start of free agency on July 1, Iguodala was up front with the Warriors about wanting to join their roster. That day, he and his agent, Rob Pelinka, met down in Los Angeles at Pelinka's office with Myers, Joe and Kirk Lacob, and Mark Jackson, who were there to sell him on what they were planning and see if he was on board. But Myers, who'd been in dozens of these pitch meetings as an agent and could assess the tenor of them quickly, realized Iguodala was the one doing the selling. Myers had prepared some DVDs as part of the presentation and was expecting a convivial but spirited discussion—he'd known Pelinka for some 15 years as they competed for clients—but he never played a single disc. "You guys are building something that I want to be a part of," Iguodala told the group. Everyone—and especially Joe Lacob—came away confident that he possessed the character that would fit with Golden State's culture.

On the court, Iguodala was a versatile and dependable starter—maybe not a perennial superstar but someone who could shoot from deep, pass well in transition, and had enough NBA experience (nine years) to learn any offensive scheme. For the Nuggets, he averaged nearly 13 points, 5.3 rebounds, and 5.4 assists. The only other players to reach such benchmarks of well-roundedness? LeBron James, Kobe Bryant, Russell Westbrook, and Rajon Rondo.

Iguodala was also a solid premier defender against those guard/forward combo players who could slash to the basket as easily as pull up from three. He'd made the All-Defensive second team in 2010–11. He was an All-Star in 2011–12. And he'd been a team leader in Philadelphia for years (taking command of the team in Allen Iverson's wake) before being traded to Denver before the 2012–13 season. Few players like Iguodala possessed such two-way skills as well as a leader's mentality.

And yet, no matter what, Iguodala would be leaving money on the table. Denver had a standing contract offer reported to be five years and $60 million, and the Dallas Mavericks, owned by dotcom billionaire Mark Cuban and just two years removed from winning a championship, cobbled together a similarly competitive offer. Sure, Iguodala had professed his admiration right off the bat, but the Warriors still needed to finagle a fair offer.

All Myers had to do was figure a way over the next week to make some impossible math work. The Warriors were in dire financial straits. They had virtually no wiggle room under the salary cap and were less than $3 million away from crossing the luxury tax threshold. The stress was immense. More than a few nights, he came home in a panic, confessing to his wife, Kristen, that he had no idea how this deal was going to happen. "He was sitting out there and we just couldn't get it done," Myers later said. "This was one of the hardest things I've ever worked on in the NBA. . . . This thing was on life support fifteen times." Myers called or texted Pelinka constantly to keep him abreast of the smallest development.

The good news for Golden State was that Richard Jefferson and Andris Biedriņš, who together accounted for $20 million, were both in the final years of their contracts. Same for Brandon Rush, who had missed the entire 2012–13 season with a torn knee ligament and was due to make $4 million. Because Lacob had stemmed the Warriors' habit of dealing away draft picks, they now had a stockpile of them to use as trade assets. The picks could be used to entice a team to take these contracts off the Warriors' hands, thus clearing enough cap room to sign Iguodala.

The problem was that the clock was ticking on Dallas's offer. Sacramento had already offered and pulled back a four-year, $52 million deal, to avoid being used as leverage (as the Warriors once had been), and Dallas would not be similarly played. Myers targeted the teams that had enough cap room to take on Golden State's trio of unwanted contracts—that included the Utah Jazz, Cleveland Cavaliers, Milwaukee Bucks, and Detroit Pistons—but the Warriors had to be prepared to give up a lot. Utah quickly became the most likely trade partner, but they were asking for a king's ransom in future first- and second-round picks.

Finally, an hour after Iguodala almost put pen to paper with Dallas, Myers informed him and Pelinka that Golden State had a deal in place with Utah. They could hammer out the details the next day, but the Warriors would be 100 percent able to fit Iguodala in under their salary cap. It wouldn't leave room to do much of anything else in free agency, but the Warriors had their man.

When Tim Connelly, Denver's new general manager, found out, he wanted in. He agreed to sign Iguodala to a new four-year, $48 million contract and then trade him to the Warriors, thereby receiving what's known as a Traded Player Exception, which is an amount of money equal to the outgoing salary ($12 million) plus $100,000 that they could use to acquire players via trade over the next 12 months and that money would *not* count toward the salary cap. As part of the deal with Utah, Denver agreed to receive Randy Foye in a sign-and-trade for three years and $9 million and used the TPE to absorb that. At the end of the day, Denver gained about $9 million in financial wiggle room, whereas they would've received nothing had Iguodala left as a free agent. The Warriors not only gained Iguodala and unloaded $24 million of contract bloat but preserved all sorts of trade exceptions by dealing draft picks to Utah and Denver and kept their salary cap obligations reasonable. The Jazz received a smorgasbord of future picks, and those contracts would come off the books in time for the summer of 2014, a serendipitous development given the hype around free agency that year.

If it sounds complicated and somewhat byzantine, that's because it is. The NBA's collective bargaining agreement is far from simple to understand and explain. There are people in the employ of every NBA organization whose primary (sometimes only) responsibility is to understand all the complexities that each new CBA exerts on the league and the different ways they can use various tricks and loopholes to their advantage. It's why every NBA offseason quickly becomes an exercise in not just diplomacy and strategy but minutiae. That's also why it helps to have a former agent as your general manager, to have someone who understands what's at stake for all parties at the negotiating table.

The Warriors held a press conference at the team facility a few days later to announce the deal and introduce Iguodala. Myers showed up looking wiped, with sleepless eyes and a week's worth of facial scruff. The toll this trade had taken on him was clear. When he spoke he still sounded incredulous at the machinations that had resulted in the signing. "There's an element of this whole day that's surreal," Myers said. "To have a guy like this join a team that has been able to keep its core together and then add somebody of his caliber—not only his ability as an athlete, but who he is. I think, as the media and the fans get to know Andre—one of the best people you'll meet, well-respected throughout the NBA, community guy, man of faith—you don't find players like this."

Iguodala said he'd been eyeing the Warriors for years, ever since he was in Philadelphia. He liked the Bay Area's tech industry and spoke of the postbasketball opportunities it could afford him. He also recalled the 2010 FIBA World Championship and attending chapel services before every game with Curry and Oklahoma City's Kevin Durant. "Us three were always together," he said. "Kind of got a chance to see [Curry] work. He got a chance to see me work. Knew how in love he was with the game. We built a pretty good relationship." At another point, Iguodala said Curry "is like the second coming of Jesus Christ. He's like the most loved man on Earth right now."

Now the Warriors had a legitimate starting small forward, not only someone who could mentor a young Harrison Barnes as he continued his development but a versatile veteran who could slide up and down in the lineup as needed. It was Golden State's first true step along the path to "positionless basketball," where you have multiple players of varying heights and sizes whose skills overlap with one another. Barnes was sized like a small forward but could shoot threes like a two-guard and was strong enough to defend power forwards. Same for Draymond

Green, who possessed the toughness and center of gravity to post up centers on defense. Curry could oscillate between point guard and two-guard—he'd done so ever since his earliest days at Davidson—and Thompson, while not an elite one-on-one defender, was tall enough that he could switch onto small forwards without becoming a liability. It was not unlike a startup trying to build itself from the ground floor and wanting to gather a workforce with varied abilities that could sub in for one another if ever needed.

In hindsight, acquiring Dwight Howard would have scuttled any hope of the Warriors coalescing in such a way, so Iguodala was the perfect fallback option. If acquiring Bogut was the first piece of the rebuild, Iguodala's arrival was the start of finishing off the penthouse. As Myers said the day his newest star was introduced, "We feel like he's the missing piece of the puzzle for this team."

There was another benefit to acquiring Iguodala as a sign-and-trade rather than a straight free agent signing. It let Golden State maintain its salary cap number at a level that allowed it to keep what's known as a "midlevel exception," a specially designated pot of $5 million that can be used to sign players without using cap space.

One player they hoped to sign with that money was free agent center Marreese Speights, who'd played his first three seasons in Philadelphia with Iguodala before moving to short stints with Memphis and then Cleveland. Speights had played well in only half a season with the Cavs, who would not agree to a sign-and-trade with the Warriors—as the Nuggets had done with Iguodala—so Myers inked the backup big man to a three-year, $11 million deal that came out of the MLE. And as Speights went west from Cleveland, Jarrett Jack took his spot there, signing with the Cavs for four years and $25 million. (Landry would join the Sacramento Kings for roughly the same amount.)

The Warriors, after a season that stunned even the most optimistic projections, were starting to reassemble in better shape than before.

Throughout the process, Myers kept going back to that sit-down in Los Angeles, when Iguodala stunned the room by selling himself to the Warriors' brass.

"That," Myers recalled at Iguodala's press conference, "was a transformative moment for our franchise."

. . .

Beyond bringing a high-caliber, high-character player like Iguodala into the fold, the Warriors' offseason was a lot less dramatic than in years past. The team had no picks in the 2013 draft. Curry enjoyed a summer where he was actually upright and mobile for most of it. Lee's recovery from hip flexor surgery continued without complications. And Bogut, who battled through that irksome left ankle, was signed to a three-year contract extension that, with incentives, could earn him north of $40 million. Lacob had tried for nearly two years to acquire a big guy with Bogut's size and strength; he wasn't about to let him go, especially after whiffing on Dwight Howard.

The Warriors also picked up the team option on head coach Mark Jackson's contract for 2014–15. Jackson's first season was a rocky one, with nonstop injuries and personnel adjustments. His second was one of the most surprisingly fun Warriors seasons in years. To let him go into the 2013–14 season without picking up his option would've looked ridiculous after such progress was made. He would've been a lame duck, coaching for his job from night to night. The organization didn't need to place such pressure on Jackson, who was well liked by players and fans. Plus, he was a stable presence. After all of the turnover during the Cohan era, the Warriors faithful could be assured of at least a familiar face in the head coach's seat for some time.

Upstairs, the Warriors welcomed a new face. In May, the NBA announced that an ownership group led by Vivek Ranadivé, the founder of Palo Alto software giant Tibco and a Golden State minority owner since

Joe Lacob and Peter Guber bought the team, had beat out Microsoft chief executive officer Steve Ballmer to buy the Sacramento Kings. The total franchise valuation was pegged at $534 million, which beat out the record $450 million sum Lacob and Guber's group had put down for the Warriors. Ranadivé had become nationally known in 2009 when the *New Yorker*'s Malcolm Gladwell wrote at length about the unorthodox strategies he implemented while coaching his 12-year-old daughter's basketball team in Redwood City, along the northern edges of Silicon Valley. "They weren't all that tall. They couldn't shoot. They weren't particularly adept at dribbling. They were not the sort who played pickup games at the playground every evening," Gladwell wrote. So Ranadivé, who knew close to nothing about basketball, had his team implement the full-court press—a stifling, high-energy defense that often resulted in forced turnovers and easy layups for his own squad—for entire games. The team advanced all the way to the National Junior Basketball championships. Now Ranadivé, who'd been one of the Warriors' most vocal proponents of the use of emerging technology and once boasted they'd become "the premier basketball team of the 21st century," was out to spread that gospel 80 miles up I-80 East in Sacramento.

Ranadivé's replacement was straight out of Lacob central casting: Mark Stevens, a longtime Valley venture capitalist and one of the most well-known figures on Sand Hill Road. That Stevens was selected to scoop up Ranadivé's stake was hardly surprising. What was far more interesting was ESPN reporting that Stevens had bought in at a team valuation of $800 million, meaning the Warriors had effectively increased their worth by 78 percent over the July 2010 purchase price. And in the wake of the Iguodala signing, the Warriors sold 3,000 season-ticket packages, on their way to hitting an all-time high that fall of 14,500. What had seemed, not three years earlier, like a desperate overpayment to beat out a dotcom alpha-billionaire now looked like one of the savviest business deals of the decade.

Stevens's arrival was the big front office news of the offseason, but there was another new addition in Oakland—a familiar face to many already there. Sammy Gelfand, the DC whiz kid, was bumped from Santa Cruz north to the mothership and given the title of Basketball Analytics Coordinator. Along with Kirk Lacob, his immediate supervisor, Gelfand was tasked with being the direct liaison between the statheads making recommendations behind the scenes and the coaches who would assess those suggestions. That was what he'd done with the Santa Cruz Warriors, learning the delicate art of espousing the value of analytics without seeming like a pushy know-it-all. That would be critical in dealing with Mark Jackson, who, based on a comment he made in his introductory press conference two years earlier, seemed skeptical about fully embracing and implementing analytics.

"I do have a lot of faith in advanced statistics; I don't have total faith in it because you can look at the game and see a guy have thirty points, nine rebounds, and five assists and say, 'What a great job,'" Jackson explained that day. "Me, with my experience, can look at the stat sheet, watch the game, and say, 'He played horrible,' and I can break it down to you exactly why. There is a benefit to stats, but stats *do* lie, contrary to popular belief. I believe, when I look on the floor, a guy can have five rebounds and three blocked shots and you may say he got it done in that first quarter and I say he could've had ten rebounds and seven blocked shots, if he'd have given me more passion, more energy, and more effort on the end of the floor. So I will trust the numbers, but I'm going to trust my eyes more so."

In truth, Jackson hadn't totally resisted the use of analytics once he came aboard. In his first season on the bench, the Warriors' defense ranked 28th in three-point percentage allowed. Based in part on SportVU data presented by Kirk Lacob, the Warriors improved to seventh in the league in 2012–13 and to third in 2013–14. "It's hard to say if we really impacted that, or if the variability of the shots just evened out,"

Lacob later told the *San Francisco Chronicle*. "But we think we were able to help the coaches identify the root of the problem, and they were able to solve it in practice."

Lacob saw his duty to help thaw the "inherent freeze to analytics" that old-school coaches can project, and having the affable Gelfand on his side would help in that continuing mission. Though Jackson could be demanding, Lacob believed you just had to find the right way to approach him. "If you give [Jackson] a piece of paper and it says this is the best player on the free agent market or this is the third-best player on our team based on his WAR rating, he's going to be like, *No, no, I'd rather rely on what I've seen*," Lacob said in a 2012 interview. "But if you're giving him things like, *This guy is shooting better coming from this side*, that is advanced statistics. That's analytics. That he does listen to."

The people Jackson really listened to, or at least felt most comfortable around, were those on his handpicked coaching staff, a group Jackson picked less for their pedigree than for his own comfort. It was not a group that would threaten his authority as the head coach. Pete Myers, who was once known as the guy who replaced Michael Jordan in the Bulls' lineup when His Airness left the NBA to play professional baseball, worked 10 years on the Chicago bench after his playing days were over and was entering his third season with Jackson. Same for Darren Erman—a trained lawyer and Louisville native who had only four seasons of NBA coaching experience (with Doc Rivers in Boston) before heading west in 2011—and Jerry DeGregorio, who joined Jackson's staff in 2011 after eight years as a private trainer and coach.

But when top assistant Mike Malone was poached by the Sacramento Kings to be their head coach—thank Ranadivé for that one—and another assistant, Bob Beyer, was hired by the Charlotte Bobcats, Jackson had to hire two new coaches. One was Lindsey Hunter, who played 17 years in the NBA and won titles with Detroit and the Lakers and was brought aboard just before training camp opened. The other was Brian Scalabrine, who had played for 11 seasons before retiring to do a season of television work for the Celtics. He had no prior professional coaching experience, but he knew Bob Myers (his former agent of 10 years) and Joe Lacob (who was Celtics minority owner in 2008 when Scalabrine won a title in Boston) and could relate to the players of today, in the same way that Jackson prided himself on doing. It was an unorthodox pick but one that Lacob appreciated. After all, Jackson had no coaching experience himself and, so far, that had worked out well enough for Golden State.

Even as Lacob trusted Jackson's judgment in assembling a staff that would work in harmony, there were constant rumblings that all behind the scenes was not well. There was tension between Jackson and Malone due to the latter's rising public profile. Malone had been hyped as a possible head coaching candidate the summer before and been credited (along with Erman) by the media for turning around the defense. And the analytics staff had encountered more resistance from Jackson than they anticipated. What good was all this back-end investment in new technology if it was going to be underused on the front end?

Jackson prohibited his assistants from speaking to the media during the season, so there had been no public blowups, but there was a sense of lingering unease as the season drew near.

.   .   .

After setting the three-point record, Stephen Curry was as anxious as anyone to get back to that level again, but an exhausting playoffs had taken their toll. The good news? No offseason surgery required, so he got right back to work with Brandon Payne and the Accelerate team down near his Charlotte home. One moment, he was doing flat-bodied pullups to help with his upper body control. Other times, he was dribbling a ball in his right hand while making behind-the-back passes with his left or maybe doing waves with a heavy rope or getting pummeled with foam mallets as he repeatedly jumped with a ball in his hands and an elastic resistance belt around his waist. The NBA could feel like a world away down in that converted industrial warehouse, but the promise of something more was out there. With every exercise regimen, dead lift, and exaggerated finger roll, Curry was one step closer to affirming his place as one of the NBA's true superstars.

They just needed to keep the ankles healthy, so the team had Curry work with new performance trainer Keke Lyles to improve his strength training, mix in a little yoga, and essentially rebuild the strength in those ankles so that they didn't suffer a repeat of the past few years. And because Curry was still on the books for three more years at only $33 million, Myers had financial flexibility to keep building around him. After Iguodala, the team hoped, more stars would follow.

For that to come true, the Warriors would need to put forth another promising season. After winning 47 games and advancing to the conference semifinals, anything less than the playoffs would be unacceptable, but Jackson was also under pressure to succeed given two recent embarrassments he'd heaped on the team.

In late April 2012, with the team having just wrapped up another miserable year, Jackson dropped a bombshell on Warriors' upper management: He was being extorted for hundreds of thousands of dollars by two people, one of them an ex-stripper with whom he'd once had an affair for nearly a year back when he was a TV analyst for the New Jersey Nets. She was in possession of nude photos Jackson had texted her years earlier, as well as recordings of voicemails Jackson had left her during their relationship. After the Warriors coach paid them $5,000, the mistress and her accomplice contacted Jackson's wife of 22 years (singer and actress Desiree Coleman Jackson) and demanded more money. Jackson then told the team, which alerted the FBI. A sting operation allowed authorities to arrest the two suspects, who were booked in U.S. District Court in Oakland.

The entire debacle was leaked to the press only in late June after the arrests were made and the team was forced to acknowledge both Jackson's impropriety and its role in apprehending the suspects. "I recognize the extremely poor judgment that I used both in having an affair six years ago—including the embarrassing communication I exhibited during that time—and in attempting to deal with the extortion scheme at first by myself," Jackson said in a statement. "I apologize for any embarrassment I may have caused my family, friends, and, of course, the Warriors." It was particularly embarrassing since so much of Jackson's public image was wrapped up in professing himself as a man of deep faith. He was a pastor, helped run a Southern California church he and his wife founded, and was constantly making references to religion in his dealings with the media and his team.

A year after the stripper extortion plot, Jackson's faith again became a public issue. In April 2013, when NBA player Jason Collins announced in the pages of *Sports Illustrated* that he was gay, Jackson's public comments rankled many in the Warriors organization, including at its highest levels. "As a Christian man, I have beliefs of what's right and what's wrong," he told reporters during the playoff series against Denver. "That being said, I know Jason Collins, I know his family and am certainly praying for them at this time."

That didn't sit well with team president Rick Welts, the highest-ranking out-gay team executive in American professional sports. In an interview with a Bay Area public television station a few months later, Welts was asked if Jackson's comments disappointed him. "Yes," he said, "and Mark and I have the kind of relationship where we could have a conversation about that. . . . It did disappoint me, but I think since [then] we've talked it out and we're in a good place."

But between being extorted by a former mistress, making public comments that seemed intolerant at best and homophobic at worst, and relationships with various front office personnel that had frayed, Jackson was entering the 2013–14 season with at least two strikes on his record. He'd had his option picked up, but that was no guarantee for his future. A vigorous start to the new season stood to benefit all parties.

. . .

After a 31-point blowout of the Lakers at Oracle Arena on opening night, the Warriors cruised through the early going of the season. They burst out to an 8-3 record—one win at Oracle coming on an Andre Iguodala buzzer-beater against Oklahoma City—but lost five of their next six, due in part to Iguodala's straining his left hamstring. He missed the next 12 games; Golden State lost seven. Soon, there was even tension between Iguodala and the team about his return. "We're in the same chapter," Iguodala said after missing one mid-December practice. "Not on the same page." Fans had seen this movie before; it never ended well.

But Iguodala returned a few days later and the team was reinvigorated. The Warriors won 12 of their next 14 and entered the mid-January doldrums on a roll. With 25 wins and 14 losses nearly halfway through the season, the Warriors weren't playing like a one-year blip. They looked like a seasoned team that was playing for keeps.

Curry, healthy and with more complementary components around him than ever before, was thriving in Jackson's offense, with 23 points and nine assists a night. Iguodala, despite the injury, started to settle into a groove, scoring more than 10 points a night with five assists and four rebounds. Klay Thompson was averaging 19 points thanks to 41.4 percent shooting on threes. Harrison Barnes, relegated to a bench role except for when Iguodala was injured, was good for 11 points every time out, and the frontcourt duo of David Lee and Andrew Bogut had played in 38 of 39 games so far and was contributing a combined nightly production of 28 points and 20 rebounds. At maximum strength the Warriors were still not an elite team, but they could defeat anyone on any night.

They were even getting better about overcoming the inevitable midseason controversies that always popped up. Before one mid-February game, Jackson was asked about Bogut's having to sit out with yet another of his freakish injuries, this one a bone bruise and inflammation in his left shoulder. The Warriors center said he suffered it during a late January win against Utah, but Jackson inferred Bogut was being less than forthright about the malady's origins. "As far as I know, it was not on the court," Jackson said. "It wasn't in practice. It wasn't in a game. I'm not really sure. It may have been sleeping, and I say that in all seriousness, but it's important for us to make sure we continue to treat him, it's legitimate, and then let's be smart with it."

Bogut was furious when he heard what Jackson had said. "The sleeping comment is absolutely ridiculous. I don't know where it came from," he told the media. "It's definitely not the case I just woke up, slept on my shoulder wrong and have a bone bruise and swelling in my shoulder from sleeping. Very highly unlikely, I believe." At the same time, David Lee was nursing shoulder and hip issues while Jermaine O'Neal had an inflamed wrist. That meant a few midseason starts for Draymond Green, who started in place of Bogut that night in a 43-point blowout of Philadelphia.

Two days later, LeBron James and the defending champion Miami Heat strolled into Oracle, and the Warriors' confidence was at a high. With a record of 31-21, Golden State had its best mark after 52 games since the "We Believe" season of 2007–08. Hope abounded with the All-Star break just a game away, but the Heat, at 36-14, were still a notch above. With James flanked by three other future Hall of Famers—Dwyane Wade, Chris Bosh, and Ray Allen—Miami had knocked off San Antonio in a classic seven-game championship series the season before and was steamrolling through the Eastern Conference en route to its fourth-straight Finals appearance. With an encouraging showing against the Heat, the Warriors could serve notice as a legitimate force in the NBA.

Coming down to the final minute, the Warriors more than held their own. With 7:52 left in the third quarter, Miami led by 21, but Golden State went on a 28–9 run over the remainder of the frame to cut the deficit to two heading into the fourth. And with 15 seconds left to play, it looked as if Curry's layup and free throw (courtesy of a foul from Mario Chalmers) would decide the game. The Warriors led, 110–108, but Miami had one final shot.

After dribbling into the offensive end, Chalmers passed off to James with nine seconds on the clock. With only Andre Iguodala guarding him and no double-team in sight, James had a decision. Klay Thompson was shadowing Chalmers (an excellent three-point shooter at 39 percent) in the corner and would not leave him unguarded. James could try to force the double-team and then pass off to his young point guard; he decided to take on Iguodala instead. Signed in part for his elite perimeter defense, the Golden State small forward did all he could, keeping a right hand high, but James's step-back three flew by, just beyond his reach.

With Joe Lacob standing a few feet away in front of his courtside seat, James watched as his shot swished through with one-tenth of a second left for a 111–110 win. The reigning MVP finished with 36 points, 13 boards, and nine assists for Miami. "At the end of the day," Jackson said, "we witnessed greatness."

As the first half of the season came to a close and Curry, a first-time All-Star selection, prepared to depart for the festivities in New Orleans, one couldn't help but notice there was something about playing in Oracle Arena that brought out the absolute best in LeBron James.

. . .

Even before the loss, Joe Lacob didn't feel Mark Jackson was getting the most out of the Warriors and made his opinion known through a newspaper interview just hours ahead of James's game-winner. Speaking to the *San Jose Mercury News*, Lacob affirmed his confidence in Jackson but let it be known the team was not doing as well as he'd expected. The goal coming into the year, he said, was to finish in the top four of the Western Conference; they were a few games off that pace due to some inopportune losses. "The way to look at it bottom line—net-net, as we say—is that we are 31-21 and we have not played as well as we need to play. We've been very inconsistent at home," he vented, even while throwing in a bit of arcane business jargon. "The road's been fine, but at home we've lost a couple games . . . maybe another four games that we just absolutely should've won. We didn't. And I'm not sure why. The team wasn't ready in those games. I can't explain it, why we don't play so consistently at home as we should. We have a great home-court advantage, great fans, great atmosphere. It's not clear."

When asked specifically about Jackson and his coaches, Lacob said the team would wait until the season was over to make any final judgments. "I do think our coach has done a good job. We have had some big wins, a lot of wins on the road, and that's usually a sign of good coaching," he said. "But some things are a little disturbing. The lack of being up for some of these games at home—that's a concern to me." Jackson was officially—and publicly—on notice.

A few weeks later, as the playoffs were coming into focus, another Jackson-made bombshell hit the team. On March 25, assistant coach Brian Scalabrine, still in his first season on staff, was personally demoted by Jackson. The front office, according to reports, urged Jackson to reconsider but gave him the due deference to make the move, even one so late in the season.

All Jackson would publicly say about the matter was that the two men had a "difference in philosophies." With 11 games left in the season, Scalabrine was exiled to the D-League staff in Santa Cruz.

Not two weeks later, another improbable scandal rocked the coaching staff. Assistant coach Darren Erman—Jackson's defensive architect and someone who had spent months working with Draymond Green to unlock his untapped potential as a stopper—was terminated for "violation of company policy." It was later reported that he had secretly taped at least one conversation between members of the coaching staff. Because California requires two-party consent on such things, the Warriors' hand was forced in firing him, but it was a bad look for the organization and another reminder of what used to occur regularly in the Chris Cohan era. Just days before the playoffs were set to begin, the Warriors were a team, at least off the court, in disarray.

On the court, the Warriors were doing fine. They won five of their last seven games to secure the No. 6 playoff seed and finish with 51 wins, their most in 22 seasons. Health was the reason why: All five starters—Stephen Curry at point guard, Klay Thompson at the two, Andre Iguodala at small forward, David Lee at power forward, and Andrew Bogut at center—each started at least 63 games. Thanks to all that playing time together, Curry (261) and Thompson (223) hit more combined threes than any teammates in NBA history. The Warriors were a top-12 team in both offense and defense while running the sixth-fastest pace in the league.

The only real setback struck with two games left to play, when Bogut, who was already recovering from a groin injury, was diagnosed with a broken rib and ruled out indefinitely. The expectation was that he would at least miss the first round of the playoffs, so Jermaine O'Neal would start for the time being.

Bogut was so frustrated by yet another freak, ill-timed injury that all he could do was joke about his upcoming offseason workout regimen. "I'm going to dedicate the summer to learning how to play while avoiding contact at all costs, I guess, moving out of the way, not taking charges, and not trying to block shots," he said. "There are some players in the league who are very good strategically at avoiding contact, so I guess I need to watch them and bring that into my game."

Bogut would be missed, but the Aussie's absence was no death knell for the Warriors, who had more depth than in recent years and were confident they could survive long enough to witness his return.

But that reality would require advancing past the potent Los Angeles Clippers.

. . .

Most first-round matchups in the NBA playoffs are fairly pedestrian. Occasionally you get a No. 4 vs. No. 5 matchup that's intensely competitive. Once every few years, a lower seed (No. 7 or even No. 8) will push a top-seeded contender to the brink, maybe even shove him out with a monumental upset. But nothing memorable usually sprouts from these middle-of-the-road No. 3 vs. No. 6 pairings. Sure, the Warriors and Clippers finished No. 1 and No. 2, respectively, in the Pacific Division, separated by six games in the standings, but they were evenly matched. Golden State had Curry and Thompson; the Clippers had All-Stars Blake Griffin (drafted No. 1 ahead of Curry) and Chris Paul, the most lethal true point guard in the league since Magic Johnson. Most assumed this one would go seven games, and the basketball gods did not disappoint.

Where the deities did outdo themselves, however, was concerning a titanic bit of news that surfaced after Game 3. By that point, the Clippers were up 2–1 and the series had already shifted back to Oracle. After stealing a close win in Game 1 in Los Angeles and getting blown out by 40 in Game 2, the Warriors returned home only to see a frantic fourth-quarter comeback fall short and lose a heartbreaker, 98–96, despite two Curry threes in the final minute. The Warriors wouldn't have been even that close if they hadn't dug themselves out of an 18-point third quarter hole, but that was when Jackson subbed out Jermaine O'Neal and David Lee and had Draymond Green slide up to center and Harrison Barnes play power forward. That "small-ball" lineup, where the undersized Green matched up with the opposing big, immediately sparked a 10–0 run and helped fuel that frantic fourth-quarter rally that fell just short.

The series thus far was playing out true to expectations, and Game 4 seemed as if it would be merely a continuation of recent events.

That was when TMZ (and, soon after, Deadspin) leaked audio recordings of Clippers owner Donald Sterling uttering a litany of racist statements about African-Americans (including Magic Johnson) to his girlfriend. Sterling had long cultivated a reputation as one of the league's most repugnant owners and this news went viral within hours. By the time Game 4 was ready to tip, the Sterling controversy had enveloped the NBA landscape, and Oracle Arena had become ground zero. When the Clippers came out for pregame shootaround, they took off their jackets to reveal their warm-up jerseys worn inside out, so the word "Clippers" would not appear across their chests. Now this first round matchup had been infused with something that transcended sports and became a cultural event that the world was watching.

The sideshow clearly affected the Clippers. Before the game, head coach Doc Rivers had used some variation of "I don't know" or "no idea" more than a dozen times in taking questions from reporters. The players themselves looked sluggish, as if their mental energy had been drained by all the off-court extracurriculars. The Warriors jumped out to a 15-point lead after one quarter and never looked back. Curry finished with 33 points, including five threes in the opening quarter to start the afternoon off, while Iguodala had 22 points and nine assists. Green, making just his second-ever playoff start, replaced O'Neal in the lineup as David Lee slid up to center, a small adjustment to give the team extra energy. (On the ESPN telecast, Jeff Van Gundy repeatedly called it the "speed lineup.") Green's defense on Griffin, who was held to just 21 points after back-to-back games of 30-plus, was a particular revelation, and Golden State won easily, 118–97, to tie the series. "I didn't do my job tonight," Rivers said after the game, "and I take that personally."

But the Clippers, recharged by coming home, comfortably won Game 5, 113–103. After falling behind by 10 after one quarter, the Warriors never led again. Jackson even implemented yet again his "small-ball lineup"—Curry, Thompson, Green, Barnes, and Iguodala—for the first six minutes of the fourth quarter to try to use athleticism and defense to cut into the deficit, but it was for naught.

With its season on the line, Golden State returned to Oracle for Game 6 and eked out the narrowest of victories, 100–99, as a sellout crowd sporting more than 3,000 mini-megaphones (thanks to a promotional giveaway) blasted the court with a wave of ear-melting cheers all night long. Green, starting for the third time in a row, played the most well-rounded game of his young career, chipping in 14 points, 14 rebounds, four assists, and five steals, the first glimpse on a national stage of his promising development. Curry, with 24 points and nine assists, sealed the win by purposely bricking his final free throw with four-tenths of a second on the clock.

Oracle Arena had never cheered so loudly for a missed Warriors shot.

After the win, Jackson spoke as if in both present and past tense, like he harbored an inkling this could be his last game at home as Warriors head coach. "I'm proud of my guys. It's been an incredible, incredible ride," he said. "And now, against a 3-seed with two of the top 10 players in the world, and a future Hall of Fame coach, we are going to Game 7, in spite of all the sideline music." He cited his team's toughness and willingness to step up in the face of adversity. "Mo Speights? Ready. Hilton Armstrong? Ready. Jordan Crawford? Ready. Draymond Green, a gamer. David [Lee] responded. I'm proud of these guys, and it wasn't our best night." It was like a longtime coworker sending out a sappy good-bye email on their last day in the office and feeling compelled to thank everyone who came to mind.

Jackson added, with more defiance than confidence, "I look forward to Game 7."

. . .

The Warriors hadn't won a Game 7 on the road since 1948—not since Joe Fulks was dominating the old BAA and wowing East Coast crowds with his newfangled "jump shot"—and history would again stand in their way this time around. The loss of Bogut eventually became a burden too big to bear, as Los Angeles shot 55 percent from the field. Despite 33 points from Curry and 24 from Green, the Warriors couldn't keep up with the fast-paced Clippers, who scored 39 in the fourth and prevailed, 126–121, to end the Warriors' season. Golden State actually led by one with 2:22 to go, but Los Angeles kept scoring at the rim as needed. Blake Griffin and DeAndre Jordan combined for eight points over the next 90 seconds to seal the win.

Jackson was resolute after the game, seemingly ready for any decision Lacob might make concerning his employment. "I'm totally confident and have total faith that, no matter what, I'm going to be fine," he said. "That's even if I'm a full-time pastor."

Lacob had a lot to consider. On one hand, the Warriors had just had their best two seasons in more than 20 years and were playing their best and most vibrant basketball since the Run-TMC days. The players clearly loved Jackson's style and temperament. He was a man of deep faith and that resonated with quite a few Warriors, especially Curry and Iguodala. After the close Game 1 win over the Clippers, and amid rumors swirling that Jackson's firing was a fait accompli, Iguodala said the team was playing "to save our coach." Before Game 2, most of the team attended services at Jackson's church.

But there had been so many difficult moments, in both the past (such as the extorting mistress and comments about Jason Collins coming out) and the present. Executive board member Jerry West wasn't a welcome figure at team practices. Jackson had almost no functioning relationship with Kirk Lacob, didn't want him talking to his assistants, and prohibited analytics head Sammy Gelfand from corraling rebounds for players at practice. Erman, before he was fired, was certain Jackson was badmouthing him behind his back, and Scalabrine, according to a report, hadn't spoken to Jackson for weeks at one point. Jackson had lost virtually all interest in reviewing game film or diagraming plays in the huddle. "[Jackson] did a great job, and I'll always compliment him in many respects," Joe Lacob said that fall to a room of venture capitalists, "but you can't have 200 people in the organization not like you."

On May 6, Jackson was fired. All of Jackson's assistants—the few he still had, anyway—were canned as well. "We all make the decision to change the CEO too late, right?" Lacob later explained. All along, he saw this as a business decision and nothing personal, even as his own son was among those shunned by Jackson. "No matter how many times you've done it, we're always in the situation. We're always waiting longer than we should wait. And I'm very cognizant of that after all those years [as a venture capitalist]. And in sports, it's no different than a business. You really kind of have to get ahead of it."

Jackson was, as *Sports Illustrated* deemed him, "the right man at the right time . . . though he was the wrong man for the long run." Appearing the next day on Dan Patrick's nationally syndicated radio show, Jackson implied he was canned for not acquiescing to Lacob's demand that he overhaul the coaching staff and implicitly criticized the organization for interfering with his authority. As Patrick likened anti-Jackson whispers coming from inside the Warriors to "propaganda," Jackson emphasized that he didn't "try to get out of my lane and be running reckless all around the building."

Lacob later admitted that the long-running tumult surrounding

Jackson and his staff was a breaking point between the two men: "Carte blanche. Take my wallet. Do whatever it is to get the best assistants there are in the world. Period. End of story." But Jackson wouldn't budge. "His answer . . . was, 'Well, I have the best staff.' No, you *don't*."

Jackson wished whoever inherited his team well, even while lobbing one last grenade into his successor's chair. "That's a championship-caliber team," Jackson told Dan Patrick. "That's a team that's prepared and ready. Somebody will inherit some incredible players and some incredible individuals. It will be entertaining to see what their next step is, because 51 [wins] is not enough."

Warriors fans were stunned by the news. What sense did it make to fire the most successful coach since the first coming of Don Nelson? Lacob didn't get much benefit of the doubt for his decision in the local media. Despite all the public acknowledgment that Jackson had screwed up numerous times and was far from a perfect leader, the move was seen as reactionary and ego-driven. They thought letting a personality conflict dictate personnel matters could set the organization back years.

One particularly damning rebuke appeared in the *San Francisco Chronicle*, in which longtime columnist Bruce Jenkins let Lacob have it with both barrels. Speaking of the Warriors' recent years of success, Jenkins contended that "to reject all that, because of a man's personality, speaks of a very risky gamble. And I don't buy this notion that, with a new coach, these same Warriors reach the NBA Finals next year.

"Dead wrong. Zero chance of that."

# 7 ★ ★ ★ ★ ★ ★ ★

# STRENGTH IN NUMBERS

The 2014–15 season

**W**hen Joe Lacob made the wildly unpopular decision to fire Mark Jackson as head coach of the Warriors, the future of the franchise depended on whom he next chose to roam the Oracle Arena sidelines. That might sound hyperbolic, but the team was firmly teetering on yet another one of those cliff edges that it had so often plummeted over in years past. Over that 18-year stretch with only one playoff appearance, the team had 11 different head coaches. It's like a young quarterback whose offensive coordinators keep getting poached by other teams. There's a constant state of unease and flux, no time to develop chemistry or anything remotely lasting.

Jackson, the 11th in that line of succession, was supposed to break the cycle, but hubris had been his undoing. In an organization that sought to encourage dialogue and hold people accountable as much as lift them up, Jackson preferred his bubble of authority, which was well within his rights. A head coach can run the team as he sees fit, but an owner can choose any head coach he wants. Lacob knew this from every executive board meeting he'd ever attended. Leaders must be allowed to lead, but upper management has to realize when the best move is the most difficult one to make.

Lacob's next coach had to be a winner. He could not afford to blow this. There had been much offseason turmoil already, and the season was barely over. In addition to Jackson's departure, the team announced during the series against the Clippers that the original arena plan, which had been announced with so much fanfare two years earlier, had to be scrapped. The new plan still called for an arena in San Francisco but now in the southeastern part of the city, in a more industrial neighborhood and a far cry from the picturesque waterfront views Lacob boasted of back in 2012. It was a setback for the team and a reminder that the process of privately financing a sporting complex with a 10-digit price tag was rife with potential pitfalls.

That was an issue for the future. The head coaching vacancy was far more pressing, but eight days after Jackson was let go, the Warriors made their choice, a man with five championships as a player, one of the most recognizable faces in the NBA, and—of course—not a single second of coaching experience to his name.

. . .

"What should a front office look like?"

The MIT Sloan Sports Analytics Conference in Boston has long boasted the smartest forward-looking discussions in the entire industry, and the "Basketball Analytics" panel, which always pulls together some enchanting mix of outspoken coaches and general managers, is a particular high point every year, almost without fail. But the 2014 assemblage, moderated by *Grantland* writer Zach Lowe, produced one of the smartest basketball-related discussions ever conducted in the public sphere. There was assistant general manager Mike Zarren and head coach Brad Stevens, both of the Boston Celtics, talking at length about the science behind their team's practice schedule. There was former Miami Heat head coach Stan Van Gundy, who railed against advanced stats that don't pass the eye test. Also on the dais was former Toronto Raptors and Phoenix Suns general manager Bryan Colangelo, who put real dollar amounts (perhaps $500,000 or more) on how much teams should be investing in their analytics departments.

Rounding out the group was Steve Kerr, an on-air analyst for Turner Sports. As the second of two former Suns GMs on the stage, Kerr was more than qualified to take up Lowe's question and convey his insights as to how the modern NBA front office structure should operate. "I think what I would be looking for," Kerr said, "is somebody who can combine a basketball knowledge with the numbers. Somebody with an actual basketball and analytics background could slide right in and now we have easier conversations."

Kerr told a story from his days in Phoenix. During the 2009–10 season, his final year with the team, Kerr was exploring a way to trade All-Star Amar'e Stoudemire. After he'd tried (and failed) to convince the Warriors to take him for the draft rights to a young Stephen Curry, Kerr was desperate to find a suitor as the trade deadline approached. As part of that process, his staff was trying to identify a potential trade target. One of his charges suggested J. J. Hickson, a 21-year-old power forward in his second season with the Cleveland Cavaliers. As a new addition to the first unit, he'd been playing starter minutes for the Cavs and averaging nine points but had a killer field-goal percentage. Hickson was, according to this Suns employee, shooting better at the rim than Stoudemire. The numbers said so!

Kerr was incredulous. "You're kidding me, right?"

"No, it's right here, 65 percent to 62 percent."

Kerr didn't buy it. There were few players in the NBA more skilled at cleaning up at the rim, finishing off those pesky three- and four-footers that so many bigs can't handle with finesse but the sure-handed Stoud-emire did. Kerr pulled up a Synergy video of Hickson's shot attempts that were zero to five feet from the rim. Turns out they were almost all dunks. Hickson wasn't even trying shots with any distance.

Kerr never forgot the lesson of that impromptu film session. As he told the rapt Sloan crowd, "I would want somebody who could actually look at the numbers and figure out pretty quickly, 'That number won't work because it doesn't apply to Hickson because he doesn't shoot from two to five. Amar'e's much better. Let's move on to a different number.' There's so much information but how do you get through it all? I think it would help a lot to have somebody with both backgrounds."

Colangelo came away impressed. "Steve is clearly multitalented and possesses a rare blend of intelligence, personality, and likeability," he says. "His cerebral, calm, and confident demeanor makes him an easy guy to talk to and believe in."

Kerr's confidence came from doing his homework. For more than a year, he'd been dumping every effective concept and strategy he'd ab-sorbed throughout his long and winding career into a Word document as well as (with the help of a friend) compiling a video library with clips of plays he would install as an NBA coach. By the spring of 2014, Kerr had collected dozens of plays and a smorgasbord of coaching knowledge from some of the game's brightest minds. He was happy calling games for TNT, but if a coaching opportunity came along that was right for him and his family, Kerr wanted to be ready. By May, he had pieced together a thorough and wide-ranging PowerPoint presentation; one of the first slides was titled "Why I'm Ready to Be a Head Coach."

In its totality, Kerr's résumé represented not just a wealth of basket-ball knowledge gleaned from years of playing under and working along-side some of the most successful coaches in the sport but a culmination of one of the most eclectic lives one is likely to encounter.

Born in Lebanon, Kerr was the third of four children born to Ann

Zwicker and Malcolm Kerr. His parents had met a decade earlier at the American University of Beirut, often referred to as the "Harvard of the Middle East." Malcolm, himself born in Lebanon in October 1931, received his master's from AUB in 1955. They soon married, and Malcolm earned a doctorate in international relations from Johns Hopkins in 1958. They stayed in Beirut until 1961, when he joined the UCLA faculty and they moved to Southern California.

By that time, Malcolm was on the fast track to establishing his bona fides as one of the world's leading scholars on Middle East relations. His book *The Arab Cold War* was considered a landmark publication, and even though the Kerrs technically lived in the United States, they returned to Beirut often. It was during one of these sabbaticals abroad that Stephen Douglas Kerr came along in September 1965, and extended periods of his formative years were spent not just at the Kerrs' home in Southern California but in such countries as Egypt and Tunisia. While abroad, Kerr was stunned by the poverty one didn't see growing up in a sleepy surf town like Pacific Palisades. He watched kids play soccer with rocks as goal markers, the ball nothing more than bundled rags. "It made me more compassionate and it also made me appreciate our own country," Kerr told an interviewer in 2016, "for not only the comforts and the freedom we live in but just for the joy that we were allowed every day. Most people don't grow up with great joy in their lives; they're struggling to survive. That struck me pretty hard at a young age."

With his older brother, John, available to grab rebounds and play catch, Steve fell into sports from a young age. At Palisades High School, Steve was a third baseman and relief pitcher for the baseball team as well as the starting point guard for the varsity basketball squad. And even though Malcolm wasn't much of a participant himself, save for some one-on-one on the driveway hoop and recreational tennis with friends, he championed Steve's love of sports. He would keep Arabic readings in his lap to read during the commercial breaks of college football games, and sports references even found their way into his own academic writings, no matter how heady the topic. "In the good old days," Malcolm wrote in a 1971 book preface, "most Arabs refused to take themselves very seriously, and this made it easier to take a relaxed view of the few who possessed intimations of some immortal mission. It was like watching Princeton play Columbia in football on a muddy afternoon. The June war [of 1967] was like a disastrous game against Notre Dame which Princeton impulsively added to its schedule, leaving several players crippled for life and the others so embittered that they took to fighting viciously among themselves."

After nearly 20 years of on-and-off living in Southern California, Malcolm Kerr took a post at the American University in Cairo in 1979. Lebanon was in the midst of civil war and had become too dangerous, so setting up the family in Egypt was a compromise of sorts. Steve stayed there through his freshman year of high school before returning to California to play basketball.

In the summer of 1982, Malcolm Kerr accepted the position of president of AUB, the institution that had most shaped his life and worldview. Even though tensions in the regions were bubbling higher by the day, it was a dream job that he couldn't turn down. As Malcolm once told Ann, "The only thing I'd rather do than watch Steve play basketball is be president of AUB."

Meanwhile, Steve Kerr thrived at Palisades High, which had sent star Kiki VanDeWeghe to UCLA and the NBA's Denver Nuggets just a few years earlier, though his prospects for getting a scholarship to play Division I hoops were slim. He was 6-foot-2, shot well from the outside, and could run an offense, but was scrawny at barely 175 pounds and looked as if he'd be dominated by bigger, more agile upperclassmen. He had fallen in love with UCLA as a kid, ever since his father had taught at the school during the heyday of head coach John Wooden and standout players like Bill Walton. His earliest memory of sports is going with his father to see

John Lucas's Maryland squad come to Pauley Pavilion on December 1, 1973, and watching UCLA escape with a dramatic one-point win to extend its record win streak to 77 games. (Kerr remembers feeling confused that the fans sounded disgruntled as everyone walked home that night. When Steve asked his father why they seemed so mad after a win, Malcolm Kerr replied, "Well, the expectations are a little higher than that.")

When he was 12, Kerr was a UCLA ball boy for a couple of seasons—just as a certain UC-Irvine alum was across campus working toward his master's in public health—but playing for the Bruins was always the longest of shots. Maybe he could walk on somewhere else? That was almost more than Kerr could hope for.

But in June 1983, a month after graduation and with no destination for the fall, Kerr was working out at a basketball showcase at California State University–Long Beach and caught the eye of Lute Olson, the incoming basketball coach at the University of Arizona. In the hierarchy of the mighty Pac-10, the Wildcats were a perpetual afterthought. Since joining the conference five years earlier, the team had produced only one winning record. In the 1982–83 season, Arizona hit rock bottom, winning just four of 28 games, so school officials poached Olson from the University of Iowa, where he'd coached the team to five straight NCAA tournament appearances, including the Final Four in 1980.

With Arizona, Olson was inheriting a mess and he needed quality players to rebuild the program. He was looking not just for talent but for character as well. "Jerks draw jerks," Olson would say. "Great kids draw great kids." The new coach had one scholarship left to hand out when he saw Kerr play. Though Kerr and Olson immediately connected with each other, Steve wasn't convinced the coach wanted him, so he tentatively accepted the only scholarship offer to come along, from Cal State Fullerton. Malcolm Kerr, then back in California and sensing some great tension in Steve, called Olson and smoothed over the whole situation just in time.

A month later, thanks to a father's intervention, the pride of PaliHi had taken his talents to Tucson, despite never having visited the campus.

Just getting there was a nightmare. Kerr had gone to Beirut to see his father before the fall semester started. He was scheduled to fly home on August 12, but as he and his mother were in the airport terminal, shells starts raining down from above. "You can never know what death sounds like until you hear one of those shells hit near you," Kerr recalled a couple of months later. "It was the sound of death. I'll never forget it."

The airport was shut down for at least a couple of weeks, so Malcolm Kerr made a few calls. Three days later, Steve was driven 10 hours by car through Syria and on to Jordan, where he would fly to Cairo and then the United States. Despite the myriad military checkpoints along the route, Steve was finally airborne.

Malcolm Kerr had been planning on coming stateside (along with Ann) to see Steve play against UCLA at Pauley Pavilion in early March, but on January 18, 1984, two men (later purported to be members of Hezbollah) approached Kerr—in the same on-campus building where he and Ann had met 30 years earlier—and shot him dead. He was just 52 years old. President Reagan praised Kerr for working "tirelessly and courageously to maintain the principles of academic freedom and excellence in education." It was the lead story in that day's *Los Angeles Times*: COLLEGE CHIEF SLAIN IN BEIRUT. The next day's *New York Times*, on page A1: UNIVERSITY HEAD KILLED IN BEIRUT; GUNMEN ESCAPE.

Today, a memorial stone dedicated to Kerr sits on the AUB campus and reads:

*In memory of*
MALCOLM H. KERR
1931–1984
*He lived life abundantly*

Two days after Kerr's murder, Arizona was slated to host rival Arizona State in Pac-10 conference play. Lute Olson's Wildcats were having a miserable first half of the season, losing 11 of 13 games, including all four Pac-10 matchups thus far. The Sun Devils, meanwhile, were a more respectable 7-7 and had won 10 straight meetings with the Wildcats.

Shortly after Kerr received the middle-of-the-night call from a family friend that his father was dead, Olson (at the urging of his wife, Bobbi) had him picked up and brought to their house. Kerr slept there for the next two nights as he tried to process what had happened. "[Lute] had lost his father so he told me his story, which was really helpful," Kerr says. "He just wanted to give me space to do whatever I wanted. I felt like the best thing to do was just to play, get away from it."

Olson thought Kerr would take a couple of weeks off, but his broken-hearted freshman was determined to play. He cried beforehand in the locker room, the players coming over one at a time to place a hand on his shoulder. No one would've faulted him had he sat this one out, but there was Kerr standing with his teammates during a pregame moment of silence. Kerr bowed his head, moving only to use his warm-up jacket to wipe away the tears streaming down his face.

Olson subbed Kerr into the game before eight minutes had elapsed, and what could've been just another midweek Pac-10 battle between rivals became the impromptu christening of a folk hero.

With Arizona clinging to a three-point lead, Kerr launched a long jumper from 25 feet out. *Swish.*

Kerr's next shot from the right elbow, 15 feet out? Nothing but nylon.

Arizona State head coach Bob Weinhauer knew he was witnessing history. Having guided Penn to a Final Four appearance five years earlier, he was familiar with improbable performances. "To see someone perform in that situation, under that duress, with that pressure," Weinhauer says, "that's a special, special thing. I've never forgotten it."

Arizona won in a blowout, 71–49, to give Olson his first-ever Pac-10 conference win. Kerr finished with a career-high 12 points and when he was subbed out with 1:39 left in the game, the fans inside the Mc-Kale Center gave him a standing ovation. And after each of his baskets, the public address announcer, Roger Sedlmayr, let out a bellowing "Steeeeeeeeeeve Kerrrrrrrrrr!"

And the crowd reciprocated every time: *Steeeeeeeeeeve Kerrrrrrrrrr!*

Two days after the death of Malcolm Kerr, the legend of Steve Kerr was born.

In the weeks that followed, he kept making buckets. Eight days after the emotional win over Arizona State, Kerr pumped in 15 points (another career-high) on the road against the University of Oregon. He'd always preferred shooting long jumpers from 20 and 25 feet out, but this newfound accuracy was a breakthrough. One of Olson's assistant coaches, Scott Thompson, instructed Kerr during practice to shoot all of his jumpers within 15 feet of the basket. "Adrenaline," he told Kerr, "will add ten feet."

Maybe it sounded kooky, but it worked. Kerr played in 28 games, averaged seven points, and shot 51.6 percent from the field. In his sophomore season, Kerr started 29 of 30 and averaged 10 points (third-best on the team) on 56.8 percent shooting. As a junior, Kerr started all 32 games and finished second on the team in scoring with 14.4 points.

As Kerr improved, the Wildcats started winning more games. Arizona went 21-10 in Kerr's sophomore season and made the NCAA Tournament for the first time in eight years. (It was the first of 23 straight NCAA tournament appearances under Olson.) For Kerr's junior year, the Wildcats were picked to finish eighth in the conference but went 23-9 and won their first Pac-10 regular-season title in school history.

But a few weeks before his senior season was set to begin, Kerr was playing in the 1986 FIBA World Championship in Spain (with Olson as his coach) when he blew out his right knee in the semifinals as he jumped and tried to pass off to teammate Charles Smith. A defender cut in front of Kerr, who was forced to reorient his body in midair. In doing so, he landed awkwardly on his overly torqued right knee and snapped both the anterior cruciate and medial collateral ligaments on impact. Kerr collapsed and writhed on the court as he screamed in agony. He could only limp to the bench with some assistance under each arm, Smith holding up the right with Oscar Schmidt, the legendary Brazilian baller, supporting the left.

The Americans would win gold, but Kerr was already back in America by then, prepping for surgery. Though unable to stand there with his teammates at the end—and unable to stand at all—Kerr showed he could play. "Every day I was pretty much amazed at what he could do and what he brought to the table," says Hall of Fame center David Robinson, another of Kerr's teammates, "especially since he's not an imposing guy."

By his excelling in Spain, the glint of an NBA career for Kerr seemed more real than ever—but with a major caveat. One of the first things Tim Taft, USA Basketball's team physician, told Kerr after diagnosing his injury was that he might never play ball again. "I'm thinking, *Thanks a lot, doc*," Kerr says with a laugh. "Thanks for the pep talk."

Taft wasn't off base with his initial skepticism. Through the 1970s, athletes with ACL and MCL tears often never played again. But in the early eighties, advances in ligament reconstruction had progressed to the point where surgery and rehab could help, albeit with no guarantees. "With a big injury like that for a point guard, at that time," Taft says, "it would not have been at all surprising for that to have been a career-ending injury." Had Kerr's ill-timed leap happened just five years earlier, his NBA prospects would have been dashed in a blink.

After the surgery, Kerr was given every assurance that he could be back playing in nine months, but that meant sitting out the 1986–87 season with a medical exemption. During that time, Kerr became a de facto student coach for the Wildcats. "We thought we were going to be really good so it was a tough blow to the team when he went down," says Bruce Fraser, who played out his senior season with Kerr relegated to the sidelines. Arizona went 18-12 and made the NCAAs for a third-straight season. "When he was off that year, he wasn't on the floor coaching, but I think he's always thought he would coach."

By the time Kerr returned to the Wildcats for the 1987–88 season, the stars had aligned. Arizona was loaded, as Kerr reunited with the dynamic Sean Elliott, a Tucson native who would become the school's all-time leading scorer. Tom Tolbert, a senior who had transferred the year before from UC-Irvine, had also developed into a reliable big who could score and rebound at will.

Working in Kerr's favor was that the NCAA had finally (and controversially) adopted the three-point line, set as an arc 19 feet and nine inches away from the basket on all sides. That meant Kerr's long-range prowess could be more valuable than ever and—if he could keep up his efficiency—maybe the NBA was now a possibility. There would be time to ponder that later.

For now, the Wildcats were an unstoppable dynamo. They raced out to a 12-0 start, knocking off three top-10 teams along the way, and were ranked No. 1 in the country. They entered the NCAA Tournament with a 31-2 record and as the Pac-10 conference champs. They were also cocky with personality to spare. At pep rallies, the starters would sing one of these cheesy, anodyne raps that became popular for a time with sports teams of that era. (Kerr's own verse: "Give Kerr the ball / give Kerr a hand / I'll drill it in from three-point land.") Even the bench players had their own nickname—the "Gumby Squad," coined by Fraser—and were known for their in-game antics on the sidelines. The season felt like a five-month-long coronation, the national championship a fait accompli.

And even though Kerr had finished just fourth on the team in scoring at 12.4 per game, his three-point shooting was unfathomably good. Entering March Madness, Kerr had made 102 of 167 threes. That's a whopping 61.1 percent, positively stratospheric in any era for a long-distance shooter. Just about 75 percent of all of his scoring came via threes. In his year away from the game, Kerr's greatest skill as a player had been fully weaponized, and a new era of college basketball had dawned. It was up to him to take full advantage.

Kerr, tempestuous as a child, had developed a thick skin and learned to channel his anger through basketball. Ann Kerr says her son "could contain his emotions more carefully when he had to run back and forth on the court all the time." There was no better display than late in his senior year, during a February game in Tempe against Arizona State, when a dozen or so students started taunting him in warm-ups with phrases such as "PLO!" and "Go back to Beirut!" as well as other references to his father's death. With tears welling up in his eyes, Kerr had to sit down for a few minutes to calm himself. He'd heard similar remarks from ASU students over the years but nothing this hurtful.

Kerr went 6-of-6 on three-pointers in the first half and finished with 22 points in a blowout win, 101–73. After the win, Kerr called those specific fans "the scum of the earth" and admitted they motivated him to play better: "I was looking for my shot a little more. At halftime, I kind of got control of my temper. Maybe I should get mad more often." A few days later, Arizona State athletic director Charles Harris sent Kerr a personal letter of apology, but by then the Wildcats already had eyes on wrapping up the Pac-10 tournament title (which they did with ease) and making an emphatic statement in the NCAAs.

With four wins over the first two weeks of the tourney, the Wildcats pushed their record to 35-2 and earned a trip to their first Final Four in school history. Their reward? A date with Mookie Blaylock, Stacey King, and a stacked University of Oklahoma team that averaged 104 points, in part, by forcing a ridiculous 24 turnovers per game.

Kerr, facing the end of his collegiate career with an opportunity to win a championship, played better as the rounds progressed, yet he tried to maintain some perspective. A few months earlier, with the 12-0 Wildcats atop the national rankings, Kerr joked to a reporter that winning a championship might not be the best thing for him. "Everything in my life would be downhill after that," he deadpanned.

Alas, the Wildcats' season came to a bitter end as they lost to the Sooners, 86–78. It remains their best season (record-wise) in school history, but the chance was there for more and they could not capitalize. Kerr had one of the worst games of his life, unable to find any rhythm amidst the Sooners' smothering full-court press. The most lethal three-point shooter in college basketball missed 10 of 13 shots from beyond the arc. Kerr gave everything he had—he was the only Wildcat to play all 40 minutes—yet it was for nothing. He scored only six points. "I got completely off track, just not being in rhythm," Kerr says. "It was the pressure of the moment. I kept firing away, I kept trying to find it, but I couldn't find it. Without a doubt, not even close, the most frustrating game of my life."

Olson thinks the pressure of having Ann Kerr there in attendance affected her son. Fraser, by then a graduate student coach on Olson's staff, saw Kerr go through a perfect warm-up routine and saw no foreshadowing of what was to come. "Usually, if a guy is nervous, he's going to be missing in warm-ups, too," Fraser says. "Oklahoma got off to a good start and their press affected us and maybe that affected his timing. If he shoots it well, we probably win the whole thing, just because we were the best team."

Kerr was devastated, convinced he had let the team down. "He felt like it was his fault, and we were right there," Fraser says. "You see the frustration in his face when that happens, but when you have a shooter like that, you're always waiting for the next one to go in."

Regardless of the reason, if Kerr had simply hit threes at his seasonal average—or even only a smidge worse—Arizona would've advanced to play for a national championship.

"I will always blame myself for us losing that game," Kerr told author John Feinstein in the seminal 1988 book *A Season Inside: One Year in College Basketball*, of which Kerr was a focal point. "People keep coming up to me and saying it wasn't my fault but I really don't believe that. I really think—and I always will—that if I had shot well, we would have won that game. What people don't understand is, I can live with it. It will always bother me a little bit but that's all. I didn't choke or anything. I just had a bad shooting day. I'm a shooter and my shot was off at the worst possible time.

"Because of what's happened in my life, I'm not going to brood for that long about a college basketball game, even the most important one of my life. Was I down? Absolutely. Pissed off? You bet. But done in? No way. I've bounced back from losses a whole lot bigger than that one."

.   .   .

Steve Kerr would go on to have one of the most unconventionally successful careers of any NBA player in history. In the 1988 draft, he was selected by the Phoenix Suns late in the second round (50th overall). Team president Jerry Colangelo (father of the aforementioned Bryan) was criticized for selecting the Arizona fan favorite as some sort of courtesy pick. "He showed enough that he deserved a shot," Colangelo says. "That's the point, and he had enough skill. His great shooting ability was enough to warrant that opportunity."

Kerr played only 26 games in his rookie year, was often placed on the injured list, and then summarily shipped off to Cleveland, where he played three seasons for the Cavs, who traded him to Orlando, where he played half a season with a rookie center named Shaquille O'Neal. After five seasons with only middling success, Kerr was happy at home with Margot and newborn son Nick, but his career was at a crossroads.

He thought about calling Lute Olson and giving up the NBA to start a coaching career.

In September 1993, Kerr signed a free agent contract with the Chicago Bulls. In the 10 seasons that followed—in Chicago, Portland, and two stints in San Antonio—Kerr would play more than 760 games between the regular season and playoffs and start only once, but he flourished as a dependable sixth man who could provide scoring off the bench in bunches. Kerr also became the most accurate three-point shooter in the league, shooting 52.4 percent in 1994–95—a single-season record that stood for 15 years. The next year, he shot 51.5 percent from deep as the Bulls won a record 72 regular-season games and their fourth championship of the Jordan era.

A year later, Kerr redeemed himself for the Final Four fizzle.

With Game 6 of the 1997 Finals tied with just 28 seconds to play, everyone inside the United Center assumed the ball would go to Jordan for the potential game-winner—or, more precisely, *championship*-winner, since the Bulls led the series three games to two. As the timeout was almost over, Jordan, draped in a white towel and sipping from a Gatorade cup, looked over at Kerr two chairs down and mumbled under his breath for him to be ready just in case.

"If he comes off," Kerr shouted back, referring to his defender, Utah guard John Stockton, "I'll be ready."

Jordan, already looking away, nodded.

Brent Musberger yelled on the ESPN Radio telecast, "It'll be a scoop if anybody but Michael Jordan takes this shot!" And it looked as if the obvious scenario might play out. Kerr passed off to Scottie Pippen, who passed to Jordan out on the left side with 11 seconds left. But sure enough, as Jordan thought he might, Stockton came over for the double-team.

Kerr was wide open at the top of the key.

Jordan found him with seven seconds left and Kerr calmly swished a 20-footer to give the Bulls an 88–86 lead they would not relinquish. Jordan was named Finals MVP, but it was Kerr's shot that had won an NBA championship.

At the postparade celebration, Kerr gave his version of how the final sequence was drawn up and said that head coach Phil Jackson told Jordan to take the last shot: "And Michael said, 'You know, Phil, I don't feel real comfortable in these situations so maybe we ought to go in another direction.' So I thought to myself, *Well, I guess I gotta bail Michael out again.*" Jordan and Jackson were already in stitches, but it was Kerr giving a little shrug as he said the last part—about having to bail out the greatest player in NBA history—that really sent the Chicago crowd into hysterics. The affability and good humor that had served Kerr through the darkest of times were on display for the crowning moment of his professional career.

"Did Steve have physical gifts that jump out at you immediately? No, he didn't," says B. J. Armstrong, who played two seasons in Chicago with Kerr. "But the more time you've spent around Steve, you began to see things."

The Bulls won the title again in 1998, which made three in a row for Kerr. Midway through the 1998–99 season, Kerr was traded to San Antonio and won yet another title that June. Four titles in four years for Kerr, making him the first and only non–Boston Celtic to ever accomplish the feat. Aside from being able to boast a title-winning shot Kerr was now the answer to a sports bar trivia question.

After a few more seasons, Kerr could sense two decades of competitive basketball betraying him, especially in his long-ago surgically repaired right knee, so when the opportunity came to rejoin head coach Gregg Popovich in San Antonio for the 2002–03 season, he knew it would be his last rodeo. "I could feel my body breaking down," Kerr says.

Kerr played in 75 games, more than in any year since 1996–97, but even at only 12 minutes a game, Kerr still knocked down threes at a 40 percent clip. His looming retirement filled him not with fear but with freedom. Without having to worry about playing for contracts—"I didn't anticipate anybody would be dumb enough to offer me another"—Kerr played solely for the singular joy of every game left. "It's a great feeling to have success behind you and no pressure ahead of you," he says. "Just ride it out and you play. I felt liberated that year and I played like it."

Kerr played sparingly through the playoffs. Entering Game 6 of the Western Conference Finals against the intrastate rival Dallas Mavericks, Kerr had compiled only 13 minutes across five playoff games. Around teammates, he started calling himself "Ted," a reference to the cryogenically preserved Ted Williams. From lack of use, Kerr could feel his 37-year-old body going into deep freeze.

The Spurs were one win away from another trip to the Finals but were scuffling badly. They had blown a 17-point lead at home in Game 5 and were down late in Game 6. The Mavs, led by All-Stars Dirk Nowitzki and Steve Nash, looked as if they had all the mojo to win and force a deciding Game 7 in San Antonio.

That's when Popovich called Kerr's number one last time.

With starter Tony Parker playing at less than full capacity, thanks to some bad room-service crème brûlée from the night before, Popovich subbed in Kerr for the first time all night with 3:44 left in the third.

Kerr promptly assisted on a Stephen Jackson three, then made one of his own, a high-arching shot from the corner. "Somebody closed out on me really hard," he says. "Sometimes when you make a shot with a lot of arc, you kind of get in your cage quickly. In a weird way, you just sort of get tuned in."

With 10 minutes to play and the Spurs behind by 12, Kerr assisted on a Manu Ginobili three, then another Jackson three. Another triple from Jackson and the Mavs' lead stood at 71–68.

Off a pass from Ginobili, Kerr nailed a straightaway three to tie the game.

Then he hit another three.

And *another.*

When Nick Van Exel's layup with 2:51 left finally halted a 23–0 run by the Spurs, Dallas had been held scoreless for more than eight minutes and was down by eight. Kerr finished with 12 points, his highest output in more than six months. San Antonio outscored Dallas in the fourth, 34–9, and won by a comfortable 12-point margin to reach yet another Finals.

"It was an incredible moment. You had to be there to understand what this moment meant for all of us," says David Robinson, who was also retiring after 14 seasons of his own. "It was the epitome of who Steve is. Here's a guy who wasn't playing at all. He hadn't sniffed the court, but when he was called on, that man came up huge. We were having a blast with it because that was so Steve. He's just that guy. That's why Michael Jordan called on him. If there's anybody you can count on, you need somebody to trust, he's the guy."

Kerr's conference finals conflagration also didn't surprise Popovich. "The guy is there before and after practice, running and shooting until he's dripping wet," he told reporters before the Finals. "He hasn't stopped practicing every day, working every day, even though he hasn't played."

For years, the Spurs coach and team president sought to fill his roster with players who were not only talented but of high character. "Life is too short to be with jerks," Popovich said. "This is a business, and it's not the most important thing in the world."

Kerr played only 20 minutes in the Finals against the New Jersey Nets, but the Spurs easily won the title in six games. With five championship rings, Kerr retired as the most accurate three-point shooter (45.4 percent) in NBA history, and he, Margot, and their three kids soon moved from San Antonio to set down roots in the San Diego suburb of Rancho Santa Fe.

In 2004, Kerr was part of the ownership group that helped Robert Sarver (himself an Arizona alum) purchase the Phoenix Suns for a then-record sum of $401 million. Three years later, Sarver hired Kerr (then a successful TV analyst) as his general manager. All the while Kerr had considered coaching but decided the timing wasn't right. Maybe when his three kids were a little older. With his family still near San Diego, Kerr tried to take Phoenix from its fast-paced days (immortalized in Jack McCallum's book *Seven Seconds or Less*) into a new era under point guard Steve Nash, center Amar'e Stoudemire, and coach Mike D'Antoni. The Suns' high-flying offense made them one of the NBA's most exhilarating teams, but Kerr wanted the Suns to play more defense.

Over the next three years, the Suns' proficiency waffled between merely mediocre and next-level. Phoenix won 55 games in Kerr's first season as GM, but his trading away Shawn Marion for an aging Shaquille O'Neal proved disastrous. The Suns were knocked out in the first round of the playoffs, and D'Antoni resigned to lead the New York Knicks. New coach Terry Porter was fired just four months into the following season and replaced by offensive guru Alvin Gentry. The Suns won 46 games but missed the playoffs. They rebounded in 2009–10, despite having failed to acquire Stephen Curry from the Warriors in the days after the draft, and won 54 games. They advanced to the conference finals before falling to the Lakers in six games.

Kerr resigned as general manager after the season. "Once he was a GM, he realized that wasn't his lane in this business," says Bruce Fraser. Three years in Phoenix had drained Kerr, who missed being around his family. Still just 44, time was on his side for a return to the NBA should the right opportunity come along. Until that day came, Kerr hoped to spend as much time with his wife and kids as possible, maybe take another gig calling games, as he had for three years at TNT between his retirement and joining the Suns' front office.

On June 29, 2010, news broke that Kerr was returning to TNT as an analyst. "I still get to enjoy the game itself but also be in a better position," he said that day.

Two weeks later, Joe Lacob—an old golfing buddy of Kerr's going back to the late nineties—announced he was buying the Golden State Warriors.

. . .

By May 2014, Steve Kerr was the hottest head coaching candidate on the planet. As TNT's lead on-air analyst, his reputation as one of basketball's minds grew, and he was never shy in sharing his opinion. Just a couple of weeks after taking the job, Kerr ripped LeBron James's "Decision" to join Miami—"It just isn't right to host a show to announce you're abandoning your hometown"—and questioned whether the Heat could win a title out of the gate: "You've got to find a shooting guard, a couple of big men who can defend, and it takes time to develop a team—a real team." (Kerr's words seemed prescient when Miami lost in the Finals to Dallas a year later.)

Above all, Kerr was cool, calm, eminently likeable, and clearly knew his stuff. He was now 11 years removed from his last game, but with his svelte frame, closely cropped blond hair, and irrepressible smile, Kerr still looked the part of the backup point guard who won five titles. The smart money had Kerr moving east to coach the New York Knicks, where Phil Jackson, his old Bulls coach and a mentor, was team president.

But now here was Kerr in a conference room in Oklahoma City, where he was calling the playoff series between the Thunder and the Clippers. Huddled with Joe and Kirk Lacob, Bob Myers, and Travis Schlenk, Kerr outlined the tactics he'd implement as head coach of the Warriors. Over three hours, Kerr talked about scouting reports he had prepared, rotation tweaks he would make, improvements to sleep and diet that might be explored, and how he'd integrate analytics into his day-to-day duties.

For his staff, Kerr wanted to hire David Blatt (a 20-year head coach across Europe and a brilliant offensive mind), Alvin Gentry (his former head coach in Phoenix), and Ron Adams (an NBA assistant coach for nearly 20 years and one of the league's foremost defensive whizzes). Everyone was blown away by Kerr's confidence and preparedness. His presentation reached some 60 pages, with about a third of that being Warriors-specific and added just in the last few hours. The Warriors' execs couldn't stop talking about the document as they flew out of OKC. "There were a lot of little things that first-time head coaches don't even think about," Kirk Lacob later told the *San Francisco Chronicle*, "but he had already considered all of it in great detail."

The next day, Kerr and the Warriors agreed on a five-year, $25 million contract. He would have to divest the small percentage of the Suns that he still owned, but he would not be commuting from San Diego as he had when in Phoenix. Kerr had, against all expectations, spurned his friend and mentor in New York to take over a more talented team with immense expectations. Mark Jackson was right: 51 wins would *not* be enough. Lacob expected greatness and he expected it soon.

Kerr knew the best way for that to happen was to try to win over the players as fast as possible, to get them to buy into what he was selling. He spoke with Stephen Curry by phone before news broke of his hiring and, over the next few weeks, flew personally to see players like Andrew Bogut (in Australia) and Harrison Barnes (in Miami). He made sure to publicly credit Mark Jackson, which was seen by the players as a show of respect and a nod to what they had already accomplished as a group thus far, and let them keep certain Mark Jackson–era traditions, such as a massive motivational poster hung high in the locker room that read "mUSt be jUSt about US."

For Kerr, going to Oakland rather than New York also meant he wouldn't be pressured into running "the triangle," a convoluted, old-fashioned offense that was popularized by Phil Jackson and assistant coach Tex Winter with the Chicago Bulls over many years (including when Kerr won three titles there) and predicated on timing and positioning. Now, Kerr would incorporate *parts* of the triangle (the kind of high-post action that Geno Auriemma, the legendary University of Connecticut women's coach, has perfected) and elements of its foundation (precise passing, locational awareness) that were, Kerr thought, essential to success in the modern NBA.

But there was more to life than coaching the triangle, and Kerr had learned a lifetime of knowledge from many of the game's greatest minds, either as a player or as an employer. Gregg Popovich, Lenny Wilkens, and Mike D'Antoni, as well as Phil Jackson, all had aspects of their respective strategies that Kerr could pick and choose from, like a basketball nerd's buffet line: loops, drag screens, back cuts, floor spacing, all served on a bed of quick, constant motion. An offense that could emulsify these sensibilities into one magic brew couldn't be further from what Mark Jackson had installed, which was a traditional-style offense reliant on high pick-and-rolls, isolation down low, and scripted threes for Curry and Thompson. It was a predictable, stagnant kind of hoops that didn't maximize the team's true talents. A timely pick-and-roll could serve as an elegant weapon—and would retain a place in Kerr's offense—but there was so much more the Warriors could execute.

To help institute all this new thinking, Kerr needed dependable assistants he could trust. Blatt, who was atop Kerr's list, was deep into negotiations with the Warriors but jumped at the chance to coach a rebuilding Cleveland Cavaliers squad when that vacancy was offered to him in mid-June. (That whole dynamic irrevocably changed three weeks later when LeBron James came home to the Cavs.) Kerr's other targets, Gentry and Adams, both agreed to come aboard. With Gentry helping conceive the new-look offense and Adams hunkering down on improving an already-decent defense, Golden State's new direction was gaining form and function.

Kerr rounded out the staff with familiar names and fresh faces:

- Luke Walton, who played 10 years in the NBA and won two titles with the Lakers, was hired as an assistant coach. A former University of Arizona standout who played one year alongside Andre Iguodala, the 34-year-old Walton was also the son of UCLA legend and Hall of Famer Bill Walton. Just a year removed from the NBA, Walton understood both the players and the modern game. But aside from a few months as an assistant at the University of Memphis during the 2011 NBA lockout, Walton had zero coaching experience.

- Bruce Fraser, a Phoenix Suns scout and former personal coach to Steve Nash, was hired to work on player development. A former Arizona teammate of Kerr's (and one of his best friends), Fraser brought a laid-back Long Beach disposition to practice and often went by "Q," a nickname acquired in his college days for the myriad questions he could ask. (Fraser was also responsible for setting up Kerr with his wife, Margot, on a blind date in college.)

- Jarron Collins, who played 10 years in the NBA, including a year with the Suns when Kerr was general manager, was also hired to work on player development. Collins, before he was represented by Bob Myers, was a star at Stanford along with twin brother Jason, whose April 2013 announcement in *Sports Illustrated* that he was gay had led to those controversial, quasi-homophobic comments from Mark Jackson.

Lacob was overjoyed that Kerr was not repeating the mistakes of his predecessor. He'd hired a cadre of assistants who were experienced, open-minded, adaptable, and just plain enjoyable to work with. Lacob saw how companies could disintegrate from the inside simply because people couldn't stand their coworkers. That usually stemmed from a leadership issue, and Kerr seemed destined to go down a more constructive and collaborative path. Above all, he wanted his players to channel their passion for the game, remembering that basketball, above all else, was supposed to be fun.

That attitude was vital right from the get-go. While he had his faults and likely would have lasted only another full season, if that, Jackson had engendered team chemistry where none existed and showed them how to be winners in the NBA. Going forward, the Warriors were not a sure thing to play any better basketball or win any more games than they had under Jackson, but any future success would not be possible without his contributions, despite the irreconcilable differences that precipitated his ouster.

And despite the late-season flameout at the hands of the Clippers, the Warriors, thanks to some radically improved play, had cemented their place as one of the league's up-and-coming franchises, a team on the precipice of contending with the NBA's perennial powerhouses. All the signs had been there for months. In January 2014, Zach Lowe penned a *Grantland* feature headlined WHY NOT THE WARRIORS? It was a bold, compelling argument, centered on the idea that Golden State "has everything to make it work." His contention was that the addition of Iguodala had turned their starting five into an elite first unit, one that "may well be the best lineup in the entire NBA," as Lowe deduced from looking into the advanced metrics. They were still very much a middling team in a tough Western Conference, but the foundation had been poured and was starting to settle.

"The raw material of a contender is here," Lowe concluded. "Im-

agine that: a potential contender in Golden State. You don't have to imagine anymore."

. . .

Almost as soon as Kerr arrived in Oakland, the Warriors were faced
with the most pressing personnel decision since Lacob reluctantly gave
the go-ahead to trade Monta Ellis to Milwaukee two and a half years
earlier.

The Minnesota Timberwolves were dangling Kevin Love like a carrot in front of the Warriors' noses, but they wanted Klay Thompson in
return. On the surface, a case could be made for Golden State to trade
the beloved Splash Brother for Love, a three-time All-Star who was not
just an elite scorer (26 points per game) but also an excellent three-point
shooter, having knocked down 37.6 percent of his attempts on high volume just a season ago. Listed at 6-foot-10, Love was a coveted "stretch-
four," a power forward who could shoot from the perimeter and space
out the floor by forcing his defender to come out of the paint to play
defense. That, in practice, would unclog the area down low of at least one
big and free up the Warriors to attack the rim if they so desired.

There were a few problems, though. One was that Love was a year
older than Thompson. He also wasn't a shooting guard like Thompson,
so it wasn't as simple as swapping one in for the other. And this Warriors
ecosystem, which had maintained some sense of balance through even
the most tumultuous parts of the Mark Jackson era, would invariably be
upset in some way. Finally, Kerr was promising to restore a fundamental
emphasis on defense and Love was not regarded as a good defender at
all. Timberwolves opponents scored 5.6 more points per 48 minutes and
shot 1.2 percent better from the field when Love was on the court as opposed to the bench. The Warriors' own internal analysis also confirmed
Love's defensive shortcomings.

Sure, Love could score in bunches, shoot threes like a sniper, and was a UCLA alum (like Bob Myers), but internal resistance was firm. Two people above all others held the line against green-lighting the trade: Steve Kerr and Jerry West. In business and sports, sometimes it's the moves you *don't* make that can affect your organization more than the ones you do. In this case, two persuasive dissenters made a compelling case that Thompson was the preferable player, the one better suited to both the Warriors' style of play and their future plans. West, in particular, was adamant that Thompson remain a Warrior. In no uncertain terms, he made it clear to all who'd listen that he would resign his position should Thompson be shipped off. The public was just as divided, as some fans thought Love might be the missing piece to a championship. Others—such as NFL Hall of Famer Ronnie Lott, who posted a You-Tube video to personally urge Joe Lacob to keep Curry and Thompson together—were not so convinced.

"We encourage very strong debate," Lacob later said, "but then it's my job to make the decision. I certainly listen most of the time to what the group decides and then we just do it and we go. I do think that is what's different. That's what separates us. That's the Silicon Valley way, the entrepreneur way. That is not the big company way."

In the end, Lacob heeded the advice of both his new coach and his most senior adviser. All trade discussions were nixed, and, after training camp, Thompson was signed to a four-year contract extension worth some $70 million. Kerr and West (and, I suppose, Lott) got their wish and the Splash Brothers would remain side by side for at least another three seasons, while Love was traded to Cleveland later that summer after LeBron James rejoined the franchise from Miami.

Even as the Warriors worked to resolve Thompson's status one way or the other, Myers moved to shore up the weaker spots in his roster. In July, he signed veteran point guard Shaun Livingston to be Curry's backup. The onetime high school phenom from Peoria, Illinois, didn't shoot threes and was most known for the horrific broken leg he'd suffered in 2007 (which required a year and a half of rehab), but he was 6-foot-7 with long arms, never met a midrange jumper he didn't adore, and was regarded as a good teammate devoid of ego and pretense. Playing for eight different franchises in nine years will give you a new perspective on NBA life, and Livingston was open to any role the Warriors asked of him. Curry now had a legitimate backup who could keep the offense humming in his stead.

In September, the Warriors signed Leandro Barbosa, a wing scorer who was entering his 12th season in the league. Though only 6-foot-3 and sporting a funky shooting style, the Brazilian Blur, as he was known, was fast off the dribble but could just as easily knock one down from deep (a career 39 percent three-point shooter) if he caught you napping on defense. Barbosa had played for four different teams, but his best years came when he was in Phoenix, which was how Kerr became familiar with him and his work ethic. Between Barbosa and Livingston, Kerr now had experienced second-unit contributors ready to check in at his request.

But Kerr knew he could make the second unit stronger still, even as he improved the starters. That's when, after just two preseason games and midway through his first training camp ever as a head coach, Kerr sat down Andre Iguodala—the $48 million man who had started all 758 games over his 10-year NBA career and averaged nearly 15 points every time out—and asked if he'd cede his starting role as small forward to Harrison Barnes. Even for an experienced coach with a decade or more behind the bench, this was a daring request.

Iguodala was initially hesitant, as any employee with established credentials would be, but Kerr convinced him of the utility of moving up Barnes (to help accelerate his overall development, which Kerr believed had been stymied) and having Iguodala lead a second unit consisting of Livingston, Barbosa, Draymond Green, and Marreese Speights—four legitimate rotation players whose minutes could be staggered with various combinations of starters, allowing Kerr and assistant coach Alvin Gentry to mix and match players from both units as needed.

Kerr was persuasive enough and Iguodala, to the surprise of some inside the organization, accepted what was essentially a no-fault demotion. As the former All-Star told *Sports Illustrated*, "I agreed with his larger vision. . . . I've been in this league eleven years and I want my professionalism to be something that stands out." Lacob and Myers had talked for years about bringing in high-character guys who would put the team before themselves, and Iguodala exemplified that notion distilled to its essence. (It probably also helped that Kerr and Iguodala, as a couple of University of Arizona alums, shared a certain kinship.)

With Iguodala penciled in as a reserve, the Warriors won their next preseason game—in Los Angeles against Kobe Bryant, Steve Nash, and the Lakers—by 41 points.

With the rotation set, Kerr completing his playbook, Curry and Thompson united for the foreseeable future, and a bench unit that was good enough to start for the league's worst teams, the Warriors looked ready to finally capitalize on their years-long upward trajectory.

There was no small amount of pressure on Kerr to keep the good times rolling. Curry and others were saying all the right things regarding their new coach and appreciated his deference to what Jackson had helped establish, but establishing trust takes time. Plus, the optics of a white man with no previous coaching experience replacing an African-American coach who was beloved by his players and fired for reasons that were, at best, difficult for the larger fan base to comprehend, presented a moment where it all could've come crashing down. When the season started, people of color comprised 76.7 percent of players but just a third of the 30 head coaches. Kerr didn't allow such external considerations to weigh on him, but they were there all the same.

. . .

The Warriors flew through the preseason, winning six of eight match-ups, and it looked as if Kerr's offense predicated on ball movement and predictive motion would be a smash hit. Curry and Thompson were getting open looks as never before, Barnes was facilitating from the small forward position, and even Lee and Bogut, as the two bigs up front, were rebounding and passing with aplomb. They were scoring more than 110 a game, six points higher than last season's average. Of course, preseason statistics are almost useless, since every team is tweaking rotations and playing time irrespective of in-game situations, but more scoring (so long as it's not compromising your defense) is always preferable to less. And with just a few days before the opener—on the road against Vivek Ranadivé's Sacramento Kings—Golden State looked a juggernaut waiting to take the league by storm.

Then David Lee came down with a strained hamstring, similar to the one that had kept him sidelined toward the end of the previous season. Once it became clear he wouldn't be ready for opening night, Kerr called on Draymond Green to start in his place at power forward.

When considering franchise-altering decisions that seemed inconsequential at the time, you'd be hard-pressed to propose anything that beats the Green-for-Lee switcheroo. Green had been, to that point, little more than an emotional role player who could play lockdown defense at times, show off some long-distance range, and pass like a point guard. Coming out of Michigan State, he was the ultimate "tweener," bigger than your typical shooting guard yet undersized as compared to the league's premier small and power forwards. In sports, just as in any major field of business, executives say they value versatility but will not hesitate to label you if that's more convenient. It's risk aversion put into action, as evinced by Green's mere 18 starts (playoffs included) in two full seasons of play.

Green was also fiery like a 10-year veteran, possessing an on-court attitude that veered into cockiness. It was the raw manifestation of his feelings about dropping into the second round of the draft. In time, he could recite from memory all 34 players picked ahead of him—not just their names but who took them, in what order, and what had happened with their careers in the years since. That the Warriors ultimately passed on Green not once (Harrison Barnes at No. 7) but twice (Festus Ezeli at No. 30) was no small thing either, but he knew Oakland was the perfect place for him.

Kerr, in turn, was the perfect coach for him. As someone who constantly had to prove his worth over 15 seasons in the NBA—and was known for an irrational confidence that sometimes surfaced as unbridled rage—Kerr saw himself in Green. And two years before he became his coach, Kerr watched Green play Summer League games in Las Vegas and confessed to one Warriors staffer: "I don't know what position Draymond Green plays, but I know I want him on the floor."

Playing time was scarce early on for Green, but he always seemed to leave an impression. (Even in practice, Green rarely backed down from anyone.) Just six weeks into his rookie season, the Warriors embarked on their first East Coast road trip of the season. They'd won the first four games before heading south to face the defending champion Miami Heat. Green was laboring through a lackluster start, playing in all 21 games but averaging fewer than three points on barely 13 minutes. As the first big off the bench that night, Mark Jackson matched him against none other than LeBron James, who, in recent months, had racked up an NBA title, earned Finals MVP, won an Olympic gold medal, and was named *Sports Illustrated*'s Sportsman of the Year.

No big deal.

All night long, Green handled his assignment with aplomb, enveloping James on baseline dribble-drives, pull-up threes, and post-ups. He couldn't totally neutralize James—who can?—but Green played the defense of someone four or five years into an NBA career. Early in the fourth, James managed to convert a tough drive at the basket and draw a foul on Green. The King then unleashed the kind of psychological trash talk that made Michael Jordan so lethal. He jawed at Green, "You too little!" On this one play, yes, Green didn't establish enough position to keep James from extending toward the hoop, but the rookie's defensive impact was undeniable. In the 16 minutes James played that night with Green on the bench, he shot 4-of-5 from the field. In his 26 minutes with Green in the game? Just 8-of-18. James's three rebounds on the night were also a season-low.

With just two seconds left in the game, it was Green who slipped away from Shane Battier (who had moved to help defend Klay Thompson), received a pass from Jarrett Jack as he cut to the rim, and converted an easy lay-up. Was Green "too little" to even be noticed, that he could scoot to the hoop at will against the best team in the NBA? Regardless, the Warriors prevailed, 97–95. Green played a career-high 30 minutes, chipped in seven points, held the reigning MVP to just 23 points while he was on the floor, and nailed the game-winner. The Heat would go on to win the title again that season, but Green, on this night, had started to make his name known.

Kerr knew what it was like to rely on heart and guile to overcome doubters. He saw in Green the same struggle he'd experienced in gaining respect from his NBA peers. In his case, though, it often involved his own teammates. Kerr once received a black eye from Jordan in a Bulls practice when trash talk between him and His Airness escalated. The shiner notwithstanding, Kerr knew he'd gained Jordan's respect by not backing down from his lip, and Green possessed that same mentality. Kerr's and Green's mannerisms overlapped in many ways. "I wouldn't necessarily say I'm arrogant," Green told *Grantland* later in the 2014–15 season. "I'm just confident. I wouldn't necessarily say I'm an asshole.

I just don't take no shit. I wouldn't necessarily say I'm disrespectful. You've just got to earn my respect."

. . .

The Warriors began the season with Green at power forward, matched up with Andrew Bogut at center and Harrison Barnes at small forward. With Curry and Thompson in the backcourt, Golden State sought to take the league by storm right from the get-go. And did they ever, winning their first three games—over Sacramento, the Los Angeles Lakers, and Portland—with ease.

By this time the SportVU tracking system had started to fully mature, reaching all corners of the NBA. Now, teams had powerful analytical tools at their disposal that could quickly determine the defensive value of, say, Draymond Green compared to David Lee. The latter had never been considered an elite defender, but the upgrade in playing Green over Lee could now be accurately calculated. While Lee was sidelined, it was a recurring debate whether Kerr would sub him back in with the starters. It was no small thing that Lee was making $15 million, more than anyone on the roster, but by the time Lee was healthy enough to play, Green was an irreplaceable cog in Kerr's machine.

Just a couple of months into the season, Golden State was regarded as the best team in the NBA. After starting off 5-2, they reeled off 16 wins in a row, finally succumbing on the road in Memphis. They then won 14 of their next 19 to hit the season's midway point with a record of 35 wins and six losses. Curry, at nearly 23 points and eight assists a night, was a legitimate MVP candidate. Thompson's scoring output was nearly identical. Andrew Bogut missed a 12-game stretch with right knee inflammation but the Warriors went 9-3. Iguodala embraced his role as a sixth man and de facto leader of the second unit, averaging 27 minutes—just five minutes fewer than a year earlier—and seven points, while Barnes thrived with the starters. The third-year man from UNC was shooting 49.2 percent from the field (his career average was 41.9 percent) and making 42.6 of his threes (again, up from 35.2 percent for his career).

Kerr's Iguodala/Barnes flip-flop had paid off. His decision to keep Green in the starting lineup, even after Lee had been cleared to return, was validated. They had the best record in the league and the third-best Offensive Rating. They also had the best Defensive Rating in the NBA, allowing just 96.9 points per 100 possessions—an astounding feat considering they also played the fastest pace (more than 101 possessions per game) of any team. Their Net Rating—the number of points per 100 possessions by which they outscored their opponents—was on track to be the highest ever recorded. The website Basketball Reference put the Warriors' odds of winning a title at close to 40 percent, far better than any other team's.

It had taken less than three months for Golden State to become the prohibitive favorite to win its first championship in four decades.

.   .   .

With Kerr coaching the team, the Warriors, as an organization, were more open than ever to trying out new techniques that might benefit the team down the line. Bruce Fraser, Kerr's former Arizona teammate and now assistant coach, connected him with a man named Chris Johnson. For the past six years, Johnson had worked as a clinical neuropsychologist for the U.S. Navy and was running their Operational Neuroscience Lab down in San Diego. He had UCLA roots, having earned a PhD in psychology from there in 2005, and did two years of postdoc study at Yale. Johnson also grew up a fan of the Jordan-era Chicago Bulls, which made him an instant fan of Kerr.

Over the next few months, Johnson served as a part-time team psychologist, showing up in the Bay Area twice a month, conferring with players as needed, even texting them out of the blue simply to make sure they were in a good headspace. Johnson emphasized the importance of staying focused, not succumbing to the allure of perfectionism, and making good decisions under stress.

Another way Kerr hoped to manage stress was by advocating better sleep and rest habits. Player conditioning was a topic that had long fascinated Kerr. During his 2014 Sloan panel, he mused about the potential to design conditioning programs for players "based on not only how much you got played but the stress on his body." Maybe the quantification of bodily stress wasn't quite there yet—although using devices such as chest-based accelerometers in practice was a good start—but sleep was a surefire way to counteract the rigors of the NBA schedule. That was especially true for the Warriors, who, by virtue of their extreme geographical placement, would travel the most of any team during the 2014–15 regular season—some 54,954 miles in all.

Before the season, Kerr was prodded by Keke Lyles, the team's director of athletic performance, to follow through on consulting some kind of sleep expert. Luckily for the Warriors, they had one of the country's foremost experts on the sleep habits of athletes based in the Bay Area. In the summer of 2011, a Stanford researcher named Cheri Mah published research showing the benefits college basketball players could experience with just a few adjustments, such as increasing their sleep to 10 hours a night and taking 30-minute daytime naps as needed. Mah found that sprint times went up, fatigue levels went down, and both free-throw and three-point percentages showed marked improvements.

With more than a decade of sleep experience under her belt, Mah worked with the Warriors to suggest ways they could counteract the effects of their difficult schedule. She urged the players to cut down their game-day naps from two or three hours down to 30 minutes or so. She advised them to stay off their phones late at night before bedtime. The Warriors also looked to rearrange their travel schedule to cut down on, say, long overnight flights back from road games, which can wreak havoc on a player's circadian rhythms. "You're trying to link what happens at nighttime with performance during the daytime," Mah says. "Those were my strategies—of taking it home, trying to get the performance angle, building in small changes that we continue to build on over time—and it seemed to be pretty effective."

In the year since he joined the Warriors, Andre Iguodala had already felt the benefits of such practices—he would even go so far as to lower his thermostat to 57 degrees to keep his core body temperature cool—and he was a willing advocate for better sleep, even if some of the other players (such as Andrew Bogut) were more opposed to tweaking long-standing habits. "I'm not necessarily trying to overhaul everything that they've ever known," Mah says of her approach, but having Iguodala's support was key to everything. "There's a trickle-down effect across the rest of the team. For him to have the success that he did while advocating for it, obviously that's helpful."

The team also worked on aggregating more sets of objective data related to the players' health and conditioning. Again, this was something Kerr had thought about for years, and now he was with an organization with the resources and inclination to press forward with such tech-centric initiatives. They partnered with a Finnish startup, Omegawave, to assess heart-rate variability using facial electrodes. Catapult Sports, an Australian firm, helped outfit the Warriors with wireless GPS sensors that could track acceleration, the force exerted on bones and joints, and directional changes in real time during practice. (The CBA forbade teams to track individual player data during *games*, but practice was safe ground.)

These gigabytes of data were then combined with the Warriors' own internal evaluations—a simple test administered daily that the players filled out and handed back—to determine their game-readiness. How they'd been sleeping, how sore they felt, how quick their thinking was—all of these factors fed into the ultimate determinations. Kerr and his staff could then look at these readouts and make an educated conclusion about when a player might need a reduction in minutes or even a night off.

Close to March, with the playoffs about six weeks off, the evaluations started to show troubling signs. Curry and Thompson, in particular, were close to "red-lining." The staff was worried that an injury or severe drop-off in performance might be imminent. Myers and Kerr were informed that it was their decision, ultimately, but from what the data was showing, the Splash Brothers needed a break sooner rather than later.

Curry sat out two games, one in late February in Indiana, the other in mid-March in the high altitude of Denver. Thompson also sat out the Denver game—"I know there are people here in Denver who are probably coming to see Steph and Klay play, in particular," Kerr said, "but unfortunately we can't base our own team's welfare on that"—and then sprained his right ankle three days later in a win over the Lakers. He missed the next three games, the first time in his NBA career he'd missed time due to injury. The team won all three without him, but Thompson returned to play the final 13 games of the season without issue.

Thompson, among others, had thrived under Kerr's system. Even with the emphasis on defensive switching, even with the new, slimmer set of offensive schemes, Thompson was more proficient than ever. In January, he went supernova at Oracle against the Sacramento Kings. With Iguodala getting a night off and Curry scoring only 10, Thompson provided more than enough offensive oomph, finishing with 52 points, including 37 points·in the third quarter—more than any NBA player had ever scored in one quarter. Thompson made all 13 field-goal attempts in the quarter, including nine threes. (A 10th three in the last few seconds was waved off since it came just after a whistle stopped play.)

Not two weeks later, Curry dropped 51 on Mark Cuban's Dallas Mavericks, thanks to 10-of-16 shooting on threes. Just past the season's halfway point, Curry had nearly 150 threes on 40.4 percent shooting, but he shot a staggering 49.3 percent on three-point attempts over the final 33 games to finish with 286 and break his NBA record of 272 set two years earlier. During an April practice just a day before the regular-season finale, Curry sank 77 three-pointers in a row and 94 of 100 overall. He also led the NBA in free-throw percentage (.914) and steals (163).

Draymond Green also finished the season strong. If his ability to do almost anything on the court was unveiled in the first half of the season, it was magnified during the second. Over the Warriors' final 41 games, of which he played 39, Green averaged 11.7 points, 8.5 rebounds, 3.8 assists, and 1.6 steals, an improvement in each category over the team's first 41. The only other player to reach those statistical benchmarks over his team's second half? Oklahoma City's Russell Westbrook. Once you accounted for his defense, Green, with his multidimensional abilities, had become Golden State's ultimate X-factor.

Meanwhile, harmony had once again taken root in and around the Warriors' practice facility. As Ron Adams would work with Green on one hoop, Bruce Fraser would feed shots to Curry on another. Sammy Gelfand would go down to the court to grab rebounds for Shaun Livingston after responding to a Bob Myers email asking for any ideas he thought the Warriors should implement. And if Jerry West or Kirk Lacob happened to walk through practice, they were a welcome sight. Everyone was encouraged to offer insights, and coming to work every day didn't feel like, well, *work*. This was the vision Joe Lacob had when he and Peter Guber plunked down nearly a half-billion dollars into this sad-sack organization: When everyone enjoys the work they do, the team reaps the rewards.

So far, so good.

. . .

"The most important thing," Bob Myers once told me, "when you sit in our seat up in the front office, is that your players respond to your coach. There's no doubt that our team responds to him. He's got the right balance of having this competitive edge, and he's got this great feel for the pulse of the team—when to push, when to pull, and how to sustain that through the whole season."

Myers's assessment of Steve Kerr was spot-on. There was every reason the Warriors could've cratered during the 2014–15 season, any number of decisions that could've backfired, but each was made with knowledge and confidence. Maybe he was learning on the fly how to be his own kind of coach, but the game of basketball? He'd known that inside and out for decades.

"Many coaches and people in their profession are constantly seeking this holy grail, and it can grate on your personality. It can create paranoia, can create insecurity," Myers added. "[Steve] had accomplished so much as a player. Not many guys can put a ring on each finger of a hand, but that gives you confidence and a self-assuredness that isn't arrogance or cockiness but a level of confidence. A lot of players in the NBA that are seeking a championship, they trust in him that he can provide a pathway for them to try and get that. It's very hard to do and everything has to come together, but I think in him they see a person that has their best interest in mind, that has a perspective on basketball versus life. I think it's refreshing for them."

On March 16, with a month's slate of games yet to play, Golden State became the first team in the West to clinch a playoff spot. It came while they were playing the Lakers at Oracle Arena. As a result of Oklahoma City's loss to Dallas, the Warriors' magic number reached zero. The news was announced during a timeout just before halftime, the word CLINCHED flashing on the in-arena video boards. They beat Los Angeles to move to 53-13.

The Warriors reeled off 10 more wins in a row to stretch their streak to a cool dozen. They finished the year with 67 victories against only 15 losses. Golden State ended up a full 11 wins better than anyone in the Western Conference and became only the 10th team in NBA history to win that many games in the regular season.

When Kerr is handed the box score over by the bench after each quarter, he mainly looks at three things: the Warriors' assists, their turnovers, and the other team's field-goal percentage. These are the stats that resonate most with him, and while Golden State was a middle-of-the-pack team with regard to turnovers, they led the NBA with 27.4 assists per game and held other teams' shooting to a league-low 42.8 percent. They were also top-six in rebounds, steals, and blocks. That they ranked second in offensive efficiency wasn't terribly surprising, but that they became the first team in 37 years to finish tops in both defensive efficiency *and* pace of play was utterly astounding. The Warriors were defying all the conventional maxims of modern basketball while making the sport look spirited and carefree.

Though it was widely assumed Curry would win the Most Valuable Player award, there were vocal dissenters, notably his old coach, Mark Jackson, who said he'd pick Houston's James Harden if he had a vote. Andrew Bogut had the most honest response when asked about Jackson's prediction coming a day after April 1: "Well, it was April Fool's Day." (Jackson, who worked Warriors games for ESPN all season, often needled the team. During a January broadcast, when Jeff Van Gundy gushed about the job Kerr was doing, Jackson emphasized that "you cannot disrespect the caterpillar and rave about the butterfly.")

But Curry did win MVP easily, capturing 100 of 130 first-place votes. He was the first Warrior to earn the award since the team moved out west and only the second in franchise history, after Philadelphia rookie Wilt Chamberlain in 1960. He'd become the first player to record multiple career games of at least 50 points and 10 threes, and his per-game average of 32.7 minutes was the lowest ever recorded in an MVP season, proof positive that the team's emphasis on health and well-being didn't require much self-sacrifice.

Draymond Green, the accidental starter who morphed into the team's heart and soul, finished second to San Antonio's Kawhi Leonard for Defensive Player of the Year honors. Klay Thompson's 239 threes were the ninth-most ever recorded in a season. Harrison Barnes played all 82 games and averaged double-digit points for the first time in his career.

With the playoffs just three days away, Golden State was battle-tested but healthy. The five starters had all played at least 65 games and were reporting no significant injuries, a testament to the Warriors' training staff and analytics department for getting the players to buy into such new-wave methods. Before the season, Kerr proclaimed their philosophy as "strength in numbers," a guiding principle that propelled the team to the NBA's best record.

In preparation for the playoffs, Kerr pulled out an old chestnut, one he'd stolen from Gregg Popovich in San Antonio. The Spurs coach liked to preach the gospel of "appropriate fear," the feeling for when you play someone you're expected to beat. The worst thing in the world would be to give away a game to an inferior opponent. Kerr dropped that phrasing periodically over the course of the year in an effort to keep his team focused. And after barely skating by Minnesota (the league's worst team) in the last week of the season, Kerr casually invoked it once more: "I just think they're ready for the playoffs," Kerr said. "They want it, and I'm very confident that when that happens, when the playoffs come, our edge will be back. Our appropriate fear, as we talk about, will be there and we'll be sharper."

Now, the Warriors, as the No. 1 seed in the West and possessors of the best record in all of basketball, would subsist on "appropriate fear" as far as it could possibly fuel them.

# 8 ★ ★ ★ ★ ★ ★ ★

# KINGSLAYERS

## The 2015 playoffs

For the first time since 1977, the Warriors had made the playoffs three years in a row, and they seemed poised to not only fulfill Lacob's goal of making the Western Conference Finals but even potentially win the whole enchilada for the first time in four decades. They'd finished the regular season with the 10th-best record in NBA history and recorded the highest year-on-year improvement (plus-16) of any 50-win team in league history, but such accomplishments would feel hollow if they didn't get within reach of a championship.

First up were the upstart New Orleans Pelicans, led by former No. 1 overall pick Anthony Davis, a mammoth University of Kentucky star who, despite being just 21, had ravaged opposing NBA power forwards and centers for three years. He'd led the league in blocks two years in a row while averaging 24 points and 10 rebounds. Complementing him was a trio of capable guards in Tyreke Evans, Eric Gordon, and Jrue Holiday. Evans had beaten out Stephen Curry for Rookie of the Year honors back in 2010 and was the team's second leading scorer at 16 a night, while Gordon (13.4 points per game) and Holiday (14.8) were legit threats from the perimeter. And with Ryan Anderson, a 6-foot-10 backup power forward who could stretch the floor and knock down threes like a wing, the Pelicans had the deep-threat scorers to rain down enough shots to make any game tighter than it deserved to be. New Orleans even handed Golden State its 15th and final loss of the regular season, a 103–100 nail-biter on April 7 wherein only two Warriors scored in double digits and Davis dominated with 29 points, 10 boards, four blocks, and no turnovers.

Nonetheless, Golden State swept New Orleans out of the playoffs in a week's time. After two pedestrian wins at Oracle, the Warriors were down by 20 heading into the fourth quarter of Game 3 in the Crescent City. They not only forced overtime but won, 123–119, as Curry finished with 40 points and nine assists; was the game's high scorer in the third quarter, fourth quarter, and overtime; and dropped two threes in the final 12 seconds of regulation to force the extra frame. It was the first time in franchise history that Golden State won a game after being down by at least 20 points entering the fourth; its previous record in such instances was 0-358.

Sure, the Pelicans were not the staunchest competition, but it was the kind of game that gave the Warriors an air of inevitability. They were truly never out of a game, not when they were down 17 points with six minutes to play, not ever. And behind 39 points and nine assists from Curry in Game 4, the Warriors closed out the series with a 109–98 win to partake in seven full days of rest before meeting their next opponent.

· · ·

The Memphis Grizzlies would be a far tougher test for Golden State in the second round. They were constructed more in the mold of a traditional NBA squad. They shot the second-fewest threes per game and didn't have a 20-point scorer on their roster. But they were balanced— five players averaged double-digit scoring in the regular season—and boasted the third-best defense in the league, allowing just 102.2 points per 100 possessions. That was almost as good as the Warriors, but Memphis's offense, unlike Golden State's, thrived at a grinding pace, the fifth-slowest of any NBA team. The Grizzlies could break the Warriors' reliance on rhythm and reduce the game from one of back-and-forth transition and fast breaks to staid possessions that lived and died in the halfcourt. To break through, Golden State would have to either dictate pace or adapt on the fly to beat Memphis at its own game, whichever seemed more effective in the moment.

The Warriors won Game 1, 101–86, but the contest was far more competitive than a typical 15-point coasting. Curry's 22 points topped all players, even though Golden State shot better than 50 percent from the field and 46 percent on threes. The Grizzlies dictated the pace, but their execution was lacking on both ends of the court.

In Game 2, Memphis flipped the script and shocked Golden State with a 97–90 win that was more in keeping with their team style. No Warrior topped 20 points on the night as Golden State shot just 42 percent overall and a measly 23 percent on threes. Twenty turnovers led to 22 points for the Grizzlies. After the game, the mood inside the Warriors' locker room felt as if a highly touted heavyweight had hit the canvas for the first time. "Everybody expecting us to go undefeated in the playoffs, no one expects us to lose a game at home," said a somewhat sarcastic Draymond Green outside his locker, "and now the whole world is collapsed and the Bay Area's just been hit by an earthquake." Green was being cheeky, but the shock inside Oracle was real.

Kerr felt the team lost its poise, and 20 turnovers was beyond unacceptable. "They deserved to win," Kerr said of Memphis after the loss. "They kicked our butts."

But the real butt-kicking came three days later, when Memphis rolled to a 99–89 win. After the Grizzlies took a 55–39 lead into halftime, the Warriors had to claw back all night long and fell decisively short. Their shooting percentages were basically a carbon copy from Game 2, and Curry scored a miserable 23 points on 21 shots. The Grizzlies grabbed more rebounds, committed fewer turnovers, and even outassisted the Warriors. It was a complete breakdown in all facets for Golden State. The Memphis defense, led by Tony Allen, Zach Randolph, and Marc Gasol, was swarming and relentless. The Warriors were now, somewhat inexplicably, down in the series, and Kerr had to crack the Grizzlies' defensive code before the Warriors' hole deepened.

Assistant coach Ron Adams—the lead architect of the Warriors' defense and a man once described as "a caricature of the coach-as-intellectual, a thinker whose academic pursuits inform his hoops"—had an idea. Allen, even at 6-foot-4, was the Grizzlies' best one-on-one defender. Neutralize him—or better yet, figure a way to force him to the bench— and that would free up the Warriors' offense. Adams's suggestion to Kerr was to take 7-foot center Andrew Bogut and assign him to defend Allen. More specifically, Bogut would engage *only* should Allen come into the lane. As long as Allen stayed along the perimeter, he could take all the tantalizing, wide-open shots he wanted.

Why might this defensive cross-match work for Golden State? Because Allen had been terrible on jumpers all season (shooting just 32 percent) and was downright atrocious on threes in his playoff career—making barely 10 percent of such shots across more than 100 postseason games. If the Warriors were going to lose Game 4, they were going to force Allen's jumper to beat them, all while Bogut was free to help defend other players traversing the interior. The more shots Allen missed, the more pressure head coach Dave Joerger would feel to remove his best lockdown defender from the game. With Allen exiled, the Warriors could operate in space, get prime looks on threes, and have a better chance of beating the Grizzlies' bigs (Randolph and Gasol) down low.

The strategy worked to perfection. With Bogut barely noticing Allen on the perimeter, the Grizzlies wing launched up three three-pointers in the first quarter—more than he had in any game through the entire season—and clanked all of them. Meanwhile, with room to operate, Curry punched in 21 points and four assists as the Warriors led by 17 at halftime.

Allen was barely visible in the second half, missing all three of his shots early in the third quarter. Not five minutes had elapsed when Joerger benched him for almost the entire rest of the game, save the last 10 seconds of the third. In the end, despite 21 turnovers and getting outrebounded (49–45) and outassisted (24–22), the Warriors rolled to a 101–84 win. After combining for 12 threes on 52 attempts in the previous two games, Golden State sank 14 of 33 long-distance shots (42.4 percent). Allen's absence was obvious all around.

"You probably don't see the opposing team's center playing your starting shooting guard very often," said Joerger the next day, adding that Allen was experiencing hamstring pain and could potentially sit out Game 5 and beyond. Now, Allen had sat out the last two weeks of the regular season with a strained hammy but returned to play in every playoff game thus far and looked fine physically in Game 4, at least enough so that Joerger never mentioned any injury recurrence in his postgame comments with the media. Still, Allen was almost certainly hurt to some extent, because it's inconceivable the Grizzlies would've dispensed with the services of their best wing defender due to one little bit of defensive maneuvering by Golden State. Nevertheless, the sequence of events was odd and ultimately disadvantageous for Memphis.

Just before tipoff of Game 5 at Oracle Arena, Allen was officially scrapped from the lineup and the Warriors reeled off a 98–78 victory. The game's pace was agonizingly slow by Golden State standards—just 87 possessions on the night—but the Warriors adapted by raining down threes on Memphis, making 14 of 30 (46.7 percent) of them. When the

Grizzlies raced out to a double-digit advantage with less than two minutes remaining in the first quarter, the Warriors ripped an 11–0 run to
inch ahead, 26–25. The Grizzlies never led again.

Kerr called that first quarter–ending run a "miracle." He didn't like
seeing his team so anxious in the opening minutes. Regardless, the Warriors outscored the Grizzlies in every quarter. With a chance to close out
the series in Memphis, Kerr had just one message for the team. "You
don't mess around," he told them. "You get it *done*."

It wasn't another 20-point blowout, but the Warriors did what they
needed to in Game 6, finishing off the Grizzlies, 108–95, to advance
to their first Western Conference Finals since 1976. Allen was back in
Memphis's starting lineup but pulled before six minutes had elapsed,
his mobility clearly limited, although Bogut was once again ignoring
him on the perimeter, and in an elimination game, the Grizzlies simply
couldn't afford to play four-on-five on offense. Golden State's defense
allowed just 37 percent shooting and 25 percent on threes.

Curry's 32 points were more than enough for the Warriors. His 26
threes in the series? One more than all of the Grizzlies combined.

It was perhaps a more formidable challenge than expected, but the
Warriors headed home with three straight wins over an opponent that
forced them to adapt in real time. Kerr could see the series slipping away
and that something drastic was needed. And for an assistant like Ron
Adams to receive such public credit was remarkable. More tweaks and
adjustments would come in the near future, but a cohesive workplace
culture that encouraged all voices along the chain of command to speak
up had saved the Warriors' season.

Soon enough, it would do so again.

. . .

The basketball gods, in their infinite wisdom, sent the Houston Rockets
to the conference finals rather than the Los Angeles Clippers, who had

ridden the league's most efficient offense (112.4 points per 100 possessions) to 56 wins. The Clippers were tops in two-point field-goal percentage and third in both three-point efficiency and assists, all while committing the second-fewest turnovers. As ranked by True Shooting Percentage, which accounts for the value of three-pointers and free throws in its determination, the Warriors (57.1 percent) and Clippers (56.5 percent) were first and second overall. Had they been matched up against each other just a year after all the fireworks of the 2014 playoffs, the hype would've been borderline unbearable.

Both the Rockets and the Clippers finished the season with a 56-26 record. The Rockets earned the No. 2 seed by virtue of winning the Southwest Division, their first division title in 21 years. But it was the Clippers who raced out to a 3–1 series lead with one convincing win after another—by 16, 25, and then 33 points in Game 4. The Rockets— having already lost Patrick Beverley (a top-shelf defender) and Donatas Motiejunas (a low-post scoring threat) for the year and relying on the superlative play of MVP candidate James Harden—won the next two to force a decisive Game 7.

And despite heroics from Chris Paul (26 points and 10 assists), Blake Griffin (27 points and 11 rebounds), and DeAndre Jordan (16 points and 17 rebounds), the Clippers fell short, 113–100, when it mattered most. Harden was electric, with 31 points and eight assists, but the unlikely three-point shooting of Josh Smith (31.6 percent in the regular season) and Trevor Ariza (35 percent) torpedoed the Clippers' hopes. Ariza made 13 of 26 threes over the final three games of the series, including 6 of 12 in Game 7 and two in the pivotal fourth quarter. Down by 20 late, Los Angeles trimmed the lead to eight before Ariza's three with 56 seconds left sealed the win. Smith also shot 50 percent on threes (7-for-14) over those three Houston wins to close out the series, and the Clippers were again left wondering when they would advance to the first conference finals in franchise history.

But the Clippers' loss was the Warriors' gain, as Golden State was now matched up against a team whose health was far less than 100 percent and that had just expended a massive amount of energy to stave off a tough opponent in seven games. With only one full rest day, the Rockets traveled to Oakland while the Warriors had three full days at home to recharge after the grueling Memphis series.

And these Rockets were, in many ways, kindred spirits. As constructed by general manager Daryl Morey, the cofounder of the MIT Sloan Sports Analytics Conference, they were the living embodiment of the modern basketball analytics movement that preached shots at the rim (because they're high-percentage) and threes (because they're worth more than twos) above all other offensive actions. According to SportVU data, threes composed 39.4 percent of their regular-season shots compared to 30.9 percent for Golden State, and shots 10 feet or closer to the rim totaled 48.4 percent of all their field-goal attempts, whereas that number was 43.3 percent for the Warriors. That means nearly 88 percent of all their shots were either up close or deep for three—an astoundingly high percentage, but that was Morey's way.

While the Rockets resembled the Warriors on analytic steroids, where they fell short was in their efficiency. On the fourth-most three-point attempts per game, Golden State led the league in percentage (39.8 percent). And though Houston led all teams in three-point attempts, they were only 14th-best in converting them (34.8 percent). The Rockets were still making more threes per game than the Warriors based on volume (11.4 to 10.8), but more misses meant more chances for defensive rebounds—Golden State ranked No. 4 in that category—and more chances to score on the fast break, where, of course, the Warriors ranked No. 1 at 20.9 points per game.

Against a Rockets team that ranked eighth in Defensive Rating (103.4 points allowed per 100 possessions) but was shorthanded because of injuries and slammed with fatigue, the Warriors were confident about their chances.

Right away, it was clear the Rockets had not come to Oakland simply to get pushed around by the top seed. After a quarter and a half of Game 1, the visitors led by 16 points, but the Warriors reeled off a 25–6 run over the next six minutes—punctuated by a 20-foot Curry buzzer-beater—to command a three-point halftime lead.

Shaun Livingston scored 18 points that night, including 10 during the critical second-quarter comeback, which happened once Kerr went to a modified version of his "small-ball" lineup, giving Iguodala's usual spot to Livingston, who's an inch taller. "When we go small," the 6-foot-7 backup point guard said after the game, "it's not necessarily *small*." That alignment put Green at center, and neither the towering Dwight Howard (who had a wonky left knee by that point) nor his backup, Clint Capela, could contain him. Green finished with 13 points, 12 rebounds, and a team-high eight assists. Only the play of James Harden and Josh Smith (10 and eight points in the fourth quarter, respectively) kept the game close, but a late 7–0 run by Curry, who finished with 34 points, helped the Warriors pull away, 110–106.

Game 2 looked as if it should've been a Warriors blowout, especially to look blindly at select box score stats after the game: Golden State had 31 assists, tied Houston in rebounding (39), and shot 53.2 percent from the field. What would've concerned the Warriors was that Harden (38 points, 10 rebounds, nine assists) and Howard (19 points and 17 rebounds) connected on 21 of their 32 shots (65.6 percent).

But the Rockets' problem was that no one else contributed close to that kind of efficiency. Trevor Ariza and Josh Smith combined for 8-of-25 shooting and just 17 points. Golden State won the battle of the bench scoring, 20–15, while Bogut chipped in five blocks. That foundation of depth and defense made all the difference in this one. Curry scored his customary 33 points and Harden flubbed the final possession with the ball in his hands as the buzzer sounded on a thrilling 99–98 Warriors win. Whatever Houston tried, Golden State thwarted.

Golden State won a Game 3 laugher in Houston, 110–85, behind Curry's 40 points on 19 shots. The Rockets, who so often lived by the three-pointer, died by it on this night, missing 20 of 25 shots from deep. They could apply no defensive pressure, as the Warriors committed just one turnover in the first half, the first time they had one turnover or fewer in any half of basketball since December 2012. And with the win, they were now virtually assured of making the NBA Finals, since 116 teams in league history had gone up 3–0 in a best-of-seven series and not one had ever blown it. With just two losses across 13 postseason games, the Warriors were now sporting a better winning percentage in the playoffs (.846) than in the regular season (.817).

Naturally, they dropped Game 4. There figured to be one game in this series where the Rockets played to the level that had knocked off the Clippers in such stunning fashion, and this was it. Even as Curry, Thompson, and Green all topped 20 points, Harden blew up for 45 points on just 22 shots. Ariza and Smith combined for 37 points and the Rockets finally got the secondary contributions they needed for a 128–115 win.

More concerning for the Warriors than the loss was that Curry took a nasty spill in the second quarter with the Rockets ahead by 19. The MVP bit on a pump fake by Ariza and flew up in the air and then down on his head and neck. He returned to play most of the second, but it was a heart-stopping moment. Curry remained in the locker room after halftime with Bob Myers, the team's medical staff, and even his father, Dell, who had maneuvered his way from the stands. And though Curry returned to the floor midway through the third and played the final 18 minutes of the game, the Rockets' cushion proved insurmountable. After the game, Curry said it was the scariest fall he had ever experienced in a game but that he'd be fine: "You just want to gather yourself, regroup, and trust the process."

Now the series shifted to Oakland for what felt like a coronation.

. . .

It hadn't been five minutes since she left the Oracle Arena court that Riley Curry, all of two years old, went back into the Warriors' sparsely occupied family room. Most all other friends and loved ones were still on the court celebrating, taking selfies, and high-fiving with yellow confetti ribbon in their hair, but Riley had grandpa Dell, whose 16 years in the NBA educated him on how to exit a raucous court with ease, to help her back to quieter spaces.

As he carried his granddaughter, Dell gave Riley a kiss on the cheek and smiled. It was the face of not only a grandfather's love but the pride that comes with watching your eldest son lead a team that was now within reach of a championship.

Indeed, it was Steph, as always, who helped the Warriors secure a complete and clinical win, 104–90. Curry was everything the Warriors needed him to be, with 26 points, eight rebounds, six assists, and five steals—an inspiring performance after his nasty spill in Game 4. That, though, was a fast-fading memory. In the here and now, the Warriors were going to the NBA Finals.

"I always think of Pat Riley's great quote: 'When you're coaching in the NBA, there's winning and there's misery,'" Steve Kerr said after the win. "He's right. Winning feels like a relief more than anything most of the time. But to get to the Finals, first time in 40 years for the Warriors, it's more than relief. It's joy. Our players are feeling it."

Kerr was dead-on. The mood inside the locker room was gleeful and then focused. There was music, then there wasn't. Smiles were abundant but no one acted overly exuberant. Curry was stunned to see Harden's turnover total (12) when a reporter handed him the box score. Green plugged his Snapchat account. Everyone took their time getting dressed. The sense of accomplishment was palpable, insofar as one can assess such moods, but there was no doubt the ultimate goal remained unfinished. "Very proud and happy with how we played tonight," Curry said. "We've got to take a week off to get ready and get our minds right and our game plan right."

The Warriors had bested the Rockets in every phase. Dwight Howard played center for 42 minutes yet Golden State won the rebounding battle by a 59–39 margin. The Warriors had more fast-break points (26–20), points in the paint (50–34), and second-chance points (18–8). Andrew Bogut had one of his funkiest stat lines in years: zero points on 0-for-1 shooting, 14 rebounds, and two blocks in 19 minutes. Even Harrison Barnes, who was averaging only 10 points in the playoffs, finished with 24, his best output in two months.

The only cause for concern was when Klay Thompson, whose 15 first-half points led all scorers, was kneed in the head in the fourth quarter, when the Warriors two-guard faked a shot and Trevor Ariza bit hard. Despite feeling concussionlike symptoms after the game, he would recover in time for the Finals. Besides, Golden State now had several days to heal for the biggest test any of them had faced in their lives.

After the win, holding Riley in his arms once again as he had after Game 1, Curry gave his most reflective comments yet on how this team had moved from Mark Jackson to Steve Kerr.

"It's been a tough summer," Curry said. "It's been well-documented we came off a seven-game series against the Clippers and it was a shock to have a coaching change, but I assessed it as kind of two separate decisions. I didn't agree with the first one, but you've got to make the right hire, and I think they did that. Obviously, they did that. We hit the ground running in training camp with his philosophy of ball movement, player movement, obviously keeping the defense that we've established the last two years the same and taking it to another level. [Kerr] is a humble guy that understands he took over a talented team, and he's very fortunate that we've had some experiences under our belt and we can—we're not rebuilding or anything, so we're poised to have a great season, and I think we've exceeded a lot of people's expectations.

"But this is something that, as players, we've been eyeing, and it's nice to have ourselves where we are: four wins away from a championship."

All they had to do was take down the best basketball player in the world.

.  .  .

The Cleveland Cavaliers, as they stood on the morning of June 4, 2015, were a force for any team to reckon with, no matter how good they thought they were. LeBron James was playing in his fifth consecutive Finals and had been the Cavs' shining star through six weeks of playoff hoops, averaging 27.6 points, 10.6 rebounds, 8.3 assists, 1.8 steals, and 1.3 blocks over 14 games.

But that production had come at a price, as James was launching up 25 shots per game, six more than in the regular season, and making just 42.8 percent, a decrease of six percentage points. His three-point shooting, too, had cratered, falling from 35.4 to 17.6 percent. He was shouldering a mammoth load, but advancing this deep into the playoffs was contingent on winning games by any means necessary. If that meant chucking up 40 shots to get 35 points and you outscored the other team by one, so be it.

All season long, Kyrie Irving and Kevin Love, his fellow musketeers, both three-time All-Stars, were ready to follow James's example. Aside from missing two games in the Eastern Conference Finals with a tendinitis flare-up in his knee, Irving had been spectacular through three rounds, averaging 18.7 points and a whopping 48.1 percent on threes. Love, meanwhile, had been knocked out for the season back in the first round against Boston, when his left shoulder was wrenched from its socket by Celtics center Kelly Olynyk as the two tussled for a loose ball. Three days later, Love had surgery that would sideline him for at least four months. He'd struggled mightily in his first season in Cleveland and his numbers across the board fell precipitously, but Love looked better in those first three games against Boston—all wins for the Cavs—as he averaged 18 points, nine boards, and 47 percent on threes.

And yet, without their starting power forward, the Cavs soldiered on through a slate of would-be contenders. After sweeping Boston, they knocked off Chicago in six games before sweeping the 60-win, top-seeded Atlanta Hawks in a dominant display of force. In those four games alone, James fell a fraction of an assist shy of averaging a triple-double: 30.3 points, 11 rebounds, 9.3 assists. It had been 51 years since the city of Cleveland had won any kind of professional sports championship, and James was playing at a level where you believed anything was possible.

Beat Golden State four times out of seven? Unlikely, especially without Love, but surely possible.

Meanwhile, the Warriors used the rest days following the Western Conference Finals to heal up after their accumulation of bumps and bruises. Between Curry falling on his head in Game 4 and Thompson getting a knee to the noggin in Game 5—both plays courtesy of Houston's Trevor Ariza—Golden State had its share of injury scares, but was no worse for wear as the Finals approached. As someone who could boast five fingers' worth of championship rings, Kerr knew how to get his team focused and prepared. There wasn't much he could do to quell their nervousness, their frenetic anticipation of a new experience, but the trick was to keep them grounded in the moment, to not let them get too far ahead with their thoughts and actions. You don't think about Game 2 until you win Game 1, and so on. Kerr told stories from his title-winning days in Chicago and San Antonio, and he asked Luke

Walton to share a few from the two years he won titles with the Lakers. "Once you get out on the floor, you just start playing, and everything returns to normal," Kerr said the day before Game 1. "It's still just a basketball game, but you've got to get to that point, and the best way to do that is to try to ignore the chaos as much as you can." As he told his team in the locker room just moments before tipoff, "When we go out there, we're gonna be loose. We're gonna let it fly. We're gonna have some fun. We've earned this trip and every second of this should be enjoyable."

With the Cavs in their first Finals in eight years and the Warriors a couple of generations removed from their previous trip, both teams looked eager to make a good showing early in Game 1.

The Cavs raced out to a 14-point lead that the Warriors were able to shave to three by halftime. In the waning seconds of the third quarter, Iguodala stole the ball from James and raced the other way for a seam to tie the game, 73–73, heading to the fourth. "He's not stronger than LeBron," Kerr said after the game, "but he is *very* strong. He may not have the same weight—you know, he's giving up 50 pounds or so—but Andre knows what he's doing." Iguodala later said that the adrenaline of guarding James in the Finals was so pressure-filled that you couldn't absorb it. It reminded him of the kind of carefree balling a child might enjoy. "When you get into a flow, as a kid, you play in socks," he said. "You play in socks all the time in your room, so you go back to those days and just playing ball."

And when Curry, who finished with a team-high 26 points, pulled up from 20 feet and coolly sank a jumper with 53 seconds left to give Golden State a 98–96 lead, it looked as if that would be enough. But Timofey Mozgov's two free throws with 32 seconds left tied the game up. At the other end, Curry had his driving layup blocked from behind by Kyrie Irving. Both James and Iman Shumpert had chances in the final six seconds to win the game but neither converted.

Cleveland's fortunes took an irrevocable nosedive with 2:20 left in the overtime as Irving, who not only had 23 points and six assists but defended Curry marvelously all night, slipped while driving to the rim and awkwardly twisted the same left knee that had forced him to sit out a couple of conference finals games against Atlanta. The Warriors, already up by four, came down the court and Barnes sank a left-corner three to push the lead to seven. Irving limped off to the locker room, the Cavs didn't score *at all* until there was less than 10 seconds to play, and the Warriors secured a 108–100 win.

An MRI the next morning confirmed that Irving had a fractured kneecap. His playoffs were over. With him and Love out, Cleveland was without its second- and third-best players for the remainder of the Finals. In Irving's stead, the new starter was Matthew Dellavedova, an Australian import who was in his second NBA season and had played college ball in the Bay Area, 10 miles east of Oakland at St. Mary's. It meant a precipitous dropoff from Irving's production—the backup averaged just five points and three assists in the regular season—but the Cavs had no choice. That Dellavedova had also developed a reputation as something of a dirty player due to a couple of high-profile incidents in the Eastern Conference Finals was also something Coach Blatt had to live with.

Even with Irving playing most of Game 1, the Warriors were able to execute their game plan. The Cavs had held their playoff opponents to just 28.1 percent on threes, but Kerr's squad nailed 10 of 27 (37 percent) from long range. They outrebounded Cleveland, 48–45, and committed only 12 turnovers. Their offense wasn't dynamic—just 24 assists on 39 shots in 53 minutes—but a Finals win was a Finals win. James finished with 44 points but needed 38 shots to get there; Golden State would take that every time.

Still, overtime games often play out as toss-ups, and in Game 2, the coin flipped the other way. This time, the Cavs were in control late, up by 11 with 3:15 to go, until the Warriors started clawing back. With 10 seconds left, Curry, who had missed 14 of 18 shots on the night to that point, was able to split LeBron James and Tristan Thompson at the top of the key and drive for an uncontested finger roll to tie the game at 87 and force another overtime ending.

But Curry's miserable night only continued in the extra frame, as he missed all four shot attempts, the final one coming with seven seconds left and the Warriors down by one. The 19-footer might've won the game but—due to Dellavedova's waving hands—the shot airballed right into James's arms beyond the basket.

Cleveland prevailed, 95–93, as LeBron James's triple-double of 39 points, 16 rebounds, and 11 assists—all other Cavs tallied three assists *total*—was just enough. "It's not cute at all," James said of Cleveland's slow-paced play. "If you're looking for us to play sexy, cute basketball, then that's not us. That's not us right now. Everything is tough. . . . And for us to win a Finals game shooting 32 percent from the field, it's just a testament of how gritty we can be."

Klay Thompson led the Warriors with 34 points, albeit on an in-efficient 28 shots. Curry missed 13 of 15 three-point attempts, more than any player had ever missed in an NBA Finals contest, breaking John Starks's record of 11 set during Game 7 in 1994. "Sometimes the ball doesn't bounce your way," Kerr said of his struggling superstar. "It doesn't go in, it's fine. You keep playing. I've seen it with everybody. I've seen it with Michael Jordan, Tim Duncan. It doesn't matter who you are. Nobody is immune from a tough night." Kerr himself only had to think back to the 1988 Final Four—when 10 of his own threes didn't fall versus Oklahoma—but he was certain Curry's shot would return.

The problem was that few other Warriors were stepping up; the team had little focus and no energy. In Game 3 at Cleveland—for which Joe Lacob had the entire Warriors front office staff flown out—Golden State scored just 55 points through three quarters and trailed by 17 headed to the fourth. Curry then blew up for 17 points in the final frame, making the final margin much closer than it seemed. "I've never seen someone that can shoot the ball off the dribble like himself, ever," said James after the game.

As clutch as Curry was by game's end, James was scintillating from start to finish. His 40 points, 12 rebounds, and eight assists were the ingredients of utter dominance, and his two steals off Curry in the final minute helped secure the 96–91 win.

The Warriors had been down 2–1 to Memphis in the conference semifinals, but this was a far more pressing proposition. The Cavs were dominating the pace and James was operating on a whole other plane of basketball existence. Though barely shooting 40 percent from the field, James was averaging 41 points, 12 rebounds, and eight assists through three Finals games. He was making threes at a 35 percent clip and drawing contact at will, taking 13.3 free throws per game. (As a team, the Warriors were averaging 19.7 free throws against the Cavs.)

Golden State's poor shooting was not helping any—Harrison Barnes's 0-for-8 goose egg in Game 3 was one example—and would likely improve, given enough time, but they were doomed if they couldn't slow James down.

When asked to assess the pressure on his team on a scale from 1 to 10, Kerr smiled. "The pressure is like a 5.13," he said. "I don't know. We're in the NBA Finals. There's pressure for everybody."

"You get to write the superlatives," he added, "and we get to try to figure out how to slow them down."

. . .

The night before Game 4, Nick U'Ren was in his hotel room in downtown Cleveland, scrolling through old video clips, when he found a way to save Golden State's season.

LeBron James's transcendent play had been effective through three games not just in the counting stats he was putting up but in the way the Cavs' offense had taken the Warriors' defense out of its rhythm. The game ground to a halt whenever Blatt's team fed James for one post-up and iso after another. The Warriors had little chance to force turnovers, to get out in transition, and score on the fast break, but this series was not going to be won by whoever gathered the most rebounds or accumulated more assists.

What mattered more than anything was stopping LeBron James.

And that's why U'Ren was looking at video. Ever since he graduated in 2009 from the University of San Diego, where he'd been the men's basketball team manager, and was hired in Phoenix by Kerr (then the Suns' general manager) as an intern, U'Ren had made his NBA life about video. Back then, before SportVU took the NBA by storm, the video tagging process was painstaking and meticulous. U'Ren had to laboriously separate game footage—offense here, defense there—and manually tag all of the relevant actions occurring in the video. Only then was it usable for the front office or coaching staff.

Before he left as GM, Kerr ensured that U'Ren was put on the staff full-time. He was still with the Suns four years later when Kerr landed in Oakland, and the new Warriors coach hired U'Ren as a special assistant. He'd handle video, of course, but also things like Kerr's daily schedule and music playlists for practice. He'd work with Bruce Fraser during Curry's end-of-practice drills. Kerr liked having positive people around who worked hard but could also laugh and not take everything seriously. Kerr half-jokingly dubbed U'Ren his "chief of staff" and encouraged him to speak up if he felt he could contribute.

Now, here was U'Ren scanning video of the 2014 Finals, when Kerr's mentor, San Antonio coach Gregg Popovich, had made a startling lineup switch that changed his own team's fortunes. With the series tied at a game apiece, Popovich sensed his team needed to get back to basics: passing, defense, and just being smarter. He moved center Tiago Splitter, who had started 50 regular-season games and 18 of 20 in the playoffs, to the bench in favor of 32-year-old journeyman Boris Diaw, who had started just 24 games and none in the postseason. The Spurs won the next three games by 19, 21, and 17 points to win yet another championship. James's numbers across the board went down. Diaw nearly posted a triple-double in Game 4 and became a folk hero after the series. Popovich dubbed the strategy "medium ball." Splitter had three inches on the 6-foot-8 Diaw, but the Spurs' passing and defense kicked up to another level. James said then it was playing against "four point guards basically on the floor at once."

But the Warriors' situation—being down by a game instead of evened up—was worse, and what U'Ren proposed in his late-night call to assistant coach Luke Walton was far more drastic than swapping one big for another. He thought Kerr should consider benching 7-foot center Andrew Bogut in favor of starting 6-foot-6 wing Andre Iguodala. Bumping Bogut to the second unit might mean taking a hit on grabbing rebounds and protecting the rim, but Iguodala was an elite defender who could shadow James's every move. That meant the 6-foot-7 Draymond Green would act as the de facto center and defend Timofey Mozgov while 6-foot-8 Harrison Barnes would draw power forward Tristan Thompson. Walton was on board and wanted Kerr to think it over as soon as he awoke. He texted him at 3:00 a.m.

The next morning, over breakfast, the tactic was debated inside and out. Of course, it wasn't a lineup that was entirely foreign to the Warriors. During the regular season, this lineup of Curry-Thompson-Barnes-Iguodala-Green had played together for 102 minutes spread out over 37 games. It was Kerr's fifth-most-used lineup of the season and had outscored opponents by 21.8 points per 100 possessions, an excellent Net Rating in any regard but far from Golden State's most efficient five-man assemblage. And for this lineup to work, Iguodala's defense on James needed to be heroic.

Kerr gave the move his blessing. Beyond the belief that Iguodala could keep James in check, the coach thought it would help space the floor, open up passing lanes, maybe light a spark under a team that had looked downright gloomy at times. Kerr wouldn't fess up to the change when asked about any lineup tweaks before the game. It was only a few minutes before tipoff, when league rules mandate the starting lineups be submitted, that the move was made public. Golden State's entire year rested on this decision. "If this doesn't work, it's your fault," Kerr joked with U'Ren before the game. "And if it works, I'm taking the credit."

The Cavs jumped out to a 16–9 lead. Tristan Thompson had four rebounds in less than five minutes. U'Ren sat nervously behind the Warriors bench, worried not so much that he might look as if that the team didn't seem to be responding. It was then that assistant coach Chris DeMarco leaned over and told him not to worry. The Warriors were getting good looks at the rim and shots that weren't falling now soon would.

He was right. Golden State ended the quarter up by seven, a lead that stretched to 12 by halftime. James had 10 points in the first half on 4-of-12 shooting. He came alive in the third quarter, scoring 10 points on 3-of-8 shooting, but Iguodala held him without a point in the fourth. He finished with 20 points while Iguodala scored a season-high 22, Bogut played less than three minutes on the night, and the Warriors won in a rout, 103–82.

Even though U'Ren's "small-ball" lineup configuration didn't put up outrageously good numbers that night—according to the advanced stats, they played the Cavs essentially even during 14 minutes on the court—the benefits were real. Golden State, as a whole, played far better defense overall—Cleveland had its lowest-scoring game of the playoffs—and now the series had swung in its favor. The Warriors' seven turnovers were their fewest in any game of the regular season or playoffs. The psychological effect of seeing Iguodala outplay James had lifted them from their collective funk. "It's just a street fight," Draymond Green said.

"Nobody's doing anything dirty, but they're battling and we're battling, and that's why this series is so exciting."

The Warriors were now going home for Game 5. All they had to do was win the remaining games at Oracle Arena and the championship would be theirs.

After the game, Kerr quasi-apologized to the media for lying to them before the game about starting Bogut. "I don't think they hand you the trophy based on morality. They give it to you if you win," he said. "So sorry about that." He also gave U'Ren full credit for suggesting the move. "He's a major part of our staff, and I don't care where an idea comes from," Kerr said before Game 5, as if speaking from an employee handbook penned by Joe Lacob himself. "Doesn't matter wherever the idea comes from. If it's a good one, then we'll use it."

. . .

Steve Kerr stuck with Andre Iguodala in the starting lineup going forward because you don't fix what isn't broken. James's play did pick up after his Game 4 debacle, as his 40 points, 14 boards, and 11 assists in Game 5 marked his third triple-double of the playoffs. Nearly a third of Cleveland's ball touches on the night went through James's mammoth hands, yet he committed only two turnovers.

But the Warriors were operating at peak performance. Curry played his best game since the conference finals, scoring 37 points on just 23 shots. After a lockdown third quarter in which Cleveland scored only 17 points, Golden State coasted to a 104–91 win to take a 3–2 lead in the series. Iguodala had 14 points, eight boards, and seven assists. Bogut? He never got into the game. Cleveland's control of the series—looking so decisive less than a week earlier—was long gone.

The final dagger came when Curry knocked down a silly, spectacular three with 2:46 left to put the Warriors up by 10. Shadowed by Dellavedova, Curry set up the shot with a series of dribbles and crossovers that appeared possible only by polarized magnets propelling the ball away with such a forceful cadence. It was a vicious sleight of hand, fully indicative of the high level of hoops that this series, in its finest moments, had come to typify. Curry would later deem that shot his personal favorite of his career.

After the game, Curry was asked if that three might live on as some kind of signature moment in which this series took a decisive turn. He wouldn't take the bait. As Curry said, "I'll probably have a better answer for that question after we win the championship."

Not *if* the Warriors win the title. *After*.

The series shifted to Cleveland for Game 6, and this time it was Golden State that raced out to an early lead. Nine points from Curry had them up by 13 after the first quarter, but the Cavs, behind 11 points from James, cut the Golden State lead to two at halftime. The Warriors won the third quarter, 28–18, thanks to eight points from, of all people, Festus Ezeli. That unlikely contribution pushed the lead to 12 with just 12 minutes to go.

Cleveland, at the brink of ultimate defeat, emptied its tank in the fourth quarter. James threw up 12 shots and scored 10 points, even while missing all four three-point attempts. J. R. Smith came off the bench to score 15 in the fourth, and it was his fourth and final three of the night that cut the Warriors' lead to four with just 33 seconds to go, but free throws from Curry and Iguodala soon iced the game. The Cavs missed a trio of threes in the waning seconds and time ticked down. Curry grabbed the final rebound and threw the ball high in the air. Steve Kerr met David Blatt at midcourt to shake hands while his players screamed and jumped and held each other in triumph.

After 40 long years, the Golden State Warriors were champions again.

For both his defense on James and his timely offensive outbursts, Iguodala was named Finals MVP. The Cavs' strategy in Game 6 was to envelop Curry and Thompson and force players like Iguodala to beat them. Well, he scored 25 points, dished out five assists, and was, by series' end, the third-highest scorer in the Finals with 16.3 points a night. For the player who accepted a backup role after starting every game his entire career, the award was the ultimate validation. "I'm not even thinking about anything. My mind's just blank," he said. "This has been a long ride."

For Klay Thompson, the son of a former No. 1 overall pick who'd won multiple titles, the sharpshooter with the cowboy-cool demeanor, the moment was almost too much. "It just feels good to say we're the best team in the world," he said. "It's been a collective effort and we're going to enjoy it tonight, man. We deserve to."

For Draymond Green, the second-rounder whose game transcended traditional NBA labels, the night was about completing an improbable journey that started in Saginaw, Michigan. When the Warriors needed him to deliver, Green put up 16 points, 11 rebounds, and 10 assists for his first career playoff triple-double. "A lot of people said I could never play in this league. Too slow, too small, can't shoot well enough, can't defend nobody. What does he do well? He doesn't have a skill," he said. "I've got heart, and that's what stands out. It was just one of those moments where it's like I've always been doubted my entire life. . . . They can still say, oh, he's too small, he's too this, he's too that. They can never take this away from me."

For Shaun Livingston, a title meant a career that had finally come full circle. All the greatness predicted of him coming out of high school never came to pass, but he was now forever a champion. "To be here as a world champion with my brothers, man, it's a loss for words," he said. "It's been such a long journey. I've had two careers, really. It felt like two lives that I lived. To be here now as a world champion, it's the greatest feeling in the world. It makes the journey worth it."

For veterans like Leandro Barbosa, Marreese Speights, Andrew

Bogut, and David Lee, all staring at the downward slope of their professional lives, the celebration was a lifelong release from years spent chasing an elusive goal. For younger players like Harrison Barnes and Festus Ezeli—both from that loaded 2012 draft class that also produced Green—the win meant a career free of the kinds of pressures that snowball over time without a ring on your finger.

For Bob Myers, the night meant vindication for his move to the front office, a hiring that once turned heads across the industry. He brought a different experience to the job and learned as he went, but the moves he made built a basketball powerhouse for a new era. It was little surprise that, during the playoffs, Myers was named by the NBA as the 2015 Executive of the Year. And the Warriors' investment in analytics and attention to rest and conditioning had paid off, as an ESPN study later concluded the Warriors had lost the fewest minutes to injury of any team in the league that year.

For Steve Kerr, the victory was the culmination of a life sown with both the greatest successes and the lowest failures, and now he was the first coach since Pat Riley in 1982 to win a championship in his debut season on the bench. He had also just coached the first champion to ever lead the NBA in pace, a clear sign of how the Warriors were fundamentally different from any of their peers.

For years, Kerr put off coaching until his three kids were older, until he was ready, until the perfect opportunity with the right people came along. It had been 12 years since he advanced this far in the playoffs, and for all his talk about experience, the grind still took its toll, the bulb of pain in his back a nascent sign of troubles to come. "I almost forgot just how grueling the stretch is," he said. "I mean, two straight months of emotional stress and physical stress. Just the roller-coaster ride that you're on. There are days when you think, boy, I don't know if this is going to happen."

In the moment, Kerr could appreciate that the Warriors benefited from the defending champion Spurs' getting knocked out in the first round and from injuries to later opponents such as Houston and Cleveland. "Things went our way, but we took advantage of that," Kerr added. "Every year that's the case: A team falls, a team soars, there's injuries, bounce of the ball, whatever. In the end, none of it matters. The only thing that matters is that we got the job done." For Kerr, getting to celebrate this moment with not just his wife but his three kids—none of whom were even teenagers yet as of his last title with San Antonio—meant the world to him.

For Stephen Curry, the promise of a career built in his father's shadow had, at last, been fulfilled. With 98 threes in 21 games, Curry set the all-time record for most threes in a single playoffs, smashing the old mark of 58 set by Indiana's Reggie Miller in 2000. Curry was now an MVP, regarded as one of the most devastating shooters in NBA history, and, for all time, a champion. He was the longest-tenured Warrior, the lone survivor of the Chris Cohan regime. A few minutes after the final horn, he kissed and hugged Ayesha and Riley out on the court, the realization of what had transpired slowly starting to sink in.

"I think we can actually appreciate what we were able to do this year from start to finish," Curry said. "It's hard in the moment to really understood what 67 wins means in the grand scheme of the history of the NBA, how hard that is, but then also to cap that off with a championship playoff run. So we'll appreciate, I think, that whole journey a lot more now, be able to reflect. I think we definitely are a great team and a team that should go down in history as one of the best teams from top to bottom. We have a lot of things to be proud of this season.

"I'm just so happy, man. God is great."

. . .

They started arriving at 3:00 a.m.

From Pacifica to Petaluma, from San Jose to Sonoma, and everywhere in between throughout the Bay Area, a half-million people, according to the police, crowded into downtown Oakland on a Friday morning to kick off a celebration 40 years in the making. They came to salute the Warriors for completing one of the most historically dominant seasons in NBA history. They came to, once and for all, exorcise the demons bestowed by past ownership. They came to remember the beloved Golden State stars who never got this far: Chris Mullin, Mitch Richmond, Jason Richardson, Tim Hardaway, Baron Davis, and dozens more. They came to thank Stephen Curry for sticking around. They came to thank Joe Lacob and his ownership group, who made good on his promise to turn the organization around within five years.

And it did take only five years—rather, four years, seven months, and one day, as Lacob reminded the crowd—to deliver a once-improbable championship.

Everyone got their turn at the podium that day in the glaring Oakland sun. The star was Kerr, who again played the comedian role he'd perfected in 1997 when he took credit for "bailing out" Michael Jordan with the game-winning shot. This time around, Kerr recounted how he'd taken the job just nine months earlier and worried about all he'd have to improve upon in such a short time: "Not much talent. Very little shooting. Not much defense. The versatility was suspect. More than anything, just shaky character. I mean, look at these guys." He then ran through the litany of everything the Warriors did so well, the winking and nodding practically visible from Concord. His parting words, to a wave of laughter: "So, in nine months, I did all that, so thanks!"

But for everyone who spoke that afternoon, three days after the dream had been made real, the moment may have meant the most to Joe Lacob. With Lake Merritt gleaming in the distance and Warriors fans hanging on his every word, he got up and spoke for 10 minutes. The chorus of boos born on March 19, 2012, that nearly derailed his time as owner before it began in earnest felt like decades ago. He thanked everyone up and down the organization. He thanked the fans—"our greatest asset!"—for sticking through the lean times and the players for representing the organization so well. He last thanked his fiancée, Nicole Curran, for putting up with the "insanity" that comes with running a professional team.

Then, as if to magnify the sheer importance of it all, Lacob parted with both a proclamation and a promise.

"*This . . . was . . . no . . . accident.* Nothing about this was an accident."

He paused to look down at his notes before exiting.

"And it will *not* be an accident when we do it again!"

# 9 ★ ★ ★ ★ ★ ★ ★

## LEVEL UP

### The 2015–16 season

Any normal Warriors offseason would be rife with some sort of drama or controversy or injury rehabilitation that would keep fans (and some executives) tense through the summer and fall.

But Golden State had finally won the championship that had long eluded the organization. The Warriors were on top of the basketball world for the first time in four decades.

Now what?

What usually happens when a team wins a title—and this is applicable to almost any major professional sport, whether it's baseball here or soccer in England—is that the team invariably fractures in some way, not through ego (although that *can* happen) but through simple economics. When you win, the value of your best players skyrockets. And if one of your stars happens to be heading into free agency, you can all but bid him good-bye.

But the Warriors lucked out in this regard. All of their core players were already under contract at least through the 2015–16 season. David Lee, who had a season left on that July 2010 deal approved by a Lacob ownership group still under wraps, was traded to Boston for a couple of spare parts in Chris Babb and Gerald Wallace, who was traded three weeks later for backup Jason Thompson. They drafted freshman Kevon Looney, a gifted but unpolished power forward out of UCLA, with their first-round pick. They re-signed Leandro Barbosa and brought in third-year shooting guard Ian Clark, both on one-year deals. They gave former Chicago Bulls star Ben Gordon a look but waived him two weeks into training camp. Except for a couple of far-end bench spots, this would be the same Warriors team that had just won it all.

One issue, though, was quite pressing. Draymond Green was now a free agent. His fellow 2012 draft class members, Harrison Barnes and Festus Ezeli, were each first-round picks and thus signed four-year rookie deals, so they had one season to go before free agency. (The team did offer each player an extension before the 2015–16 season; each rejected their respective offer.) But as a second-round pick, Green had signed only a three-year deal back in 2012. The Warriors could still match any offer made to him, but Green was officially on the market.

From the start, both sides wanted to hammer out a deal that was mutually beneficial. Considering his low draft position along with an unexpectedly meteoric development, Green had been comically underpaid through his first three seasons in the league. In fact, he had yet to even crack $1 million in salary in a given year. On the day the Warriors won the championship, Green was the 12th-highest-paid player on the roster.

Now, Myers could make him one of the highest-paid power forwards in the league. Under the rules of the collective bargaining agreement, the most Golden State could offer him in a max deal was five years at around $93 million. The maximum Green could get from another club was four years at $69 million. How much the Warriors would ultimately pay Green had become something of a running joke inside team headquarters and especially once the team won the title. There was little concern that a deal would be reached; the open question was, for how much?

In the end, the two sides agreed to a deal that worked out well for both team and player. At five years and $82 million, Green would make $14.3 million in his first year and command the second-highest salary on the team. Taking a haircut of around $11 million gave the Warriors the kind of financial flexibility that would keep them from going too far into the luxury tax and allow them a measure of wiggle room to keep improving the roster going forward.

After a career year, Golden State's emotional leader was finally getting a salary commensurate with his talents, and the team would have more space when the cap jumped the following summer. When Green video-called his mother to tell her the news, Mary Babers-Green put her hands over her face and immediately started crying.

The Warriors' roster was now complete. They were, for the most part, the same collection of players that had trounced the league from beginning to end, except now they were a year more experienced and comfortable in Steve Kerr's offense. In fact, they brought in another familiar face to help in that pursuit. Steve Nash, the two-time MVP who had played for Kerr in Phoenix, was hired as a player development consultant. Curry had played at Nash's summer camp when he was at Davidson and had pumped him for info about playing like an NBA-level point guard back at a time when he was just getting fully acclimated to the position. Nash also knew about Bay Area basketball culture, having been a college star at Santa Clara University, located in Silicon Valley. Back then, as Netscape Navigator was revolutionizing the tech world, Nash would navigate the Santa Clara campus by dribbling a basketball in between classes to help him refine his ball-handling. (A year later, he switched to dribbling a tennis ball; the basketball just wasn't challenging enough.) And 10 years before Curry excelled at Davidson, Nash himself was an undersized point guard—6-foot-3, same height as Curry—who was lethal with a pass or three-point shot but couldn't garner the respect reserved for players in the elite conferences. Though he lived in Los Angeles, Nash would come north periodically to attend practices and offer insights as only one of the best players of the last two decades could.

Curry, for his part, once again didn't have to spend all summer rehabbing. Brandon Payne, approaching his fourth year as Curry's personal trainer, moved to Emeryville for the summer (on Curry's dime) so the MVP could maximize workout time. He started working out with a strobe light apparatus where you had to execute dribbling drills while flicking your hand over designated sensors that would light up at random, like playing a new-age version of the old Simon handheld light-up game. At Payne's urging, Curry also started doing drills while wearing Eclipse goggles that acted as a constantly shifting shutter on his eyes, shapes getting sharp then cloudy with all kinds of peripheral movement in between. "Stroboscopic sensory training," it's called. Think of it as resistance training for both the eyes and reflexes, akin to a football player stretching with a Lycra band or a baseball player swinging a bat in the on-deck circle with a weighted doughnut. These are exercises that exacerbate and complicate normal athletic acts so that, when you remove those hindrances, the move becomes easier, muscle memory is more confident, and you're less affected by outside stimuli. It makes the normal feel easier, more routine.

And with the arrival of Lachlan Penfold, a progressive sports science expert from Australia who was tapped to replace the departed Keke Lyles as head of physical performance, the team was diving headlong into new tech initiatives more than ever before. Some Warriors started doing sessions in saltwater-infused sensory deprivation pods that could mimic weightlessness and help with relaxation, recovery, and maybe even visualization. As Curry told ESPN, "It's just me and my thoughts for an hour, playing Russian roulette of the mind." The team also partnered with a San Francisco company called Halo Neuroscience, which made headphones that delivered slight electrical current into the wearer's head to put, according to the company's website, "the brain's motor cortex in a temporary state of hyper-learning that lasts for an hour." That could theoretically help with everything from dexterity to lower-body strength to explosiveness. There was little the Warriors wouldn't consider trying.

It seemed, at least according to the predictions markets, that they would need every advantage to repeat as champs. As the season was ready to tip off, Cleveland, which had fallen in the Finals just four months earlier, was the odds-on favorite to win it all—a 28 percent chance, according to the website FiveThirtyEight. Golden State, at 18 percent, was a distant second.

But that was speculation for months down the road. For the moment, with opening night against New Orleans approaching, the Warriors seemed to have everything they needed for a run at back-to-back titles.

Everything, that is, except for their head coach.

. . .

The rigors of a long NBA season can take their toll on anyone. When injuries happen to players—think of Kyrie Irving's broken kneecap from Game 1 of the Finals—it's all too obvious, but the grind invariably affects other related parties, including coaches. So it was that Steve Kerr ruptured a disk in his back during the Finals and finally underwent surgery in late July. The pain had become too much. He couldn't do yoga or play golf. And while it meant scuttling much of his remaining summer plans, the procedure would heal Kerr in time for training camp.

Five weeks later, Kerr's health was deteriorating fast. The surgery had caused a spinal fluid leak and, with it, a flood of agonizing pain. Headaches, dizziness, irritability—this was not how he planned to spend the months after his first title as coach. An early September surgery fixed the leak but the pain persisted, so much so that it consumed his thoughts. Just a couple of days into training camp, Kerr knew that basketball couldn't command his necessary attention.

In early October, a month after Kerr's second surgery, the Warriors announced he would take an indefinite leave of absence. "We don't anticipate the recovery process will be long term," Bob Myers said, "but as of today, we don't know the exact time frame. We'll evaluate his progress daily."

Kerr said he would remain as involved as his health permitted—attending practices and film sessions and such—but he wouldn't return to the sidelines until the pain either had dissipated or was sufficiently manageable. "At this point," he told the media, "I simply want to get healthy and back to my normal daily routine on and off the court."

Alvin Gentry had been Kerr's top assistant in his first season in Oakland, but the New Orleans Pelicans lured him south to be their head coach. Kerr opted not to hire a replacement during the summer, so Luke Walton, all of 35 years old and with one season of NBA coaching experience on his resume, was elevated to interim head coach for as long as Kerr was away. Walton would still have Ron Adams, Jarron Collins, and Bruce Fraser to collaborate with on the sidelines during games, and Kerr would still be around Oracle before games and during halftime.

But once that ball was tipped to start the game, Walton—just a couple of years removed from his own NBA career—was in charge.

His youthful enthusiasm drove him in those early weeks on the bench. Like Kerr, he helped run plays in practice but would engage almost as if he was still one of the guys. (He particularly enjoyed trash-talking Draymond Green, knowing that it would bring out the best in him come game time.) Walton's style wasn't a dramatic departure from Kerr's, but his offensive approach allowed for more freelancing. The occasional bout of anxiety aside, Walton grew more confident as the season progressed and was masterful in keeping the players engaged.

And did the Warriors ever thrive. They won their first 24 games of the season, a feat no NBA team had ever accomplished. Tacking on wins from the final four regular-season games from a season ago, the 28-game win streak was the second-longest in league history, behind only what the 1971–72 Lakers accomplished. On Halloween night 1971 in Los Angeles, the Lakers, despite 38 points from Gail Goodrich, fell to Golden State by just four points. They then won their next 33 games, including a trio of victories over the Warriors. The Lakers didn't lose for a 65-day stretch, though thanks to the passage of time from one season to the next, the Warriors' win streak technically lived on for 249 days.

And even after their first defeat—a deflating effort in Milwaukee that capped off a seven-game road trip and followed a double-overtime win in Boston the night before—the Warriors still kept winning. They pushed their record to 29-1, then 36-2, then 39-4 after a Midwest road trip that included a 34-point thrashing in Cleveland followed by a 31-point win in Chicago before returning home. Golden State had won all 19 home games at Oracle Arena, with each one morphing into a joyous 20,000-person party before long. Nicole Curran, Joe Lacob's fiancée, would lead the players' wives and girlfriends in postgame tequila shots just off the court at the Bridge Club. It felt as if the Warriors had a legitimate shot to win all 41 regular-season home games, which no team had ever done.

For nearly three months, Golden State had played the most dominant stretch of team basketball since the Chicago Bulls, led by Michael Jordan at the peak of his powers, won 72 games against only 10 losses over the 1995–96 season. For two decades, that Bulls team (which also boasted backup point guard Steve Kerr) had been regarded as the best team in NBA history.

The Warriors were coming for that throne.

That they were doing this without their head coach on the sidelines to call plays, make substitutions, and devise strategy in real time says much about the groundwork Kerr had laid in just one season, about the

competence of his coaching staff and that they could keep the team playing so well in his stead, about the players and their ability to internalize
what Kerr had taught them and to execute almost as if on instinct.

Curry's first half of the season was spellbinding, his numbers unlike
anything he'd ever accumulated. After 30 games, he had already made
140 three-pointers and was essentially halfway to his single-season
record of 286. He was averaging 30 points, 6.5 assists, and two steals.
He'd scored 40 or more points seven times in his first 41 games. Having missed only two games in late December with a leg bruise, Curry
headed into the second half healthy and full of confidence.

Green was also having a sensational start to the season. Many players, after having signed their first mammoth contract, drop off or perhaps exhibit slightly less motivation now that they've been paid. Not
so for Green, who put up averages of 14.5 points, 9.5 rebounds, and
7.4 assists with Walton coaching games. His defense was elite, with 1.3
steals and 1.3 blocks per game, and Golden State's opponents' numbers
were down across the board with him on the floor. He was shooting
41.4 percent on threes, but also facilitating and stretching the floor. The
Green-Curry pick-and-roll became the most lethal play call in the NBA,
literally undefendable if executed even marginally well.

And the "small-ball" lineup that had served the Warriors so well
in the Finals now had a nickname—the Death Lineup, coined in late
November by the local media—that was more than apropos considering
the results. Though Harrison Barnes had missed 16 of the Warriors' first
43 games due to a sprained ankle, the Death Lineup had played enough
together to cement its reputation as the league's most-feared five-man
combo. Over that time, they played 95 minutes together across 20 games
and produced the best Net Rating of any full lineup in the NBA. Per 100
possessions, the Death Lineup was outscoring the opposition by 60.2
points, an astronomical difference. Overall, the Warriors boasted three
of the four most efficient lineups in the league.

Then, in mid-January, having won 39 of their first 43 games, Kerr announced to the team, nonchalantly during a prepractice film session, that he would be returning to the sidelines. He had tried everything to alleviate his pain—including medicinal marijuana—but only time had helped him reach a point where he could finally come back. It wasn't a complete surprise to the team, as Kerr had joined them on the recent road trip, but the players were elated all the same. Seeing their coach in such a clearly compromised state had been difficult. It was part of their enduring motivation, not just to win but to win for *him*.

Now, Kerr was back. The Warriors were whole once more.

Golden State beat Indiana by 12 that night, then walloped San Antonio by 30 two nights later. Curry averaged 38 points between the two games and made 14 threes in all. With Kerr again in charge, the Warriors stood to become a bigger, better version of the monolith that was taking the league by storm.

Over the next month or so, the Warriors won 13 of their first 14 games with Kerr back on the bench, pushing their record to an obscene 52-5. In the span of five days in early February, the Warriors were honored at the White House by President Obama, returned home to beat Oklahoma City despite 40 points and 14 rebounds from Kevin Durant, then attended Super Bowl 50 the next day in nearby Santa Clara. The week after that, Curry, Thompson, and Green all played in the All-Star Game in Toronto.

Then came a game that defined Golden State's scintillating season.

· · ·

In late February, the Warriors trekked to chilly Oklahoma City for a nationally televised Saturday night showdown. It was the final leg of a tiring, seven-game road trip and tempers were running a little high, especially for Draymond Green. Of any player adapting to Kerr's return, it was Green who endured the most difficult transition. As players like

Curry, Thompson, and Marreese Speights had benefited from Kerr's return, Green's assists, usage rate (a metric that conveys how much of an offense is run through a specific player), and overall scoring all suffered noticeable drop-offs, while his turnovers and fouls went up. Most obvious was that Green's three-point shooting dried up. Under Walton, 33.1 percent of Green's shots came from beyond the arc. Since Kerr had returned, that number plummeted to just 22 percent.

Heading into play against OKC, Green was clearly dissatisfied with his game, and the first half against the Thunder hadn't gone well. He missed all three of his shot attempts and had two passes picked off, including a baffler with just a minute left in the second quarter when he tried to hit Brandon Rush in the left corner. André Roberson picked off the pass and handed the ball to Russell Westbrook, who dashed down the court for a layup.

The Warriors went to the locker room down 11, and Green exploded on Kerr. "I am not a robot!" he screamed at the coach. As ESPN later reported, when Kerr told Green to have a seat and calm down, Green went ballistic: *Motherfucker, come sit me down!*" Green said he wouldn't shoot the rest of the game if Kerr wished it so. His frustration of the past month, over his diminished role, had finally boiled over. And because locker room doors are not hermetically sealed, sideline reporter Lisa Salters heard the loudest of Green's rantings and reported a portion of said screed on the nationwide ABC telecast when the second half commenced. It was an unprecedented moment in the Kerr era, but not for the Warriors franchise. This kind of blowup was par for the course under previous coaches. Such incidents had derailed seasons in the past, and it was now an open question whether the 2015–16 squad would suffer a similar fate—as millions at home watched along.

Golden State went on a 6–0 run to start the third. Then catastrophe nearly struck: Curry drove the lane and dished off to Barnes for a layup, but not before Westbrook jumped and landed on Curry's left ankle at an awkward angle. The MVP limped off to the locker room with head trainer Chelsea Lane and security guard Ralph Walker. The Warriors nervously awaited his return, should it come at all.

Curry missed five minutes of game time and Golden State was only down seven when he returned. He swished a trifecta of threes over the next four minutes and the Warriors were only down five headed to the fourth.

With just a few minutes to go, Golden State made its move. When Westbrook, despite shooting a miserable 2 of 12 in the second half, converted a nifty layup with 4:51 left to put OKC up by 11, Kerr called on the Death Lineup. From that point to the end of regulation, the Warriors outscored the Thunder, 18–7. Durant's three with 15 seconds left looked as if it might seal a win for the Thunder, but a Klay Thompson finger roll with 12 seconds left cut the lead to two.

Westbrook then rushed the inbounds pass to Durant, who was swarmed by both Barnes and Andre Iguodala. As the two Warriors kept from fouling him, Durant heaved the ball downcourt. After Thompson deflected the pass, Green saved it from rolling out of bounds. With 3.4 seconds left, Thompson corralled the ball and passed to Iguodala, who pulled up from 20 feet to tie the game but was fouled by Durant with less than a second on the clock.

Iguodala made both free throws, and the game went to overtime.

The Thunder scored five quick points in 33 seconds, but a Curry drive to the hoop with 4:13 to go forced Durant to commit his sixth foul and sit out the remainder of the game. Curry then came down and hit one three—to tie his single-season mark of 286—then another for the record as he fell to the ground to tie the game at 110 with 2:29 to go.

Back and forth they went until OKC set up for a potential game-winner. Tied at 118 with 10 seconds left, Westbrook drove on Thompson and tried to bank in a 14 foot pull-up jumper that went askew and into Iguodala's arms. He threw a pass out to a waiting Curry.

Kerr opted not to use his last timeout and instead let Curry and the Warriors engineer their own fate.

With 3.5 seconds left, Curry dribbled across the midcourt line.

With 2.5 seconds left, Curry pulled up from 37 feet away.

With 0.8 seconds left, Curry's shot sailed through the netting.

"Curry, way downtown, *BANG! BANG!*" yelled Mike Breen on the broadcast. "Oh, what a shot from *Curry!*"

The MVP ran to his bench, then aimlessly toward the far end of the court, screaming and pumping his arms and doing a shoulder-shimmy. Curry had scored 46 points on just 24 shots. His 12 threes tied the single-game record, matching Kobe Bryant and Donyell Marshall in that esteemed club. Watching from his home in Charlotte, Brandon Payne was flush with pride, having seen that kind of shot from Curry a million times in practice. "As soon as he let it go," Payne says, "I knew it was good."

Final score: Golden State 121, Oklahoma City 118.

It was the most audacious performance of Curry's career, and while it might seem silly to suggest that shot saved a season for a team whose record was 52-5 heading into that night, the suggestion is not entirely without merit. Between Green's halftime meltdown, Curry's apparent ankle injury, and the fact that the Thunder (41-17) were no slouches themselves, you never know where the season could have headed. It was certainly Golden State's biggest win since Game 4 of the 2015 Finals. And once again, they had survived the awesomeness of Durant, who fouled out with 37 points and 12 rebounds. After the game, ESPN's Ethan Sherwood Strauss tweeted, with a whimsical eye toward the unknowable machinations of a coming offseason sure to be dictated by Durant's free agency, "I can't even fathom KD and Curry existing as a joined force."

Green missed all eight of his shots but did compile 14 rebounds and 14 assists. After the game, his numbers started trending back upward again until season's end, and his attitude noticeably improved in the weeks that followed. That precipitous drop in percentage of Green's shots from three-point land? For the rest of the season after the halftime incident, 33.6 percent of his shots were three-point attempts, an even higher clip than when Walton was in charge.

The team downplayed the incident, with Kerr telling reporters two days later, "It's the NBA. Every team I've ever been on has had stuff like this. Every team. Championship teams or not, it happens."

· · ·

Aside from all the ancillary dramatics that night, the win came the same night that the Warriors clinched a playoff berth, the first time since the 1987–88 Lakers that a team had done so before the calendar flipped to March. (Technically, the deed was done an hour before Curry's overtime three, by virtue of San Antonio's win in Houston 450 miles south, but Golden State didn't need to know.)

More important, the Warriors kept winning, including 15 of 17 games in March. They entered April with a 68-7 record, and with five wins over their final seven games they could eclipse Chicago's once-thought-unbreakable record of 72 regular-season wins. Even more incredibly, the Warriors were still undefeated at Oracle Arena, winning all 36 games they'd played there. Overall, they hadn't dropped a regular-season game in Oakland since an overtime loss to Chicago in January 2015. An NBA-record 54 home wins in a row had followed that misstep.

Maybe the Warriors should've known a down night was in the offing when Kerr's attempt on April Fool's Day morning to prank Draymond Green into thinking he would be sitting out that night didn't go well. "I didn't get much of a laugh and Draymond glared at me," Kerr said. "I told him I was going to give him the night off because he needed to rest. He just glared at me and I said 'April Fools' and nobody laughed. . . . They usually go over better than that, but just crickets."

Joke bombs notwithstanding, the Boston Celtics prevailed that night at Oracle, 109–106, as both Curry and Barnes missed potential game-tying threes in the final 10 seconds. Turnovers (22 of them) doomed the Warriors, but as frustrating as the loss was, Boston was a playoff-bound team that could win on the road in any arena any given night. "It's a weird feeling," Curry said of losing at home after so long. "We've just got to be able to move on from it."

Four nights later, coming off an easy rebound win over Portland, Golden State dropped a stinker at home to the lowly Minnesota Timberwolves, who came into the game just 25-52 on the season. They had some undeniably talented young stars in the making—former No. 1 overall draft picks like Andrew Wiggins and Karl-Anthony Towns—but it was a team the Warriors should've easily beaten. Instead, they fell in overtime, 124–117.

The loss kept the Warriors at 69-9 on the year. They had four games left and no margin for error if they were to capture the wins record. Their path wouldn't be easy. After hosting San Antonio, they'd hit the road for Memphis before facing San Antonio again. A potential 73rd win would come at home versus Memphis in the season finale. The Grizzlies had been hammered by a rash of injuries and were a far less intimidating iteration of the team that took a 2–1 series lead over the Warriors in the conference semifinals a year earlier. Out of the playoff hunt, Memphis was playing solely for pride.

The Spurs, meanwhile, would be a tougher foe. Playing without Andrew Bogut, the Warriors labored through a frustrating 87–79 loss in San Antonio back on March 19. It was a typical Spurs win—gritty, low-scoring, and eminently perplexing for their opponent. Curry had his worst game of the season, finishing with just 14 points on 18 shots; he missed 11 of 12 threes. Klay Thompson had 15 points on 20 shot attempts and missed six of seven threes. It was the Warriors' lowest-scoring game of the year and second-worst shooting performance. By the time they returned, the Spurs were 39-0 at home on the year and winners of 48 straight at AT&T Center. The Warriors had still not won a regular-season game in San Antonio since 1997. To have any chance of reaching 73 wins, they'd have to break a 19-year losing streak.

But first things first. At Oracle, the Warriors handled the Spurs with relative ease, 112–101, for their 70th win. Curry led all scorers with 27 points and, after the win, addressed the idea that the Warriors were forgoing rest and potentially sacrificing playoff health in the chase for 73. "Two teams in the history of the game have reached where we are now," he said. "This is our journey. The goal is to win a championship and nobody should sacrifice that for anything in this regular season, but if you're able to play and feel like you can go out and give what you got and continue to build momentum into the playoffs, then we'll do it."

Golden State's 71st win was far harder than expected, necessitating a comeback from nine points down with five minutes to play. But threes from Curry, Barnes, and Iguodala fueled the late rally, and Green's putback off a missed Curry layup with one minute to go was the deciding bucket. Green made all three of his shots in the fourth quarter en route to a team-high 23 points on the night. Despite 18 lead changes and a measly six turnovers from Memphis, Golden State survived.

Win No. 72 was another classic Warriors-Spurs matchup, but Curry was more than up to the task, unlike in that dispiriting loss in March. Behind 37 points from the MVP, the Warriors improved their scoring in each quarter as the game progressed—from 14 to 21 to 27 to 30—and won, 92–86, for their first regular-season victory in San Antonio since Bill Clinton had just taken his second oath of office. (The victory also capped Golden State's road record at 34-7, the best in NBA history.) After the game, Kerr paid homage to the late tennis pro Vitas Gerulaitis by adapting his most famous quote: "Nobody—and I mean *nobody*—beats the Golden State Warriors 34 straight times on their home floor. Nobody!"

And on April 13, 2016, Golden State crushed Memphis, 125–104, to cap off its historic regular season with an unprecedented 73rd win against only nine losses. In a mirror image of his captivating late February game in Oklahoma City, Curry again finished with 46 points on 24 shots, this time in less than 30 minutes on the court. In making 10 of 19 threes, Curry ended the year with 402 three-pointers, improving on his old mark of 286 by a brain-numbing 41 percent.

Five years to the day after news leaked about Bob Myers's hiring as assistant general manager just hours after I stood in the rafters above Oracle Arena for a glimpse at motion-capture cameras that promised a better kind of basketball analysis, the Warriors had ascended to unprecedented heights. "I'll say the same thing I said 20 years ago: I don't think this one's ever going to be broken," said Kerr, a reserve guard on the 1995–96 Chicago Bulls squad that won 72. "We wanted to get this record. The guys wanted it."

Kerr noticed how the Warriors' play had dropped off as the regular season rolled toward its conclusion, how they had become so reliant on threes, even as their success rate remained at a high level. The turnovers, as evinced by the home losses to Boston and Minnesota, had started creeping up to unacceptable levels on too many occasions, but it's hard to point out such minor flaws when you're winning game after game. Sometimes a coach has to decide not just when to point out mistakes but when not to point them out, when calling attention to them could be a net negative. So Kerr let it slide.

The Warriors had cemented their place as one of the all-time great passing teams in NBA history. They finished the regular season with 2,373 assists (the 16th-best single-season mark ever) and were only the second team of the past 20 years to join the ranks of the top 100 single-season assist totals. They had 43 games of 30 or more assists, the most in 31 years. (Next closest was Atlanta, with 18.) They had 13 games of 35 or more assists, more than any team in 28 years. (Behind them?

Minnesota, with just three.) Kerr's motion-dependent hybrid offense, even more potent in its sophomore season, had transformed the Warriors into an eighties throwback, reminiscent of an era when 125-point games were not uncommon. (Golden State also posted 18 of those outbursts, more than anyone since 1990–91.)

The historic number of assists was a by-product of the Warriors' extreme offensive efficiency but also their focus on corralling missed shots. The defense wasn't as sharp as the season before—the Warriors dropped from first in Defensive Rating to a three-way tie for fourth— but they led the league for the first time ever in defensive rebounding, which meant more opportunities for scoring in transition. In the past, when the Warriors led in overall rebounding, it was usually paired with their also leading in *offensive* rebounds, which meant they benefited from missing a whole mess of shots. This time, the Warriors were just 21st in offensive boards, a testament to their high shooting percentage.

The Death Lineup, hampered early on by the Barnes injury, played only 172 minutes together across 37 regular-season games. Among all five-man lineups that played at least that many minutes, the Death Lineup was the best in the NBA, posting a Net Rating of 44.4. It was the highest Net Rating for any five-man lineup going back to at least the 2000–01 season.

The Warriors averaged 13.1 threes per game, the most in NBA history. Their 1,077 threes made them the first team to ever top a thousand. And of the 17 teams that previously had averaged at least 10 per game, the Warriors had the best shooting percentage (41.6 percent) of any of them. Both in volume and in efficiency, Golden State had not only exploited a glaring market inefficiency but managed to redefine the inherent lethality of the three-point shot.

Curry was the biggest single reason why. No one had ever made 300 threes in a season, yet Curry finished with a ridiculous 402. (The You-Tube video featuring all of them has a runtime of nine and a half minutes.) It was the third time in seven years he had set the single-season record for threes. The combined long-range shooting of Curry and Klay Thompson (276 threes) accounted for more than 20 percent of the Warriors' total offense in games they played together. The NBA had never seen two teammates so consistently good from long range over the course of a season.

But Curry's season was about much more than his long-range game. He posted the highest-ever True Shooting Percentage of anyone averaging 25 or more points. He had the highest Effective Field Goal Percentage of any 30-point scorer in history—better than any season for Kareem Abdul-Jabbar, Michael Jordan, or Wilt Chamberlain. And since no one had ever averaged 30 points while playing fewer than 35 minutes a night, Curry's Player Efficiency Rating (the best metric for evaluating a player's overall contributions) came in as the eighth-highest mark recorded. Only Chamberlain, Jordan, and LeBron James had *ever* accumulated a higher PER over a season. He was the first player since Allen Iverson to lead the NBA in both scoring and steals and became just the second player ever—after two-time MVP (and future Golden State consultant) Steve Nash—to finish a season shooting at least 50 percent from the field, 45 percent on threes, and 90 percent on free throws.

"We talk a lot about how we're blessed to have each other to get to play with every single night," Curry said after the win, "and as long as we stay focused on continuing to get better, continuing to do things that have gotten us to this point, who knows how far we can take this thing?" Klay Thompson said the Warriors appreciated how hard the playoffs would be, having won the title a year before: "We know what we've got to do to win."

And Draymond Green, who embraced the chase for 73 wins more vocally than any of his teammates, was downright jubilant after the game. After the final buzzer, he cradled the ball in his arms, refusing to let it go for anyone. When asked what the night meant for him, Green replied in his usual understated way. "It means that I'm a part of the best team ever," he said through a wide grin, "and not many people can say that."

That reply was wholly indicative of the Warriors' confidence level by that point. They felt invincible, maybe rightfully so. They'd handled every top competitor in the league with ease. A championship seemed inevitable.

As Joe Lacob—who had been criticized for weeks since boasting to the *New York Times Magazine* how the Warriors were "light-years ahead of probably every other team"—rushed from the court to the celebration going down in the Warriors' locker room, he held in his hands a print-out of the next day's *San Francisco Chronicle*. Over a full-page image of an exultant Curry, the headline declared BEST EVER.

# 10 ★ ★ ★ ★ ★ ★ ★

---

# THE COMEBACK

## The 2016 Western Conference playoffs

**W**ith all of the attention surrounding the Warriors' pursuit of 73 wins, the first round of the playoffs represented a sudden decrescendo. The team's media relations department issued some 350 press credentials for the regular-season finale against Memphis, about the same number they'd authorize for a conference finals game. For the first-round opener at Oracle Arena against Houston just three days later, that number fell back to its usual levels, perhaps 100 or so.

For the players, the transition to the playoffs was an opportunity to recalibrate and focus on their path to a title: Just 16 wins separated them from immortality, and they knew that a championship was the only acceptable coda for a record-breaking regular season. When Steve Kerr was on the 1995–96 Chicago Bulls team that won 72 games, they were seen during playoff practices wearing shirts (devised by Ron Harper and Scottie Pippen) that read DON'T MEAN A THING WITHOUT THE RING. The Warriors now felt that same weight of responsibility bearing down on them.

The Rockets had played Golden State tough throughout the regular season, even as the Warriors (of course) won all three matchups. Houston was a talented if dysfunctional team that could play like world-beaters one night and descend into chaos the next. They were a far less accomplished iteration of the team that had met Golden State in the conference finals just a year earlier. Leading the Rockets were James Harden, who had finished second in the league in scoring (behind Curry), and Dwight Howard, who was expected to opt out of his contract at season's end, forgo a $23.2 million player option, and decamp to another franchise at the first opportunity. The tumult had started three weeks into the season, when general manager Daryl Morey fired head coach Kevin McHale and installed 36-year-old J. B. Bickerstaff. The Rockets rebounded from their 4-7 start to finish 41-41 and sneak into the playoffs by a single game over the upstart Utah Jazz. Their prize? A rematch with the Warriors.

And while the Rockets thrived on drama, the Warriors were a loose and relaxed collection as the playoffs drew near. Kerr was intimately familiar with the challenge that awaited the Warriors. He had lived through this kind of circus once before as a member of the 1995–96 Bulls, and history remembered that group as the greatest team in NBA history. Kerr knew he had to keep everyone focused but also calm. His biggest advantage was that these players knew each other as well as any roster in professional sports. Chemistry wouldn't be an issue, but maintaining focus and health was paramount.

On the court, the matchup with Houston couldn't have been more suited to Golden State. The Rockets gave up the second-most assists per game, the sixth-most points, the most offensive rebounds, and the second-most threes per game. But they were also a swarm of pests that forced more turnovers than anyone else. And this was a team—just a year removed from the conference finals—with legit playoff experience. The chances of a convincing first-round sweep, as Golden State had done to New Orleans the previous season, seemed unlikely.

Curry, who averaged 31 points against the Rockets in the playoffs the year before, was brilliant in the first half of Game 1, scoring 24 points on just 13 shots, thanks to five threes. The afternoon felt like an easy continuation of his historic regular season.

But with a couple of minutes until halftime and the Warriors up by 24, Curry tried a one-handed floater from 12 feet up that rimmed off, and as he was turning to head back on defense, Curry felt his right ankle slip out from under him ever so slightly, just enough for him to feel an unwelcome tweak. He hobbled up court and Kerr removed him from the game at the next stoppage. Curry returned to start the third quarter but was pulled again before three minutes had elapsed. Through the rest of the game, Curry pleaded with Kerr to let him back in. He even convinced assistant coaches Luke Walton and Bruce Fraser to lobby on his behalf. All were summarily shut down. "We were not going to let him play if there's any risk of making it worse," Kerr said after the 104–78 win. "Obviously we're hoping that we're going to be in the playoffs for the next couple of months. So we don't want to take any chances."

Curry felt his chances to play in Game 2 two nights later were good, but Kerr kept him in street clothes for that—a clinical 115–106 win for the Warriors—and for Game 3 in Houston, which came down to a game-winning Harden jumper from the free-throw line with three seconds to go. Shaun Livingston started in Curry's place, as he'd done in the three regular-season games Curry sat out, and scored 16 points in each contest, but it wasn't the same Warriors team. Livingston didn't attempt a three in either game—he had attempted only 12 *all season* and made just two—and as good as Livingston could be with a midrange jumper, the spacing that Curry's outside shot brought to the Warriors was clearly missed. Kerr's rotation was, as he put it, "out of whack," but the Warriors were still ahead two games to one and Curry was cleared to play in Game 4. All seemed to be trending well for Golden State.

But in basketball, there are plays that seem inconsequential in the moment that often have extraordinary repercussions later on. The final sequence of Game 3 was one such instance. After Harden's shot, there was still time left on the game clock for the Warriors to hit a game-winning shot. Green received the inbounds pass and promptly dribbled the ball off his foot and out of bounds. It was his seventh turnover of the night, and now he had to play defense as the Rockets inbounded the ball with one second on the clock and the game essentially over. As the ball came into play and the final buzzer sounded, Green was overly aggressive in defending Michael Beasley, wrapping him up with both arms and tackling him to the ground away from the action.

The on-court officials missed the takedown but the league office didn't. The next day, Green was assessed a flagrant foul. "I didn't think it was that physical, but it is what it is," Green said after the decision was announced. "I'll just play my game. I'm not going to go out there and be tentative."

In the playoffs, disciplinary points are accrued on these types of hard fouls. Green was issued a flagrant-1, meaning he now had one point. If he should somehow reach four points during the Warriors' playoff run, the league would suspend Green for one game. "That might not seem like a big deal right now," wrote James Herbert of CBS Sports, "but the Warriors plan on a long postseason run, so it could come into play later."

. . .

With Curry back, the Warriors resembled their old selves to start Game 4. Though Curry himself struggled in the first half, scoring only six points on nine shots, the team scored 56 points and collectively hit on nine of 20 three-pointers, even when accounting for Curry's 1-for-7 showing. The offense was clicking, Curry was facilitating, Kerr's rotations had returned to their natural balance, and then the Warriors' fortunes changed again.

With just four seconds left in the second quarter and the score tied at

56, the Rockets inbounded for one final shot before the buzzer, with Trevor Ariza dribbling up court. Normally guarded by Marreese Speights, Ariza crossed up with Harden as he passed the midcourt line. In that moment, two fateful things happened. One was that Curry, who had been defending Harden, stayed with the ball-handler and switched up to defend Ariza, which was good for Golden State since Curry was clearly a better one-on-one defender than Speights. The second thing was that Houston's Donatas Motiejunas clumsily tripped over his own feet and slid on his back over the area at the top of the three-point arc—the exact spot Curry was backpedaling toward as the primary defender.

As Curry contorted his body to defend Ariza's buzzer-beating attempt, his left leg slid out on the sweat left in Motiejunas's wake. His right knee, acting on instinct, attempted to brace his body for the coming fall and buckled. Curry crumpled to the ground in agony. He hobbled out of the locker room after halftime to test his lateral movement but it didn't take long before he gave up and shook his head, telling teammates, with tears in his eyes, that he was done for the night. Curry walked gingerly back to the locker room, his hands clasped over his head in disbelief. Bob Myers kept pace just a few steps behind. In that moment, even before the MRI was scheduled, the team seemed to understand the gravity of what had occurred. But before Curry walked off the court, Green told him, "We got this. We will win this for you."

Without their biggest star once again, the Warriors stepped up. They neutralized Houston in the second half and set a record for most three-pointers (21) made in a playoff game, en route to a 27-point thrashing. The next morning, Curry was given an MRI and subsequently diagnosed with a Grade 1 sprain of the medial collateral ligament in his right knee. An MCL injury of this type mandated at least two weeks of rest before a reevaluation. There was no guarantee Curry would return for the second round. There was no guarantee Curry would return *at all*, no matter how far Golden State advanced in the playoffs.

Curry's extended absence meant the Warriors would have to reinvent themselves on the fly. They had to proceed, essentially, as if Curry would not be returning. Klay Thompson and Draymond Green would have to shoulder more of the three-point load, Leandro Barbosa and Ian Clark would play more minutes off the bench, and Shaun Livingston would have to keep the offense moving downhill, even if he wasn't as personally proficient as Curry. Anything they could count on from Harrison Barnes, who was laboring through a rough shooting stretch, would be a bonus. And the defense would have to elevate its play, with better rebounding and rim protection from the bigs.

Feeding off their performance in Game 4, the Warriors won Game 5 by a whopping 114–81 margin, led by 27 points from Thompson. Once again, Livingston started and scored 16 points, exactly as he'd done in Games 2 and 3. Green had 15 points, nine boards, eight assists, and no turnovers. For Houston, James Harden scored 35 points but had a game-high seven turnovers. Dwight Howard chipped in eight points and 21 rebounds, but played the entire fourth quarter and didn't score, while Brandon Rush and Leandro Barbosa alone combined for 16 points in the fourth for Golden State.

Without Curry, the Warriors had done all they could do: finish off the Rockets, start preparing for the second round, and hope their MVP's knee could heal in time.

. . .

Awaiting them in the next round were the upstart Portland Trail Blazers, who opened the year projected to be one of the worst teams in the Western Conference. Despite its youth and inexperience, Portland won 44 games and made the playoffs as the No. 5 seed in the West. Matched up against the Los Angeles Clippers in the first round, Portland won the series in six games, as they were decimated with injuries and without stars Chris Paul and Blake Griffin by series' end. Led by point guard Damian Lillard and shooting guard C. J. McCollum, Portland played ball with an exuberance that was reminiscent of the Mark Jackson–era Warriors, a team learning how to win with regularity while shaping its identity. They played capable defense, but while the Blazers were adept at limiting three-point attempts—just 23 per game, tied for eighth-lowest—their opponents' shooting percentage on those threes (37.1 percent) was third-highest in the NBA. Even without Curry, Kerr would have to stress the importance of launching as many good, deep looks as possible. In lieu of their typical volume, the Warriors' efficiency would carry the day.

Curry sat the first three games of the series, with the home team prevailing in each matchup. Golden State won the first two at Oracle Arena, by 12 and then 11 points. Thompson and Green combined for 60 points in the opener, while Game 2 was decided by a lockdown fourth quarter that went the Warriors' way, 34–12. Green was again the catalyst, finishing with 17 points, 14 rebounds, seven assists, and four blocks, while Thompson led all scorers with 27. Lillard dazzled the home crowd in Game 3 with 40 points and 10 assists, as the Blazers pulled out a crucial 120–108 win, which meant, just as in the Houston series, the stage was now set for a potential Curry comeback in Game 4.

This time, the Warriors were more careful. It had been exactly two weeks since Curry's MRI. Game 4s always represent a tricky spot. If you're up 2–1, you can essentially put your opponent away with one more win, as your expected series win percentage rises to around 90 percent when you're up 3–1, but if you're down 2–1, all it takes is one win to even up your odds.

And while Curry was not 100 percent, he was healthy enough to play. Kerr sought to cap his workload at around 25 minutes, depending on how he felt. Curry wouldn't start—they'd stick with Livingston, at least at tipoff—but he'd be subbed in as soon as it made sense.

What happened next was one of the most riveting single-game performances in recent NBA history. Curry had a rough first half, essentially splitting time at the point with Livingston, and scored only 11 points on 13 shots. And though Golden State took a one-point lead heading to the fourth, thanks to a 29–18 third quarter, Curry was having a miserable evening, missing all nine of his three-point attempts. His NBA-record streak of 152 straight games with at least one three was in serious jeopardy. More important, the game was still very much in doubt. A loss here, coupled with Curry's subpar health, would put Golden State in actual jeopardy of succumbing to Portland.

Then, Curry woke.

He made his first three of the game with 4:35 to play, giving Golden State a 103–100 lead. Then he answered a long Lillard three with another to keep the Warriors within one with two minutes to play. And with under a minute to go and down by three, Curry ran under the basket and kicked out to a waiting Harrison Barnes, who calmly stepped back and dropped one in from 26 feet out. Curry would have one last chance with the game tied at 111, but his running floater from 11 feet rimmed out. When Green's last-second putback also went askew, the game went to overtime.

What transpired next was fantastical, even by Curry's standards. His one-handed floater from 11 feet banked in just 33 seconds into the overtime. A minute later, a no-dribble three from the top of the arc tied the game at 116. Thirty seconds later, his offensive rebound and putback off a Barnes miss tied the game again. A steal by Green and feed to Curry for a breakaway layup with 2:21 left gave the Warriors a lead they wouldn't relinquish. Curry next curled around a screen from Green and sank a three from 26 feet straight out. The Blazers, down by five, called a timeout and Curry, as he walked away in triumph, pulled out his mouthpiece, shimmied his shoulders a little, then yelled, to no one and everyone, "I'm *here*! I'm *back*!"

Curry then used another high screen to get just enough separation to throw up a 25-footer from the right side that fell through. Suddenly the Warriors were up by eight with barely a minute to go, Curry had scored 15 points in the overtime, and Blazers owner Paul Allen stood agape in the front row of the Moda Center. Two late free throws from Curry sealed the 132–125 victory, and the Warriors' backup point guard finished his one-night-only show off the bench with 40 points, nine rebounds, and eight assists in less than 37 minutes.

Curry's 17 points in the five-minute overtime? The most any player had scored in a single overtime period.

Ever.

In the way championship teams do, the Warriors rose to the moment with Curry back on the floor. Green had 21 points, nine boards, five assists, and seven blocks. Thompson had 23 points, and even Barnes nailed a clutch three off a pass from Curry near the end of regulation. Kerr started the overtime with Festus Ezeli at center to give the Warriors some rim protection while the score was close, then subbed in Iguodala for the final 3:06 of the game. With Curry as the ultimate spark plug, the Death Lineup outscored the Blazers 16–9 the rest of the way.

The next day, Curry was announced, to the surprise of not a single soul, as the league's Most Valuable Player for the second year in a row. What did reverberate through the NBA was that the vote was unanimous, making Curry the first MVP in league history to earn such a distinction. His speech this time around wasn't the emotional affair of a year earlier. Instead of the ballroom below the Warriors' practice facility, this ceremony was held on a dais constructed on the Oracle Arena floor. After some brief intros, he took the mic and thanked Joe Lacob and Peter Guber for creating a workplace that was focused and fun, Steve Kerr and the coaches for giving him the freedom to play his game, and Bob Myers for showing that he cared about the players, not just as athletes but as people.

Curry didn't go through and thank every Warrior one by one (as in

2015), but he did convey his appreciation for their work ethic, friendship, and sacrifice. There was a sense that, having gone through all his recent medical travails, he was not taking this moment for granted, that everyone was aware of how fleeting and capricious this all can be. After the flight back from Portland and the extended minutes of Game 4 after missing four whole games, Curry could sense the pain in his sore knee as he spoke.

"Every single one of us has different personalities and different roles on the team, but we have such a great combination that it's obviously work," Curry said, "but I think we need to appreciate what we have right now. We want to keep it together, and obviously want to see the end of this year out and finish our job and achieve our goal, but I hope we take a moment every single day, when we come into the practice facility or come into games, to appreciate the bond that we have and how much fun we have going out there and playing every single day."

Then he implored them to finish off the season in style, to see this unprecedented feat through to its end. "Regardless of what happens down the stretch of the season, we will be a team that will be remembered for what we accomplished. No team has done what these 15 guys on this stage have done in the history of the game. . . . So let's keep it going, let's win the championship and find a way to get it done and really set our place in history with the opportunity that we have in front of us."

The Warriors closed out the Blazers the next night, 125–121. Curry started, played just under 37 minutes, and finished with 29 points and 11 assists, but it was his 14 points in the fourth quarter that sealed the win. Thompson finished with a game-high 33 points on 6-of-9 shooting from deep, and Green had 13 points, 11 boards, and six assists. The win was classic Warriors, outlasting a strong opponent on their own floor, snuffing out hope late, and somehow making it seem easy. C. J. McCollum had 16 points in the final quarter, but Damian Lillard, the

Oakland native, missed six of seven shots over that same time frame and that was costly. To beat the Warriors, you often needed multiple transcendent performances; one was almost never enough.

And amid all the uncertainty and the injuries piling up—in this game alone, Green tweaked his ankle while Bogut was knocked out with a hamstring pull—the Warriors were now just eight wins shy of finishing off the greatest season in basketball history.

Achieving those next eight wins, though, represented an infinitely more difficult task.

. . .

Throughout the 2015–16 season, the chatter involving Golden State's playoff run revolved around an inherent hope that the basketball gods would provide an epic conference finals pairing with San Antonio. Since the earliest games on the schedule, the Warriors and Spurs were clearly the best of the West, and the three competitive regular-season contests—the low-scoring Spurs win in San Antonio in March and the Warriors' two victories over the final four games—only stoked the desire for such a matchup to materialize.

But the basketball gods are a fickle bunch, and while the Warriors held up their end by dispatching Houston and Portland, the Spurs fell short by dropping their second-round series to No. 3 seed Oklahoma City in six games. Kevin Durant and Russell Westbrook, the Thunder's dominant duo, each averaged more than 25 points and six rebounds a game, while center Steven Adams chipped in more than 11 points and nearly 12 boards a night.

Oklahoma City's margins, though, were razor-thin. Thanks to a 32-point win in Game 1, San Antonio still had the point-differential advantage by series' end. The Spurs also finished with more steals, blocks, and assists, as well as fewer turnovers and more efficient three-point shooting. But the Thunder pulled down 45 more rebounds and held a decided advantage in free-throw shooting. Those factors were the difference, as Oklahoma City won two of the three games decided by four points or fewer. With Durant and Westbrook scoring 65 points between them, the Thunder rolled to a Game 6 win, 113–99, and avoided a Game 7 in San Antonio, where the Spurs were 40-1 during the regular season.

For the Warriors, a matchup with the Thunder would be problematic from the start. Durant and Westbrook were two of the five or six best players in the league and dominated all aspects of OKC's offense. Durant was perhaps the best two-way player in the league, a true position-less virtuoso who could shoot threes, isolate on smaller defenders, spread the floor on offense, and collapse into passing lanes on defense. On pull-up jumpers, Durant had the second-best Effective Field Goal Percentage (51.1 percent) in the league. He was still lethal sans dribbles, a top-20 player in points per game on catch-and-shoots.

Westbrook was smaller and faster than Durant, less efficient with his shot but more experimental. His unpredictability and derring-do made him a darling with certain corners of the basketball intelligentsia. Between Westbrook's creativity and Durant's pragmatism, the Thunder were a pain to game-plan for, but Kerr's strategy went something like this: If Durant and Westbrook were going to get theirs, and if Golden State could just prevent the other rotation players (Serge Ibaka, Dion Waiters, André Roberson, and Steven Adams) from blowing up and exacerbating the rebounding deficit, the Warriors could weather the Thunder. And keeping OKC's shooting to the outside would lower its efficiency. If that meant a few more open looks for, say, Waiters or Roberson on the perimeter, that was a calculated risk Kerr would take.

Another X-factor for the Thunder was their size advantage. Golden State had Andrew Bogut and Festus Ezeli to stay down low, but Oklahoma City could counter with Adams (7 feet), Ibaka (6-foot-10), and

Enes Kanter (6-foot-11), never mind that Durant, while officially listed at 6-foot-9, was a legitimate 6-foot-11, if not still a tick taller. That vertical gap manifested itself mostly on the boards. In the late February matchup—the night that Curry hit 12 threes, including the overtime game-winner from Tulsa—the Thunder won the rebounding battle by a mammoth 62–32 margin.

The data also showed they needed to take advantage of every second Durant wasn't on the court. With Westbrook on the bench, the Warriors' overall shooting percentage and three-point percentage fell. With Durant sitting, Golden State shot 13 percent better from the floor and a whopping 29 percent better from three. In that regard, Kerr would be battling with Thunder head coach Billy Donovan, in his first year at the helm after 19 years and two national championships coaching the University of Florida, to stagger his players' minutes and optimize matchups.

But to win the series, the Warriors would have to make their shots when they mattered most. In that endeavor, they utterly failed in Game 1. Curry's buzzer-beating three gave Golden State a 60–47 lead heading into halftime, but Westbrook, who had only three points at the break, blew up for 19 in the third. Klay Thompson's 25 points through three quarters gave the Warriors an 88–85 lead heading to the fourth.

From there on, the Warriors couldn't make any timely deep shots, finishing a miserable 1 of 10 on threes in the fourth quarter, with Curry missing five of six and Thompson bricking all four of his attempts.

Kerr wasn't concerned about the shooting, chalking it up to an off night, but the turnovers annoyed him. Golden State committed 14, with half coming from Curry. Conversely, the Thunder committed only one turnover in the entire second half. They also dominated the boards (52–44) as expected, but the 15–2 advantage in second-chance points all but killed any chance for a Warriors victory. Durant played more than 45 minutes, and his 17-footer with 31 seconds left sealed the 108–102 victory. It was only Golden State's third loss of the season in 48 home games.

Curry finished with a decent line (26 points, 10 rebounds, and seven assists), but his seven turnovers were uncharacteristic, as was the fourth-quarter flameout. "I think it's fun to be able to have this opportunity to come back and show what we're made of, show our resiliency," he said afterward. "It's going to be a long series."

The Warriors bounced back in Game 2, thanks in large part to the MVP's resiliency. He scored 11 points in the opening frame but also inexplicably dove headfirst into the stands after a loose ball and emerged with a welt on his right elbow that grew to near-softball-size proportions.

Curry would not be stopped. In the third quarter, he put on a scoring performance reminiscent of the Game 4 overtime in Portland. With the Warriors holding a seven-point lead midway through the third, Curry scored 15 points in just under two minutes of game clock. During that sequence alone, Durant made two turnovers and was called for a technical foul. OKC never got closer than 18 the rest of the way. Against all odds, Golden State even finished with more rebounds (45–39), and the Warriors' 118–91 win tied the series.

Durant played only 35 minutes and scored 29 points but also committed eight turnovers, with four coming on bad passes. The frustration on his face was hard to miss. "They were sending three guys," Durant said after the loss. "I was trying to make the right pass. I was turning the ball over playing the crowd. So maybe I just got to shoot over three people."

Curry finished with 28 points on an efficient 15 shots, the kind of MVP performance the Warriors needed. "It's all about our ball movement," he said. "The way that they've been defending, it's hard to kind of get a rhythm if you don't move the ball and don't play with aggression and decisiveness, and I think we were able to do that. We set great screens. We moved the ball from side to side. When I get open shots, that's the game plan. Obviously, I'm going to have to make them."

. . .

Whatever momentum the Warriors thought they had was merely wishful thinking. They dropped the next two games in Oklahoma City, 133–105 in Game 3 and 118–94 in Game 4. Kerr's squad shot 41.3 percent from the floor in both games. OKC's 38–19 second quarter sealed the first win; it was their 24–12 fourth quarter in the latter that sent the series back to Oakland for a potential clincher. Golden State's first losing streak of the entire season couldn't have been more ill-timed.

Nothing about the Warriors' game plan was working. The Thunder outrebounded the Warriors by 14 and then 16. Westbrook had 66 points and 23 assists across the two wins. Enes Kanter had a double-double off the bench in Game 3. Roberson had a career-high 17 points in Game 4. Durant was scoring (59 across both games) but also spacing the floor, playing with discipline, and using his oarlike arms on defense to clog passing lanes and disrupt Kerr's offensive sets. It was perhaps the best two-game defensive performance of his nine-year career. In the second quarter of Game 4, his double-jump-and-block on Shaun Livingston's attempted dunk, as if Durant was bouncing on a trampoline, exemplified the Warriors' acute haplessness. "This is probably the longest team in the league that we're facing," Kerr said, "and we are continuing to try to throw passes over the top of their outstretched arms. It's probably not a great idea."

Aside from the Durant conundrum, the Warriors once again had a Draymond Green problem. In the second quarter of Game 3, Green drove into the lane, lost his handle on the ball, and proceeded to kick opposing center Steven Adams right in the kiwis. The New Zealand native went down in a heap and Green was hit with a flagrant-1, but the league office upgraded that to a flagrant-2 the next day. The NBA opted not to suspend him outright—it could have, as the NBA can essentially do what it wants when it comes to meting out discipline—but Green still had three disciplinary points to his name. Another flagrant foul and he'd be automatically suspended.

"Russell said I did it intentionally, but he's part of the superstar group that started all this acting in the NBA," Green said just before his suspension was announced. "Russell Westbrook kicked me at the end of the half. He just didn't happen to catch me where I caught Steven Adams." But it had been Green's actions alone that forced the Warriors into this predicament. That he'd also kneed Adams in the groin in Game 2 as he went up for a shot didn't help his contention that it was accidental. Green made it through Game 4 without further escalation, but the Warriors simply couldn't afford any more slipups.

Now, heading back to Oakland with the season on the line, the Warriors found themselves in the most unfamiliar position of *needing* to win. Victory was no longer a luxury; it was required. "This team is outplaying us right now, and we've got to come up with some answers," Kerr said after Game 4. "It's as simple as that."

And yet there was nothing simple about the task that lay in front of them. Durant was dominating at both ends, while Westbrook was compensating for his inefficiencies with volume shooting and hyper-competitive spirit. The biggest advantage Golden State held was that it was coming home.

But Kerr had to shake things up, so he went back to basics. The small-ball Death Lineup would look a bit more traditional so as to counteract OKC's resounding advantage in rebounding. Out came Harrison Barnes (whose scoring was down 20 percent since the playoffs started) in favor of Andre Bogut.

The tweak worked wonders. Bogut played nearly 30 minutes, his most floor time in nearly six weeks, and finished with 15 points and 14 boards. The Barnes-less Death Lineup played 14 minutes together and shot a combined 61 percent (13 of 21) from the floor. Curry and Thompson needed 41 shots to score 58 points, but it was enough. The Warriors were even able to match the Thunder in rebounds, at 45 apiece.

Whither the Death Lineup 1.0? Its only extended playing time came in the final 2:28 of the game, with the Thunder desperately fouling en masse. The Warriors swished all 11 free throws over that time and sealed a 120–111 victory to save their season. Kerr's gambit had worked; Golden State lived to play another day. "I had four crappy games and tried to have a good fifth one and didn't want to have it end tonight," Bogut said in the locker room. "We've got a chance. OKC is a tough place to play. We feel like we can play there like we did tonight."

Durant and Westbrook combined for 71 points but they took 59 shots between them and also committed 10 turnovers. After the game, they gathered in the Oracle Arena pressroom and were asked by an ESPN reporter whether Curry, who had led the league in steals the past two seasons and finished this night with five, was underrated as a defender. It was an innocuous enough question, nothing *that* controversial, but as Durant started to answer, Westbrook smiled and rubbed his face as if to suppress a laugh.

"I mean, getting steals, I don't know if that's just—that's a part of playing defense, but he's pretty good," Durant gamely said before taking his comments in the other direction. "But he doesn't guard the best point guards. I think they do a good job of putting a couple of guys on Russell, from Thompson to Iguodala, and Steph, they throw him in there sometimes. He moves his feet pretty well. He's good with his hands. But, you know, I like our matchup with him guarding Russ." A couple of minutes later, Westbrook glared at the ESPN reporter as he and Durant walked off.

The question rankled Westbrook more than it did Curry, who was asked a few minutes later about Durant's scouting report. "I don't get too caught up in the one-on-one match-up," he said. "My job is to follow the game plan, and I've done that the last four years of my career trying to elevate my defensive presence and do my job." After all, it was Curry's strip-steal of Durant with 1:25 left that essentially sealed the win. Durant, going straight up on Curry, tried to drive the lane with the Warriors up eight. He lost the handle due to pressure from Curry, who scooped up the ball and ran to the other end for a layup that pushed the lead to 10. The entire sequence took 20 seconds off the clock.

Donovan called timeout and Curry headed toward the Warriors' bench, stopped, and turned to the crowd. "We ain't going home!" he shouted. "We ain't going home!"

As the game clock rolled down, the Oracle crowd chanted in booming unison, *See you Monday! See you Monday!* That was when a Game 7 would be played there, assuming Golden State survived Game 6.

. . .

The true lethality of the Warriors—and the real underlying reason why they were able to win an unprecedented number of games—is that they had so many players capable of taking over a game. That doesn't mean it always happened, but your odds go up when you have more than just a Stephen Curry or a Draymond Green or Andre Iguodala or Klay Thompson. When that band of All-Stars plays well together, Golden State's win probability rockets upward. Like a Terrence Malick ensemble epic where you could issue all four acting Oscars and still have deserving people left out, the Warriors overflowed with talent, meaning they were never to be counted out. Any one of them could carry the team to victory.

In Game 6, that role fell to Thompson, the laid-back Southern California son of an NBA champion who, as the team's media relations folks like to say, would just as soon never give another interview as long as he plays in the league. The attitude is born not of disdain but of the limits of personal comfort. Athletes like to say they'd prefer to let their play on the court speak for them, but Thompson embodies that ideal. It can come off as aloofness, but he is happiest and most at ease when shooting a basketball. Everything else—even the perfunctory act of dribbling—is secondary in that pursuit.

The Warriors' overall strategy remained largely the same. Bogut would be pressed to play more with the first unit, Barnes would switch out for Iguodala, the rebounding gap had to stay close, and enough long-range shots from Curry and Thompson had to fall. On top of all that, the Warriors needed to weather the palpable joy of the Thunder faithful, who could sense the anticipation of a Finals appearance on the back of their necks. If Durant and Westbrook played with even a fraction of the dominance they did in Games 3 and 4, Golden State was doomed.

Despite a scoreless first quarter from Curry, the Thunder lead was only three after the first 12 minutes, but they were more aggressive in the second, going hard at the rim and scoring 22 points in the paint to the Warriors' six. With the Thunder up 13 with less than five minutes until halftime, it looked as if, once again, the game would be irrevocably lost early on.

Then Thompson got going. Off a pass from Curry, he dribbled once to his left and popped in a three from the left wing to cut the lead to 10. It was his first triple since he scored Golden State's first points of the night. Not a minute later, Thompson drained another, a classic catch-and-shoot from the right wing off a Curry kick-out. With 2:10 left in the half, Curry caught a trailing Thompson in transition for another no-dribble three. The Thunder lead was only four and stayed at five heading into the intermission. OKC's offense was stagnating, as Durant and Westbrook settled for iso sets devoid of ball movement. The duo had 27 points on 31 shots at the break. Curry and Thompson weren't all that much better, with 25 points on 23 shots, but at least their 6-of-13 shooting from three-point range (46 percent) showed the deep threat had to be respected. In turn, Durant and Westbrook were a combined 0-for-8 on threes. Kerr was confident in the locker room.

Curry played truer to form by scoring 14 in the third quarter. Thompson contributed two more threes, both coming in the first minute, and he started to feel that this could be one of those special nights. He had made six threes and executed just two dribbles between them all. His last four had all been catch-and-shoots, which he preferred. Some players need a rhythm dribble before they put a shot up, but not Thompson. He avoids the hesitation whenever possible.

The Thunder, however, answered with a renewed vigor and grew their lead to eight by the end of the third quarter. Golden State had 12 minutes left to save its season. The home crowd, clad in white and reverberating with hope, could barely be contained.

As Thompson went out to start the fourth, Curry gave him one last charge of encouragement. *This is your time*, he said. *Put on a show out there. Have fun!*

Just 34 seconds into the fourth, Thompson slipped free of Anthony Morrow, curled up to the right wing, and drained a three, his seventh of the night. As Marv Albert pondered aloud on the TNT broadcast, "Now *will* this be the final 12 minutes of the season for the Warriors, who had a magical regular season?" Thompson's shot had injected some last-second doubt into Albert's declaration and the inflection on the word "will" must, in hindsight, sound chilling to Thunder fans.

Thompson's eighth three came less than two minutes later, when Iguodala screened Thompson's defender, Randy Foye. That forced Durant to switch late onto Thompson, who buried an arching shot from the right corner. Less than 90 seconds later, Bogut fished an offensive rebound out of Westbrook's prying paws, established position on the left wing, set a high screen on Dion Waiters, and passed to Thompson, who swiveled to his right, as if standing on an office chair, and launched a rainbow three that cut the deficit to five with 8:30 to go.

With just under five minutes left, Thompson made NBA history. Standing straight away from the basket, 28 feet out, he took a pass from Green and had to decide what to do. There was no play called, no screen to create separation. Barnes and Iguodala were jumbled off to his left with defenders close by. Curry was out on the strong-side wing but had Durant in his face, and Green was still stationed directly to his right and not a real option. So Thompson did what shooters do: He shot, with feet barely set, and Westbrook, even just a couple of feet away, was too late. The ball cradled in to make it 96–92, and Thompson now held the all-time NBA playoff record for most threes (10) in a playoff game.

Curry then joined his fellow Splash Brother in the fun, dropping a 25-foot three with four minutes left to cut OKC's lead to one; another with 2:48 to play tied the game at 99. But when André Roberson converted a Durant miss into an easy layup with 2:25 left, the game remained (despite Thompson's heroics) very much in doubt. That's when Iguodala initiated what was arguably his most important sequence in three years with the Warriors, first driving the lane for a left-handed finger roll to tie it up with two minutes to go.

After Westbrook brought the ball upcourt, Iguodala switched onto him and slapped the ball from his hands as the Thunder point guard spun to his left for a turnaround jumper. The reigning Finals MVP—honored in large part for how he had limited LeBron James—corralled the steal and coolly passed down the right side to a waiting Thompson, who was already standing on that familiar right wing. With Durant flailing a sky-high arm at him, Thompson held the ball for less than a second, throwing up a shot that snapped the netting for his 11th three of the evening. The Warriors, somehow, now led, 104–101.

After another Iguodala steal on Westbrook, this one with 36 seconds to go and Golden State still up by three, Curry drove into the paint on center Serge Ibaka and flicked up a looping right-handed shot that banked in and pushed the lead to five with 14 seconds to go. He then stole Westbrook's inbounds pass on the ensuing possession and was promptly fouled. Curry looked up to the crowd and held his hands aloft, five fingers extended on his right hand, two on his left. The stunned crowd of more than 18,000 didn't need a translator. Game 7 was a forthcoming reality.

Curry finished with 31 points, 10 boards, and nine assists, but Thompson was the undisputed star, scoring 41 points and making 11 of 18 from deep. After dribbling once on each of his first two threes, the remaining nine were all of the catch-and-shoot variety. As with his 37-point quarter in Sacramento a season ago, Thompson put on a shooting exhibition that perhaps only he could. Kerr, himself known for clutch threes, deemed it "some of the most incredible shooting you'll ever see."

When the moment mattered most, Thompson didn't let Golden State down as he anchored Kerr's most lethal five-man combo. The original Death Lineup played the final 6:33 of the night and outscored OKC, 21–10; Thompson alone scored as much as the Thunder over that stretch. As he walked off the court and down the tunnel to the visitors' locker room, Joe Lacob got down on his knees, bowed with uncharacteristic exuberance, and rose to bear-hug his first-ever draft pick around the chest.

"If we win [the title], that will be the game we remember," Barnes told *Sports Illustrated* a few days later. "That will be the best game of any of our lives."

. . .

There was nothing preordained about the Warriors' first Game 7 of the Steve Kerr era, and their first since the Los Angeles Clippers bounced them from the first round in 2014 in what would be Mark Jackson's final game as head coach. But there was little discernible tension at Oracle Arena in the hours before the game. Festus Ezeli worked on free throws. Ian Clark played one-on-one with assistant coach Chris DeMarco. As the bigger names came out for their warm-ups, team president Rick Welts walked the outer perimeter of the court with partner Todd Gage, the two of them smiling and occasionally stopping to chat with guests or pose for pictures. Speaking to various team officials, any pressure on the Warriors seemed devoid of real weight. They had now rolled the Thunder twice after being blown out. What was once more?

Kerr left nothing to chance. Minutes before tipoff, Andre Iguodala was announced as a starter, in place of Harrison Barnes. It was the same tactic he used starting with the second half of Game 6. For this night, Iguodala had one goal: defend the ever-living hell out of Kevin Durant.

The Thunder played well enough in the first half, outscoring the Warriors in each quarter, and took a 48–42 lead to the locker rooms, but they had led by as much as 13 before Golden State clawed back with a 9–3 mini-run over the last two minutes of the second. Despite the deficit, the Warriors had neutralized Durant. Iguodala held him to only nine points, and all five of his shot attempts were midrange jumpers of varying difficulty. That Durant hadn't shot a free throw was evidence enough that he wasn't able to get to the rim, to be aggressive and force his offensive will. Even in his 12th season, and starting just his second game since the Warriors had won the championship in Cleveland a year ago, Iguodala could be counted on for a night of lockdown defense few others could deliver.

Golden State, as if biding its time, finally broke through with a 29–12 third quarter as Curry nailed a trio of threes. Westbrook played the entire frame but was held scoreless on three field-goal attempts; Durant could muster only six points on five shots.

The Warriors led by 11 heading to the fourth but OKC stormed back to shave the lead down to four with 1:40 to go, after a Durant bank shot from 14 feet. On the next trip down the floor, with three seconds left on the shot clock, Serge Ibaka fouled Curry on a desperation three-point attempt from the left wing. Curry made all three free throws and capped off the night with a crossover spot-up three from the right side with 27 seconds left. Iguodala, who played 43 minutes and held Durant to a manageable 27 points on 19 shots, embraced Curry at midcourt as the celebration around them began in earnest.

Golden State 96, Oklahoma City 88. The comeback was complete.

After becoming the 237th team in NBA history to go down 3–1 in a playoff series, the Warriors were only the 10th ever to survive and advance. On average, such a feat happens only once every *seven years*. Yes, home teams have an 81 percent success rate in Game 7s, but Golden State had beat long odds just to get to that point, tweaking their play just enough to keep OKC off balance and allowing Klay Thompson to excel as the best, truest form of himself. In all, the Game 6 hero finished the seven-game set with 30 three-pointers, the second-highest total for one player in a playoff series in NBA history.

The only player ever with more? Curry, in this series, with 32.

"Everybody left their soul out on the court," Durant said. "We have no regrets." It would be, unbeknownst to anyone, his 732nd and final game for the Thunder. The next time he returned to play at Oracle, the circumstances would be dramatically different.

For Golden State, the win meant new life and a chance—one that had seemed unfathomably remote just five days earlier—to defend their title. They'd banded together in the darkest of hours and emerged on the other side, scarred but undeterred, perhaps a bit weary but ready for one more fight. "All that matters right now for us," Curry said, "is we've put ourselves in a great position to realize another goal, and we've got to get it done."

As for facing the Cavs again, Curry knew they had just two days to prep for a vastly different foe, albeit one that was plenty familiar. "I think the way this series went from Game 1 to Game 7," he said, "we're ready for anything."

# 11 ★ ★ ★ ★ ★ ★ ★

## "BECAUSE GOD SAID SO"

### The 2016 NBA Finals

The improbable comeback over Oklahoma City made a return trip to the NBA Finals feel like a small miracle for Golden State, but the Cleveland Cavaliers had also played their way through some potential season-ending obstacles. The Cavs' near undoing had nothing to do with injuries to key players or the need for a remarkable playoff resurgence. Their troubles happened months earlier, in a personnel change that altered the very fabric of the team.

On January 18, the Warriors came to Quicken Loans Arena for the first time since Game 6 of the Finals seven months earlier and thrashed the Cavs, 132–98. Stephen Curry had 35 points on 18 shots, Andre Iguodala had 20 off the bench, and Draymond Green had 16 points, seven boards, and 10 assists. LeBron James? A measly 16 points on 16 shots and the kind of achievements you never want to hear after a game. It was the worst home loss of his career. James finished with his worst ever point differential in a game: Cleveland was outscored by 35 with James on the floor. The Warriors racked up the largest in-game deficit James had ever witnessed in an NBA game—the Cavs were down by 43 points early in the fourth quarter. "It was a good old-fashioned A-kicking," James said in the locker room. "Tonight was an example of how far we've got to go to get to a championship level."

That beatdown came on a Monday night. By the weekend, head coach David Blatt—despite Cleveland's 31-10 record at the season's mid-point, still the best record in the Eastern Conference—was fired. The personality conflicts had become too much. (Among other things, Blatt had a propensity for constantly reminding staffers and media of his bona fides and extensive experience as a head coach in Europe.) And he had been hired by general manager David Griffin before James announced in *Sports Illustrated* that he was returning to his hometown team; it was never a pairing that made sense.

In Blatt's stead, the Cavs promoted assistant coach Tyronn Lue, who spent 12 years in the league as a serviceable backup point guard and was an assistant coach for Doc Rivers in both Boston and Los Angeles before heading to Cleveland to work under Blatt. More important, Lue was a James-approved selection. They had a natural chemistry, which was critical if Lue was to command James's respect. According to one report, in one of Lue's first games as head coach, he told a talkative James during one timeout to "shut the fuck up, I got this."

The Cavs started to play more efficiently on offense. Their pace didn't really accelerate, but their scoring sure went up—five more points per 100 possessions. Cleveland's Net Rating stayed the same—meaning they were also *giving up* five more points per 100 possessions—but the style of play suited James more.

And even as a higher percentage of James's shots were coming at the rim—more than 70 percent of his shots after the All-Star break came within five feet of the basket, nearly three percentage points higher than before—the Cavs' three-point shooting boomed upward. In 41 games with Blatt as coach, Cleveland averaged 28.2 threes per game and shot 35.9 percent. In 41 games with Lue, the Cavs took 31 threes per game and their success rate actually went *up*, to 36.6 percent. They finished the year seventh in three-point percentage. The gap between them and the Warriors, who made 41.6 percent, was still significant, but they were attempting only two fewer threes per game than Golden State. And in the playoffs, you go to your bread and butter, what is more comfortable.

For Lue's squad, that meant raining down as many threes as possible.

In a first-round sweep of the Detroit Pistons, the Cavs shot 41.3 percent on nearly 35 threes a game. And when they swept the Atlanta Hawks in the next round, they attempted 38 threes a night and made more than half (50.7 percent). In Game 2 of the series, they even set the all-time record for most threes made in a playoff game (25), breaking the mark Golden State had set (21) a few days earlier.

Cleveland fell to earth a little against the Toronto Raptors in the Eastern Conference Finals, averaging 29 three-point shots per game and making 38.9 percent. It was a surprising regression, considering the Raptors allowed the NBA's second-highest three-point percentage, but James also started attacking inside with abandon. During the regular season, James shot 57.4 percent on two-point shots; that went up to 70.1 percent against Toronto in this series. With James moving in and J. R. Smith, Channing Frye, and the revitalized Kevin Love leading the three-point barrage, the Raptors were powerless to stem the Cavs' inside-outside onslaught.

Cleveland prevailed in six games, blowing out Toronto in each of the final two matchups, so the Finals rematch that everyone craved was made real. The Cavaliers were out for redemption. The Warriors hoped to cement what they believed was their place in history.

Something had to give.

.  .  .

ESPN's Basketball Power Index had the Warriors at 75 percent favorites before the series started, but the matchup was still expected to be competitive. The Cavs were healthy and bombing threes with unbridled confidence. The Warriors had the unanimous MVP and were riding the emotional high of overcoming the 3–1 series deficit to Oklahoma City. It's impossible to get inside an athlete's head at any given moment, but the Warriors emitted a bravado in the two off-days before the Finals. "I think we know what to expect on this stage," Klay Thompson said, "and I don't think anyone's going to be nervous out there like we were last year." Curry, too, felt more at ease. "The first time, it's a whirlwind," he said. "I know we're prepared for pretty much anything."

With that attitude, the Warriors stomped the Cavs in both Games 1 and 2 at Oracle Arena to take command of the series. Despite Curry and Thompson combining for just 20 points in the opener, the Warriors' bench was prolific, as Shaun Livingston, Andre Iguodala, and Leandro Barbosa chipped in 43 points between them, and Golden State rolled to a 104–89 victory. Three nights later, the Cavs were blown out, 110–77. Despite 20 turnovers, only 26 assists on 44 made field goals, and just 10 free throws attempted, Steve Kerr's club appeared unstoppable. Golden State dominated on threes (15 of 33) and outscored Cleveland in the paint, 50–40. In a role reversal, Draymond Green (28 points) was the game-high scorer while Curry was Golden State's top rebounder with nine. Even Andrew Bogut finished with five blocks. Inside and out, backward and forward, the Warriors were a juggernaut.

For his part, LeBron James was scoring only 22 points a night through two games. The Cavs, who had carved a path to the Finals with one three after another, were a measly 27 percent (12 of 44) from deep against the Warriors. Golden State's point differential (plus 48) was the largest such cushion one team ever held after the first two Finals games, and of the 31 prior teams to take a 2–0 Finals lead, only three had failed to win the championship.

Still, the Warriors were saying all the right things publicly, even though they had (going back to the 2015 Finals) defeated James seven straight times. "We haven't won anything really," Curry conceded after the Game 2 drubbing. "We took care of home-court advantage, which is what we're supposed to do. There's still a lot of basketball left. . . . I'm only worried about Game 3."

Curry's concerns were well founded. If there was one game the Warriors were almost certainly going to drop, it'd be this one. The Cavs could expect to harness all the emotion of coming home—the putrid performances of Games 1 and 2 notwithstanding—and Quicken Loans Arena, at its most boisterous, is one of the more intimidating road venues in the NBA. All signs pointed toward a Cleveland win in Game 3, and the teams stuck to the presumed script.

Everything that could go wrong for the Warriors did. They made just nine of 33 threes (27.3 percent). They committed 18 turnovers. They were outrebounded by 20. They were down by 17 after one quarter and not a single player cracked 20 points on the night.

With 32 points from James and 30 from Kyrie Irving, the Cavs' tenacious play led to an emphatic 120–90 win. Kerr had thought the team would come out more emotional, but he realized after the loss that he didn't have them prepared to play. "We were soft tonight," Kerr said. "And when you're soft, you get beat on the glass and you turn the ball over. Those are the telltale signs. So we can't be soft in Game 4 if we want to win."

The open question for the Cavs was when Kevin Love would play again. In the second quarter of Game 2, Harrison Barnes clocked him in the back of the head with his left elbow while leaping for an offensive rebound. The All-Star power forward was kept out of Game 3 as a precaution, meaning that the Warriors also couldn't run pick-and-roll to exploit his suspect perimeter defense, but Lue smartly inserted Richard Jefferson into the starting lineup. Though he was making his first start of the 2016 playoffs, Jefferson had racked up 121 playoff games throughout his career. Taking turns defending Green, Barnes, and Livingston, Jefferson had contributions that went beyond the nine points and eight rebounds that showed up in the box score. He spaced the floor and was aggressive on the glass. It was a very Warriors kind of effort for the one-time Warrior.

But another play in Game 3, toward the end of the third quarter, signaled a shift in the series' direction, that Cleveland wouldn't go so quietly. With less than 12 seconds to go in the quarter and the Warriors down by 19, Livingston drew a foul on Iman Shumpert, and Curry scooped up the loose ball after the whistle just to throw a layup in. James, standing right under the rim, jumped and blocked Curry's shot at the backboard glass. A meaningless sequence of events to most, but one James thought provided a psychological benefit to his side. "When you have the greatest shooter in the world trying to get an easy one or trying to get in rhythm, it's our job to try to keep him out," James said. "If you're a great player and you see the ball go in, no matter if it's after the play or during the play, then you start feeling it. Not that you feel good because you know what you're capable of, but it helps. So I didn't want him to see the ball go in."

Curry was not seeing the ball go in as much as he was accustomed to. In fact, he was having a miserable Finals. Through three games, he had yet to break 20 points on any single night. He had accumulated more turnovers (15) than assists (13). Despite 90 minutes of court time, Curry had only two steals and four free-throw attempts. His lingering leg injuries from the opening-round series against Houston, combined with the grind of the seven-game matchup against OKC, had hampered his mobility on drives to the basket. The explosiveness was gone, although Curry wouldn't admit that he was clearly operating in a limited state. "I'm fine," he said after Game 3. "We're in good shape. . . . We have a great opportunity on Friday to keep control of the series, and that's going to be a challenge for us."

The Warriors were more crisp and controlled in Game 4, even with Love coming off the bench and Jefferson entrenched with the starters. Kerr went to the Death Lineup early (not five minutes into the game) and often (17 minutes that night), which helped facilitate a defensive pressure that was absent in Game 3. Curry finally had an MVP-type performance: 38 points on 25 shots, 7-of-13 from three, 9-of-10 on free throws, six assists, and only three turnovers. He looked spry, in control, and healthier than he had in weeks. The team fed off his energy, assisting on 23 of 33 made shots for a nice 69.69 percent clip. The Warriors played like their truest selves, making more threes (17 of 36) than twos (16 of 45).

James and Irving each played more than 43 minutes and combined for 59 points, but it wasn't enough. Cleveland had lost its first home game of the 2016 playoffs and at a most inopportune time. The Cavs were now down 3–1 in the Finals and would need to execute a few near-impossibilities to win a title. They'd have to beat Golden State twice at Oracle Arena, where the Warriors had compiled a 50-3 record that season. They would have to win Game 6 against the team that had won more regular-season road games than any other team in NBA history. They'd need to defeat Golden State three straight times to survive; the Warriors hadn't lost any three games in a row since November 2013. And no team in the Finals had ever coughed up a 3–1 series lead and lost. Of the previous 32 teams to go up 3–1, each had won the title.

The Warriors now had 88 wins between the regular season and playoffs—more than any team had *ever* accumulated in a season. With just one more, they would be considered the greatest team in the history of basketball.

. . .

The fates of many sports teams have been subject to the whims of history, to the unencumbered impulses of man. What can, at first, seem innocuous can create wide-ranging repercussions over a period of time, one little blip cascading into another.

For the Warriors, their fateful occurrence came with less than three minutes to go in Game 4, with a win firmly in hand, on a play that was otherwise unremarkable save for one ill-conceived action.

With the Warriors up by 10 and Stephen Curry dribbling near mid-court, Draymond Green moved high to set a screen on LeBron James, who was guarding Curry. James fought through the screen and locked arms with Green, the two looking like offensive linemen tussling at the line of scrimmage. As Curry passed to Harrison Barnes in the right corner, James knocked Green down with a left forearm to continue his pursuit of Curry. As Green was rising, James stepped directly over his head and shoulders. Green then brushed his right arm right up into James's underside, which caused the Cavs superstar to turn and jaw in Green's face. After Andre Iguodala's pull-up a few seconds later missed, Green and James both went up hard for the rebound; each was called for a foul. With play finally whistled dead, James was incensed, screaming at Green, who calmly walked away as a CPD officer came onto the court from under the basket and Ralph Walker, the Warriors' head of security, came to Green's side from the other end. A few steps away, Tyronn Lue stood silent, content to let his marquee player state his case. James was livid that Green had tapped him in the nether regions, even as referee Dan Crawford was just a few feet away, had witnessed the entire incident, and deigned to call no foul.

After the game, James was reminded of Green's tenuous disciplinary situation—how one more flagrant-foul ruling would result in a one-game suspension—and whether he believed the play warranted such punishment. "It's not my call," said James, not taking the bait even as he lowered his own lure in the stream. "That's the league office. They'll take a look at it. We all saw it in the locker room. You know, like I said, as a competitor, I love going against Draymond, and I'm all about going out there and leaving it out on the floor. But when it gets a little bit more than what it should be, that's what caused me to have words with him."

As the series shifted back to Oakland for a potential clincher, the league office waited almost two full days to issue its ruling. The Warriors knew that Green's absence for even one game could be devastating. Through four games he had played 80 percent of Golden State's minutes, during which time the Warriors were outscoring the Cavs by a staggering 13.6 points per 100 possessions and had notably better assist and rebound rates. With Green on the bench the advantage flipped, with Cleveland outscoring Golden State by 9.6 points per 100 possessions. Green's impact through four Finals games was undeniable.

The day before Game 5, just as the Warriors were starting practice, Bob Myers got the call from the league office in New York. He phoned Steve Kerr at the team's facility in downtown Oakland. Kerr pulled Green aside late in practice before telling the entire team the news: Green had been assessed a flagrant-1 for his backhanded slap to James's sensitive area. Kiki VanDeWeghe, the league's executive VP of basketball ops and designated discipline czar, put out a statement affirming that while the play, on its own merits, didn't warrant a suspension, Green had accumulated too many flagrant-foul points over the course of the playoffs, officially turning the end-of-game tackle on Houston's Michael Beasley in the opening round into one of the most meaningfully pointless plays in postseason history. If the Warriors were to clinch a championship the next day, it would happen without their emotional core and most versatile player.

"I do think it's curious that somebody who gets knocked out in the first round and who's been on vacation for seven weeks is under the same penalty system as somebody who is still playing in the Finals now," Kerr said a few minutes after hearing the news. "I'm not sure why that is the case. It seems like a strange rule. It's not anything we're going to bring up with the league. Maybe it's something to talk about in the off-season. It does seem a little strange."

Internally, the Warriors were furious. They thought the league was interfering on the sport's biggest stage without sufficient cause. In the moment the play itself wasn't even deemed punitive enough for a personal foul. More than anything, the Warriors saw the call as direct interference into what had been a hard-fought series. Now they were left scrambling to fill a gaping void in their rotation.

Klay Thompson was plenty vocal about it when asked. "Obviously people have feelings and people's feelings get hurt even if they're called a bad word," he said in reference to James's postgame comments. "I guess his feelings just got hurt. I mean, we've all been called plenty of bad words on the basketball court before. Some guys just react to it differently." James, ever the diplomat, laughed off Thompson's assertion that his feelings were hurt in any way: "I'm not going to comment on what Klay said, because I know where it can go from this sit-in. It's so hard to take the high road. I've been doing it for 13 years. It's so hard to continue to do it, and I'm going to do it again."

Green's suspension was the topic that dominated the rest of the Finals, but the Warriors were still in prime position to take the series. Their second unit, at least for one night, would have to play sublime basketball. Kerr slid Iguodala into the starting lineup, to at least try to keep some defensive pressure on the Cavs' two scoring threats, James and Irving. Shaun Livingston would be the first man off the bench, and if the Warriors could even shoot a decent percentage on threes, the title would be theirs. Despite the league's decision (and incredibly late issuance of said discipline), the Warriors felt good about their chances. Green had to stay off-site, so the plan was for him to hole up next door at the Oakland–Alameda County Coliseum—in a luxury suite with Bob Myers—and be ready to run up the Oracle Arena tunnel and onto the court should the Warriors win.

"I thought [the Cavaliers] were dead in the water going into Game 5," assistant coach Ron Adams said a couple of months later, "and then things changed."

. . .

You could argue the Warriors lost the 2016 Finals the moment Stephen Curry slipped on a slick pool of sweat in Houston during Game 3 of the first round. Or when Draymond Green needlessly tackled Michael Beasley at the end of Game 4. Or when Oklahoma City went up 3–1 in the conference finals, thus forcing the Warriors to expend an untold amount of energy just to survive and advance. Or even the NBA's sense of dramatic timing on Green's suspension.

But there's a compelling case to be made that the Finals officially became Golden State's doomed exploit at the 10:30 mark of the third quarter in Game 5. That was when, with the Cavs holding to a three-point lead, J. R. Smith drove unchallenged toward the rim and rose for a layup from the left side. As he elevated, Andrew Bogut met him in the air at the apex of his jump. Smith then crumpled in half underneath, so the 7-foot Aussie slammed down on him and rolled in an awkward heap. His left knee locked in place as his weight dropped downward, and Smith crashed right into the joint. Bogut lay writhing out of bounds for two more possessions before time was called. He limped off to the locker room with assistance from two staffers, one under each arm.

From then on, the Warriors scored only 33 more points in 22:30 of game play, which was as much as James (13) and Irving (20) scored for the Cavs over that same stretch. Golden State would miss 18 of 20 three-pointers while Cleveland made four of nine. And while the Cavs didn't grab a single offensive rebound for the rest of the game, the Warriors couldn't take advantage. James finished with 41 points, 16 boards, and seven assists, though Irving, who also pumped in 41, was arguably better, dropping in contested threes and running bank shots with the confidence of someone who knew he could do no wrong. It was a stunning display of clutch efficiency and the Cavs needed every iota, as their bench scored only 12 points. (Though he returned to the starting lineup, Kevin Love was a nonfactor with two points in 32 minutes.)

Cleveland won handily, 112–97, and Irving's 17 makes on 24 attempts made him only the second player in Finals history to score 40 points on better than 70 percent shooting. (The other? Wilt Chamberlain in 1970.) He and James became the first teammates in Finals history to each score 40 or more in one game. James called Irving's night "one of the greatest performances I've ever seen live."

That was the sort of one-two punch Cleveland needed, even with a depleted Warriors roster, and the momentum was all theirs. For Irving, it was a moment of redemption for the Finals he missed a year earlier. "To repeat a performance like this would definitely be tough," Irving said, "but whatever it takes to win." Indeed, his impact on these Finals was far from finished, but he had already delivered once.

For the Warriors, they were still ahead 3–2 in the series and technically in control of their own destiny, but they lost Bogut for the remainder of the playoffs. Even with Green back, they wouldn't have Bogut available to eat up minutes, set screens, pass from the paint, and (most critically) protect the rim. As soon as Bogut went down, the Cavs started going inside more, making 50 percent of their two-point shots for the rest of the night. Kerr plugged in every available big he could—James Michael McAdoo, Festus Ezeli, Anderson Varejao, and Marreese Speights all saw minutes at center in the second half of a potential title-winning game—and nothing worked. "Generally speaking, you're going to stay with your best players as much as you can," Kerr said, "but it just wasn't our night and we didn't get anything going. We couldn't find any combinations." The hope was that Green's return in Game 6 would put some life back into the team.

. . .

As the rain drizzled in from off Lake Erie on the morning of June 16, a wisecracking train conductor wished his passengers well as they disembarked at Cleveland's downtown Tower City station. "Go Cavaliers! We need a miracle tonight," he said, followed by a deep, audible sigh: "Keep hope alive."

Hope was a good thing, but having LeBron James was even better. As the game got under way and Quicken Loans Arena reached the offensively loud volume it's famous for, the Warriors looked dazed and confused. They missed their first seven shots as the Cavs raced out to an 8–0 lead. After 12 minutes, they led 31–11, allowing the fewest points in the first quarter of a Finals game and the fewest first-quarter points Golden State had scored in a playoff game. The Warriors were down by 16 at halftime, and though the deficit was only nine heading to the fourth they could draw no closer than seven. The Cavs kept them at bay and the ravenous crowd inside the Q ate up every moment.

Bogut's presence was missed. With him out, Kerr opted to start Iguodala, meaning the Death Lineup would play major minutes out of the gate, which is not what the Death Lineup was designed for. At its best, it was a weapon designed to push, say, a five-point lead to double digits in a couple of minutes. It wasn't optimal for long stretches, it wasn't meant to help claw the Warriors back from big deficits, and it certainly wasn't intended to start games. That hadn't been Kerr's modus operandi since taking over, but events forced his hand. The move backfired and the game quickly devolved into the kind of rhythm-hunting that had plagued Golden State in the scattered second half of Game 5. Even more concerning was that Iguodala's back tightened up, limiting him to only 10 second-half minutes after playing 20 in the first. That hampered any chance of a late comeback, which never seemed close to materializing anyway. The Cavs were too focused, too powerful on this night and won, 115–101.

James finished with another 41 points and 11 assists. Irving fell to earth a bit, with 23 points on 18 shots, but Tristan Thompson welcomed Bogut's absence, posting 15 points on 6-for-6 shooting, as well as 16 rebounds. While Stephen Curry (30 points) and Klay Thompson (25) were effective, the Warriors received few other contributions. Draymond Green's night was well-rounded (eight points, 10 boards, six assists), but Harrison Barnes missed all eight of his shots and was scoreless in 16 minutes. Shaun Livingston scored three points, while Andre Iguodala chipped in only five. The defending champs were now on equal footing with the Cavs, just the third team ever (and first since the 1966 Los Angeles Lakers) to force a Game 7 after going down 3–1.

The frustration had boiled over for Curry with 4:22 left and the Cavs up by 12. As James corralled the ball off a missed Klay Thompson free throw, Curry lunged for the steal and made contact with James's right forearm, causing the Warriors point guard to foul out. Curry was so exasperated at the referee's call that he grabbed his mouthpiece and inadvertently flung the gnarled protective wear into a group of fans sitting courtside. Curry was ejected and immediately apologized to the fans—Tyronn Lue laughing nearby all the while—as Ralph Walker came onto the court and escorted the MVP from a hostile setting, the crowd pummeling him with vitriol as he made his way toward the arena tunnel. It was Curry's first time fouling out since December 2013 and his first career ejection.

"It got the best of me, but I'll be all right for next game," Curry said. "I had some stuff I wanted to get off my chest tonight after the way the game went and that was it." Kerr was slightly more direct in his assessment of Curry's outburst and what caused it. "Let me be clear, we did not lose because of the officiating," he said. "They totally outplayed us and Cleveland deserved to win. But those three of the six fouls were incredibly inappropriate calls for anybody, much less the MVP of the league."

Kerr was asked if he was okay with how Curry comported himself in those final minutes. "Yeah, I'm happy he threw his mouthpiece," he said. "He should be upset. Look, it's the Finals and everybody's competing out there. There are fouls on every play. It's a physical game. I just think that Steph Curry and Klay Thompson—the way we run our offense, we're running, we're cutting through the lane, we're a rhythm offense. If they're going to let Cleveland grab and hold these guys constantly on their cuts and then you're going to call these ticky-tack fouls on the MVP of the league to foul him out, I don't agree with that."

The Warriors were reaping the benefits of building an early series lead. The Green suspension and a complete bottoming out of Game 6 had not derailed their hopes. There would be no more games at Quicken Loans Arena, which was already being prepped for its next big event (the 2016 Republican National Convention) just a few hours after the game ended, as all the video screens inside the arena turned red.

Golden State had one more game at Oracle Arena, where they were 50-4 on the year, to win it all and retain their championship swagger. It would be the 19th Game 7 in Finals history, of which road teams had won only three.

"A home game to win the NBA title," Kerr said. "It's as good as it gets."

· · ·

"All right! Congratulations to MVP. Question one for MVP. Go MVP . . ."

With more than four hours before Game 7 was scheduled to tip off at Oracle Arena, and the NBA was scrambling like hell to get everything ready. As the gaggle of TV and cable networks swarmed the periphery of the court, making sure lighting was right and mics were ready to record, a production crew took up residence at midcourt and practiced for the postgame trophy presentation and MVP announcement, meaning they had to prepare for two scenarios. The far more likely scenario was rehearsed first: LeBron James winning MVP as Golden State won the title. By this point, it was accepted as fact that James would win MVP no matter who prevailed that night. The only player to win the award as part of the losing team? Warriors executive board member Jerry West, who won it in 1969 even though his Lakers fell to the Celtics in seven games. West averaged nearly 38 points and more than seven assists in that matchup. James, through six games against the Warriors, was averaging 30.2 points, 11.3 rebounds, 8.5 assists, 2.7 steals, and 2.2 blocks, but his overall effect on the series was incalculable. The Warriors could only hope to blunt his impact as much as possible.

The NBA also had to be prepared in case the Cavs won, meaning the MVP would be right there on stage already. But that's one they practice every year, so it seemed like they were just going through the motions, with a couple of producers doing role play.

"Question one, we're very happy."

"Question two, are you still very happy?"

"Question two, we're still very happy. We're the champs."

"Stand by, one last question for MVP. Here comes question three for MVP."

"Question three, we are *still* the champs."

"Very good, I think we have another player. Do we have another player around?" A random production assistant stepped up. "One more player, here we go. Supporting player number one, question one . . ."

Everyone was feeling a little punchy by this point. Game 7 of the Finals. It was June 19, Father's Day afternoon. The playoffs had stretched to their furthest possible point and the attention of the basketball world was now about to converge on Oracle Arena for one of the most anticipated games in NBA history.

One way or another, this was the end.

.  .  .

The tension that had permeated Oracle through much of the playoffs was frenzied as hours turned to minutes before tipoff, but Kerr tried to keep everything even-keeled. He did his usual hour of game-day morning yoga with assistant coach Luke Walton. Head trainer Chelsea Lane kept him apprised via text of Iguodala's back, and all signs pointed toward his playing big minutes. The day's mantra: *Relax and be loose.*

Kerr opted to start Festus Ezeli as a true center to replace Bogut rather than keep Iguodala in and have the Death Lineup kick things off. It was a gamble, since Ezeli had given him nothing, just 14 points and 12 rebounds over six Finals games, but he was the best natural rebounder Kerr had left. Iguodala would also be needed as a late-game defender on James. The new starting lineup was composed of five players—Curry, Thompson, Green, Barnes, Ezeli—all drafted by the Warriors between 2009 and 2012, none higher than No. 7 overall. If they were to win another title, this crop of homegrown talent needed to rise to the moment.

The Warriors came out energized and were down only 23–22 after one quarter. Their three-point shooting (4-of-5) was saving them so far. Green then scored 12 straight Warriors points midway through the second and turned a two-point deficit into a late four-point lead. The Warriors stretched that advantage to lead 49–42 at halftime. The pace was plodding and slow—preferable for the Cavs—but Green was carrying the Warriors with 22 points, six boards, and five assists. He had made all five of his three-point shots, and Golden State was 24 minutes from another championship.

J. R. Smith came out piping hot early in the third, scoring eight points in less than three minutes. With 8:53 left in the third, Kerr decided to give Barnes and Ezeli a rest on the bench and bring in Iguodala and—of all people—Anderson Varejao. The move backfired badly. Over the next four and a half minutes, the Warriors had one rebound to the Cavs' five. They made three turnovers and committed four fouls. They didn't shoot a free throw and missed four of five three-pointers. A tie game became a six-point Cleveland lead, and though Golden State's modified Death Lineup (with Shaun Livingston in for Klay Thompson) clawed back to take a one-point lead going into the fourth, the Warriors looked gassed.

With less than seven minutes to go, Curry crossed over Tristan Thompson at the top of the arc and let one fly from 27 feet out that tied the game at 83. It was the only points he'd score in the fourth quarter but they were massive. The next time down the floor, Klay Thompson swished one in from the left corner that would've been a three had he not planted his right foot down on the line as he pump-faked Iman Shumpert. Then Green followed with an offensive board and layup off a Curry miss. Golden State was up by four with 5:37 to go.

But Ezeli's disastrous night hit its low point, as James took advantage of a mismatch off a switch and faked a three from the wing to initiate contact. Ezeli flew into James's body, the foul was called, and the Cavs star hit all three free throws. Then Curry came down and threw a behind-the-back pass out of bounds that was intended for Thompson. "Bad play, and he knows it," Mark Jackson said on ABC. "A bad decision. These are the plays that he's got to eliminate, especially closing out games." On the ensuing possession, Green was guarding James when Tristan Thompson came up high to set a screen. As a result, Ezeli inexplicably switched *again* onto James, who didn't hesitate in dropping a long three to give Cleveland a two-point lead. It was James's only triple of the night, but it was also perhaps the most important shot of his career.

Klay Thompson answered with a nifty drive to the rim from the top of the arc and the game was tied at 89 with 4:39 to go.

For the next three minutes and 46 seconds, neither team scored.

The atmosphere inside Oracle became viscerally anxious as both teams missed their next six shots. Since neither could corral a single offensive rebound, it was nonstop back and forth at light speed. Picture a rollicking game of air hockey at your local arcade, but with the stakes multiplied by untold millions.

When Iguodala grabbed a rebound off an Irving miss with 1:56

left and decided to run the length of the court for a layup, it seemed like maybe that would be the difference for Golden State, but James pursued him like an outback predator who'd skipped breakfast. As Iguodala, James's defensive nemesis from a year ago, passed off to Curry and streaked down the middle toward the rim, James stalked him from the weak side, sneaking in from his blind spot high on the left. As Curry passed it back to Iguodala, James flew in across the paint and slapped the ball off the glass. Iguodala had double-clutched the layup ever so slightly to avoid the swatting hand of J. R. Smith, and that gave James the microseconds he needed to swoop in and reject the shot. It was James's only block of the night but a seismic one that felt instantly iconic.

Neither team looked capable of scoring again. In football, you'd call it "running out the clock," but this was not due to passivity or calculated strategy. The Warriors let loose four threes in that time; any of them dropping through might've made the difference, but none were true. Curry's attempt with 1:14 left didn't even skim the rim. Lue called timeout to set up the Cavs' next play, one that could decide basketball history.

. . .

The coach wanted Kyrie Irving to drive for a layup. With just 69 seconds on the clock and both teams mired in a shooting slump, the thought was to get him room to maneuver toward the rim for a nice high-percentage shot. Lue also wanted Curry (with his mobility clearly hampered) to guard Irving, but after the inbounds it was Klay Thompson defending Irving. So J. R. Smith came over to set a screen that forced Curry to switch onto Irving. With the matchup the Cavs wanted, Irving could now take his time and blow past a physically limited defender for a drive to the basket. Maybe he gets the layup. Maybe he draws a foul. Either way, the odds were in Irving's favor.

But when Curry backed up just enough to give Irving some space to operate, the Cavs point guard, the one who had made nervous small talk with Joe Lacob not even five years ago at the draft lottery, pulled up from the right wing and launched a three. Curry—because of either Irving's quick release, his own health, the shot clock now in single digits, or the overwhelming shock of it all—barely jumped, getting a helpless hand up in the air that was short. As Curry turned and stood in place, the ball sailed on through the netting. In terms of championship probability added—as a *Wall Street Journal* analysis later determined—it was the biggest shot in NBA history.

With 53 seconds to go, the Cavs were up by three. The lead might as well have been 30.

Curry brought the ball up and, this time, the Warriors forced the Cavs' mismatches. With Irving guarding Curry, Green came over to screen, which forced Kevin Love to switch onto Curry. Now the league's greatest long-distance shooter had the defender *he* wanted—but Love shadowed every movement. Curry went to his right, then his left. Love stayed at a safe distance, not biting.

Curry passed off to Green to reset the play. Green passed it back. Just 37 seconds to go. The shot clock down to seven. Curry had to do something fast. The crowd gasped for one more breath. The MVP took two dribbles to his left, crossed over to his right, and pulled up from 25 feet out.

·  ·  ·

What is six inches?

It's not much, but how much could a half-foot affect your life?

For Stephen Curry, it meant the difference between tying up Game 7 and the sickening realization of heartbreak.

When his shot sailed about six inches to the right and bounced off the rim and down into LeBron James's arms, the Warriors' fate was sealed. Green fouled James on a thunderous slam attempt with 11 seconds to go and James made one of two free throws. After a couple of feeble shot attempts with hardly any time left, the clock mercifully hit zero for Golden State.

With a 93–89 win, Cleveland had prevailed. Golden State's quest for history had come up short. The league's highest-scoring offense was shut out for the final four minutes and 39 seconds of the game. Kevin Love, who'd giggled at Lacob's misfortune on that March 2012 night fueled by 20,000 boos, again had the last laugh.

As Adam Silver addressed the stunned Oracle Arena crowd—and congratulated them on bearing witness to "one of the greatest games in NBA history"—Kerr addressed his team in the locker room. "We've had so many moments of joy together, and it was like, wow, we're actually having a moment of sorrow as a team," he said after emerging. "It's a great reminder that, first of all, it's not easy to win a championship. But, as I said, it's life. Things happen. You move on."

Green and Iguodala said some encouraging words behind closed doors, but the team was too stunned to absorb much of anything. Klay Thompson, who missed eight of 10 threes, answered his first four questions with some variation of "I don't know." Ezeli, who was held scoreless in 11 minutes, twice said, "It was just not our time."

Iguodala said Golden State fell short because Cleveland was meant to win. He was asked to elaborate why he thought that.

"Because God said so."

. . .

Against all odds, as LeBron James liked to say, the Cavaliers brought the city of Cleveland its first championship in 52 years. They became the first road team to win a Finals Game 7 since the 1978 Washington Bullets. James, as Finals MVP for the third time in his career, became the first player to lead both teams in a playoffs series in points (208), rebounds (79), assists (62), steals (18), and blocks (16). His 27 points,

11 boards, and 11 assists made him the third player ever to record a triple-double in a Game 7. And just as the Warriors became the 10th team ever to come back from a 3–1 series deficit when they beat OKC in the conference finals, the Cavs were now the 11th.

"Not a whole lot you can say other than how proud you are of the team and that there's a reason you celebrate as crazily as you do when you win, because it's really hard," Kerr says. "We were right there at the end, but that's life."

Green's Game 7 performance (32 points, 15 boards, and nine assists) encompassed perhaps the best game of basketball he ever played, but he was alone in that excellence. Curry, whose 32 threes not only set the Finals record but tied his own NBA record for one series, finished with just 17 points. Klay Thompson, whose 98 threes across four playoff rounds tied Curry's record from a year ago, scored just 14 points. Harrison Barnes capped off a forgettable postseason with just 10 points. The 89 points were the fewest Golden State had scored in the entire playoffs, and their nine playoff losses were as many as in the 82-game regular season.

Curry, who held his head in his hands in the locker room before returning to the court to congratulate the Cavs, tried to encapsulate what he was feeling. "It sucked to watch them celebrate, and we wish that would have been us," he said. "But at the end of the day, you congratulate them for accomplishing what they set out to do, and it will be a good image for us over the summer and all next season to remember so that we can come back stronger. That's all you can do."

"I blame myself for everything," Green said when asked about the impact of his Game 5 absence. "That's just who I am. I think as a leader that's important. Hey, I'm not afraid to take the blame. I do think that's where the series turned, but it happened. Move on from it. . . . I learned from it and I'll be better. But I'm not afraid to say that it's my fault. I think it was. But this ain't the last that you'll see from us."

After the official media interviews had ended, I had hoped to get one more look inside the Warriors' locker room. As I walked past the friends and family suite, a collection of booze and mixers was being wheeled away by arena security, many of the bottles still quite full.

As I tried to turn and walk up the tunnel to the Warriors' locker room, a guard poked his hand into my chest: "Whoa, whoa, where do you think *you're* going?"

I could see the blue locker room doors had closed. Hardly anyone was congregating nearby. Normally, there's a mob of well-wishers, agents, childhood friends, and family members milling around, but tonight it had already gone deathly still. A celebration that seemed certain just a few days ago would never come.

"Nobody's coming out of *there* anymore," the guard added. "They're *gone*."

# 12 ★ ★ ★ ★ ★ ★ ★

## INDEPENDENCE DAY

### The Summer of 2016

**W**alking out of Oracle Arena after Game 7, several hours after the throngs of fans had long departed, my mind drifted to what Steve Kerr had once said in the aftermath of losing to Oklahoma in the 1988 Final Four, when his 2-for-13 performance sank Arizona's bid for its first NCAA championship game appearance.

*I will always blame myself for us losing that game.*

*I didn't choke or anything. I just had a bad shooting day.*

*I'm a shooter and my shot was off at the worst possible time.*

*I've bounced back from losses a whole lot bigger than that one.*

I thought that no matter what the future held for this Warriors team, there was no better coach in place to help them through this, one of the most improbable and devastating losses in the history of American professional sports. No NBA team had ever blown a 3–1 series lead in the Finals, and the 73-win Warriors, who boasted the first-ever unanimous MVP, were the first.

Because they lost by such a tantalizingly close margin, it was hard not to blame Curry, for whom even a mediocre night on offense would've meant a historic championship for the franchise. The MVP was uncharacteristically inefficient, with 17 points on 19 shots. But by Game 7, Curry was nowhere near the player he was in the regular season. The NBA's leader in steals could barely defend on the perimeter, the lift in his legs sapped by injury. At least the summer would provide a respite. Then he'd get back to training with Brandon Payne after hosting his annual kids' summer camp. Soon enough, next season would arrive, the hunt for a title beginning anew.

Kerr thought about what he could've done differently. As was the case against David Blatt a year earlier, Kerr had faced an adaptive coach in Tyronn Lue, with each man looking to one-up his counterpart at every turn. Each team had a valuable rotation player effectively rendered useless by series' end—Marreese Speights for Golden State, Channing Frye for Cleveland—but the Warriors couldn't hold up after losing Andrew Bogut in Game 5. Kerr hoped Anderson Varejao's passing and Festus Ezeli's rebounding would make up for the Aussie's absence. Four days after the Finals, Kerr finally watched the Game 7 tape and was haunted by what he saw. Late in the game, they couldn't get anywhere into the paint; everything was shot from the outside. The pressure had gotten to the Warriors, who fell back on their worst tendencies as the game hung in the balance. Those lapses of judgment that Kerr couldn't point out in the midst of a historic regular season had come back to bite them. At least there'd be time to correct such shortcomings in training camp.

What would the Warriors even look like then? They had remarkably little turnover after winning the title, but this offseason would be radically different. Ezeli and Harrison Barnes, having both turned down contract extensions at the start of the season, would be restricted free agents, meaning the Warriors could match any offer. Bench players, like Leandro Barbosa, would be unrestricted free agents. Bogut would be entering the final year of his contract. Same for Curry. They drafted Damian Jones, a 7-foot center from Vanderbilt, and paid the Milwaukee

Bucks $2.4 million for their second-round pick at No. 38 and the draft rights to Patrick McCaw, a 6-foot-7 guard from UNLV. Reloading via the draft was fine to a point, but the Warriors needed more.

How they navigated the free agent waters depended on how much space they could finagle under the salary cap. In any other year, Golden State's wiggle room might've been fairly minimal, but in a turn of good fortune, the cap flew up that summer from $70 million to $94.1 million. That was due to the massive influx of TV money that was heading toward the NBA's coffers. When ESPN and TNT signed a nine-year, $24 billion TV deal in February 2016 to extend their broadcast rights, it represented an enormous increase in basketball-related income (BRI). And according to the collective bargaining agreement, the players get half of all BRI.

With these increases, the NBA raises the salary cap level to make sure the proper amount of BRI is heading to the players' pool, but what the players' union needed to decide was whether it wanted the cap increase to be "smoothed out." In other words, raise the gap gradually over time or in faster, dramatic lump sums? Given the choice, a union wants its members to get paid as soon as possible, so smoothing came off the table. Hence, a 34 percent cap spike from 2015–16 to 2016–17.

That meant everyone suddenly had a surplus of money to spend during the summer of 2016. And because each team had to hit the minimum required salary level—equal to 90 percent of the cap, or $84.7 million—salaries were set to skyrocket as never before.

Lacob was ready to do whatever was necessary to keep the Warriors elite and was determined to turn the hell of losing Game 7 into a positive. "Failure is really important," Lacob said later that fall. "You need to fail at some point. You need to know what it feels like, how horrible it feels, to fail, to not succeed, to be criticized. And then you're able to take it next time." The Finals loss had crushed him . . . for an hour. Then he started thinking about the upcoming draft and (above all) pursuing the great prize they'd talked about for as long as anyone could remember, the most marquee of all the free agents: Kevin Durant.

As Oklahoma City's enormous (and enormously talented) power forward, who had spent all nine years of his career with the franchise, was hitting the open market, the Warriors believed they had a better-than-average shot at nabbing him. Recruiting Durant had been discussed internally for the better part of two years because Golden State execs figured they would get a seat at the table no matter how the playoff bracket shook out.

The Durant-to-Golden-State narrative bubbled up with fervor midway through the season, so much so that Durant was forced to directly address the speculation when the Thunder came to Oracle Arena in early February. "It's hard not to enter your mind," he said from the visitors' locker room. "There's a lot of uncertainty to what's going on because I haven't really thought that far. I just try to focus on playing basketball. When I lock in, I'm trying to be better every single day, just trying to come in and help my teammates every single day. I think that's what my thought process is always focused on. And once that time comes, I'll make that decision."

A few months later, on-court circumstances couldn't have worked out better, with both Durant and the Warriors suffering massive playoff heartbreak, but how the economics fell in Golden State's favor bordered on sheer serendipity. Klay Thompson had signed a max deal in 2014, but Curry's 2012 contract extension was as team-friendly as possible. Draymond Green's 2015 contract wasn't *quite* the max; he'd taken a haircut worth $11 million. All those accumulated savings—plus the cap's going up so steeply—amounted to a perfect storm for free agency. (ESPN's Kevin Pelton dubbed it "a historic fluke.")

Durant's joining the Warriors—thereby creating a modern-day super-team—was not just feasible but seemed to make sense. In two years with Kerr at the helm, the Warriors' offense was a juggernaut, and

Durant (standing in for a departed Harrison Barnes) would only magnify their proficiency. The Death Lineup pick-and-roll with Curry and Green? Swap in Durant for Green as the roll man and now you've got defenders guessing how to guard the two best pure scorers in the NBA on one play. Curry's spot-up jumper or Durant's iso dominance? And what about a Thompson catch-and-shoot, Andre Iguodala corner three, or Green cutting to the hoop? At their best, the Warriors, with four All-Stars under 30 and a Finals MVP, would be unstoppable. It would mean letting go of Festus Ezeli and Harrison Barnes (who knew he was gone from the way his exit interview went) and finding a trade partner willing to take on Andrew Bogut and his $12 million salary, but an ESPN projection concluded that the Warriors (with Durant) would win 76 games. And as Durant sat at home watching Game 7 of the Finals alongside Rich Kleiman, his agent, he was envisioning the same thing.

The Warriors, knowing that potential future championships were at stake, took nothing for granted. Steve Kerr had a video package of clips prepared to show Durant how he might fit into his offense. The team partnered with NextVR—a Southern California virtual reality company that boasts Peter Guber as a board member—to produce a simulation that would show Durant what it was like to be a Warrior, to run out the tunnel and into Oracle Arena, to be in the huddle with everyone as Kerr diagrammed plays, and so forth, all while Drake lyrics in the background subliminally played their part: *Cause I got a really big team / And they need some really big rings . . . Are we talkin' teams? / Oh, you switchin' sides? / Wanna come with me?*

After spending the night before in New York City, the Warriors arrived at Durant's rented house in the Hamptons eight deep: Joe and Kirk Lacob, Bob Myers, Steve Kerr, and the four All-Stars of the Death Lineup. On Durant's side, there was Kleiman, longtime friend and confidant Charlie Bell, and Durant's father, Wayne Pratt.

They talked for the next two hours, and the immediate future of the

Golden State Warriors had all the uncertainty of a jump ball free-falling to earth.

. . .

Bob Myers thought the Warriors blew their chance. Sure, they gave the pitch meeting everything they had, but there was just no way Kevin Durant—*the* Kevin Durant!—would sign with them. It simply couldn't happen.

Back at his in-laws' house in South Lake Tahoe, Myers's brain was racked with second thoughts as he paced the floor on the morning of July 4. The meeting hadn't gone exactly as planned. The virtual reality headset that would give Durant a taste of life as a Warrior? Malfunctioned from the start. Kleiman jumped in to take control: "Why the *hell* would you guys want Kevin?"

From there, everyone took their turns. Curry talked about facilitating shots and not caring who was getting all the attention. Iguodala, who had also won a gold medal alongside Durant in London in 2012, stressed to him that joining the Warriors would also mean the most fun he'd ever had in his life. As Joe Lacob sat next to Durant's father, Kerr showed Durant some video plays to illustrate how he'd use him in their offensive schemes. Green told him not to sweat the public's reaction, that they would defend him through anything. "Just know you not in it by yourself," he said. "You take some backlash, we taking it with you." Thompson started riffing how Durant's presence would create the most open shots *Thompson* had ever seen before catching himself and steering the pitch back toward how Durant would also benefit, but everyone had a good laugh. Durant's reps asked about business opportunities in Silicon Valley. Renderings of the new San Francisco arena were shown. It was a cordial back-and-forth that lasted about an hour. The players then talked among themselves for an hour after that. Durant later said it looked as if the players had walked into the room holding hands. That's how genuine their camaraderie felt.

For the most part, Durant didn't talk all that much that afternoon. After parting ways with Durant and his reps, Myers headed to the team plane not truly knowing what to think. On a confidence scale of 1 to 10, Myers tells me he was probably a 3: "He's a very quiet guy. They didn't show any of their cards."

The meeting had been on a Friday afternoon, with several teams to follow over the weekend. (Oklahoma City had met with Durant for five hours on June 30 and would get last crack at him on Sunday afternoon.) The Warriors flew back to points west—Joe Lacob to his summer home in Montana, Curry and Iguodala to Chicago, and Myers to Tahoe—but the pitch never truly stopped. Myers made sure the Warriors were following up in every way that might help.

Late that Friday night, Curry sent Durant what Myers called "one of the best text messages I've ever seen," a heartfelt promise that Durant would fit in with them, that they truly wanted him, that no one cared about attention or sacrificing stats, that what mattered was winning a championship. Durant also got calls from Steve Nash (a longtime friend) and Jerry West, who chewed his ear for a half-hour, speaking of regret over his multiple failures in the Finals—Durant had lost once, in 2012 against LeBron James and the Miami Heat—and told him to think about his legacy, of wanting to be regarded as a great all-around player, the implication being that Golden State provided a more fulfilling environment for his diverse skill set.

Internally, West pushed hard for Durant's recruitment because he was convinced his presence would solve one of the Warriors' most glaring issues, namely, that their best scorers did not get to the free-throw line enough. From the perimeter, yes, they were lethal, but when you're deep in the playoffs—perhaps fatigued, physically or mentally or both—

West knew you could always rely on driving to the basket, drawing contact, and getting yourself to the charity stripe for a couple of freebies. Curry averaged just 4.6 free throws per game during the season, the second-fewest in NBA history for a 30-points-per-game scorer. In those waning moments of Game 7, West saw the Warriors become completely dependent on the often-fickle deep three. A player like Durant would act as a hedge against Golden State's temptation to fall back again on such a risky strategy.

Above all, West urged him to block out the noise. "Kevin," he said, "just follow your heart." West's counsel had paid countless dividends in his five years with the Warriors, but his call that day with Durant was everything Lacob had hoped for when he hired him. "You're recruiting somebody, whether it be in a Silicon Valley tech company or whether it be in basketball," Lacob would say of enlisting West's help to persuade Durant, "you're going to use everything you can at your disposal to do things that would hopefully convince the party to join." Lacob also enlisted a small, select group of former Warriors to call Durant and vouch for the organization.

The first clue Myers received that the Warriors might get lucky was on the afternoon of Sunday, July 3, when Durant called him to talk. Myers put him on hold to call Lacob and patch him through. The owner was out in a boat on the lake that borders his Montana home and wasn't sure the reception would hold up. The only salient portion of that call Myers remembered was when Durant said something to the effect of "So when I come . . ." Myers called Lacob back to verify he wasn't going insane and had heard the same thing. Neither was completely sure, and hope, at that point, was a dangerous thing. They had already started work on contingency plans. Even as whispers circulated Sunday night that Durant was leaning toward Golden State, Myers decided to just wait for the official call, which would come the next morning.

Finally, a little after 8:00 a.m. Pacific time on July 4, Myers was wandering around outside his in-laws' house—no more than 50 feet from the exact spot he was back in 2013 when he got the call that secured the Iguodala deal—when his cell phone rang.

It was Rich Kleiman, Durant's agent. "Do you have a second to talk to Kevin?"

"Sure." Myers steeled himself for the bad news.

Durant got on the line. "I just want to tell you that you guys are a first-class organization and I appreciate all the things you are and who you guys are but . . ." Myers' brain raced at that *but*.

*Oh man, here it comes*, he thought.

"But I'm coming to the Warriors."

Myers was overjoyed. He thanked Durant, hung up, and let out a celebratory yell that caused one neighbor to ask if he was okay. All Myers had time to do before the news became public was call Lacob, who was sitting out on his lakeside patio in Montana when his general manager called at 9:20 a.m. local time to tell him that the Warriors had pulled off the biggest free agent signing in years. Lacob already had packed his bags and was ready to jet to the Hamptons if it would help quell Durant's indecision. His pilot, waiting on standby, could stand down.

"I grew up here," Myers says. "I just couldn't fathom a player of his caliber choosing us. We are mostly a homegrown team. Steph was drafted. Klay was drafted. Draymond and Harrison were drafted before we got Kevin. Andre was a free agent acquisition. We'd never been in my mind a place that could attract a player like him and it's very hard to get anybody in free agency. Disbelief was probably the biggest emotion, to be honest." Back in 2011, they were elated just to sign a restricted free agent like DeAndre Jordan to an offer sheet. Now the Warriors were an A-list destination, capable of attracting the biggest superstars.

After Myers, Durant called Sam Presti, OKC's general manager, to tell him the news. It was short, but tears were shed. Around that time, Charlie Bell was texting Draymond Green, who was lying in a hotel room bed in Michigan. "Let's get it," the text cryptically read. Klay Thompson was sleeping, checked his phone when he heard the news, and went back to snoozing. But all around the country, fans (and media) were frantically refreshing *The Players' Tribune*, the online publication where the announcement was to be posted.

Then it appeared.

The headline read MY NEXT CHAPTER. The story even had original art, with a photographer on-site in the Hamptons. Of the 351-word first-person piece, it was these 13 that changed the course of the modern NBA: "I have decided that I am going to join the Golden State Warriors." At 8:40 a.m. Pacific time, the Warriors players' phones blew up with congratulatory texts. Players from around the league started tweeting out reactions. In Hawaii, where the sun still hadn't risen, Margot Kerr kicked her husband awake when she saw the news.

Myers flew back to the Hamptons the next day to spend time with Durant, to get to know him and his inner circle. His wife, Kristen, asked where he was going now. "This one's kind of important," he said, "I think I should go." There was some element of risk, since players couldn't sign for three more days, and Myers would realize only later that his return could've needlessly complicated matters, but he and Durant got along well and talked over meals about basketball, their respective careers, anything that came to mind.

As they flew back to Oakland to sign the contract and meet the media for the first time, Myers asked Durant if he was messing with him with that tantalizing *but*. The newest Warrior said he thought he might try something like that but realized he had a tougher phone call to make (to Presti) and thought better of it.

On July 7, Durant met a crowd of several hundred people inside the Warriors' practice facility and spoke of how blessed he felt to be with a team that possessed such potential. Kerr and Myers joined him on the dais, while Ron Adams, his old defensive coach in Oklahoma City during his first two years there, sat in the front row and beamed. They'd stayed close in the years after Adams left OKC for Chicago and then Oakland. (After Game 7 of the conference finals, Adams pulled Durant aside and told him how proud he was of the player he'd become.) And when Durant first arrived that morning at Warriors headquarters, there was Adams, normally so stoic and composed, waiting to give him a bear hug around the waist.

"What's important—what lasts forever—is the game, the game of basketball," Durant said. "They play it the right way." As the morning wound down and Durant prepared to change into some sweats and shoot a few jumpers at the far end of the closed-off court, Joe Lacob stood to the side and indulged questions from a small scrum of reporters. I asked him what an advantage it was to have a "closer" like Jerry West to help seal the deal. Lacob bristled at my use of the term. "That's not really true. He was a part of the process," he said. "The most important guy was Bob Myers. He's the guy that led this charge and, in the annals, this will go down as his recruitment, and it should. That's his job. The players were the greatest asset, and Jerry certainly was an asset that helped." Ultimately, all that mattered was that Durant was in Oakland. Within two hours of that press conference, with the contract officially signed, the Warriors sold more than 1,000 Durant jerseys through their website.

In the days that followed, criticism of Durant's defection was constant and fierce. Players both retired (Reggie Miller and Charles Barkley) and not (Paul Pierce) took issue with Durant's perceived lack of loyalty. The local OKC press was far from kind to Durant, and even commissioner Adam Silver addressed the kerfuffle. "In the case of Kevin Durant, I absolutely respect his decision once he becomes a free agent to make a choice that's available to him. In this case, he operated 100 percent within the way of the system, and the same with Golden State," Silver said. "Having said that, I do think in order to maintain those principles that I discussed, creating a league in which every team has the opportunity to compete, I do think we need to re-examine some of the elements of our system." (Lacob's terse rejoinder came the next day while attending the Las Vegas Summer League: "Let them talk.")

With five of the seven richest contracts in NBA history being verbally agreed upon less than a day after free agency started, there was a heightened interest around the NBA's new economic reality, and it seemed that everyone had a perspective. "Durant's move to California feels like some sort of reckoning," wrote the *New York Times Magazine*. "Silicon Valley has remade or is in the midst of remaking every industry you can name, so why should the N.B.A. be any different?"

A writer for the website SB Nation posited that Durant had, in a way, bolstered LeBron James's mainstream bona fides: "With Golden State now established as the Ultimate Evil of the sport, or at least its consummate uber-team, it falls on LeBron James—the one man who can stop them—to head into battle next season with yet another goal that goes well beyond a season championship. Unless there's a massive reversal of opinion concerning the Warriors next season (unlikely), James will find himself tasked with defending basketball from all that this team stands for. Mercenary players, annoying tech money, dirty play, nut punches . . . these are now not only our sworn enemies, but LeBron's, as well."

The media's obsession with dissecting Durant's image was nothing new. For years, he had been built up as a foil to James—the wilder, more exciting sports icon—whereas Durant (despite his DC roots) was the humble, midwestern alternative.

But as Tommy Craggs wrote in *Slate* back in 2010, that kind of Durant narrative-building was often disingenuous: "He is as pure a scorer as we've seen, and you could drop him in with all the other great self-styled scoring forwards in NBA history—Adrian Dantley, Bernard King, Alex English, even George Gervin—except that at 21 he's probably already better than those guys. He is certainly more intuitive than just about any of his contemporaries. Carmelo Anthony, for instance, jab-steps and jab-steps and jab-steps on offense, as if cycling through different drafts of his possessions. Durant looks, considers, and attacks. There is nothing humble or understated or gracious about that."

Unsurprisingly, the most full-throated defense came from new teammate Draymond Green, always eager to express his opinion but exceedingly astute in dissecting the role of the modern athlete. "Nobody complain when somebody leave Apple and go to Google," Green said. "Aren't they in competition with each other? Nobody talk junk about the CEO who leaves Apple and goes to Google. As a basketball player, you are the CEO of a business. You are a business. Kevin Durant is a big business. He is the CEO of that business. So him going to play basketball for a different team, the CEO decided to leave where he was at and go somewhere else.

"But there's so many guys in this league that are so stupid they don't think like that. They don't think business-wise. It happens every day in the world. But in basketball, it's a problem. Aren't you competitive in your day job if you work for Apple? Don't you want to outdo Google? What's the difference on the basketball court? It's your day job. You want to do what's better for you."

And in addition to doing what was in his best interest, Durant also wanted to win, to know what it was like at the top of a mountain he'd never fully scaled. "I've been second my whole life," Durant told *Sports Illustrated* in 2013. "I was the second-best player in high school. I was the second pick in the draft. I've been second in the MVP voting three times. I came in second in the Finals. I'm tired of being second.

"I'm not going to settle for that. I'm done with it."

. . .

With the Summer Olympics in Rio de Janeiro fast approaching, Kevin Durant wouldn't be able to stick around the Bay Area very long, but three weeks in Brazil would allow him to play alongside some now-future teammates like Draymond Green and Klay Thompson, who had already made it well-known how he viewed things changing with Durant's arrival. ("We all want to see each other do well, but I'm not sacrificing shit," he told Yahoo! Sports, "because my game isn't changing. I'm still going to try to get buckets, hit shots, come off screens. I want to win and have a fun time every game we play.")

Thanks to a bit of fortuitous planning from months before, the USA Basketball exhibition tour was stopping at Oracle Arena in late July. It had been just five weeks since the horror of Game 7 and three weeks since Durant was introduced to the Bay Area. The fans congregated on this night to welcome their new star and feel some sense of closure from the wounds of June. A week before the game, team president Rick Welts, in referencing the Game 7 loss, called Durant's signing "the greatest consolation prize in the history of the NBA."

At 5:24 p.m., accompanied by assistant coach Ron Adams, Durant took the court at Oracle as a Warrior for the first time, even if he wasn't wearing blue and gold just yet. Stephen Curry, Andre Iguodala, and Bob Myers sat courtside as spectators, at times lapsing into fits of laughter. Just six seconds in, Durant knocked down the first shot of the game, a three from the left wing off a pass from, of all people, Kyrie Irving. Durant scored 10 in the first quarter, finished with 13, and the United States beat China by 50. After the game, some 2,000 fans crowded around the periphery of the court, simply to catch their first public glimpse of Curry since the title slipped away.

"I'm not going to lie, it felt a little weird for these fans to be cheering me on like that," Durant said after the game. "Obviously being somewhere for so long and then making a change, but it felt great. I appreciate all of the basketball fans that come and enjoy us playing. But it was cool, man. It was different."

Seeing Durant in action just two months before Warriors training camp gave the situation a sense of realness, and the idea of how he would integrate into Kerr's schemes was a basketball strategist's fever dream.

Curry and Durant finished the 2015–16 season ranked first and second in both True Shooting Percentage and Player Efficiency Rating. Over the last four seasons, Curry, Thompson, and Durant ranked first, second, and 12th in threes. Of all players in 2015–16 who had at least 30 post-up possessions, Durant scored the most points per possession (1.23) of anyone. On spot-up shooting, Curry was second in points per possession, Thompson 22nd, and Durant 39th. With Green's passing from the center position and Iguodala's versatility, the Death Lineup would be an unstoppable force of basketball excellence with off-ball movement, back cuts, and pick-and-rolls that would leave opposing defensive coaches in cold sweats the night before. They could pass until someone—anyone!— was open, inside or out, iso or in motion. They could endlessly switch on defense and feel confident in the resulting matchup. As Kerr knew, you could play that lineup only maybe 12 to 15 minutes a night because of how taxing it can be (especially for Green at center), but that's still only a third of these players' minutes per night in one of the most fearsome five-man lineups ever devised. No wonder the Warriors were giddy to start the season.

A couple of weeks into training camp, the Warriors were honored with the Entrepreneurial Company of the Year (Encore) award from the Stanford Graduate School of Business Alumni Association. Lacob said that night that the award meant as much to him as winning the title a year earlier: "The truth is, we're not really a basketball team. In this day and age, we're much more than that. We're a sports, media, and technology entity." When the Warriors media guide came out two weeks later, you only had to flip to page five to see a photo of Lacob with the Encore in hand.

It was the culmination of a year of accolades and achievements that few sports teams ever experience. Besides Curry's winning the MVP unanimously and Kerr's earning Coach of the Year honors, the Warriors were named Best Analytics Organization at the Sloan conference in March; Kent Lacob and Sammy Gelfand were there to accept the award. (As *Sports Illustrated* wrote, "The team seemed to be mentioned in every panel and presentation, generating awe as easily as they generate points.") The Warriors were the most popular team on the NBA's League Pass subscription service and Curry's jersey was the top seller in 48 states—all except, you guessed it, Ohio and Oklahoma. In March, when *Fortune* released its list of the "World's 50 Greatest Leaders," Curry and Kerr were co-listed at No. 15, the only sports-centric people to be honored (other than Alabama football coach Nick Saban) and one spot behind Bono.

In May 2016, *Sports Business Journal* reported that the Warriors were valued, according to a limited partnership sale, at $1.6 billion, meaning Lacob and Guber had, in less than six years, increased the team's value by some 256 percent over the original purchase price. And Chase Center, the team's privately financed 18,000-seat arena in San Francisco, appeared on track to break ground in early 2017 and open in the fall of 2019. That same month, the publication also named the Warriors its Sports Team of the Year for the second time in three years, based on their on-court success but also for business reasons. Season-ticket renewals were at 99 percent, local TV ratings were the highest of any market, their social media presence had more than doubled in one year's time, and revenue from new corporate partnerships was up 20 percent. It was no surprise when Lacob was named Sports Executive of the Year.

The Warriors had become, in many ways, a model for all other professional sports franchises. Using a spirit preached by Lacob and championed by Peter Guber, the Warriors were successful, profitable, beloved, and sustainable. They'd gotten there by making smart decisions and never being afraid to innovate. As Guber himself said during a conference at Stanford in March 2016, "We live in a constant state of 'beta.'" So long as that attitude prevails first and foremost, the Golden State Warriors figure to hold their place as one of the elite organizations not just in sports but (as evinced by the Encore Award) in all the business world.

As the 2016–17 season drew near, Bob Myers was asked about the long-term sustainability of Golden State's success. Could they truly become, say, a new-age San Antonio Spurs, always reloading and seemingly immune to whatever new trends may arise? "I think we're going in the right direction but you have to be careful because things swing really fast in sports," he said. "An injury, a decision—people are viewing things as going swell now, but it can change, so you got to stay humble and keep doing what you do and hope that people recognize you for it. It's professional sports. You think you got it all figured out, and then whatever it is, fate, misfortune remind you that we're all susceptible to a downturn.

"We want to enjoy this and see how far we can take it."

. . .

It's 11:00 a.m. on a drizzly morning in Oakland. Here the Warriors have come, to the conclusion of an endless offseason. It's October 25, the day the Warriors will embark on a year that promises rewards bigger than anything they've imagined. To that end, everyone is keeping up a semblance of normalcy, adhering to their tried-and-true routines after game-day shootaround. In the far corner, Draymond Green practices midrange jumpers with new assistant coach Mike Brown, far from the madding crowd of reporters, TV crews, and staffers who've assembled to cover this spectacle. With Luke Walton having left to become head coach of the Lakers, Brown is one of several new faces around, but he's not the one everyone has come to see.

That would be Kevin Durant, who's shooting long threes with another new assistant, the recently retired NBA guard Willie Green, who feeds him a fresh ball after each attempt. On another rim to their right, Shaun Livingston shoots corner threes as Sammy Gelfand, the Warriors' analytics whiz kid, grabs loose balls with an eager smile. Closer to the media scrum, Stephen Curry cycles through his customary three-point drills around the arc as assistant coaches Bruce Fraser (the de facto "Curry Whisperer") and Nick U'Ren (who helped legitimize the Death Lineup in the 2015 Finals) keep track of makes and misses. Ron Adams works on defense with Andre Iguodala, who gets second-unit mates Kevon Looney, Patrick McCaw, and Ian Clark to follow him to another rim like a band of ducklings lagging behind. As always, Klay Thompson fine-tunes his catch-and-shoot technique with assistant coach Chris DeMarco.

This is the postpractice setup that works for the Warriors, and they are loath to futz with it too much, especially this early in the season. The familiarity helps quell the uncertainty that a new slate of games can bring. As they didn't end the previous season under the best of circumstances, they'll take any comfort they can get right now. But there are new faces who must learn how things are done here. Gone are Andrew Bogut and Harrison Barnes (to Dallas), Leandro Barbosa (back in Phoenix), Marreese Speights (south to the LA Clippers), Brandon Rush (north to Minnesota), and Festus Ezeli (landed in Portland). Their replacements—David West, Zaza Pachulia, and JaVale McGee—mingle here and there as they acclimate to their new digs.

Eventually they disperse, slouching toward the workout room, trails of sweat forming along their backs, to reappear a few hours later at Oracle Arena. As the Cleveland Cavaliers are receiving their championship rings 2,500 miles to the east, the Warriors steel their focus. One by one, they trickle out onto the court to begin some light pregame shooting. They all know full well that the only goal for this season is a championship, an honor both achieved and squandered in the past 16 months. Now they've reloaded and critics say their very existence has ruined competitive balance, harmed the very fabric of what makes basketball fun. They will be the most covered, most scrutinized basketball team in the history of the sport—another fact of life they cannot control.

What they can dictate is how they play every game, run the fast break, switch seamlessly onto opposing defenders, and so forth. Soon, these actions will feel instinctual, but that will come after an adjustment period. It won't be perfect from the outset, but Golden State is good enough for now. No team has come close to averaging 116 points per game in 25 years, yet that seems entirely possible for these Warriors.

Aside from otherworldly talent, the team has some tech initiatives that could play a role. Their practice court is now outfitted with technology from two different startups that promise to analyze their play as never before. An Alabama-based company called Noahlytics uses a sensor positioned 13 feet above the rim to analyze every shot a player takes around the arc at 30 frames a second and map it on a monitor installed a few feet away on a wall. Five years earlier, SportVU was deemed revolutionary because the motion tracking could log a player's movements on the court. Noahlytics can actually map the angle of any shot *and the exact plane* of where the ball crosses down and through the rim and out below. The Warriors were one of four teams to try out that piece of tech near the end of the 2015–16 season, but they were the first NBA team to install the SmartCourt system from an Israeli startup named PlaySight. SmartCourt allowed the Warriors to record practice, stream it live online to people off-site, and store tagged plays in the cloud for either immediate or later review. Myers liked it so much that the system was also installed at their D-League facility in Santa Cruz.

But while technology helps and the Warriors will take every advantage they can, it means nothing if they don't win. The Finals taught them that in the most painful way imaginable. More than 400 threes from one player? A record 73 wins? The first unanimous MVP? And now, signing Kevin Durant? Doesn't mean a thing without the ring. Michael Jordan himself told Joe Lacob as much when they dined over the summer. As His Airness decreed, "Seventy-three don't mean shit."

As the minutes ticked down to tipoff with the San Antonio Spurs,

Oracle was awash in antsy anticipation. The 190th consecutive sellout crowd filed into the arena not really knowing what to expect. The players methodically worked on their jumpers, baby hooks, and layups, as Dave East's remix of Fat Joe and Remy Ma's "All the Way Up" blared overhead. The chorus came around—*I'm all the way up / All the way up / Nothing can stop me / I'm all the way up*—and sounded prophetic.

Regardless, the Warriors sat atop the National Basketball Association with 29 teams eager to knock them down. Five years ago from this moment, Golden State could boast no homegrown All-Stars, Olympic gold medals, recent playoff appearances, or all-time records. They had come very far in a short period of time and there was more to do, but the season—one they hoped would affirm their place in basketball history—had arrived.

As Zaza Pachulia and Pau Gasol prepared for the jump ball from referee Dan Crawford, who had worked Game 7 of the Finals, Joe Lacob stood a few feet away, nervously bouncing on the balls of his feet in front of his usual courtside seat. Peter Guber was three seats to his left, also standing with anticipation. Stephen Curry stood in the backcourt, gnawing on his mouthpiece and retying the strings on his shorts, while Kevin Durant pointed to the sky and walked across the Warriors logo to his new usual spot, prompting another rush of cheers from the crowd.

When everyone was ready, Crawford tossed the ball high in the air.

A new season had begun.

# EPILOGUE

## The 2017 NBA Finals

The champagne is making my eyes tear up from 50 feet away.

Up ahead, past the blob of slow-shuffling media and beyond a hallway lined with sepia-toned photos of past Golden State greats—Wilt Chamberlain, Tom Meschery, Al Attles, Chris Mullin, Rick Barry, and finally Nate Thurmond—the Warriors are bouncing around their locker room as they celebrate the fifth championship in franchise history. There's enough Moët champagne to run up a six-digit tab, even as bottles of Stella Artois, Blue Moon, and Corona are passed around by team employees. Players mingle with their wives, kids, and parents. Executives and coaches hug each other like they'll never let go. Only those on the inside truly know the full measures it took to finish out a title run that the NBA largely treated as a fait accompli.

If only it were that simple. Sure, the Warriors ran off a 67-15 regular-season record—same as in 2015, when they also rolled toward a title—that was replete with memorable performances. In November against New Orleans, Stephen Curry set the NBA record with 13 threes in one game. In December against Indiana, Klay Thompson scored a career-high 60 points despite playing fewer than 30 minutes in the game. In February against Memphis, Draymond Green recorded the first triple-double in league history that didn't involve double-digit points (12 rebounds, 10 assists, 10 steals). On any given night, you were apt to see some feat that no basketball fan had ever witnessed.

But there were also stumbles along the way. San Antonio stomped them on opening night by 29 points. They blew a 13-point fourth-quarter lead in Cleveland on Christmas Day. And after Kevin Durant went down in late February with a sprained knee ligament, they lost five of their next seven games, their worst sustained stretch of play in Steve Kerr's three years as head coach. With a month to go in the season, they had slipped to second place in the conference standings. Golden State had played eight games in eight different cities in 13 days of travel that spanned the continent from one coast to the other. They were injured, exhausted, and the season was suddenly in limbo.

But in one of the most stunning stretches of late-season play in the modern era, the Warriors won their next 14 games, with Durant returning for only the last of those. Then with Thompson sitting out the season's penultimate game—and Kerr resting Curry and Green in the fourth quarter—Golden State finally dropped one, to the Utah Jazz, but had already locked up home-court advantage through the playoffs. The loss was meaningless. With Durant healthy again, the No. 1 seed in their pocket, and a mere 16 wins separating them from ultimate redemption, the Warriors set about taking back what they felt was stolen from them a year ago.

Their approach was different this time around. With no chase for 73 wins bearing down on his players, Kerr more closely heeded the advice of his training staff and made a concerted effort to manage in-game minutes and plan scheduled rest for players up and down the roster. "Every season is different unto itself," Kerr said before that Utah loss on April 10. "This season reminds me a lot of our first year when the last few games we already had the one-seed locked up. . . . We are trying to do the same thing this year in terms of monitoring minutes and making sure we are healthy and rested. Similar to two years ago, but very different from last year."

Just so long as the season resulted in a very different ending from 2016.

· · ·

As the blue and yellow confetti rained down inside Oracle Arena, Kerr embraced general manager Bob Myers with tears in his eyes and unconditional joy in his heart. This postseason had been the most painful of his entire NBA career. In missing the first 43 games of the 2015–16 season with a fluid leak in his spinal column that caused chronic pain and daily migraines, Kerr ceded in-game bench duties to Luke Walton. But with his upstart assistant now the head coach of the Los Angeles Lakers, Kerr desperately wanted to get through all 82 regular-season games without issue.

Not only did he coach every one, he missed just a single practice.

But there were good days and bad. Sometimes the tell was that he wasn't wearing a tie on the sidelines. He always deflected when anyone asked about his health. Especially on the road, Kerr would find himself cornered by well-wishers who just wanted to check in and see how he was doing: *You doing good? How ya feeling?* He always smiled and assuaged their concerns. It was more manageable, yes, but always lurking. After coming home from the grueling mid-March road trip, Kerr was supposed to speak with me at the team practice facility, but he couldn't stay. There was a doctor's appointment that even the team's media relations department didn't know about. Ten days after that, as I asked a source close to Kerr why he so often seems happy and carefree, the response shook me: "I don't think *happy* is the right word for Steve."

Why is that? "Well, he's having a hard time now with his health."

Three weeks later, Kerr's back gave out again. Sitting on a 2–0 lead in the first-round series against Portland, he announced he was stepping aside. Assistant coach Mike Brown, who'd once coached a young LeBron James to his first career Finals appearance and had years of bench experience to his name, became acting head coach. The affable and gregarious Brown was hired in part as a hedge against Kerr's health failing again, but this succession was going into motion at the most critical point in the season. They were still 14 wins shy of a title, and the competition would only get exponentially harder from there on.

But win the Warriors did, finishing off Portland in a four-game sweep before imposing the same fate on Utah. Even with Gordon Hayward and Rudy Gobert (albeit slightly hobbled from an injury suffered in the first round), the Jazz were overmatched from start to finish. The Warriors, now 8-0 in the playoffs, were halfway to a title, but San Antonio loomed in the conference finals. Even in dealing with their own injuries—Tony Parker was out for the playoffs with a ruptured quadriceps tendon, while MVP candidate Kawhi Leonard rolled his left ankle hard just a few days earlier and sat out the deciding Game 6 against Houston—the Spurs still had Gregg Popovich at the helm. Kerr's mentor was regarded as the best head coach in the game, but he would be matching up against Brown, who'd been his assistant a year ago.

So the basketball gods finally gave the fans a series that was years in the offing, but fortunes turned hard in the Warriors' favor when Leonard's ankle finally gave out. In the third quarter of Game 1, as the Spurs' lead swelled to as much as 25 points, Leonard landed on the foot of teammate David Lee, the ex-Warrior who was sitting on the Spurs bench just off the court. Leonard crumpled in obvious pain but stayed in the game. A couple of minutes later, Leonard landed awkwardly again, this time on the foot of Zaza Pachulia, who closed out aggressively as Leonard came down from a jumper. Reckless or not on Pachulia's part, Leonard's already compromised ankle could take no more. The Warriors stormed back to win Game 1 and took the next three games as Leonard, in street clothes, could only watch from the Spurs' bench.

Twelve playoff games, 12 wins. Just four to go, and they would have a chance to finish off their run against (who else?) the Cleveland Cavaliers, who romped through the first three rounds with a 12-1 record.

A third meeting in three years. A rubber match to decide NBA supremacy. With both teams healthy and rested—all those sweeps meant a lot of downtime in between each series, including nine days off for the Warriors before the Finals—the question of who was the NBA's best would definitively be decided.

With just four turnovers in Game 1, the Warriors were as disciplined as they were dangerous. Their 31 assists showed they could move the ball and score at will against a porous Cavs defense. A 113–91 thrashing and the Warriors were off and running. They were just three wins away from 16-0—the first undefeated postseason in NBA history.

But one hour and 45 minutes before the start of Game 2, news dropped that made dozens of gathered media members murmur and shift in their press seating. The back door to the interview room swung open and in strolled not Brown (who'd won 11 straight games) but Kerr. With hardly any advance notice, the Warriors head coach was headed back to the bench. Not even his players knew yet.

"Hi, everybody," Kerr said with a grin. "Any questions?"

. . .

After the final buzzer sounds, Kevin Durant doesn't know what to do first, but there's LeBron James, so they embrace for a few seconds. James has just become the first player to *ever* average a triple-double in a Finals, but it's a forgotten footnote for now. Durant was utterly dominant against the Cavaliers, averaging 35 points, eight rebounds, and five assists. In Games 1 and 2, he often drove the lane for uncontested slams. In Game 3 in Cleveland, it was Durant's dramatic pull-up three over

James with 45 seconds left that anchored an 11–0 Warriors run to end the game and secure an insurmountable 3–0 series lead. Even his 35 points in Game 4 helped turn that 21-point loss into something slightly more respectable.

But Durant's lethality was fully unleashed in the Game 5 clincher back at Oracle Arena. With all the pressure in the world on his shoulders, he was sensational, dropping 39 points on 20 shot attempts and keeping the Cavs at bay through a manic, back-and-forth fourth quarter that wasn't decided until the final minute.

With about 45 seconds left, Curry danced along the left wing above the arc as Kyrie Irving tried to move with him step for step. A year earlier, it was Irving who nailed the three that damned Golden State to a summer of second-guessing. This time, Curry, who finished with 34 points on the night, would seek his revenge. He hopped around, to his left, around to the right, left, right, left *again*, looking for that sliver of an opening. Curry finally juked one last time, saw his angle, and, with six seconds on the shot clock, let the ball fly from 25 feet out.

*Swish.*

Curry flew down the court, leaped in the air, and bounced hips midflight with Draymond Green. Andre Iguodala, who played 38 inspiring minutes and scored his most points (20) in nearly three months, looked right at Durant, who raised all seven feet and four inches of his arms high above in jubilation. After a decade in the NBA, after a long year of criticism and ridicule, Durant had on the most spectacular of stages.

And so he hugged James, then found his mother, Wanda, to embrace her, too. Then he found Curry, the undisputed star of this team, the man who pledged to put everything aside, all ego and pretense, to acclimate Durant and help him fulfill his mission of finally winning a title.

It hadn't been easy for Durant, whose personality was unlike any other in the Warriors locker room. His sense of humor could be tough to parse, and there were times when a surprising sensitivity would surface.

When one lighthearted postgame discussion about expensive suits led a reporter to harmlessly joke that "we poor sportswriters can't afford all that," Durant quickly retorted, "Man, you don't even *know* what poor is." He would also often push back on media members who asked weak press conference questions. (Fair enough, though.) Durant didn't quite embody the happy-go-lucky ethos that had been codified with Kerr's arrival, but he grew more comfortable as the season went on. Even sitting out five-plus weeks with the late-season knee injury was something he ultimately viewed as a positive. "I think that was good," Durant said after his first game back, "just to get away, kind of have a mental vacation from it all."

By the time the Warriors reached the Finals, Durant was a singular force, not only in his own play but in how he opened the floor up for Curry, Thompson, and others. It had taken all season but Durant was now fully integrated into Kerr's motion offense, thanks in large part to his adaptability and work ethic. "You can talk about whatever you want to talk about, but nobody comes in and cares about the game or loves the game as much as I do or works as hard as do I at the basketball game," Durant said afterward, his glittering Finals MVP trophy standing near him. "I knew at some point in my life that it will come around for me. So I just tried to stay with those principles and keep grinding."

As I inched my way toward the locker room, the Moët making my eyes water with each closing step, Durant emerged and gave Rich Kleiman, his business partner, a mammoth bear hug, the sheer happiness evident on his face. The tears of ecstasy in the locker room behind him, the sopping puddles of bubbly pooling on the floor, the high fives and the smiles—it was largely because of Durant, but it was also due to Kerr and Curry—who was three weeks away from signing a $201 million contract, the richest in NBA history—and Myers, whose dress shirt was drenched and practically see-through as he drank from a comically large champagne bottle, and Sammy Gelfand, the analytics whiz who made the rounds inside the locker room, shaking hands with anyone he could find, and still dozens more people down the line.

At the top of that hierarchy sat Joe Lacob, who watched from courtside as the Warriors became the first Oakland sports franchise in 43 years to win a championship on home soil. After he and Peter Guber lifted the Larry O'Brien trophy for the second time in their lives, Lacob was asked by ESPN's Doris Burke whom he wished to thank for making this title a reality.

"There is no doubt," he calmly began, "that who we have to acknowledge the most are *these guys right here!*" With Lacob now wildly gesticulating over his shoulder, the crowd went nuts, the scathing boos of five years ago little more than myth in this moment. "Fantastic team! Every single one of them! We *love* 'em! They're great players, Steph and Draymond and everybody else. And Kevin, thanks for coming!"

From down the dais, Durant replied, "Yes, sir!" He then kissed the championship trophy, already cradled in his enormous arms, for the first time in his life.

# NOTES

**PROLOGUE**

1 *As the ball left Stephen Curry's hands:* The descriptions of Game 7 in this prologue come directly from my being inside Oracle Arena on that day.

2 *eighth-best in NBA history:* A PER around 25 indicates an excellent, All-NBA-caliber season. Above 30 and you're talking about a historically good season. Curry's PER was 31.46. By comparison, when Russell Westbrook averaged a 30-point triple-double for the 2016–17 season, his PER was 30.6. The only other modern NBA player who appears among the top-10 all-time single-season PER totals is LeBron James (Basketball-Reference.com).

2 *three-point attempt from the side tunnel:* Ron Kroichick, "Stephen Curry's long tunnel shot has become Warriors fan favorite," *San Francisco Chronicle*, February 21, 2017.

3 *eight of 15 teams:* The Western Conference didn't grow to 15 teams until the 2004–05 season, so this stretch of playoff absences is more pronounced than one might think.

5 *millions in pure profit:* In valuing the Warriors at $2.6 billion in February 2017, *Forbes* estimated that their operating income jumped from $44.9 million (2015) to $58 million (2016) and then $74.2 million (2017).

**1: NEW BLOOD**

8 *named for a long-gone team:* The Philadelphia Warriors originally played in the American Basketball League in 1925.

8 *38 percent more:* Fulks averaged 23.1 points while Bob Feerick could only muster 16.8 points as the league's second-best scorer.

8 *"the Babe Ruth of basketball":* Russ Davis, "Basketball's Hottest Shot," *Saturday Evening Post,* January 3, 1948. Fulks so infuriated opponents that one player was quoted in the piece with this advice: "The only way to stop Fulks is to break his legs."

9 *unleashed the infinite possibilities of a one-handed jump shot:* William McDonald, "Kenny Sailors, a Pioneer of the Jump Shot, Dies at 95," *New York Times,* January 30, 2016.

9 *"the greatest assortment of shots I've ever seen in basketball":* Phil Jasner, "Joe Fulks: NBA's 1st Superstar," *Philadelphia Daily News,* March 22, 1976.

9 *a meeting held high in the Empire State Building:* "Pro Court Loops Merge," *Plainfield* (N.J.) *Courier-News,* August 4, 1949.

9 *the NBA was born:* The NBA has officially absorbed BAA records and results into its own historical archives, which can result in some apparent contradictions. For example, a banner hanging in the Warriors' practice facility commemorates their place as "1946–47 NBA Champions" despite the NBA being two years away from existence at the time.

10 *winning the 1974–75 Finals:* Weirdly enough, none of the Warriors' Finals games were actually played at the Oakland Coliseum Arena. Due to a scheduling mishap, the Warriors had to play all their games at their old home, the Cow Palace in San Francisco.

10 *1966–67:* This was a truly memorable six-game matchup against Wilt Chamberlain, the former Warrior who finally won his first title in eight seasons. He averaged 18 points and 29 rebounds in the series, even as Nate Thurmond (14 points and 27 boards a night) nearly proved his equal.

10 *Larry Bird:* The Warriors could've picked Bird with the fifth pick in the 1978 draft, opting instead to select Purvis Short, who played 12 seasons and stands as the club's eighth-best scorer of all time.

11 *"Nellie Ball":* Don Nelson, "Nellie Ball," *Players' Tribune,* July 19, 2016.

11 *a Bay Area icon:* Mieuli was also known for his vehement opposition to the NBA's adoption of the three-point line. In remarks reported by the Associated Press ("Warrior Owner Makes Drafts, Rips New Rule," *Santa Cruz Sentinel,* June 26, 1979), Mieuli said, "Whatever good it's going to do, the price was too high. We've separated ourselves from the main body of basketball." A month later, Mieuli still hadn't calmed down. "I simply do not want my name in the annals of the 22 small men who in the summer

of 1979 had the audacity to change the game of basketball," he said, according to UPI, which described the owner's comments as "another one of this world-meanderings" ("Mieuli Still Fuming," *Petaluma Argus-Courier*, July 31, 1979).

12 *After his parents divorced:* Mark Fainaru-Wada, "The man who owns the Warriors," *San Francisco Chronicle*, February 10, 2002.

12 *Cohan paid $21 million:* Ibid.

13 *immediately began asking anyone in sight for some shred of intel:* Ric Bucher, "Warriors' Minority Partner Buys Team," *San Jose Mercury News*, October 9, 1994.

13 *his name didn't even appear in the team's media guide:* Phillip Matier and Andrew Ross, "Why Warriors' Silent Partner Began to Talk Back," *San Francisco Chronicle*, July 23, 1994.

13 *"I want to assure our many fans":* Bucher, "Warriors Minority Partner," 1994.

13 *"I guess I've been in business":* Associated Press, October 11, 1994.

13 *Cohan undermined Nelson publicly:* Mark Heisler, "Golden State Sends Webber to Washington," *Los Angeles Times*, November 18, 1994.

13 *Nelson privately told his coaching staff:* Tom Friend, "Nelson Leaves The Warriors As Result of Webber Rift," *New York Times*, February 14, 1995.

14 *floated the possibility:* Associated Press, "Warriors consider move to San Jose," *Santa Cruz Sentinel*, December 10, 1994.

14 *Cohan deftly evaded:* Mal Florence, "Obviously, He Didn't Want to Talk About It," *Los Angeles Times*, February 14, 1995. (Writing in the *San Francisco Chronicle*, Bruce Jenkins concluded that Nelson's departure wouldn't make much difference anyway: "They could bring in a corpse to coach this team and it couldn't get any worse.")

14 *"didn't appear to be responding":* Friend, "Nelson Leaves the Warriors," 1995.

14 *"Policimo":* Dirk Facer, "24 second clock," *Deseret News*, October 12, 1997.

14 *"I just got to the point":* David Steele, "Warriors Fire Sprewell for Attack on Coach," *San Francisco Chronicle*, December 4, 1997.

14 *Cohan sued Nelson:* Associated Press, January 7, 1999.

15 *"a horrible reaction":* Matt Steinmetz, "Warriors Owner Opens Up," *Contra Costa Times*, December 5, 2001.

15 *in breach of contract with the OACC:* Fainaru-Wada, "The Man who owns," 2002. Much of the information in the preceding paragraph and this one—including the controversy around Cohan's dealings with the city and the later quote from Scott Haggerty—comes from this lengthy investigative report.

16  *Midway through the fourth quarter, a ceremony took place:* Mike Wise, "Twin Towers Star as the West Comes Up Big," *New York Times,* February 14, 2000.

16  *Cohan stood at center court:* David Steele, "Warriors Almost Left Unscathed," *San Francisco Chronicle,* February 14, 2000.

16  *"As soon as the roar for Jordan subsided":* Ray Ratto, "Warriors' Cohan hits the bottom," *San Francisco Examiner,* February 14, 2000.

16  *As Cohan felt the humiliation:* Steinmetz, "Warriors Owner Opens Up," 2001.

16  *five-year-old son:* Dax and younger brother Chad would both go on to play four years of lacrosse at Duke. Their sister, Christina, also graduated a Blue Devil.

17  *"didn't catch my eye":* Ralph Wiley, "Why West went south," ESPN.com Page 2, May 2, 2002.

17  *Robert Rowell was just 27:* Most of the biographical details were gleaned from a copy of the Warriors' 2003–04 Media Guide, which contains an extensive biography of Rowell.

17  *a rising star in sports business:* John Lombardo, "Forty Under 40: Robert Rowell," *SportsBusiness Journal,* November 5, 2001.

18  *rumblings that summer revolved around Kevin Garnett:* Tim Kawakami, "KEVIN GARNETT to the Warriors, folks (it could be)," Bay Area News Group, June 28, 2007.

18  *cuts and scrapes on his legs:* Marc Stein, "Cuts, abrasions lead some to question cause of Ellis' injury," ESPN.com, September 3, 2008.

19  *publicly chastise Mullin:* Associated Press, October 11, 2008.

19  *the most lucrative in Bay Area sports history:* Tony Cooper, "Jamison stays for big bucks," *San Francisco Chronicle,* August 29, 2001.

20  *"We view this as a win-win for everyone":* NBA.com, November 17, 2008.

20  *"I wanted to be out pretty bad":* Associated Press, November 16, 2009.

20  *Rowell promised season-ticket holders:* Brad Weinstein, "Team would bust tax level in effort to keep Arenas," *San Francisco Chronicle,* February 23, 2003.

21  *Cohan might be getting serious about selling the team:* Tim Kawakami, "Warriors big picture: Is Cohan getting ready to sell?" Bay Area News Group, July 3, 2009.

21  *sold 20 percent of the team:* Associated Press, July 13, 2004.

21  *the Internal Revenue Service came after him:* Mark Fainaru-Wada, "Warriors owner accused of tax evasion, fights IRS," *San Francisco Chronicle,* May 17, 2007.

22  *most logical suitor was Larry Ellison:* Tim Kawakami, "Warriors sale: The Ellison/20% minority investors Super-Group could all but seal this deal," Bay Area News Group, June 5, 2010.

22  *third-richest man in America:* Ellison trailed only Bill Gates and Warren Buffett, according to a *Forbes* ranking (March 10, 2010).

22  *tried to buy the Seattle SuperSonics for $425 million:* Berry Tramel, "OKC group agrees to buy Sonics," *The Oklahoman*, July 18, 2006.

22  *Peter Guber, the famed Hollywood producer:* Some of Guber's most well-known credits are *Rain Man* (which won Best Picture), *The Color Purple, Midnight Express, Gorillas in the Mist, The Witches of Eastwick,* and *Flashdance,* but his greatest contribution to the cinema might be helping to convince Jack Nicholson to take the role of the Joker in Tim Burton's *Batman.* As Guber recounted in his 2011 book *Tell To Win* (pp. 113–14), he and Burton took the studio jet to Nicholson's home in Aspen to seal the deal. Once there, the Oscar-winning actor told them to prepare for horseback-riding the following day. When Burton said in confidence that he didn't know how to ride horses, Guber corrected him, "You do now!"

23  *"Chris and I both felt":* Marcus Thompson II, "Warriors' $450 million surprise," Bay Area News Group, July 16, 2010.

23  *not even eclipsing $500 million:* This was confirmed by a league source.

23  *about to board a helicopter for Delphi:* Marcus Thompson II, "The long journey of Warriors' owner Joe Lacob," Bay Area News Group, October 28, 2015.

23  *Lacob lived his earliest years in New Bedford:* Tim Weisberg, "New Bedford native Joe Lacob not resting on his laurels as NBA owner," *New Bedford Standard-Times,* April 14, 2013. Most of the biographical details in this paragraph (as well as the quotation) come from this extended interview with Lacob.

24  *knew he would one day own an NBA team:* From an interview Lacob and Guber did for the Warriors' YouTube account ("Warriors Weekly: Behind The Scenes With Joe Lacob And Peter Guber—11/22/10").

24  *"One of the great breaks in my life":* Marcus Thompson II, "Warriors owner Joe Lacob has a plan—and patience," Bay Area News Group, March 10, 2011. Lacob, perhaps unsurprisingly, has returned to New Bedford only twice since leaving nearly fifty years ago.

24  *started out with Cokes and then ice-cream sandwiches:* Marcia C. Smith, "From Angels peanut vendor to NBA owner," *Orange County Register,* November 22, 2010.

24  *the bags could be double- and triple-stacked:* From an interview and Q&A session Lacob did (along with Cavs owner Dan Gilbert) at Zynga headquarters in San Francisco on June 5, 2015.

25  *took a mathematics class taught by Edward O. Thorp:* Bruce Schoenfeld, "What

Happened When Venture Capitalists Took Over the Golden State Warriors,"
*New York Times Magazine*, April 3, 2016.

25 *"The big thrill"*: Paul O'Neil, "The Professor Who Breaks the Bank," *Life*,
March 27, 1964.

25 *published in the journals*: "Acquisition deficits induced by sodium nitrite
in rats and mice," *Psychopharmacology*, February 28, 1979; "Modulation of
memory processes induced by stimulation of the entorhinal cortex," *Physiology & Behavior*, July 1977.

25 *47, by his own count*: Lowell Cohn, "Joe Lacob's grand ambition for Warriors,"
*Santa Rosa Press Democrat*, January 22, 2011.

26 *"Hell of a good piece of advice"*: Lacob said this during an interview and Q&A
session with LinkedIn employees on September 22, 2016.

26 *"I liked the science"*: From an interview Lacob gave to "Alan Olsen's American
Dreams," presented by Groco CPAs and Advisors, November 29, 2012.

26 *the largest-ever IPO*: Thomas Lueck, "Cetus in Record Offering; Market Response Is Cool," *New York Times*, March 7, 1981.

27 *earned Mullis the Nobel Prize*: Kary B. Mullis, "Nobel Lecture," December 8,
1993 (Nobelprize.org).

27 *"I was in the right place"*: Lacob interview with Olsen (2012).

27 *"We're extremely committed to that investment thesis"*: Matt Richtel, "Green Energy Enthusiasts Are Also Betting on Fossil Fuels," *New York Times*, March 16,
2007.

28 *"a drunken sailor"*: Dan Primack, "Kleiner-Backed Terralliance Begins To Im-
plode," peHUB.com, April 2, 2009.

28 *the company was in free fall*: Adam Lashinsky, "How a big bet on oil went
bust," *Fortune*, March 26, 2010.

28 *changed its name in early 2010 and again the following year*: Terralliance became TTI Exploration before morphing into NEOS GeoSolutions in January
2011.

28 *less than subtle*: Zoran Basich, "Let's Hope Joe Lacob's Golden State Warriors
Is No Terralliance," *Wall Street Journal*, July 15, 2010.

28 *"We compete with Bill Gates every day at Kleiner Perkins"*: Earl Gustkey, "Investor Keeps the Faith in ABL," *Los Angeles Times*, November 4, 1997.

28 *filed for Chapter 11 bankruptcy*: Associated Press, December 23, 1998.

28 *slated for San Jose in January 1999*: Associated Press, January 1, 1999.

28 *purchased a minority stake*: Celtics statement issued on January 18, 2006
(NBA.com).

29  *sat in the front row at Staples Center:* Marcia C. Smith, "Orange County boy returns to area as part owner of Celtics," *Orange County Register*, June 12, 2008.

29  *Cohan released his final statement:* "Galatioto Sports Partners Secure Purchase Agreement," July 15, 2010 (NBA.com).

30  *Lacob returned their calls that same day:* Marcus Thompson II, "Joe Lacob: 'We're all about winning,' " Bay Area News Group, July 15, 2010.


## 2: IN THE NAME OF HIS FATHER

32  *Curry's two late free throws:* Terry Armour, "Streak-busters," *Chicago Tribune*, April 9, 1996.

32  *the Charlotte Hornets' all-time leader in points scored:* Entering the 2017–18 season, Curry remained the franchise's leader not only in points but also games (701), field goals (3,951), and three-pointers (929).

32  *the same Akron, Ohio, hospital where LeBron James had been delivered:* Mark Purdy, "Tracing the LeBron James, Stephen Curry roots in Akron, Ohio," Bay Area News Group, June 8, 2015.

32  *"I saw drugs, guns, killings; it was crazy":* Grant Wahl, "Ahead of His Class," *Sports Illustrated*, February 18, 2002.

33  *Dell Curry made nearly $20 million:* Per Curry's player page on Basketball -Reference.com.

33  *frequent one-on-one showdowns with Vince Carter:* From Carter's interview with ESPN, aired on April 9, 2016.

33  *idolized guards like Allen Iverson, Steve Nash, and Reggie Miller:* Jessica Camerato, "Curry Remembers How HOF Finalist Iverson Inspired His Career," CSN Philly, April 3, 2016; Robby Kalland, "Steph Curry on His Basketball Heroes, The Warriors' 'Different' Season, and Getting Rest," *Dime Magazine*, March 22, 2017.

33  *"I found myself subconsciously picking up things":* Todd Shanesy, "Looks can be deceiving," *Spartanburg Herald-Journal*, January 13, 2007.

33  *5-foot-5 in sneakers by eighth grade:* Alex Ballingall, "Stephen Curry's Grade 8 season at tiny Toronto school remembered," *Toronto Star*, February 26, 2015.

33  *only 5-foot-8 (and maybe 150 pounds) by his sophomore year:* David Fleming, "Stephen Curry: The Full Circle," *ESPN the Magazine*, April 23, 2015. Much of the description of this time in Curry's life in this paragraph and the next (including the "summer of tears" quote) comes from this story.

34  *"The gifts that he has"*: From interviews given to the Warriors' YouTube channel, featured in a video titled "Stephen Curry's High School Years," uploaded
on December 3, 2015. The quotes in this paragraph from Shonn Brown and
Chad Fair, as well as confirmation of his yearbook quote and school records
for steals and three-pointers, come from this video.

34  *senior-year page in the yearbook:* His yearbook page postscript, in asking for
three things he'll be remembered as, also read: "Swoosh . . . baller . . . sweet to
everyone . . ."

35  *stopped regularly attending Hokies games:* Grant Wahl, "The Next Step for
Steph," *Sports Illustrated*, September 22, 2008.

35  *"kids don't pass the eye test":* Pat Forde, "How Stephen Curry went from ignored college recruit to possible NBA MVP," Yahoo! Sports, April 23, 2015.

35  *"A lot of Division I schools":* Ibid.

35  *His son Brendan played with Steph:* Ben Cohen, "The Stephen Curry Approach to Youth Sports," *Wall Street Journal*, May 17, 2016.

35  *"I saw brilliance":* From an interview McKillop gave to ESPN's Jeremy Schaap
for an E:60 segment that aired on April 24, 2014.

35  *The coaches practically danced around the room:* Pat Forde, "Spurned by ACC,
Curry dances with Davidson," ESPN.com, March 3, 2007.

37  *"He's for real":* John Wawrow, Associated Press, March 15, 2007.

37  *"the star of the tournament whose legend continues to grow":* Schaap, 2014.

38  *four future NBA players in their starting lineup:* Those were Darnell Jackson,
Mario Chalmers, Brandon Rush, and Darrell Arthur. (Coming off the bench
were future NBA players Cole Aldrich, Sasha Kaun, and Sherron Collins.)

38  *the entire history-making season almost never happened:* Scott Fowler, "Steph
Curry not tough? The injury that almost derailed Davidson's NCAA run,"
*Charlotte Observer*, May 20, 2016. Much of the ensuing anecdote about
Curry's injury in the next two paragraphs comes from this story.

40  *"Curry is less athlete than folk hero":* Tommy Craggs, "The Year of Magical
Shooting," *Slate*, March 12, 2009.

40  *the 25th-best scorer in NCAA men's basketball history:* Curry would've had
an outside shot at breaking the all-time scoring mark—set by LSU's Pete
Maravich nearly 40 years earlier—if he had stayed for his senior year. Curry
scored 974 points in his junior year and ended up just 1,032 shy of Pistol
Pete.

40  *Several Charlotte TV stations:* Associated Press, April 23, 2009.

40  *"His first step is average at best":* Jonathan Givony, Kyle Nelson, and Joseph

Treutlein, "NCAA Weekly Performers, 2/28/09," DraftExpress.com, February 28, 2009.

40 *"an interesting case"*: Matt Kamalsky, "Situational Statistics: This Year's Point Guard Crop," DraftExpress.com, May 8, 2009.

40 *"Far below NBA standard"*: Stevan Petrovic, "Strengths/Weaknesses," NBA Draft.net, December 15, 2008.

41 *"Was Curry capable of blowing by defenders in college?"*: Doug Gottlieb, "Curry's skills may get lost in translation," ESPN.com, May 11, 2009.

41 *wanted to beef up the frontcourt*: From an interview Riley gave to the Warriors' YouTube channel, conducted on June 22, 2009.

41 *fifth-youngest roster in the NBA*: Per Basketball-Reference.com, the only teams younger than Golden State (25.0 years) in the 2008–09 season were Chicago (24.9), Oklahoma City (24.5), Portland (24.0), and Memphis (23.3).

41 *"A draft pick is an asset"*: The quotes in this paragraph from Riley come from an interview he gave (as well as audio captured) to NBA.com as part of its predraft coverage that aired on NBA TV ("NBA Draft '09: Opening Chapter"), accessed via Internet Archive in July 2016.

42 *grew up the sons of farmers*: Con Marshall, "The Riley twins: From Indiana farm to Chadron State to NBA," *Chadron Record*, October 22, 2013. Most of the biographical details in this paragraph come from this story.

42 *30-mph winds and freezing snow showers*: Donald W. Nauss, "Commuter Plane Crashes Near Detroit, Killing 29," *Los Angeles Times*, January 10, 1997.

42 *he heard a voice inside his head*: Perry A. Farrell, "Grizzlies' executive skipped Flight 3272," *Detroit Free Press*, January 16, 1997.

43 *"It reinforced my faith"*: Rusty Simmons, "Profile: New Warriors GM Larry Riley," *San Francisco Chronicle*, June 1, 2009.

43 *"The worst decisions"*: "NBA Draft '09: Opening Chapter" video footage.

44 *"Curry looked smooth, smart, and extremely talented"*: Jonathan Givony, "NBA teams take to Chicago for combine," NBA.com, May 28, 2009.

44 *Riley had also scouted Curry in person*: Harvey Araton, "Coveting Sharpshooter, Knicks Just Missed," *New York Times*, December 14, 2014.

44 *"I didn't feel like there was anybody at the five spot who could fit into our rotation"*: Michael Lee, "For Grunfeld and Wizards, Trade Was a 'No-Brainer,'" *Washington Post*, June 25, 2009.

44 *compiled mock drafts from around the internet*: Accessed via Internet Archive (www.nba.com/warriors/news/2009_mock_drafts.html).

45 *feel the butterflies puttering around his stomach:* "NBA Draft '09: Opening Chapter" video footage.

45 *there was immediate befuddlement:* "NBA Draft '09: Inside the War Room" video that aired on NBA TV, accessed via Internet Archive in July 2016. The scene details in this paragraph and the following one come from this video footage.

46 *prevent his client from ever becoming a member of the Warriors:* Marc J. Spears, "The story of how Stephen Curry's agent and dad didn't want the Warriors to draft him," Yahoo! Sports, May 4, 2015.

46 *liking what he saw in Mike D'Antoni's high-scoring offense:* Tim Kawakami, "Stephen Curry and the night that transformed the Warriors," Bay Area News Group, February 13, 2014.

46 *"We had a lot of discussions":* Tim Kawakami, "Former Suns GM Steve Kerr on the Stoudemire for Curry almost-trade in 2009: 'We were very far down the road,'" Bay Area News Group, February 11, 2014.

47 *they heard cheering from the team's war room:* Dan Bickley, "Forever Linked," *Arizona Republic,* March 2, 2016.

47 *a hopeful headline:* A NEW LOOK IN THE WORKS: SUNS DRAFT CLARK, EYE TRADE FOR CURRY, *Arizona Republic,* June 26, 2009.

47 *Austin got a call from someone in the Suns front office:* Spears, "The story of how Stephen Curry's agent," 2015.

48 *"not going to win that way":* Tim Kawakami, "Monta Ellis on pairing with Stephen Curry: 'We can't . . . (We're) not going to win that way,'" *San Jose Mercury News,* September 28, 2009.

48 *"Everybody knows it's a business":* From an interview Ellis gave to the Warriors' YouTube channel ("Live with Monta Ellis at Warriors Training Camp— 09/29/09"), conducted on September 29, 2009.

48 *took it as a veteran player making it known:* Gerald Narciso, "Stephen Curry Talks About the Alleged Beef With Monta Ellis," *Dime Magazine,* November 16, 2009.

49 *taken his demand for a trade public:* Marcus Thompson II, "Warriors' Jackson wants to be traded," *San Jose Mercury News,* August 29, 2009.

49 *suspended by Nelson for two preseason games:* Associated Press, October 10, 2009.

49 *"I can't be a role model":* Rusty Simmons, "Jackson abandons captaincy," SFGate.com, October 13, 2009.

49 *"I'm kind of jealous":* Karen Crouse, "And to Think, He Was Almost a Knick," *New York Times,* November 11, 2009.

49  *Curry even led a spirited rendition:* From YouTube footage ("Steph Curry sings Happy Birthday to Monta Ellis 10/26/2009") uploaded on October 26, 2009.

50  *took a three-hour nap that afternoon that helped calm his nerves:* Stephen Curry, "My Rookie Season: Stephen Curry's NBA Debut," GQ.com, November 5, 2009. Most of Curry's insights from that day and what he was doing and feeling before and after the game come from this diary entry.

51  *gave an interview to ESPN to rip Don Nelson:* Chris Broussard, "Jackson's agent goes after Nelson," ESPN.com, November 9, 2009.

51  *"it's harder than hell to trade that guy":* Henry Abbott, "Don Nelson: 'It's harder than hell to trade that guy,'" ESPN.com, November 13, 2009.

51  *"Everybody knows the situation here":* Rusty Simmons, "Game 7: Warriors at Indiana (final)," SFGate.com, November 11, 2009.

52  *Curry tweeted:* twitter.com/StephenCurry30/status/5639862962.

52  *with 25 family and friends who'd requested tickets:* Stephen Curry, "My Rookie Season: How Stephen Curry Spent His Time in New York City," GQ.com, November 19, 2009.

52  *caused the All-Star power forward to jaw in his face:* Video footage uploaded to YouTube ("Stephen Curry blocks David Lee and David Lee cries about it") on November 15, 2009.

52  *watching old footage of his Davidson days:* Stephen Curry, "My Rookie Season: Stephen Curry's Thanksgiving Plans," GQ.com, November 26, 2009.

53  *James came to see Curry play in the Sweet 16 in Detroit:* Stephen Curry, "My Rookie Season: Stephen Curry Hangs at LeBron's Pad," GQ.com, November 24, 2009. Most of the details in this paragraph and the next regarding Curry and James's visit, as well as their history, come from this story.

53  *it was Curry, playing for the opposing team, who sank a contested three-pointer for the win:* Ryan Jones, "LeBron Camp Report," *Slam Magazine*, July 9, 2008.

54  *"There is something bright at the end of the tunnel":* Rusty Simmons, "Stephen Curry keeps undermanned Warriors in it," *San Francisco Chronicle*, March 6, 2010.

54  *use what's known as a hardship waiver:* Rusty Simmons, "Warriors use hardship waiver," SFGate.com, November 20, 2009.

54  *"We've got a little hiccup here":* Ric Bucher, "Rowell talks futures of Nelson, Jackson," ESPN.com, November 16, 2009.

54  *the same injury he had suffered 13 months earlier:* "Curry sprains his left ankle," *Charlotte Observer* (syndicated in *Chicago Tribune*), February 15, 2009.

54 *"That kind of summed up our season"*: Rusty Simmons, "Limp to victory is fitting finish," *San Francisco Chronicle*, April 15, 2010.

## 3: BETABALL

58 *Lacob himself personally signed off on the deal*: Rusty Simmons, "Lacob/Guber dawn a new day," SFGate.com, November 15, 2010.

58 *Lacob bought out the final year of Don Nelson's contract*: Marc Stein, "Sources: Keith Smart to coach Warriors," ESPN.com, September 24, 2010.

58 *Smart was familiar to the team*: He was also plenty familiar to Peter Guber, a Syracuse grad who'll never forget the sight of Smart's title-winning shot against his alma mater all those years before. "I don't forget, but I forgive," Guber would say.

58 *Nelson retired for good to Hawaii*: Scott Ostler, "For Don Nelson, life is good at his Maui home," *San Francisco Chronicle*, April 18, 2011.

59 *stripped of his decision-making power*: Marcus Thompson II, "New Warriors owners Joe Lacob and Peter Guber preach patience," *San Jose Mercury News*, November 15, 2010.

59 *in six months' time*: Al Saracevic, "Owner Joe Lacob rebuilt Warriors with Silicon Valley values," SFGate.com, June 7, 2015.

59 *grew up cheering general manager Billy Beane's Oakland A's*: From an interview Kirk Lacob did with GoldenStateofMind.com ("Interview with Kirk Lacob (Pt. 2): The Warriors, Sports VU & solving the 'communication problem'"), published on September 28, 2012.

59 *Lacob cited Mullin's hiring*: Tim Kawakami, "Joe Lacob on the New Era Warriors: 'Something very special is happening already,'" Bay Area News Group, November 15, 2010.

60 *"He is just so impressive"*: Ibid.

60 *the international experience*: Curry had previously played for Team USA at the FIBA Under-19 World Championships in Serbia in 2007. His teammates then included future NBA players Jonny Flynn, Patrick Beverley, Michael Beasley, and DeAndre Jordan.

60 *bonded with Iguodala and Durant*: From remarks Iguodala made in his introductory press conference with the Warriors on July 11, 2013.

61 *Lee needed an intense regimen of antibiotics*: "Wilson Chandler's Tooth Almost Ended David Lee's Career," *Deadspin* via *Sports Radio Interviews*, December 10, 2010.

61  *in the very next game, against the Clippers:* This game is perhaps even better known as the night of Jeremy Lin's NBA debut. The Palo Alto High School and Harvard grad came in to play the final 2:32 of garbage time, although to a raucous ovation from the home crowd.

61  *looked as if Curry had been fitted for an ankle cast:* Marcus Thompson II, "Stephen Curry reinjures ankle in Golden State Warriors' victory," *San Jose Mercury News*, October 29, 2010.

62  *"I don't think I could write a script":* From video footage of Lacob's remarks ("Warriors New Ownership Introductory Luncheon") uploaded to the Warriors' YouTube channel on November 16, 2010. The other scene details and quotes in the following paragraphs are also from this video.

63  *"This is not the cure for cancer":* Tim Kawakami, "Joe Lacob on the New Era Warriors: 'Something very special is happening already,'" Bay Area News Group, November 15, 2010.

63  *"Be careful . . . all glory is fleeting":* From an interview Lacob and Guber gave to the Warriors' YouTube Channel ("Owners' Box: Looking Back At Year One - 11/12/11"), uploaded on November 14, 2011.

64  *"They are terrible":* From an interview Lacob gave to IDG Ventures' Phil Sanderson and a room full of venture capitalists in the fall of 2015, uploaded to YouTube ("Interview With Warriors Owner Joe Lacob") on April 10, 2016.

64  *"Well, you're going to have to look down if you want to see the camera":* This entire interaction with Schlenk, as well his background and biography, is detailed in my feature story for Wired.com ("Hoops 2.0: Inside the NBA's Data-Driven Revolution"), published on April 18, 2011.

64  *"one of those guys who flies under the radar":* Paul Suellentrop, "Homegrown Travis Schlenk finds his way around the NBA," *Wichita Eagle*, April 27, 2013.

65  *a news story:* Rusty Simmons, "Al Thornton makes quick debut with Warriors," *San Francisco Chronicle*, March 5, 2011. The section that initially caught my eye was titled "High-tech basketball."

65  *a movement that would revolutionize how basketball is analyzed:* Rob Mahoney, "Optical Tracking Offers Glimpse of the Future," *New York Times*, March 7, 2011.

65  *SportVU didn't originally develop from anything sports-related:* "Hoops 2.0," 2011.

65  *partnered with a graphics firm named Vizrt to provide CNN with its Jedi-like holograms:* Jason Chen, "How the CNN Holographic Interview System Works," *Gizmodo*, November 4, 2008.

66  *an $8.5 billion business:* Daniel Kaplan, "Goodell sets revenue goal of $25B by 2027 for NFL," *SportsBusiness Journal,* April 5, 2010.

66  *"You don't want to come in and say":* "Hoops 2.0," 2011.

67  *started out as a $250-a-month intern:* Jayda Evans, "Sonics' GM Presti sets new beat," *Seattle Times,* October 28, 2007.

67  *second-youngest GM in league history:* Jerry Colangelo was 28 when he was named general manager of the expansion Phoenix Suns in 1968.

67  *SportVU first came on their radar:* The details in this paragraph and the next regarding how the Warriors both discovered and implemented SportVU were initially reported for my Wired.com story ("Hoops 2.0") in April 2011.

68  *Lacob did an hour-long Q&A:* The Lacob quotes in this paragraph and the next come from audio of his KNBR interview conducted in studio on January 27, 2011 (Warriors.com).

71  *getting left behind:* For whatever reason, the Lakers were the last remaining holdout, not sending any representatives to Sloan until the 2014 conference.

71  *a few writers in attendance started tweeting about comments Lacob had made:* The controversy resurfaced a few weeks later when the official panel video was uploaded online. The relevant portion of Lacob's comments was then transcribed and posted online by BayAreaSportsGuy.com ("Joe Lacob on bloggers and real fans, in his own words") on March 28, 2011, but over the years the video disappeared from the Sloan website. I asked Jessica Gelman (the Sloan conference cofounder and moderator of this specific panel) if a copy of the video still survived. She told me several MIT servers—including the one storing that panel—were accidentally wiped in 2015 and could not be fully restored.

72  *Lacob emailed beat writers the next day:* Rusty Simmons, "Lacob explains 'real fan' comment," SFGate.com, March 6, 2011.

72  *Lacob mingled in the halls:* Marc Tracy, "The Joy of Stats," *Tablet,* April 27, 2011.

72  *a $1.6 million renovation:* Jon Xavier, "Golden State Warriors HQ gets $1.6M in renovations," *Silicon Valley Business Journal,* July 8, 2011.

73  *Goofing around during one February practice:* Lori Preuitt, "He Shoots, He Scores," NBC Bay Area, February 3, 2011.

## 4: GROWING PAINS

75 *the Warriors had hired a new assistant general manager:* Tim Kawakami, "Reported move to hire player agent Bob Myers may be game-changer for Golden State Warriors," Bay Area News Group, April 13, 2011.

76 *a rabid Warriors fan:* Myers even keeps the ticket stub from his first-ever Warriors game—a 104–102 win over the New York Knicks on January 15, 1982, thanks to 32 points from Bernard King—in his wallet (Mark Medina, "How Bob Myers went from UCLA walk-on to architect of Warriors NBA championship," *Los Angeles Daily News,* November 23, 2015).

76 *played ball at Monte Vista High School:* Myers remains the school's most high-profile graduate, if only because supermodel Christy Turlington (1987) didn't *technically* graduate, at least if Wikipedia is to be believed.

76 *Harrick facilitated a meeting:* Chris Ballard, "The Architect: Meet the man who built the Warriors with a golden touch," *Sports Illustrated,* June 8, 2016.

76 *could intern at financial giant Bear Stearns:* From an interview Myers gave to the Warriors' YouTube channel ("Bob Myers Interview—Part 1"), uploaded on June 3, 2011.

76 *Kobe Bryant stopping by during Myers's first day:* From an interview Myers gave to KNBR's Damon Bruce on May 19, 2011.

77 *seen wearing his Warriors sweatshirt around campus:* From comments Myers made during a discussion (with Rick Welts) at the Dreamforce conference in San Francisco on September 15, 2015.

77 *acquired the firm in 2006 for a reported $12 million:* Brooks Barnes, "A Sports Agent with Hollywood in His Blood," *New York Times,* July 7, 2013.

77 *some $575 million in contracts:* Per the Warriors. In the NBA, agents' fees are capped at 4 percent max, easily making Myers a multimillionaire on these commissions.

77 *a call out of the blue from Danny Ainge:* Tim Kawakami, "Why Golden State Warriors owe Danny Ainge big time," *San Jose Mercury News,* March 15, 2016.

77 *Myers himself asked Ainge to put in a good word with Lacob:* Ibid.

77 *Myers had sensed that reluctance:* Tim Kawakami, "Bob Myers interview: How the Warriors GM was hired five years ago, what he was thinking during his interview with Lacob, and much more," Bay Area News Group, March 11, 2016.

78 *something like an apprenticeship:* Tim Kawakami, "Joe Lacob on Bob Myers: 'Bob would be expected to ascend to the GM role,'" Bay Area News Group, April 15, 2011.

78  *invited Tellem to dinner:* Tim Kawakami, "Myers on landing with the War-
    riors: One of the top five or six jobs in the NBA," Bay Area News Group,
    April 15, 2011.

78  *The super-agent knew right away:* Tellem, it just so happens, followed Myers's
    lead in 2015 when he joined the front office of the Detroit Pistons.

78  *exhibited a very public frustration:* Darren Heitner, "Bob Myers To Become
    Golden State Warriors Assistant General Manager," SportsAgentBlog.com,
    April 14, 2011.

79  *BYU sensation Jimmer Fredette and the frenzy to secure his representation:*
    Three weeks after Myers accepted the Warriors job, Fredette announced he
    had signed with agent Jeff Austin, who also represents Stephen Curry.

79  *his likeness graces the NBA's own logo:* Jerry Crowe, "That iconic NBA silhou-
    ette can be traced back to him," *Los Angeles Times*, April 27, 2010.

80  *in need of fresh income:* Steve Galluzzo, "All Things Lakers: Jerry West," *Los
    Angeles Times*, February 11, 2011.

80  *Raymond Ridder put his old boss in touch with his newest one:* Sam Amick,
    "How the Warriors got Kevin Durant," *USA Today*, July 4, 2016.

80  *"I never want to get back to where I go to bed at night, never go to sleep":*
    From an interview West gave to the Warriors' YouTube channel ("Jerry West
    Interview—5/24/11"), uploaded on May 24, 2011.

80  *his interest in potentially joining the Warriors:* Skip Bayless, "How to Rescue
    Warriors: Go West," *San Jose Mercury News*, February 24, 2002.

81  *"I've seen teams trade players that score tons of points":* Tim Kawakami, "Trade
    Monta Ellis? Jerry West just might be the guy to do it," *San Jose Mercury News*,
    June 1, 2011.

82  *Lacob settled on his man in early June:* Years later, Lacob did admit that one
    of the first people he talked to in 2010 about coaching the Warriors was Steve
    Kerr, who had just resigned as general manager of the Phoenix Suns. Accord-
    ing to comments Lacob made to 95.7 The Game's Greg Papa on February 7,
    2017, Kerr turned him down but told him to check back in about three years
    or so. (Jackson was fired after three seasons.)

82  *Jackson was almost hired by his hometown New York Knicks in 2008:* Harvey
    Araton, "Walsh Had Mark Jackson Pegged as a Future Coach," *New York
    Times*, June 7, 2011.

83  *"One week ago, for my first time as a Warriors fan, the air smelled fresh":* Kevin
    Draper, "The Spiritual Rebirth and Salvation of the Golden State Warriors,"
    TheDissNBA.com, June 28, 2011.

84  *the brains behind the creation of the annual Dunk Contest:* Roy S. Johnson, "Show Biz N.B.A. Style," *New York Times*, February 7, 1987.

84  *he came out as gay:* Dan Barry, "Going Public, N.B.A. Figure Sheds Shadow Life," *New York Times*, May 16, 2011.

84  *Gage's two children from an earlier marriage:* Rusty Simmons, "Rick Welts: Honesty best defense for Warriors exec," *San Francisco Chronicle*, November 27, 2011.

84  *"some real gems":* From comments Welts made during a discussion (with Bob Myers) at the Dreamforce conference in San Francisco on September 15, 2015.

84  *"the easiest recruiting job in the history of sports":* Ibid.

85  *Irving and Lacob were making benign small talk:* This scene, as well as Lacob's later quotes about being happy for Cleveland and being one ball shy of getting the No. 1 pick, comes from an interview Lacob gave to the Warriors' You-Tube channel ("The 2011 NBA Draft Lottery With Joe Lacob"), uploaded on May 20, 2011.

86  *His father, Mychal, had been drafted No. 1 overall by the Portland Trail Blazers in 1978:* Because of when he was drafted and by whom, Thompson became one of the many characters in David Halberstam's *The Breaks of the Game*, still regarded by many as the best basketball book ever written. Because Thompson had to sit out the entire 1979–80 season (the central time frame of Halberstam's narrative) with a broken leg suffered in an offseason pickup game, he was little more than a tertiary character, though we did learn that he drove a car with the license plate "MYCHAL" and had a natural talent for sneaking women back to his hotel room via the team bus, a fact that, as Halberstam wrote, evinced his "great courage and confidence not only on the court but off it."

87  *"That's our guy":* Chris Ballard, "Pursuit of perfection: Jerry West's fire burns as deep as ever with Warriors," *Sports Illustrated*, June 11, 2015.

87  *other players high on their board who were available:* From comments Larry Riley made on the night of the draft, uploaded to the Warriors' YouTube channel ("Larry Riley on The Selection of Klay Thompson") on June 23, 2011.

87  *Jimmer Fredette went at No. 10 to the Milwaukee Bucks:* Thompson was asked during training camp in 2015 if he ever thinks about what might've happened if the Bucks, and not the Warriors, had picked him in the draft: "I thank God every day."

87  *"out to get mine":* From a press conference Thompson made to assembled media in New York just after he was drafted, uploaded to the Warriors' You-

Tube channel ("Behind the Scenes of the 2011 NBA Draft with Klay Thompson") on June 26, 2011.

88 *average NBA player lost $220,000 of income:* "For NBA players, check's not in the mail," ESPN.com, November 15, 2011.

89 *"nuclear winter":* Howard Beck, "N.B.A. Season in Peril as Players Reject Offer and Disband Union," *New York Times,* November 15, 2011.

89 *Klay Thompson, bored out of his mind:* Sam Amick, "Lockout unsettling for rookies," *Sports Illustrated,* July 13, 2011.

89 *Curry met a local sports trainer named Brandon Payne:* Diamond Leung, "This man helps Warriors' Stephen Curry take game to new heights," *San Jose Mercury News,* December 4, 2015.

90 *became interested in the training side of the game:* Daniel Bartholomew, "Check Out the Hottest Basketball Training Facility in Charlotte," *Dime Magazine,* September 7, 2011.

90 *"His desire to learn more":* Interview with Payne on March 1, 2017.

91 *effectively doubled as Accelerate's first major client endorsement:* YouTube, "Stephen Curry training with Accelerate Basketball," uploaded on October 18, 2011.

91 *he could bounce ideas off Payne:* Leung, "This man helps Warriors' Stephen Curry," 2015.

91 *As announced at 3:40 a.m.:* Howard Beck, "N.B.A. Reaches Tentative Deal To Save Season," *New York Times,* November 27, 2011.

92 *"I'm disappointed. We need him back quick":* Associated Press, December 20, 2011.

92 *"He ran his basketball team":* Associated Press, December 26, 2011.

93 *"slumped in his courtside chair, arms folded in frustration":* Associated Press, December 31, 2011.

93 *"It's been one of those things that's been chronic with me":* Associated Press, January 4, 2012.

94 *"I just felt it wasn't right to throw him out there":* Associated Press, March 11, 2012.

95 *"The most challenging aspect of owning the Warriors has been the patience":* Warriors.com ("Joe Lacob Answers Fan Questions"), posted on July 27, 2011.

95 *online report that disclosed Lacob's plans:* Marcus Thompson II, "Joe Lacob to Interview Spurs' Mike Budenholzer," Bay Area News Group, May 31, 2011.

96 *Lacob fired two staffers over the leak:* From an interview Lacob did with venture capitalist Ted Schlein for the KPCB CEO Workshop series ("Taking the

Golden State Warriors to Greatness: Making Tough Decisions"), uploaded to Kleiner Perkins' YouTube channel on October 4, 2016.

96  *"I think you can very, very much clearly presume that we value him very highly"*: From an interview Lacob did with KNBR's Tom Tolbert and Ralph Barbieri on June 21, 2011. Lacob's quotes in the next two paragraphs also come from this interview.

97  *"Monta Ellis is a great player"*: From an interview Lacob did with the Warriors' YouTube channel ("Warriors Owners' Box—1/25/12"), uploaded on January 25, 2012. Lacob's quote in the following paragraph also comes from this interview.

98  *started conversations with Bucks general manager John Hammond the year before:* From the recording of a conference call Riley and Bogut held with Warriors season-ticket holders on March 27, 2012.

98  *contends to this day that it was always about Ellis:* Tim Kawakami, "Debunking a Warriors urban myth: No, they were not ready to trade either Curry or Ellis for Bogut . . . it was always only Ellis," Bay Area News Group, March 22, 2016.

98  *a former Warriors employee had filed a sexual harassment lawsuit against Ellis and the team:* Associated Press, December 21, 2011.

99  *actually follow through on those opportunities:* What also likely helped them land Bogut was that Larry Harris--the Milwaukee general manager who had drafted Bogut back in 2005 and with whom the center had a good relationship—had since decamped for Golden State's front office.

100  *"They were all scared to tell me that they had come to consensus"*: KPCB CEO Workshop, "Making Tough Decisions," 2016.

101  *"This kind of trade just doesn't happen every day"*: Rusty Simmons, "Warriors see Andrew Bogut as big piece to puzzle," *San Francisco Chronicle*, March 16, 2012.

101  *a tribute to Ellis, scored to Green Day's "Good Riddance (Time of Your Life)"*: Rusty Simmons, "Bucks top Warriors in Monta Ellis' return," *San Francisco Chronicle*, March 17, 2012.

101  *Talks between the Warriors and Smith's legal counsel began just a few days after Ellis was traded:* Associated Press, June 8, 2012.

102  *Lacob himself announced to season-ticket holders:* Associated Press, September 17, 2011.

102  *a terrible trade Mullin had approved back in 2008:* Scott Howard-Cooper, "Biggest sting from bad '08 trade yet to come for Warriors," NBA.com, March 6, 2012.

103 *not one but* two *separate issues featuring cover photos of Jeremy Lin:* Issues of *Sports Illustrated* dated February 20 and February 27, 2012.

104 *thought to himself, somewhat jokingly,* Maybe I'll do better than him: Tim Kawakami, "Kirk Lacob and Andrew Bogut on the night Joe Lacob got booed at Oracle, and everything that came next," Bay Area News Group, May 30, 2015.

104 *Bogut was stunned:* Bogut later told the *Bay Area News Group* (ibid.) what he was thinking during the fans' treatment of Lacob: "I guess, at that point, they were happy with losing games and having a guy score 30 a night that was a fan favorite."

104 *Kevin Love stood off to the corner with his Timberwolves teammates and could only giggle:* From video shot by a fan in attendance at Oracle Arena that night and uploaded to YouTube ("Kevin Love laughing at Joe Lacob getting booed") on March 20, 2012.

104 *"The less you say, the better off you are":* Joe Marshall, "Pouncing on a Championship," *Sports Illustrated*, January 15, 1979.

105 *"I'm not going to let a few boos get me down":* Tim Kawakami, "Joe Lacob after the booing: 'I'm not going to let a few boos get me down,' " Bay Area News Group, March 19, 2012.

105 *hated the word itself:* Al Saracevic, "Owner Joe Lacob rebuilt Warriors with Silicon Valley values," SFGate.com, June 7, 2015.

105 *replying to some 400 emails:* From an interview Lacob did with Rosalyn Gold-Onwude of NBC Sports Bay Area, uploaded on March 22, 2017.

106 *"The day is going to come":* From video footage of Jackson's postgame press conference shot by Steve Berman of BayAreaSportsGuy.com and uploaded to YouTube ("Mark Jackson on Joe Lacob getting booed by Warriors fans") on March 19, 2012.

107 *gathered on a makeshift dais along San Francisco's Embarcadero:* All of the scene details and quotes from this day come from a video uploaded to the Warriors' YouTube channel ("Warriors Announce Plans For San Francisco Arena") on May 22, 2012.

107 *Despite a $500 million price tag, the team would pay every penny:* Richard Sandomir, "Golden State Warriors Return to San Francisco," *New York Times*, May 22, 2012.

## 5: MARK'S MEN

109 *Bob Myers sat on one of the thousands of green benches dotting New York's Central Park with a pocket full of good-luck charms:* From an interview Myers gave

to the Warriors' YouTube channel ("GM Bob Myers in NYC's Central Park"), uploaded on May 30, 2012.

110 *the pairing was a disaster:* Kelly Dwyer, "Marcus Williams is still haunting the Golden State Warriors," Yahoo! Sports, February 9, 2011.

112 *crushing a hapless Nets team by 31:* As the game ended, Toronto general manager Bryan Colangelo could see Nets head coach Avery Johnson smirking with delight, even though his team had just been crushed. That's because the loss dropped the Nets to 22-44 and bumped them a slot above both Toronto and Golden State—except their draft pick was already headed to Portland thanks to the trade for Gerald Wallace that March. The Blazers happily drafted Damian Lillard with the sixth pick. Colangelo later admitted during a 2014 Sloan panel that that game was the only time in his career he could recall hoping a team of his would lose.

113 *"Widely touted as college basketball's most cerebral star since Bill Bradley":* Jason Zengerle, "Moneyballer," *The Atlantic,* April 2012.

114 *surprised everyone by opting for Dion Waiters:* Mary Schmitt Boyer, "Cleveland Cavaliers pull a draft surprise, taking Syracuse's Dion Waiters with fourth pick of 2012 NBA Draft," *Cleveland Plain Dealer,* June 28, 2012.

114 *possessed a physical maturity:* Ezeli was one of only four seniors drafted in the first round in 2012, as opposed to eight freshmen, eleven sophomores, and six juniors.

114 *averaged more than 16 points and 10 rebounds in his senior season:* In early February 2012, in a game against rival Michigan, Green actually outrebounded a decent Wolverines team (which featured future NBA players Tim Hardaway Jr., and Trey Burke) all by himself, 16–15.

115 *235 pounds:* Green actually weighed closer to 300 pounds when he was a freshman in East Lansing, but slimmed down considerably under the eye of head coach Tom Izzo (Jonathan Abrams, "The Fastest Mouth in the West," *Grantland,* April 8, 2015).

115 *modeled his game after "old-school Charles Barkley":* From an interview Green gave to the Warriors' YouTube channel ("Pre-Draft Workout Interview: Draymond Green"), uploaded on June 4, 2012.

115 *wearing 23 in college as an homage:* Associated Press, December 4, 2015.

115 *barely slept the night before:* Hugh Bernreuter, "Draymond Green calls NBA Draft wait for Golden State Warriors 'rugged,'" MLive.com, June 29, 2012.

116 *Adam Silver read his name at No. 35:* Detroit, at No. 39, would've taken Green had he fallen that far (Abrams, "The Fastest Mouth," 2015). Instead, they took

Texas A&M's Khris Middleton, who was traded a year later as part of a package of players, to Milwaukee for Brandon Jennings.

116 *performed an exploratory arthroscopic surgery on Stephen Curry's right ankle:* Pablo S. Torre, "How Stephen Curry got the best worst ankles in sports," *ESPN the Magazine*, February 29, 2016.

117 *Ferkel operated on Andrew Bogut's left ankle:* Rusty Simmons, "Ankle surgery for Curry, Andrew Bogut," *San Francisco Chronicle*, April 22, 2012.

117 *partnered with a company called Sports Aptitude:* The details here about the Warriors using BBIQ, as well as subsequent descriptions of Synergy Sports and MOCAP Analytics, come from a presentation given by Kirk Lacob at the Sports Analytics Innovation Summit in San Francisco in September 2012.

118 *answers given to 185 questions:* Travis Langley, "Player-Aptitude Reports Are Critical for NBA Prospects," Wired.com, June 22, 2011.

118 *"We need to be able to make this information useful to us":* Kirk Lacob, September 2012.

119 *Golden State put down almost $2 million:* Lou Babiarz, "WIZARDS: Taking hands-on approach," *Bismarck Tribune*, June 30, 2011.

119 *the fourth NBA team to actually own and operate its own D-League affiliate:* In four years, the number of NBA teams that owned and operated D-League teams had grown to 16, with an all-time high of 23 teams overall.

120 *you were earning a greater commission on your shot investment:* Ben Cohen, "The Golden State Warriors Have Revolutionized Basketball," *Wall Street Journal*, April 6, 2016.

121 *Bob Myers and Jeff Austin completed an agreement:* Marc Stein, "Stephen Curry gets 4-year extension," ESPN.com, November 1, 2012.

121 *"If you look at other people in my draft class":* Rusty Simmons, "Warriors sign Curry to $44 million deal," *San Francisco Chronicle*, November 1, 2012.

121 *Curry kept coming back to a phrase his father had instilled in him:* Tim Kawakami, "Stephen Curry says he sees no reason to leave the Warriors this summer," *San Jose Mercury News*, January 14, 2017.

122 *"There's really no timetable for a return right now":* From an interview Bogut conducted with KNBR's Tom Tolbert on November 27, 2012.

122 *"I wanted to play the first game of the season":* From Bogut's media scrum on November 27, 2012, transcribed from a video uploaded to the Warriors' YouTube channel ("Practice Interviews - 11/27/12") later that day.

122 *he'd actually had a version of microfracture surgery:* Marcus Thompson II, "An-

drew Bogut and the Microfracture Mystery," *Bay Area News Group*, November 27, 2012.

123 *"We don't want to fool anybody, anymore"*: Rusty Simmons, "Warriors' Bogut on 'indefinite leave,'" *San Francisco Chronicle*, November 28, 2012.

123 *they held a conference call for season-ticket holders*: From an audio recording of the conference call, which was held on March 27, 2012.

124 *"I know it's being perceived that it was mishandled and not handled appropriately"*: Marcus Thompson II, "Warriors GM Bob Myers Apologizes for Warriors' Handling of Andrew Bogut Situation," *Bay Area News Group*, November 29, 2012.

124 *"you would've thought they'd won a playoff game"*: Marcus Thompson II, "Golden State Warriors edge Denver Nuggets 106–105," *Bay Area News Group*, November 29, 2012.

125 *so palpable that it birthed a meme*: Marc J. Spears, "Origin of Stephen Curry's and Klay Thompson's 'Splash Brothers' nickname," *Yahoo! Sports*, February 12, 2015.

126 *the most anyone had scored at MSG since Kobe Bryant dropped 61 on the hapless Knicks*: Marcus Thompson II, "Warriors' Stephen Curry hits career-high 54 points in Madison Square Garden loss," *San Jose Mercury News*, February 27, 2013.

127 *"We're not going to lay down"*: Rusty Simmons, "Rockets rout Warriors by 31," *San Francisco Chronicle*, February 6, 2013.

127 *"I used to sit where you sit!"*: From audio that was picked up by ESPN's lapel mic on Jackson and aired on the broadcast.

127 *Bogut quit drinking during the season*: Scott Ostler, "Bogut gives Warriors newfound attitude," *San Francisco Chronicle*, May 2, 2013.

127 *skipped down the hallway to the locker room in postgame jubilation*: From video footage uploaded to the Warriors' YouTube channel ("Warriors Clinch Playoff Berth") on April 9, 2013.

129 *"This was an important first step for this franchise"*: Ibid.

131 *"one slithery move"*: Arnie Stapleton, Associated Press, April 20, 2013.

132 *Jackson went to his coaches with a crazy proposition he was prepared to be talked out of*: Rusty Simmons, "Warriors on target, win 131–117 at Denver," *San Francisco Chronicle*, April 24, 2013.

132 *"In my opinion"*: From interview audio uploaded to the Warriors' SoundCloud page ("Mark Jackson Postgame—Warriors at Nuggets [4/23/13]").

133 *wouldn't be able to play without the extra day of rest afforded by the travel*

*schedule:* Tim Kawakami, "Steph Curry's sore left ankle and Game 3 outlook: 'I wouldn't be able to play right now if there was a game,'" Bay Area News Group, April 25, 2013.

133 *Curry succumbed and received the shot prior to Game 4:* Antonio Gonzalez, Associated Press, April 28, 2013.

135 *"they tried to send hit-men on Steph":* From audio uploaded to the Warriors' SoundCloud page ("Mark Jackson Postgame—Warriors at Nuggets [4/30/13]").

135 *"did he play football or basketball at Michigan State?":* Associated Press, April 30, 2013.

136 *the first pain-blocking injection of his career:* Sam Amick, "Warriors hang on to beat Nuggets, move on to Spurs," *USA Today*, May 3, 2013.

140 *"It seems like every time you get on a roll":* Associated Press, May 12, 2013.

141 *"God has His hands on this team":* ASAP Sports transcript, May 12, 2013.

142 *Kirk Lacob could see that the Warriors were gassed:* From remarks Lacob made at the Sports Analytics Innovation Summit in San Francisco on September 10, 2015.

142 *"With the way I played this season":* ASAP Sports transcript, May 16, 2013.

142 *Joe Lacob huddled in the back of the Warriors' locker room with reporters:* From video footage of Lacob's remarks uploaded to YouTube ("Warriors owner Joe Lacob following the team's Game 6 loss") on May 17, 2013.

## 6: LEARNING TO FLY

146 *Iguodala felt the calculus worked in his favor:* Zach Harper, "Nuggets' Andre Iguodala says he'll opt out, become a free agent," CBS Sports, March 31, 2013.

147 *met down in Los Angeles at Pelinka's office:* From remarks Myers made during Iguodala's introductory press conference on July 11, 2013.

147 *prepared some DVDs as part of the presentation:* Anthony Slater, "Kevin Durant, Joe Lacob shed more light on Durant's free agency decision," *San Jose Mercury News*, October 11, 2016.

147 *"You guys are building something that I want to be a part of":* From Myers at Iguodala's press conference on July 11, 2013.

147 *a standing contract offer reported to be five years and $60 million:* Rusty Simmons, "Iguodala hopes to give Warriors flexibility," *San Francisco Chronicle*, July 11, 2013.

148 *More than a few nights, he came home in a panic:* From Myers at Iguodala's press conference on July 11, 2013.

149 *an hour after Iguodala almost put pen to paper with Dallas:* Simmons, "Iguodala hopes," 2013.

149 *Tim Connelly . . . wanted in:* Christopher Dempsey, "Nuggets to get Randy Foye in sign-trade deal with Andre Iguodala," *Denver Post,* July 8, 2013.

152 *ownership group led by Vivek Ranadivé:* While it's unknown precisely what Lacob and Guber each paid to become Warriors co-owners, it turns out that Ranadivé didn't have to pay all that much to acquire the Kings, just around $54.5 million himself to acquire a 15.08 percent stake, which was enough to be named controlling owner (Sam Amick, "Vivek Ranadive's early years with Kings forgettable," *USA Today,* October 9, 2016).

153 *Malcolm Gladwell wrote at length about the unorthodox strategies he implemented:* Malcolm Gladwell, "How David Beats Goliath," *New Yorker,* May 11, 2009.

153 *"the premier basketball team of the 21st century":* Rusty Simmons, "Owner Ranadivé pushes technology for Warriors," *San Francisco Chronicle,* January 30, 2012.

153 *Stevens had bought in at a team valuation of $800 million:* Darren Rovell, "Source: Warriors worth $800 million," ESPN.com, August 16, 2013.

153 *an all-time high that fall of 14,500:* Eric Young, "Warriors sell 14,500 season tickets, set franchise record," *San Francisco Business Times,* November 5, 2013.

154 *"I do have a lot of faith in advanced statistics":* From comments Jackson made at his introductory press conference on June 10, 2011.

155 *"we think we were able to help the coaches identify the root of problem":* Rusty Simmons, "Golden State Warriors at the forefront of NBA data analysis," *San Francisco Chronicle,* September 14, 2014.

155 *"That's analytics. That he does listen to":* GoldenStateofMind.com, "Interview with Kirk Lacob (Pt. 2)," 2012.

155 *a trained lawyer:* Warriors.com, "Darren Erman Interview," September 23, 2011.

156 *tension between Jackson and Malone:* Tim Kawakami, "Mark Jackson and Michael Malone: Year 2 on the Warriors' staff could be interesting," Bay Area News Group, July 26, 2012.

156 *prohibited his assistants from speaking to the media during the season:* Rusty Simmons, "Assistant Scalabrine reassigned after clash with Jackson," *San Francisco Chronicle,* March 27, 2014.

156 *dribbling a ball in his right hand while making behind-the-back passes with his left:* These exercise descriptions largely come from a series of videos recorded

at Accelerate by *Sporting News*' DeAntae Prince and uploaded to YouTube on August 13, 2013.

157  *the team had Curry work with new performance trainer Keke Lyles:* Torre, "How Stephen Curry got the best worst ankles in sports," 2016.

157  *extorted for hundreds of thousands of dollars by two people, one of them an ex-stripper:* Beau Yarbrough, "Warriors coach Mark Jackson admits to affair with ex-stripper," *San Jose Mercury News*, June 28, 2012.

158  *NBA player Jason Collins announced in the pages of* Sports Illustrated *that he was an out gay man:* Jason Collins, "Why NBA center Jason Collins is coming out now," *Sports Illustrated*, April 29, 2013.

158  *"As a Christian man":* Jackson's comments were reported by many news outlets when they were made on April 29, 2013.

158  *"It did disappoint me":* From an interview Welts gave to KQED's Scott Shafer, uploaded to YouTube ("KQED NEWSROO14M: An Interview with Golden State Warriors President and COO Rick Welts") on February 20, 2014.

159  *"We're in the same chapter":* Associated Press, December 12, 2013.

160  *"As far as I know, it was not on the court":* Diamond Leung, "Warriors' Bogut says Jackson comment 'ridiculous,'" Bay Area News Group, February 10, 2014.

162  *"net-net":* An arcane bit of Wall Street jargon, the kind you'd only hear at a bar full of finance bros or at lunch with venture capitalists.

162  *"we have not played as well as we need to play":* Tim Kawakami, "Joe Lacob on Mark Jackson and the Warriors' season so far: 'Our coach has done a good job . . . but some things are a little disturbing,'" Bay Area News Group, February 11, 2014.

162  *Scalabrine . . . was personally demoted by Jackson:* Adrian Wojnarowski, "Warriors coach Mark Jackson forces reassignment of assistant Brian Scalabrine," Yahoo! Sports, March 25, 2014.

162  *"difference in philosophies":* Diamond Leung, "Warriors' Mark Jackson reassigns assistant Scalabrine," Bay Area News Group, March 25, 2014.

162  *spent months working with Draymond Green:* Connor Letourneau, "Warriors' Draymond Green vies for Defensive Player of Year," *San Francisco Chronicle*, April 11, 2017.

163  *"violation of company policy":* "Assistant Erman fired for violating Warriors' team policy," SFGate.com, April 5, 2014.

163  *secretly taped at least one conversation:* Chris Broussard, "Darren Erman secretly taped talks," ESPN.com, April 29, 2014. On the day this was reported,

three weeks after the firing, Erman was rehired by the Celtics as their director of NBA scouting. General manager Danny Ainge said he was "not concerned at all" about bringing Erman back on staff (Baxter Holmes, "Celtics hire Darren Erman as scouting director," *Boston Globe*, April 29, 2014).

163 *"I'm going to dedicate the summer to learning how to play while avoiding contact at all costs"*: Associated Press, April 14, 2014.

165 *Clippers owner Donald Sterling uttering a litany of racist statements:* Timothy Burke, "NBA Owner Sterling To Girlfriend: Why Bring Black People To My Games?" *Deadspin*, April 26, 2014. The tapes lead directly to the NBA's forcing Sterling to sell the team that summer to Steve Ballmer for $2 billion.

166 *blasted the court with a wave of ear-melting cheers:* I covered this game and was in attendance at Oracle Arena. (The sound was quite painful.)

167 *most of the team attended services at Jackson's church:* Diamond Leung, "Warriors players rallying around Jackson," Bay Area News Group, April 20, 2014.

168 *Jerry West wasn't a welcome figure at team practices:* Zach Lowe, "The End of Mark Jackson and a New Beginning for the Warriors," *Grantland*, May 7, 2014.

168 *almost no functioning relationship with Kirk Lacob:* Reported by Tim Kawakami on Twitter on May 6, 2014, and confirmed to me by a team source.

168 *prohibited analytics head Sammy Gelfand from corraling rebounds for players at practice:* Zach Lowe ("The Champs Are Here: A Guide to the Elite and Unlikely Cast of Characters Who Defined the 2014–15 Golden State Warriors," *Grantland*, June 17, 2015) reported that it was a "young front office official"; a team source confirmed it was Gelfand.

168 *Scalabrine . . . hadn't spoken to Jackson for weeks:* Broussard, "Darren Erman secretly taped talks," 2014.

168 *Jackson had lost virtually all interest in reviewing game film or diagraming plays in the huddle:* Chris Ballard, "Warriors Come Out to Play," *Sports Illustrated*, February 23, 2015.

168 *"I'll always compliment him in many respects"*: Diamond Leung, "Golden State Warriors co-owner Joe Lacob details reasons for firing coach Mark Jackson," Bay Area News Group, December 5, 2014.

168 *"We all make the decision to change the CEO too late, right?"*: Ibid.

168 *"the right man at the right time"*: Ballard, "Warriors Come Out to Play," 2015.

168 *Jackson implied he was canned for not acquiescing to Lacob's demand:* This audio from Jackson's interview comes from *The Dan Patrick Show*'s YouTube channel ("Mark Jackson on the Dan Patrick Show (Full Interview) 05/07/2014"), uploaded on May 7, 2014.

169  *"Carte blanche. Take my wallet"*: Leung, "Golden State Warriors co-owner Joe
      Lacob details reasons," 2014.

169  *One particularly damning rebuke:* Bruce Jenkins, "Meddling Joe Lacob to
      blame for firing of Mark Jackson," *San Francisco Chronicle*, May 7, 2014.

## 7: STRENGTH IN NUMBERS

172  *the original arena plan . . . had to be scrapped:* John Coté, "Warriors shift arena
      plans to Mission Bay," *San Francisco Chronicle*, April 22, 2014.

172  *one of the smartest basketball-related discussions ever conducted*: Seriously,
      anyone even remotely interested in basketball or analytics should watch this
      discussion on YouTube ("SSAC14: Basketball Analytics").

174  *Colangelo came away impressed:* From my email interview with Bryan Colan-
      gelo in March 2017.

174  *For more than a year:* Ballard, "Warriors Come Out to Play," 2015.

175  *"It made me more compassionate"*: From an interview Kerr did for David
      Axelrod's "The Axe Files" podcast, posted on November 23, 2016.

175  *older brother, John, available to grab rebounds and play catch:* From my inter-
      view with Ann Kerr-Adams in March 2017.

175  *Arabic readings in his lap to watch during the commercial breaks of college foot-
      ball games:* Maureen Dowd, "Educator Slain in Beirut Is Mourned in Prince-
      ton," *New York Times*, January 30, 1984.

176  *"In the good old days"*: Malcolm H. Kerr, *The Arab Cold War: Gamal 'Abd
      al-Nasir and His Rivals, 1958–1970* (Third Edition), p. v.

176  *"The only thing I'd rather do than watch Steve play basketball"*: From Kerr-
      Adams's 1996 book, *Come with Me from Lebanon: An American Family Odys-
      sey*, p. 10.

176  *His earliest memory of sports:* From my interview with Steve Kerr in March 2017.

177  *a certain UC-Irvine alum was across campus:* Joe Lacob was earning his mas-
      ter's degree at this very same time.

177  *Kerr was working out at a basketball showcase:* From my interview with Lute
      Olson in March 2017.

177  *"Jerks draw jerks"*: Bob Logan, "Olson, Arizona 1 big happy family," *Chicago
      Tribune*, January 3, 1988.

177  *Malcolm Kerr . . . called Olson:* Olson interview, March 2017.

178  *"You can never know what death sounds like"*: Rich Dymond, "Beirut bomb-
      ings leave scars, Wildcat says," *Arizona Daily Star*, October 15, 1983.

178 *Malcolm Kerr had been planning on coming stateside (along with Ann) to see Steve play against UCLA:* Mary Curtius and Jack Jones, "Kerr Aware of Risks Facing Him in Beirut," *Los Angeles Times,* January 19, 1984.

178 *members of Hezbollah:* John Branch, "Why Steve Kerr Sees Life Beyond the Court," *New York Times,* December 25, 2016.

178 *Reagan praised Kerr:* Ronald Reagan: "Statement on the Assassination of Malcolm Kerr, President of the American University of Beirut," January 18, 1984. Online by Gerhard Peters and John T. Woolley, The American Presidency Project.

179 *Olson (at the urging of his wife, Bobbi) had him picked up:* Olson interview, March 2017.

179 *"[Lute] had lost his father so he told me his story":* Kerr interview, March 2017.

179 *"To see someone perform in that situation":* From my interview with Bob Weinhauer in March 2017.

180 *the public address announcer, Roger Sedlmayr, let out a bellowing "Steeeeeeeeeve Kerrrrrrrrrr!":* Greg Hansen, "Beloved Wildcat Kerr leads UA past ASU just after father's assassination," *Arizona Daily Star,* August 24, 2016.

180 *"Adrenaline . . . will add ten feet":* Rich Dymond, "Kerr's scoring rising," *Arizona Daily Star,* January 28, 1984.

181 *"Every day I was pretty much amazed at what he could do":* From my interview with David Robinson in March 2017.

181 *he might never play ball again:* From my interview with Tim Taft in March 2017.

181 *"I'm thinking, Thanks a lot, doc":* Kerr interview, March 2017.

181 *"With a big injury like that for a point guard":* Taft interview, March 2017.

181 *"We thought we were going to be really good":* From my interview with Bruce Fraser in March 2017.

182 *one of these cheesy, anodyne raps:* This particular rap was written by Harvey Mason Jr., a junior guard for the Wildcats who would later go on to win several Grammys as a successful record producer.

182 *the "Gumby Squad":* Associated Press, April 1, 1988.

183 *Kerr, tempestuous as a child, had developed a thick skin and learned to channel his anger through basketball:* Ann Kerr-Adams interview, March 2017.

183 *a dozen or so students started taunting him in warm-ups:* Bob Young, "Hecklers no worry for Kerr," *Arizona Republic,* February 28, 1988.

183 *sent Kerr a personal letter of apology:* Bob Cohn, "ASU sends apology for remarks," *Arizona Republic,* March 1, 1988.

184  *"Everything in my life would be downhill after that"*: Logan, "Olson, Arizona,"
     1988.

184  *"I got completely off track"*: Kerr interview, March 2017.

184  Olson thinks the pressure of having Ann Kerr there in attendance affected her
     son: Olson interview, March 2017.

184  *"Usually, if a guy is nervous, he's going to be missing in warm-ups, too"*: Fraser
     interview, March 2017.

185  *"I will always blame myself for us losing that game"*: From John Feinstein's 1988
     book, *A Season Inside: One Year in College Basketball*, p. 460.

185  *criticized for selecting the Arizona fan favorite*: Lee Shappell, "Suns join in cho-
     rus of praise for Kerr," *Arizona Republic*, October 23, 1988.

185  *"He showed enough that he deserved a shot"*: From my interview with Jerry
     Colangelo in March 2017.

185  *played half a season with a rookie center named Shaquille O'Neal*: Kerr also got
     to play with a more familiar face while with the Magic: Tom Tolbert, his old
     power forward in college, and one of his closest friends to this day.

186  *thought about calling Lute Olson*: Kerr interview, March 2017. I later asked
     Olson if he would have hired Kerr on staff with the Wildcats. "Obviously I
     would've," he told me. "All the fans were hoping, once I retired, that Steve
     would come here."

186  *a single-season record that stood for 15 years*: Kerr set the mark by converting
     on 89 of 170 threes over 82 games. During the 2009–10 season, Utah's Kyle
     Korver broke the record by making 59 of 110 shots (53.6 percent) over 52
     games off the bench.

186  *"If he comes off . . . I'll be ready"*: From archived audio aired on NBA TV and
     uploaded to YouTube ("Steve Kerr—NBA Finals 1997, Game 6's Final Shot")
     on June 17, 2008.

186  *Brent Musberger yelled on the ESPN Radio telecast*: This audio can be heard
     on a YouTube video titled "Amazing Playoff Moments: Michael Jordan pass to
     Steve Kerr," uploaded on June 2, 2009.

187  *"Did Steve have physical gifts that jump out at you"*: From my interview with
     B. J. Armstrong in March 2017.

187  *"I could feel my body breaking down"*: Kerr interview, March 2017.

188  *"I didn't anticipate anybody would be dumb enough to offer me another"*:
     Ibid.

188  *started calling himself "Ted"*: Mike Wise, " 'Frozen' Kerr Catches Fire and Lifts
     Spurs," *New York Times*, May 30, 2003.

188 *some bad room-service crème brûlée*: Mike Wilbon, "Spurs' Kerr Is a Long-Shot Made Good," *Washington Post*, June 4, 2003.

188 *"Somebody closed out on me really hard"*: Kerr interview, March 2017.

189 *"It was an incredible moment"*: Robinson interview, March 2017.

189 *"The guy is there before and after practice"*: Sam Smith, "Ever-so-modest Kerr can't hide his value," *Baltimore Sun*, May 31, 2003.

190 *moved from San Antonio to set down roots in the San Diego suburb of Rancho Santa Fe*: Larry Stewart, "Kerr's Joy Tinged by Sadness," *Los Angeles Times*, May 14, 2004.

190 *"Once he was a GM, he realized that wasn't his lane in this business"*: Fraser interview, March 2017.

191 *"I still get to enjoy the game itself"*: Paul Coro, "Former Suns GM Steve Kerr returning to TNT," *Arizona Republic*, June 29, 2010.

191 *Joe Lacob—an old golfing buddy of Kerr's*: Tim Kawakami, "Steve Kerr on taking the Warriors job, his offensive style, Steph Curry, saying no to Phil Jackson and much, much more," Bay Area News Group, May 14, 2014.

191 *"It just isn't right to host a show to announce you're abandoning your hometown"*: Scott Cacciola, "LeBron James to Sign With Miami Heat," *Wall Street Journal*, July 9, 2010.

191 *smart money had Kerr moving east*: Kerr's deal with the Knicks was all but done—short of signing paperwork—until Lacob swooped in and persuaded his old golfing buddy to give the Warriors closer consideration. "Knowing he's a real California guy," Lacob told 95.7 The Game's Greg Papa on February 7, 2017, "I couldn't imagine him in New York, to be honest. I just couldn't. I just couldn't see it, but I think it took him a few days longer to figure it out."

191 *Kerr in a conference room in Oklahoma City*: Ballard, "Warriors Come Out to Play," 2015.

192 *"There were a lot of little things that first-time head coaches don't even think about"*: Rusty Simmons, "How Warriors got their man," *San Francisco Chronicle*, February 12, 2015.

192 *divest the small percentage of the Suns that he still owned*: Diamond Leung, "Warriors' Steve Kerr on still owning small part of Phoenix Suns: 'I'm not Steve Ballmer,'" Bay Area News Group, July 12, 2014.

192 *spurned his friend and mentor in New York*: Andrew Keh, "This Teacher Spends Life Being Taught," *New York Times*, November 13, 2014. As Kerr told the *Times*, "If Phil hadn't been involved, it would have been an easy decision.

But my loyalty to him, my interest in building something with him, was pretty deep."

192  *spoke with Stephen Curry by phone before news broke:* Marcus Thompson II, "Stephen Curry Speaks About Losing Mark Jackson, Getting Steve Kerr, and the New Direction of the Warriors," Bay Area News Group, May 15, 2014.

193  *jumped at the chance to coach a rebuilding Cleveland Cavaliers squad:* Chris Haynes, "David Blatt grateful Steve Kerr allowed him to take Cavaliers' job: 'We both got what we wanted,'" Cleveland.com, May 29, 2015.

194  *often went by "Q," a nickname acquired in his college days:* Rusty Simmons, "The Curry Whisperer: Shot guru Fraser has MVP's ear," *San Francisco Chronicle*, December 10, 2015.

195  *remembering that basketball, above all else, was supposed to be fun:* Jonah Keri, "With coaches like Kerr, Carroll and Maddon, pro sports teams remember to have fun," CBS Sports, August 30, 2016.

195  *"The raw material of a contender is here":* Zach Lowe, "Why Not the Warriors?" *Grantland*, January 14, 2014.

196  *dangling Kevin Love like a carrot:* Marc Stein, "Warriors weigh deal for Kevin Love," ESPN.com, June 20, 2014.

196  *Love was a year older than Thompson:* Despite the age gap, the two men once played on the same Little League team (Connor Letourneau, "Klay Thompson, Kevin Love go from Little League to NBA Finals," *San Francisco Chronicle*, June 5, 2016). With Love pitching and Thompson hitting leadoff, the Lake Oswego Lakers (based outside Portland, Oregon) won a state title in 2001.

197  *West, in particular, was adamant that Thompson remain a Warrior:* Ballard, "Pursuit of perfection," 2015.

197  *Ronnie Lott, who posted a YouTube video:* From Lott's official YouTube channel ("A message for Joe Lacob—Let's go Warriors!"), uploaded on October 14, 2014.

197  *"We encourage very strong debate":* From Lacob's comments in a video produced by Stanford's Graduate School of Business ("Inside Sports Management"), uploaded to their YouTube channel on November 14, 2016.

197  *the Splash Brothers would remain side by side for at least another three seasons:* What's rarely discussed is how Curry almost bolted before Thompson even played a game in Oakland. In the days following the resolution of the 2011 lockout, the New Orleans Pelicans pushed hard to acquire Curry in a trade that would've sent point guard Chris Paul northwestward (Marc Stein and Chris Broussard, "Sources: Hornets line up trade targets," ESPN.com, December 7,

2011). The Warriors didn't pursue the deal very hard, especially since Paul, who had one year left on his contract, wouldn't invoke his player option for a second year. Of course, Curry wasn't the superstar then that he would become, and the team could've decided to trade him and keep Monta Ellis instead, but the Warriors stuck to their plan, and trading Curry away wasn't part of that.

198  *Iguodala was initially hesitant:* Ballard, "Warriors Come Out to Play," 2015.

199  *people of color comprised 76.7 percent of players but just a third of the 30 head coaches:* Richard Lapchick with Angelica Guiao, "The 2015 Racial and Gender Report Card: National Basketball Association," The Institute for Diversity and Ethics in Sport, July 1, 2015.

201  *recite from memory all 34 players picked ahead of him:* Jon Wilner, "How a ticked-off Draymond Green fell into the Warriors' lap," *San Jose Mercury News*, May 20, 2016.

201  *surfaced as unbridled rage:* In the waning moments of Game 5 of the 1992 Eastern Conference Finals, Kerr (then with Cleveland) threw down with none other than the Chicago Bulls' Stacey King, who'd been a star on the Oklahoma squad that dropped Kerr's Arizona powerhouse in the 1988 Final Four. In a March 2017 interview, King told me that he still hasn't forgotten how crazed Kerr's actions were on that day they met in the NBA playoffs. "He's got a hidden temper," King says. "All of us have tempers, but you don't expect it from a guy like him, a guy who's articulate, a guy who's so even-keeled. When you watch him and talk to him, he's got a great sense of humor, he has a great understanding of society, things that are going on in the world. He's very intelligent, but beneath all that, man, I tell you, there's a competitive nature. There's a rage there, and he can control it, but he wants to win at everything he does. It's like a Chihuahua thinking that he's a Rottweiler. You can't tell him that he's not a Rottweiler."

201  *confessed to one Warriors staffer:* From a story recounted by radio broadcaster Tim Roye during an interview with Green for the Warriors' SoundCloud page ("Podcast [11/28/12]—Roundtable ft. Andrew Bogut, Bob Myers, Draymond Green & More").

201  *Green rarely backed down:* Marcus Thompson II, "Golden State Warriors' Draymond Green impressing with toughness, smarts," *San Jose Mercury News*, December 4, 2012.

202  *jawed at Green, "You too little!":* Marcus Thompson II, "LeBron James 'you too little' comment motivates Warriors' Draymond Green," *San Jose Mercury News*, May 28, 2015.

202  *Kerr once received a black eye from Jordan in a Bulls practice:* James Herbert, "Landing a punch on Michael Jordan," ESPN.com, September 27, 2013.

202  *"I wouldn't necessarily say I'm an asshole":* Abrams, "The Fastest Mouth," 2015.

204  *Johnson served as a part-time team psychologist:* Baxter Holmes, "Special force at work for Warriors," ESPN.com, June 5, 2015.

205  *travel the most of any team during the 2014–15 regular season:* Per the miles-tracking page on Daren Willman's NBASavant.com.

205  *Kerr was prodded by Keke Lyles:* Janie McCauley, "Warriors seek sleep advice to keep an edge," Associated Press, March 12, 2015.

205  *Cheri Mah published research showing the benefits:* Mah, Cheri D., et al., "The Effects of Sleep Extension on the Athletic Performance of Collegiate Basketball Players." *Sleep* 34.7 (2011): 943–50. *PMC*. Web. 30 April 2017.

206  *"You're trying to link what happens at nighttime with performance during the daytime":* From my interview with Mah in February 2017.

206  *lower his thermostat to 57 degrees:* Pablo S. Torre and Tom Haberstroh, "Invasion of the Body Snatchers," *ESPN the Magazine*, October 27, 2014.

206  *"I'm not necessarily trying to overhaul everything that they've ever known":* Mah interview, February 2017.

206  *partnered with a Finnish startup, Omegawave, to assess heart-rate variability using facial electrodes:* Diamond Leung, "Besides a Stephen Curry advantage, Golden State Warriors flaunt a tech advantage," *San Jose Mercury News*, November 13, 2015.

206  *in real time during practice:* The Santa Cruz Warriors also partnered with Athos—a Bay Area startup that counted Joe Lacob and former Golden State center Jermaine O'Neal among its investors—to outfit its D-League players with compression clothing that can gather electromyography readings to measure muscle activity and physical stress. After all, the D-League's own website does refer to its role as "the league's research and development laboratory."

206  *a simple test administered daily:* Ken Berger, "Warriors 'wearable' weapon? Devices to monitor players while on the court," CBS Sports, June 3, 2015.

207  *Curry and Thompson . . . were close to "red-lining":* Kirk Lacob, Sports Analytics Innovation Summit, 2015.

207  *"I know there are people here in Denver":* Christopher Dempsey, "Warriors to rest stars Stephen Curry, Klay Thompson vs. Nuggets," *Denver Post*, March 13, 2015.

207  *37 points in the third quarter:* Rusty Simmons, "Thompson's NBA-record 37-

point quarter lifts Warriors over Kings," *San Francisco Chronicle*, January 24, 2015.

208 *Bob Myers email asking for any ideas:* Ethan Sherwood Strauss, "Q&A: Myers on how Warriors execs work," ESPN.com, March 24, 2015.

209 *"The most important thing . . . is that your players respond to your coach":* From my interview with Bob Myers in December 2016.

210 *first team in 37 years to finish tops in both defensive efficiency and pace of play:* John Schuhmann, "Warriors trying to buck trend when it comes to pace of play," NBA.com, March 6, 2015.

210 *Mark Jackson . . . said he'd pick Houston's James Harden:* From audio archived on *The Dan Patrick Show*'s official YouTube channel ("Mark Jackson on the Dan Patrick Show [Full Interview] 4/2/15").

210 *"Well, it was April Fool's Day":* Per a tweet from Ethan Sherwood Strauss, April 2, 2015.

211 *"strength in numbers" . . . guiding principle:* The Warriors also wanted it for their intellectual property. The team filed an application in June 2015 (two weeks before winning the title) to register "strength in numbers" as a trademark (serial number 86652408) belonging to Golden State Warriors, LLC.

211 *preach the gospel of "appropriate fear":* Steve Kerr, "Fearing the best," Yahoo! Sports, May 28, 2007.

211 *Kerr dropped that phrasing periodically:* Diamond Leung, "Warriors' win streak on the line with tough road stretch," *San Jose Mercury News*, December 12, 2014.

211 *"Our appropriate fear, as we talk about, will be there":* From audio of Kerr's postgame press conference posted on the Warriors' SoundCloud page ("Steve Kerr—postgame [4/11/15]").

## 8: KINGSLAYERS

216 *Assistant coach Ron Adams . . . had an idea:* Jeff Faraudo, "Warriors' strategy takes Tony Allen out of game," *San Jose Mercury News*, May 12, 2015.

216 *"a caricature of the coach-as-intellectual, a thinker whose academic pursuits inform his hoops":* Ethan Sherwood Strauss, "How Warriors built NBA's top defense," ESPN.com, February 4, 2015.

217 *"You probably don't see the opposing team's center":* Ibid.

217 *Joerger never mentioned any injury recurrence in his postgame comments:* From Joerger's postgame comments to the media, posted on the Warriors' SoundCloud page ("Dave Joerger—postgame [5/11/15]").

218  *"You don't mess around," he told them:* From Kerr's postgame comments to the media on May 13, 2015.

223  *"You just want to gather yourself":* From Curry's postgame comments to the media, as transcribed by ASAP Sports, May 25, 2015.

223  *As he carried his granddaughter, Dell gave Riley a kiss on the cheek and smiled:* I witnessed this whole scene as I walked from the Oracle Arena media room to the postgame press conference area.

227  *"When we go out there, we're gonna be loose":* From locker room video posted on the NBA's YouTube channel ("Finals All-Access: Rookie Head Coaches Kerr and Blatt Mic'd Up") on June 4, 2015.

230  *"I've never seen someone that can shoot the ball off the dribble like himself, ever":* From James's postgame comments to the media, as transcribed by ASAP Sports, June 9, 2015.

230  *"The pressure is like a 5.13":* From Kerr's postgame comments to the media, as transcribed by ASAP Sports, June 9, 2015.

230  *Nick U'Ren was in his hotel room in downtown Cleveland:* Lee Jenkins, "Meet Nick U'Ren: The Warriors staffer with the idea to start Andre Iguodala," *Sports Illustrated*, June 12, 2015.

231  *the video tagging process was painstaking and meticulous:* Stefan Swiat, "Life of an NBA Video Coordinator," Suns.com, August 19, 2010.

231  *Kerr half-jokingly dubbed U'Ren his "chief of staff":* Tim Kawakami, "Steve Kerr on his coaching staff: How he put it together, how the braintrust of the Warriors works," Bay Area News Group, May 12, 2015.

232  *"medium ball":* Marc Stein, "Boris Diaw's unlikely arc of triumph," ESPN.com, June 14, 2014.

232  *"four point guards basically on the floor at once":* Jeff Zillgitt, "Boris Diaw: From waiver wire to Spurs' NBA Finals star," *USA Today*, June 13, 2014.

232  *what U'Ren proposed in his late-night phone call to assistant coach Luke Walton:* Jenkins, "Meet Nick U'Ren," 2015. The idea had popped into U'Ren's head for the first time after the Game 3 loss, but his lineup proposal was not taken seriously at that night's team dinner (Marc J. Spears, "The mystery man behind the plan that helped the Warriors win Game 4 of the NBA Finals," Yahoo! Sports, June 12, 2015). That's when U'Ren dove into the video, convinced it would work for the Warriors as it had for the Spurs.

233  *"If this doesn't work, it's your fault":* From Kerr's practice day comments to the media on June 13, 2015.

233  *Chris DeMarco leaned over and told him not to worry:* Tim Kawakami, "Nick

U'Ren on the 'Death Lineup' and what it does for the Warriors: 'It works because there are no other players like those guys,'" Bay Area News Group, June 3, 2016.

233: *"It's just a street fight"*: From Green's postgame comments to the media, as transcribed by ASAP Sports, June 11, 2015.

234 *"I don't think they hand you the trophy based on morality"*: From Kerr's postgame comments to the media, as transcribed by ASAP Sports, June 11, 2015.

235 *that shot his personal favorite of his career:* Robby Kalland, "Steph Curry on His Basketball Heroes, the Warriors' 'Different' Season, And Getting Rest," *Dime Magazine*, March 22, 2017.

236 *"I'm not even thinking about anything"*: From Iguodala's postgame comments to the media, as transcribed by ASAP Sports, June 16, 2015.

236 *"It just feels good to say we're the best team in the world"*: From Thompson's postgame comments to the media, as transcribed by ASAP Sports, June 16, 2015.

236 *"A lot of people said I could never play in this league"*: From Green's postgame comments to the media, as transcribed by ASAP Sports, June 16, 2015.

237 *the Warriors had lost the fewest minutes to injury of any team in the league:* Tom Haberstroh, "Biggest winner of the Finals? Rest!," ESPN.com, June 17, 2015.

237 *the first champion to ever lead the NBA in pace:* John Schuhmann, "These Warriors among NBA's greatest title teams ever," NBA.com, June 17, 2015.

237 *"I almost forgot just how grueling the stretch is"*: From Kerr's postgame comments to the media, June 16, 2015.

238 *getting to celebrate this moment with not just his wife but his three kids . . . meant the world to him:* From my interview with Kerr, March 2017.

238 *"I think we can actually appreciate what we were able to do this year from start to finish"*: From Curry's postgame comments to the media, as transcribed by ASAP Sports, June 16, 2015.

238 *They started arriving at 3:00 a.m.:* Associated Press, June 19, 2015.

## 9: LEVEL UP

243 *put her hands over her face and immediately started crying:* Via Draymond Green's Instagram account, video posted July 1, 2015.

243: *pumped him for info about playing like an NBA-level point guard:* Wahl, "The Next Step for Steph," 2008.

243 *navigate the Santa Clara campus by dribbling a basketball in between classes:* Tim Crothers, "Little Magic," *Sports Illustrated*, December 11, 1995.

244   *moved to Emeryville for the summer (on Curry's dime):* Leung, "This man helps
      Warriors' Stephen Curry," 2015.

244   *"Stroboscopic sensory training":* Tom Haberstroh, "How do Kawhi Leonard—
      and Steph Curry—train their brains? Strobe lights (yes, really)," ESPN.com,
      November 9, 2016.

244   *sessions in saltwater-infused sensory deprivation pods:* Sam Alipour, "The
      NBA—and Its Future—Belongs to Stephen Curry," *ESPN the Magazine,* De-
      cember 11, 2015.

245   *There was little the Warriors wouldn't consider trying:* As excited as the Warri-
      ors were then, the partnership fizzled out quickly. As team head trainer Chel-
      sea Lane said in May 2017, "The Halo gizmos were a very quick flash in the
      pan that a couple of the guys wore once or twice" (Benny Evangelista, "SF
      Giants turn to brain-training headsets to help players improve," *San Francisco
      Chronicle,* May 30, 2017).

245   *Kerr's health was deteriorating fast:* Ramona Shelburne, "Steve Kerr has suf-
      fered more than you will ever know," *ESPN the Magazine,* April 11, 2016.

246   *enjoyed trash-talking Draymond Green:* From comments Walton made to
      media at the practice facility on October 2, 2015.

246   *occasional bout of anxiety:* Kevin Ding, "NBA's Youngest Coach, Luke Walton,
      Is on the Level with Millennial-Laden Lakers," *Bleacher Report,* September 23,
      2016.

247   *lead the players' wives and girlfriends in postgame tequila shots:* Kelly E. Carter,
      "Haute Secrets: Nicole Curran's Guide to the SF Bay Area," *Haute Living,* De-
      cember 18, 2015.

248   *already made 140 three-pointers:* Only Milwaukee's Ray Allen, some 14 years
      earlier, had ever made 100 or more threes over a team's first 30 games. Back
      then, Allen made 103 threes in 30 games. Curry sank that many in 2015–16
      in just 20 games.

248   *healthy and full of confidence:* There was a perception by some that Curry's
      propensity for shooting threes was damaging the very fabric of the sport. As
      the Warriors and Cavs played at Oracle on Christmas Day, Mark Jackson used
      his position as an analyst on the ABC telecast to endorse this thought. "To a
      degree, he's hurt the game," Jackson said on the air, citing only anecdotal evi-
      dence that high schoolers were (in his opinion, and due to Curry's influence)
      enamored only with shooting threes rather than working on other aspects of
      their game. Golden State won the game, 89–83, to bump its record to 28-1.

248   *the Death Lineup, coined in late November by the local media:* I could find two

early references to the Death Lineup before most others. One was a blog post written on November 20, 2015, by Michael Erler of *Today's Fastbreak*, which included the following description: " 'Micro-ball' or 'small-ball' doesn't do the lineup enough justice. It's more like 'death-ball.' " Three days later, Nate Duncan and Danny Leroux devoted an entire episode (titled "The Death Lineup") of their *Dunc'd On* podcast to the topic.

249  *tried everything to alleviate his pain—including medicinal marijuana:* From Kerr's remarks to Monte Poole on the Warriors Insiders podcast, posted on December 2, 2016.

249  *Kerr had joined them on the recent road trip:* Shelburne, "Steve Kerr has suffered," 2016.

250  *"I am not a robot!":* Ethan Sherwood Strauss, "Golden State's Draymond Green problem," *ESPN the Magazine*, October 31, 2016.

252  *"As soon as he let it go":* Payne interview, March 2017.

252  *"I can't even fathom KD and Curry existing as a joined force":* Ethan really did tweet this: twitter.com/SherwoodStrauss/status/703782023094075392.

253  *"Every team I've ever been on has had stuff like this":* From Kerr's media availability at the practice facility on February 29, 2016.

256  *Kerr let it slide:* From comments Kerr made to Tim Kawakami on his *TK Show* podcast, posted on June 24, 2016: "We were blowing through the schedule and winning games at a huge rate. It's really hard to point out to players—*we can't have these mistakes*—when you're setting an NBA record for wins. I think all those mistakes kind of reared their ugly heads both against Oklahoma City and against Cleveland. If anything, it's going to be easier next year during training camp to really pound home the points we need to make in terms of just being more solid and taking care of all the little things."

256  *the second team of the past 20 years:* The other team? The 2014–15 Golden State Warriors (2,248).

256  *43 games of 30 or more assists, the most in 31 years:* Since the 1984–85 Los Angeles Lakers (52 games) were at the peak of their "Showtime" powers.

256  *13 games of 35 or more assists, more than any team in 28 years:* Both the Lakers and the San Antonio Spurs posted 13 such games in the 1987–88 season.

257  *18 of those outbursts, more than anyone since 1990–91:* The Portland Trail Blazers did so that year. The 1966–67 Philadelphia 76ers (thanks to Wilt Chamberlain) hold this record with 46 such games and likely always will.

257  *led the league for the first time ever in defensive rebounding:* While factually accurate, this is a misleading distinction. The league only started breaking out

rebounds as "defensive" or "offensive" starting with the 1973–74 season. Before that, the Warriors once led the NBA in rebounding for four straight years, thanks to bigs such as Clyde Lee and Nate Thurmond. It's a near certainty they would've led the league in defensive boards in one of those seasons.

257  *The YouTube video featuring all of them has a runtime of nine and a half minutes:* It's truly remarkable: www.youtube.com/watch?v=ZQl2qdHl_vw.

258  *highest-ever True Shooting Percentage of anyone averaging 25 or more points:* Curry's TS% finished at 66.9 percent. Second-highest was Charles Barkley, who hit 66.5 percent in 1987–88. (TS% factors in three-point and free-throw shooting.)

258  *highest Effective Field Goal Percentage of any 30-point scorer in history:* Curry's eFG% topped out at 63 percent, easily besting Adrian Dantley's 58 percent in 1982–83. (eFG% factors in that threes are worth a point more than two-point field goals, which explains why Curry's mark was so much higher.)

258  *finish a season shooting at least 50 percent from the field, 45 percent on threes, and 90 percent on free throws:* As long as you stick to players who meet the minimum field-goal percentage requirement—which is 300 made shots in a season—Curry (50.4 FG%, 45.4 3P%, 90.8 FT%) and Nash (50.4, 47, 90.6) in 2007–08 are the only players who qualify. But if you switch that to players who qualify based on minutes per game—by playing in 70 percent of team games—one more name joins the club: Steve Kerr (50.6/51.5/92.9 in 1995–96), who was also Phoenix Suns general manager when Nash pulled it off. (Kerr, incidentally, would've officially preceded both Curry and Nash if he'd made just 56 more shots during his season.)

259  *"light-years ahead of probably every other team":* Schoenfeld, "What Happened When Venture Capitalists," 2016.

259  *held in his hands a printout of the next day's* San Francisco Chronicle: From video footage uploaded to the Warriors' YouTube channel ("Warriors Ground: Season Recap") on September 12, 2016.

## 10: THE COMEBACK

261  *"DON'T MEAN A THING WITHOUT THE RING":* Fred Mitchell, "Bulls' chapel popular place, but not Sunday," *Chicago Tribune*, April 29, 1996.

264  *"That might not seem like a big deal right now":* James Herbert, "Warriors' Draymond Green assessed flagrant foul for late-game tackle," CBS Sports, April 22, 2016.

265   *"We got this. We will win this for you"*: Marcus Thompson II, "Stephen Curry's injury, emotions fuel Warriors to a Game 4 blowout of Houston . . . and now DubNation waits," Bay Area News Group, April 24, 2016.

265   *most three-pointers (21) made in a playoff game*: The record stood for 10 days, which is when Cleveland knocked down 25 threes against the Atlanta Hawks. Ten of the 13 Cavaliers who played registered at least one three. It was the most threes any NBA team had *ever* made in a game, regular season or playoffs.

269   *the first MVP in league history to earn such a distinction*: When LeBron James (who fell a single vote shy of unanimity in 2013) was asked for his opinion on Curry's MVP bona fides, he launched into an explanation about the differences between a player who is "most valuable" and who is the "best player of the year." When the Finals came around, James apologized for his comments while also accusing the media of sensationalizing his response at the time.

272   *Durant had the second-best Effective Field Goal Percentage*: The only player better on pull-ups during the season? Stephen Curry (59.8 percent).

274   *eight turnovers, with four coming on bad passes*: Durant's frustrations were tied to Kerr having Green act as a roving zone defender, allowing his assignment (Roberson) to shoot from wherever he wanted so that he could freelance defensively (usually swarming to double-team Westbrook or Durant as needed). The *Oklahoman*'s Berry Tramel called it a "gimmick defense" ("Thunder must make Warriors pay for gimmick defense," May 19, 2016) but it worked in Game 4 in Memphis a year earlier, and it sure worked this time.

277   *Westbrook glared at the ESPN reporter as he and Durant walked off*: I was in the media room and looking right at Westbrook as he stepped off the dais, stared down ESPN's Michele Steele, and walked right by her as he left.

280   *Curry gave him one last charge of encouragement*: From Curry's postgame comments to the media, as transcribed by ASAP Sports, May 28, 2016.

282   *"That will be the best game of any of our lives"*: Lee Jenkins, "'The best game of any of our lives': The night that saved the Warriors' season," *Sports Illustrated*, June 15, 2016.

## 11: "BECAUSE GOD SAID SO"

288   *a propensity for constantly reminding staffers and media of his bona fides and extensive experience*: I remember hearing this firsthand during his media availabilities and press conferences during the 2015 Finals.

288 *"shut the fuck up, I got this"*: Ken Berger, "In taking control of LeBron, Tyronn Lue has created a monster in Cleveland," CBS Sports, May 18, 2016.

296 *Internally, the Warriors were furious*: I spoke with several team sources at the time who were quite displeased.

297 *in a luxury suite with Bob Myers*: This was reported by multiple outlets at the time. Oakland native (and future Raiders running back) Marshawn Lynch was also with them.

297 *"I thought [the Cavaliers] were dead in the water"*: From an interview Adams gave to KNBR's Ray Woodson and Ray Ratto on July 7, 2016.

299 *"Go Cavaliers! We need a miracle tonight"*: I was on this train and heard it myself. (I can only imagine how much that conductor enjoyed Game 6.)

301 *all the video screens inside the arena turned red*: This happened around 2:00 a.m. as I was making my way out of Quicken Loans Arena.

301 *a production crew had taken up residence at midcourt and was practicing for the postgame trophy presentation and MVP announcement*: I watched this whole scene as it happened.

303 *his usual hour of game-day morning yoga with assistant coach Luke Walton*: From Kerr's pregame comments to the media, June 19, 2016.

305 *The coach wanted Irving to drive for a layup*: Ben Cohen, "The Biggest Shot in NBA History," *Wall Street Journal*, December 25, 2016.

306 *In terms of championship probability added*: Ibid.

308 *"Not a whole lot you can say other than how proud you are"*: Kerr interview, March 2017.

308 *"It sucked to watch them celebrate"*: From Curry's postgame comments to the media, June 19, 2016.

308 *"I blame myself for everything"*: From Green's postgame comments to the media, June 19, 2016.


## 12: INDEPENDENCE DAY

311 *what Steve Kerr had once said*: Feinstein, *A Season Inside*, p. 460.

312 *Kerr thought about what he could've done differently*: Kerr on *TK Show* podcast, June 24, 2016.

312 *haunted by what he saw*: Ibid.

313 *smoothing came off the table*: Associated Press, March 11, 2015.

313 *"Failure is really important"*: Lacob, "Inside Sports Management," 2016.

313  *crushed him . . . for an hour:* From Lacob's appearance on Tim Kawakami's *TK Show* podcast, posted on July 7, 2016.

314  *discussed internally for the better part of two years:* Confirmed to me by team sources who would know.

314  *Durant-to-Golden-State narrative bubbled up with fervor:* Adrian Wojnarowski, "Sources: Warriors serious threat to sign Kevin Durant," Yahoo! Sports, February 2, 2016.

314  *"It's hard not to enter your mind":* From Durant's pregame media availability (for which I was present) in the locker room on February 6, 2016.

314  *"a historic fluke":* NBA Insiders, "5-on-5: How many titles coming for Warriors? What's next for OKC?," ESPN.com, July 4, 2016.

315  *knew he was gone from the way his exit interview went:* Tim MacMahon, "Mavs' Harrison Barnes: 'Can't say I was surprised' by Warriors exit,'" ESPN.com, November 9, 2016.

315  *an ESPN projection concluded that the Warriors (with Durant) would win 76 games:* Kevin Pelton, "Six teams that can make best pitch to Kevin Durant to win the title," ESPN.com, June 28, 2016.

315  *partnered with NextVR—a Southern California virtual reality company that boasts Peter Guber as a board member:* Diamond Leung, "How NextVR Created Virtual Reality Experience To Help Golden State Warriors Sign Kevin Durant," SportTechie.com, December 8, 2016.

315  *Drake lyrics in the background:* Sam Amick, "Kevin Durant: Chemistry, culture were huge factors in choosing Warriors," *USA Today*, July 7, 2016.

315  *and Durant's father, Wayne Pratt:* Marc J. Spears, "KD's Dad: It Was Time to 'Be Selfish,'" ESPN's The Undefeated, July 8, 2016.

316  *Bob Myers thought the Warriors blew their chance:* Scott Howard-Cooper, "Durant signing still sinking in for Golden State's Myers," NBA.com, July 13, 2016. Much of the scene that follows, with Myers in Lake Tahoe, comes from this Q&A.

316  *Malfunctioned from the start:* From Steve Kerr's appearance on Zach Lowe's "Lowe Post" podcast, posted on September 28, 2016.

316  *"Why the* hell *would you guys want Kevin?":* Amick, "Kevin Durant: Chemistry, culture," 2016.

316  *As Joe Lacob sat next to Durant's father:* Lacob especially liked Green's pitch above the others. From an interview with venture capitalist Ted Schlein for the KPCB CEO Workshop series ("Taking the Golden State Warriors to

Greatness: Free Agency Model and Talent Wars in the Valley," uploaded to Kleiner Perkins's YouTube channel on October 4, 2016): "He gave the heavy pitch, which no one else there would have done, except for me because I'm basically the Draymond Green of the business side." To which Schlein replied: "Who'd you hit in the bar at 2:30 in the morning?"

316 *"Just know you not in it by yourself"*: From Green's appearance on Adrian Wojnarowski's podcast, posted on November 21, 2016.

316 *everyone had a good laugh*: From Lacob's talk at Kleiner Perkins ("Taking the Golden State Warriors to Greatness: Free Agency Model and Talent Wars in the Valley").

317 *"They didn't show any of their cards"*: From my interview with Myers on July 7, 2016.

317 *Oklahoma City had met with Durant for five hours on June 30*: Royce Young, "The changes that led to Kevin Durant's OKC departure," ESPN.com, July 5, 2016.

317 *Myers made sure the Warriors were following up*: Lee Jenkins, "The unlikely assist that helped deliver Kevin Durant to the Warriors," *Sports Illustrated*, July 8, 2016.

317 *"one of the best text messages I've ever seen"*: From Myers's media availability on July 7, 2016.

317 *got calls from Steve Nash*: Jenkins, "The unlikely assist," 2016.

317 *West . . . was convinced his presence would solve one of the Warriors' most glaring issues*: From West's appearance on Tim Kawakami's *TK Show* podcast, posted on September 16, 2016.

318 *Curry averaged just 4.6 free throws per game during the season, the second-fewest in NBA history for a 30-points-per-game scorer*: The player who averaged the *most* free throws in a season of any 30-point scorer? That would be Jerry West, who made 10.6 per game in 1965–66.

318 *"Kevin, just follow your heart"*: From West's appearance on Adrian Wojnarowski's podcast, posted on October 19, 2016.

318 *"You're recruiting somebody, whether it be in a Silicon Valley tech company or whether it be in basketball"*: From Lacob's appearance on Tim Kawakami's *TK Show* podcast, posted on July 7, 2016.

318 *Lacob also enlisted a small, select group of former Warriors to call Durant*: From Lacob's media availability on July 7, 2016.

318 *first clue Myers received that the Warriors might get lucky*: Slater, "Kevin Durant, Joe Lacob shed more light," 2016.

318 *Myers was wandering around outside his in-laws' house . . . when his cell phone rang*: Howard-Cooper, "Durant signing still sinking in," 2016.

319 *Lacob, who was sitting out on his lakeside patio in Montana when his general manager called*: From Lacob's media availability on July 7, 2016.

319 *"I just couldn't fathom a player of his caliber choosing us"*: From Myers's media availability on July 7, 2016.

320 *"Let's get it"*: Alex Kennedy, "Draymond Green opens up on Durant: How he recruited KD and more," *Sports Illustrated*, July 4, 2016.

320 *Klay Thompson was sleeping*: Shams Charania, "What Kevin Durant's arrival means for Klay Thompson," Yahoo! Sports, August 1, 2016.

320 *MY NEXT CHAPTER*: Kevin Durant, Players' Tribune, July 4, 2016.

320 *Margot Kerr kicked her husband awake when she saw the news*: Jenkins, "The unlikely assist," 2016.

320 *"This one's kind of important"*: From Myers's appearance on Tim Kawakami's *TK Show* podcast, posted on October 8, 2016.

320 *Myers asked Durant if he was messing with him*: From my interview with Myers on July 7, 2016.

320 *Ron Adams . . . sat in the front row and beamed*: I was there and saw this first-hand. (Yes, he actually smiled!)

321 *Adams pulled Durant aside and told him how proud he was*: From an interview Adams gave to KNBR's Ray Woodson and Ray Ratto on July 7, 2016.

321 *"That's not really true. He was a part of the process"*: From Lacob's media availability on July 7, 2016.

321 *Reggie Miller*: Reggie Miller, "Kevin Durant Traded a Sacred Legacy for Cheap Jewelry," *Bleacher Report*, July 5, 2016.

321 *Charles Barkley*: From Barkley's interview with ESPN Radio, July 6, 2016.

321 *Paul Pierce*: From Pierce's interview with SiriusXM NBA Radio, October 12, 2016.

321 *far from kind to Durant*: Young, "The changes that led," 2016.

321 *Adam Silver addressed the kerfuffle*: From Silver's remarks at the Las Vegas Summer League on July 12, 2016, as transcribed by ASAP Sports.

322 *"Let them talk"*: Ethan Sherwood Strauss, "Warriors owner Lacob dismisses Silver's competition concern," ESPN.com, July 13, 2016.

322 *five of the seven richest contracts in NBA history*: By the close of business, Mike Conley ($153 million), Damian Lillard ($139.9 million), DeMar DeRozan ($139 million), Bradley Beal ($127.2 million), and Andre Drummond ($127.2 million) all signed max deals with their respective clubs. The other

two in the top seven are Anthony Davis ($127.2 million in 2015) and Kobe Bryant ($136.4 million in 2004).

322 *"Durant's move to California feels like some sort of reckoning"*: Sam Dolnick, "Kevin Durant Reboots, Goes Digital," *New York Times*, July 8, 2016.

322 *"With Golden State now established as the Ultimate Evil of the sport"*: Bethlehem Shoals, "Kevin Durant turned LeBron James into a populist hero," *SB Nation*, July 6, 2016.

322 *"He is as pure a scorer as we've seen"*: Tommy Craggs, "Non-LeBron," *Slate*, September 1, 2010.

323 *"Nobody complain when somebody leave Apple and go to Google"*: From Green's remarks to the media on October 13, 2016.

323 *"I've been second my whole life"*: Lee Jenkins, "How 'Bout Them Apples?" *Sports Illustrated*, April 29, 2013.

324 *"We all want to see each other do well, but I'm not sacrificing shit"*: Charania, "What Kevin Durant's arrival," 2016.

324 *"the greatest consolation prize in the history of the NBA"*: From an interview Welts gave to KNBR on July 19, 2016.

324 *At 5:24 p.m.:* I was present for this and recorded the time.

325 *"The truth is, we're not really a basketball team"*: Connor Letourneau, "Warriors' ENCORE Award shows franchise's success transcends sports," *San Francisco Chronicle*, October 11, 2016.

325 *named Best Analytics Organization at the Sloan conference:* Bob Myers had the best line of the conference that weekend when, during his "Future of the Front Office" panel, he quoted Davidson head coach Bob Mc-Killop: "Analytics are like a bikini: They show a lot but they don't show you everything."

326 *"The team seemed to be mentioned in every panel and presentation"*: Matt Dollinger, "Sloan 2016: 50 NBA notes, quotes and anecdotes from analytics conference," *Sports Illustrated*, March 14, 2016.

326 *Curry's jersey was the top seller in 48 states:* "Stephen Curry Tops NBA Player Sales in 48 of 50 U.S. States Entering NBA Finals," WeAreFanatics.com, June 2, 2016.

326 *$1.6 billion:* Daniel Kaplan, "Warriors valued at $1.6B," *SportsBusiness Journal*, May 9, 2016. In February 2017, *Forbes* valued the Warriors at $2.6 billion, third overall behind the New York Knicks and Los Angeles Lakers.

326 *Sports Team of the Year:* Warriors.com, "Warriors Named Sports Team of the Year and Joe Lacob Receives Sports Executive of the Year Honors," May 18, 2016.

326 *"We live in a constant state of 'beta'"*: Per Guber's remarks at Stanford Graduate School of Business's Sports Innovation Conference on March 2, 2016.

327 *"I think we're going in the right direction"*: From Myers's appearance on Tim Kawakami's *TK Show* podcast, posted on October 8, 2016.

327 *It's 11:00 a.m. on a drizzly morning in Oakland:* I was present at the practice facility and Oracle Arena for all of the scene that follows.

329 *Noahlytics uses a sensor positioned 13 feet above the rim:* Per a press release (in which Kirk Lacob is quoted) posted on NoahBasketball.com on June 9, 2016.

329 *map the angle of any shot* and the exact plane *of where the ball crosses down:* Ira Boudway, "This Machine Knows Shooting Better Than Steph Curry," *BloombergBusinessweek*, June 8, 2016.

329 *first NBA team to install the SmartCourt system:* Diamond Leung, "PlaySight's SmartCourt Expansion Into Basketball Starts With Golden State Warriors," SportTechie.com, December 9, 2016.

329 *"Seventy-three don't mean shit"*: From Lacob's interview with 95.7 The Game's Greg Papa and Bonta Hill on February 7, 2017. The milestone still means a lot to Lacob, who wears a hat that says "73" when he plays golf.

330 *as Dave East's remix of Fat Joe and Remy Ma's "All the Way Up" blared:* I was there and heard this myself.

## EPILOGUE

331 *champagne is making my eyes tear up:* Everything that is described as happening during and after Game 5 are scenes I witnessed and experienced myself.

333 *Kerr would find himself cornered by well-wishers:* This was something I witnessed when the Warriors were on the road in Minnesota on March 10, 2017.

333 *"I don't think* happy *is the right word for Steve"*: This interview occurred in late March; Kerr announced on April 23 that he would step aside.

337 *"Man, you don't even* know *what poor is"*: I was standing a few feet away from Durant and the sportswriter in question when this interaction occurred.

# ACKNOWLEDGMENTS

A book like this doesn't happen without a deep bench of superstar-level talent.

I had no clue my agent, David Fugate, was a lifelong Warriors fan when I emailed him in early 2016 with the idea for this book, but his passion guided my vision from the get-go and helped turn the nebulous thoughts bouncing around inside my head into something real.

Todd Hunter, my remarkable editor at Atria Books, championed this idea before words were put to page and then kept the whole operation afloat through to completion. I felt I was in confident, capable hands at every step, as his unending patience made this first-time author feel (to crib from Kevin Garnett) like anything was possible.

Three times over the past four years, the Warriors' media relations department has received the Professional Basketball Writers Association's Brian McIntyre Award, which goes to the team staff that "best exemplifies standards of professionalism and excellence." It's a well-deserved honor, let me tell you. Dan Martinez, Brett Winkler, Matt de Nesnera, Darryl Arata, Lisa Goodwin, and the rest of the crew are top-notch and always willing to lend a hand to a desperate reporter on deadline. Raymond Ridder, their esteemed leader, is without equal in this industry. I knew he might be skittish when I told him I'd be commencing such a wide-ranging and in-depth look at his employer, but

Raymond's response—*"We are not going to make this difficult on you"*—put me at ease during a critical moment in my reporting. He's a true professional and (with countless assists from his staff) made my job easier than it had any right to be.

Thanks as well to the Warriors coaching staff and assistants, the players who have passed through in recent years, team executives, and myriad other people down the chain who routinely make covering the Warriors feel like a dream assignment for so many of us. I would especially like to thank head coach Steve Kerr, who is truly one of the kindest and most gracious people in sports one could ever hope to encounter.

The Bay Area reporters and columnists who have covered the Warriors over the years constitute a cadre of journalists that is exceptional. Without their prior efforts, this book simply would not exist. My enduring thanks to Tim Kawakami, Chris Ballard, Ethan Sherwood Strauss, Rusty Simmons, Marcus Thompson II, John Branch, Ray Ratto, Ann Killion, Monte Poole, Sam Amick, Diamond Leung, Anthony Slater, Connor Letourneau, Mark Purdy, Jon Wilner, Daniel Brown, Carl Steward, Janie McCauley, Phil Barber, Marc J. Spears, Eric Freeman, Jacob C. Palmer, Steve Berman, Danny Leroux, Nate Duncan, Courtney Cronin, Karl Buscheck, Carvell Wallace, Ezekiel Kweku, Kevin Jones, Andy Liu, and others. I also want to thank the national writers who have given the Warriors, at one time or another, the benefit of their own immense journalistic talents: Jack McCallum, Zach Lowe, Jonathan Abrams, Kevin Pelton, Pablo S. Torre, Kevin Arnovitz, Ramona Shelburne, Tim Bontemps, Scott Cacciola, Lee Jenkins, Ben Cohen, Adrian Wojnarowski, Harvey Araton, Jason Gay, Tom Haberstroh, Howard Beck, Kevin Ding, Nathaniel Friedman, Michael Lee, Ben Golliver, Paul Flannery, Baxter Holmes, Henry Abbott, Zach Harper, Matt Moore, James Herbert, Chris Herring, Bill Simmons, and Katie Baker.

Many of the statistical assessments found in this book could not have been reported in any other era. This new age of basketball journalism owes an immense debt to a growing number of sites that allow for unprecedented data-crunching. For me, that includes indispensable destinations such as Basketball Reference, Synergy Sports, nbawowy!, Nylon Calculus, StatMuse, PopcornMachine.net, NBA Miner, and Stats .NBA.com.

Like any shooter in a rhythm, this book was often sustained solely by encouragement and confidence, and there was no shortage of friends who supplied me with both when I was running low. To Lindsey Adler, Bill Barnwell, Grant Brisbee, Jason Fagone, Cat Ferguson, Pete Gaines, Alex Goot, Elon Green, Megan Greenwell, Patrick Kennedy, Jonah Keri, Molly Knight, Will Leitch, Alexis Madrigal, Sam Miller, Matt Miskelly, Matt Norlander, Brian Phillips, Martin Rickman, Eugene Ruocchio, Beejoli Shah, Dave Shaw, Alan Siegel, Robert Silverman, Jon Tayler, Wendy Thurm, Don Van Natta Jr., Charlie Warzel, and Katie Zezima, I can't thank you enough. Next round is on me.

I've been enormously privileged to work with many attentive and exceptional editors who have transformed my rough copy into something exponentially better. My gratitude to Tommy Craggs, Tom Scocca, Jack Moore, Ben Mathis-Lilley, Steve Kandell, James Montgomery, Jeremy Stahl, Philip Michaels, Gabe Guarente, Chris Trenchard, and Matt Sullivan for all of your efforts.

I first stepped onto the campus at Boston University in 1998 knowing that I wanted to be a sportswriter but not quite sure how to make it happen. During the day, I had the encouragement and guidance of so many wonderful professors—especially Mark Leccese, whose humor and perspective I have carried with me ever since, and the late Jack Falla and David Brudnoy. And for countless nights over four years, I lived at *The Daily Free Press*, the independent student newspaper that allowed me to make mistakes, learn from them, and ultimately feel like I had started on the path toward my dream.

When I moved to the Bay Area, I was twenty-one, just a few months out of college, and without any job prospects. With two weeks to go until my first student loan payment, I answered a Craigslist posting from *Wired* magazine in San Francisco. I had no idea that when I applied to be a research intern—$10 an hour!—I had changed the course of my career in profound ways. During my eight-plus years at the magazine, including seven as a fact-checker, my *Wired* colleagues showed me how the highest-quality journalism comes together in ways that would seem magical to the uninitiated. They also became some of my dearest friends, and I thank them for their boundless wisdom and camaraderie, especially Joanna Pearlstein, Mark McClusky, Adam Rogers, Rebecca Smith de Ramírez, Rachel Swaby, Angela Watercutter, Jon J. Eilenberg, Sarah Fallon, Erica Jewell, Jason Tanz, Bill Wasik, Caitlin Roper, Mark Robinson, Bob Cohn, Peter Rubin, Robert Capps, Mike Isaac, Dylan Tweney, Nancy Miller, Betsy Mason, Jordan Crucchiola, Michael Calore, and Scott Dadich.

A dedicated working area at home is a nice perk for any writer, but sometimes you need to get away to a place that's quiet, free of distractions, and boasts a constant supply of air-conditioning. My thanks to the San Mateo and Burlingame public libraries.

To my parents, Michael and Judy, and siblings, Kristin and James, thank you for making me who I am, for instilling in me a sense of curiosity about the world, and for helping me understand the impact that sports can have on any of us.

Most important, to my wife, Becca, and my son, Tomás, thank you for your unconditional love and devotion and for being there in the clutch as the seconds ticked down. When the pressure was on, there was nothing too tough for us. Thank you for always believing in me.